SAMS Teach Yourself

FreeBSD®

in 24 Hours

Michael Urban

Brian Tiemann

SAMS 201 West 103rd St., Indianapolis, Indiana, 46290 USA

Sams Teach Yourself FreeBSD® in 24 Hours

Copyright © 2003 by Sams Publishing

International Standard Book Number: 0672324245

Library of Congress Catalog Card Number: 2002102902

Printed in the United States of America

First Printing: December 2002

04 03 02   4 3 2 1

Trademarks

Warning and Disclaimer

ACQUISITIONS EDITOR
Katie Purdum

DEVELOPMENT EDITOR
Dee-Ann LeBlanc

MANAGING EDITOR
Charlotte Clapp

PROJECT EDITOR
Andy Beaster

COPY EDITOR
Rhonda Tinch-Mize

INDEXER
Ken Johnson

PROOFREADER
Leslie Joseph

TECHNICAL EDITOR
Dee-Ann LeBlanc

TEAM COORDINATOR
Amy Patton

MEDIA DEVELOPER
Dan Scherf

INTERIOR DESIGNER
Gary Adair

COVER DESIGNER
Alan Clements

PAGE LAYOUT
Point 'n Click Publishing, LLC.

Contents at a Glance

Contents

Part III Networking

HOUR 12 Introduction to Networks

HOUR 13 Connecting FreeBSD to an Existing Network

Part IV FreeBSD as a Workstation <span></span> 255

About the Authors

MICHAEL URBAN is a biology student at the University of Minnesota where he plans to major in Ecology, Evolution, and Behavior. He is involved in research projects with African lions and is also the Webmaster for the Lion Research Center. He has worked in numerous IT jobs including Web design and technical analysis. He has experience with various Unix operating systems including FreeBSD, Linux, and Solaris.

BRIAN TIEMANN has been a constant user of FreeBSD since his student days at Caltech, where he used it to build a movie fan Web site that has continued to grow and sustain more and more load until the present day. Born in Ukiah, California, He has remained in the state all his life; he currently lives in San Jose, works in the networking appliance field, and writes ceaseless commentary about Apple, Microsoft, and the technology field. Occasionally, but not often enough, he has time to enjoy motorcycling, travel, animation, and other such interests.

About the Development Editor

DEE-ANN LEBLANC is an award-winning computer book author, and has been in the field since 1994. She's published 11 computer books and 60 articles, taught and developed courses, and more—mostly involving the Linux operating system and its related programs. Her latest book is *Linux for Dummies, Fourth Edition* from Wiley Publishing, Inc. She also has a growing wealth of experience on the editorial front, turning part of her time to technical and development editing. This combination of working both sides of the desk allows her to both write better books and become a better editor.

You can follow Dee-Ann's work and share your input through her mailing list at `http://www.dee-annleblanc.com/mailman/listinfo/general` or find out more in general at `http://www.Dee-AnnLeBlanc.com/`.

Dedications

To my parents, Chris and Bonnie, and to my sister Beth.

—Michael Urban

To my parents, Keith and Ann, and to my brother, Mike. Also to all the members of the open-source UNIX community, who continue to bring more and more legitimacy to the movement every day.

—Brian Tiemann

Acknowledgments

This book would not have been possible without the efforts of several people. I would like to thank Kathryn Purdum at Sams Publishing for her work and also for accommodating my unexpected trip to Egypt, Andrew Beaster for his work on the development, Dan Scherf for his work on the CD, and all of the other staff at Sams Publishing who worked on this book. In addition, I would like to thank Brian Tiemann for taking up the slack on some of the chapters and on author review during my unexpected two weeks in Egypt. Of course, I also need to thank all the volunteers who have spent numerous unpaid hours making FreeBSD into an operating system that is better than many commercial operating systems. Without them, this book would not exist.

—Michael Urban

We Want to Hear from You!

As the reader of this book, *you* are our most important critic and commentator. We value your opinion and want to know what we're doing right, what we could do better, what areas you'd like to see us publish in, and any other words of wisdom you're willing to pass our way.

You can email or write me directly to let me know what you did or didn't like about this book—as well as what we can do to make our books stronger.

Please note that I cannot help you with technical problems related to the topic of this book, and that due to the high volume of mail I receive, I might not be able to reply to every message.

When you write, please be sure to include this book's title and author as well as your name and phone or email address. I will carefully review your comments and share them with the author and editors who worked on the book.

Email: opensource@samspublishing.com

Mail: Mark Taber
           Associate Publisher
           Sams Publishing
           201 West 103rd Street
           Indianapolis, IN 46290 USA

Reader Services

For more information about this book or others from Sams Publishing, visit our Web site at www.samspublishing.com. Type the ISBN (excluding hyphens) or the title of the book in the Search box to find the book you're looking for.

Introduction

Until recently, home computer users and small business users had little choice when it came to what operating system they used to on their computers. You pretty much had two choices: You could either use Microsoft Windows or Apple's Mac OS. Of course, you were limited even further by what hardware you had. If you had an Apple Macintosh, you had to use Mac OS. If you had an x86 based system, you had to use Windows. UNIX systems were well out of the price range of most small businesses or home hobbyists. On top of that, they required proprietary hardware from the UNIX vendor. This locked you into a single vendor and a single choice of hardware. So for the most part, home users and small businesses stuck with Windows. If they needed to do networking, they usually went with Windows NT, or Novell Netware.

In the mid to late 1990s, however, this Microsoft monopoly on x86 operating systems began breaking. A couple of UNIX-like operating systems being developed by hobbyists working together over the Internet began to get some notice. The two most popular ones were Linux and FreeBSD. Over time, these operating systems evolved, and grew stable enough to be used in production environments on servers and workstations.

The operating systems were being freely distributed on the Internet. In addition, they ran on cheap x86 hardware that had the additional advantage of not locking you into a single vendor. Businesses, both small and large, began to take notice and started using these systems for various tasks. Among the most popular were email and Web services. Hobbyists who wanted to work with UNIX also adopted the new operating systems for use on their home computers, and they wrote software for the new operating systems.

Among the software that was written was graphical user interfaces—some of which were so advanced that they rivaled Windows for features and ease of use. With the advent of these graphical interfaces, the new operating systems started to become usable for the average user instead of just the guru. This book is geared toward that average user.

What This Book Is

This book is designed to teach the average computer user how to work effectively with the FreeBSD operating system in 24 lessons—each approximately one hour in length. By the time you have finished this book, you will have a good basic understanding of how to perform most common tasks in FreeBSD, including such things as setting up a basic Web or email server, basic FreeBSD administration, basic security, installing software, and basic navigating and file management in FreeBSD. You will also have a good understanding of how to work with the graphical user environment in FreeBSD.

What This Book Is Not

This book is not an introduction to computers. Although it does not assume that you have any previous UNIX experience, it does assume that you have a fairly good working knowledge of Windows. It does not assume that you are an expert Windows user, but it does assume that you have a working knowledge of basic concepts such as files and folders and navigation in the Windows environment using the mouse.

This book is also not designed to teach advanced concepts or cover all the included topics in depth. As such, if you already have some UNIX experience with another UNIX system such as Linux, you will probably do better looking at *FreeBSD Unleashed*, also from Sams Publishing, because this book will likely be too basic for you, and will leave you unfulfilled.

How to Use This Book

This book is designed as a tutorial on various topics of FreeBSD. You might not be interested in all the topics covered. You don't necessarily have to go through the hours in the order they are given in the book. However, certain topics will require knowledge of other topics that were covered previously. For example, before you can set up a working Web server, you must have a working network, and you also have to know how to install software so that you can get the Web server software installed. At points in the hours where knowledge is required from a previous hour, cross-references to the relevant hours will be made.

The concept of learning an entirely new operating system might seem intimidating to you at first, but the process can actually be fun, and you will probably find the rewards of FreeBSD to be well worth the effort put into learning it. Hopefully, this book will make it a little easier to learn about this powerful operating system. Now, let's get started in Hour 1 by learning about some of the basics of what FreeBSD is and why you might want to use it.

PART I

Introduction to FreeBSD

Hour

HOUR 1

Planning for and Preparing to Install FreeBSD

Before you can use FreeBSD, you need to install it on your computer's hard disk. In this hour, we will discuss the background information needed to make the best decision about how to install FreeBSD. Of course, the first thing you might want is a little bit of background on FreeBSD.

What Is FreeBSD?

FreeBSD is a freely available and open source implementation of the Berkeley version of the UNIX operating system. In many ways, it is similar to Linux, but it also has some important differences. Let's look at a few of the buzzwords and phrases that can be used to describe FreeBSD, as well as what those words and phrases mean.

FreeBSD Is a True UNIX Operating System

This means FreeBSD is in the same family of operating systems as Solaris, AIX, HP-UX, and Digital UNIX. The original UNIX operating system can trace its roots back to the 1960s. The designers of UNIX created a design so flexible and powerful that even 30 years later, UNIX (and thus FreeBSD as well) remains one of the most versatile, well-respected operating systems available.

FreeBSD Is Open Source

This means that all the source code for the entire operating system is available to you. If you are not a programmer, this might not mean much to you. However, even end users benefit from open source because thousands of programmers use FreeBSD. The fact that the source is available to them means that bugs and possible security problems are likely to be found and fixed quicker than in operating systems developed by commercial companies in which users do not get access to the source code.

FreeBSD Is Free and Has a Very Liberal License Agreement

You can download FreeBSD free from the Internet. You can burn your own FreeBSD CDs or purchase copies of FreeBSD from various sources for just a few dollars. Unlike Windows, and some commercial versions of UNIX, there are no per-user or per-server license fees for FreeBSD. You can install FreeBSD on as many systems as you want and allow as many users to access it as you want without paying a penny. If you run a business, this has the potential to save you thousands of dollars in software licensing fees.

FreeBSD Is Stable and Powerful

The old adage "You get what you pay for" doesn't apply to FreeBSD. A lot of people assume that because FreeBSD is free and is developed primarily by volunteer "hobbyists," it must be little more than a toy that cannot be taken seriously or relied upon for doing serious work. Nothing could be further from the truth. Many large corporations are relying on FreeBSD for many tasks. Some of the companies and organizations currently using FreeBSD include Sony, Yahoo!, Microsoft, the Apache project, and Hollywood special effects studios. Many people regard FreeBSD as one of the most stable operating systems available. System crashes common in Windows become a thing of the past with FreeBSD.

What Is FreeBSD Being Used for?

Because the source code for FreeBSD is freely available and FreeBSD comes with a large number of programming tools, what you can do with FreeBSD is really only limited by your imagination and skill as a programmer. However, without having any programming skill, here are some of things that you can do with FreeBSD.

Set Up a Powerful Web Server

The CD that comes with this book includes the Apache Web server, which is the most popular Web server software on the Internet. FreeBSD and Apache is widely regarded as one of the best software combinations for building a powerful and stable Web server. Yahoo!, the Apache Project itself, and Sony Japan rely on FreeBSD to power their Web sites. If you do not want set up a public Web server, FreeBSD also makes a great platform for running a corporate intranet.

Email Services

If you need an email server for your organization, FreeBSD can do the job quite well. The resource requirements of FreeBSD are very low, so it can often turn an old and outdated system into a perfectly serviceable email server. That old 486 you use as a doorstop might just have a use.

DNS and Routing Services

You can make a perfectly serviceable router or DNS server using FreeBSD—even one with sophisticated functions such as firewalling and Network Address Translation (NAT). Once again, this can be a more attractive option than purchasing a dedicated router if you have an older system sitting around that is not being used for anything. FreeBSD also has the capability to allow you to share a single Internet connection with several systems, even if you only have one connection and one IP address.

File and Printer Sharing

With the freely available SAMBA software, you can create a file or print server that is compatible with Microsoft Windows workstations. You can even create a FreeBSD server that emulates a Windows NT domain controller.

Database Services

There are several freely available SQL database servers for FreeBSD. These freely available databases are being used by some major organizations, including NASA.

Software Development/Learning Programming

If you want to learn programming, FreeBSD is a great platform to do it on. For one thing, FreeBSD comes with compilers for several programming languages. Many more can be downloaded free. On some other operating systems, these compilers would cost thousands of dollars.

Learning UNIX

If you need to learn UNIX for a class or for your job, FreeBSD can help you do it. And it can help you do it at home on your own time. FreeBSD is a real UNIX operating system that allows you to get hands-on experience.

Inexpensive UNIX Workstations

Thousands of applications are available for FreeBSD—most of them at no cost. These applications range from Web browsers to office packages to email clients to scientific applications. In addition, you can work with remote X applications running on any remote UNIX server.

FreeBSD Compared to Other Operating Systems

You might be wondering how FreeBSD compares to other operating systems. In this section, we will look at how FreeBSD compares to several other operating systems, including other flavors of UNIX and Windows.

FreeBSD Compared to Linux

Most people today have at least heard of Linux, even if they do not have a very good idea of what it is. Linux is a clone, or "work alike," of the UNIX operating system. It was originally started as a hobby project by Linus Torvalds, but has since grown to be developed by thousands of volunteers all over the world. Linux is a project that was started from scratch. As such, it is not, and never has been, based on any actual UNIX code. When people talk about "UNIX-like operating systems," they're usually referring to Linux.

From an end-user point of view, and even for most administration tasks, FreeBSD and Linux are quite similar. The main differences between the two are in the design philosophy. Here are some of the major variances:

- There is only one distribution of FreeBSD. There are more than 30 distributions of Linux: Each of the Linux distributions has slightly different ways of doing things. This can cause problems if you need to migrate to a different distribution of Linux later on.

- FreeBSD is a complete operating system. Linux is a kernel with a set of utilities included with it: Different Linux vendors have differing opinions on what should be included with a Linux distribution. Of course, if something you want isn't included, you can always download it off the Internet.

- FreeBSD is maintained by a core team. As such, what ends up in a FreeBSD release is better controlled than what ends up in most Linux releases: This can help to reduce the compatibility problems that sometimes show up with Linux.

- FreeBSD can often be easier to upgrade than Linux: When you upgrade FreeBSD, you generally upgrade the entire operating system. With Linux, you might download a kernel upgrade, only to find out that it breaks other parts of the system that you then need to upgrade separately. (This has its downsides too, though; many Linux distributions are packaged nicely so that upgrading them is easier and less prone to breakage than FreeBSD.)

- FreeBSD is considered by many to be more stable than Linux. As such, it might be more suitable for production servers. However, the trade-off is that FreeBSD is often slower to support the latest cutting edge technology and hardware devices than Linux.

- FreeBSD has less software available for it than Linux—especially when it comes to commercial software. However, this is often not an issue because FreeBSD can run most Linux software extremely well.

Another difference between FreeBSD and Linux is in licensing. Linux is licensed under the GPL, which stands for the *GNU General Public License*. This license was developed by the Free Software Foundation. One of the goals of the GPL is to foster innovation by ensuring that developers can build on existing code from other developers. (Whether it succeeds in this goal or actually inhibits innovation is a subject of religious debate.) The GPL does this by requiring that source code be made available for the product and that the author not restrict distribution of the product. Any GPL code used in a software product requires that the entire product automatically inherit the GPL license: thus, the author must make source code available and cannot restrict others from redistributing the software or making further changes to it.

If you're interested in reading an analysis of the GPL as well as how it affects and is affected by the realities of commercial software development, see "A Funny Thing Happened on the Way to the Market" by Matt Asay, at `http://www.linuxdevices.com/articles/AT4528760742.html`.

FreeBSD, on the other hand, is licensed under the BSD software license developed by the University of California at Berkeley. This license is much more liberal than the GPL. Basically, the BSD license allows you to do whatever you want with the software, including re-using it in a commercial software product and not releasing the source code. Because of this, the BSD license is often favored by commercial software developers. Apple has used a great deal of FreeBSD code in Darwin, the foundation for Mac OS X: even Microsoft has used BSD licensed software, and occasionally contributed software to BSD. This means that you re-use BSD licensed code in your own software and then license the software under a completely different license. The only requirement is that the BSD code maintain the BSD copyright information and an acknowledgment of the original authors.

Ultimately, the major differences between FreeBSD and Linux come down to philosophical differences about software licenses and such. Both operating systems are quite capable, and both can serve the needs of most users quite well.

Other BSD Operating Systems

Although FreeBSD is by far the most popular of the BSD based operating systems for PC hardware, there are several others.

The most popular BSD-based operating system, and indeed the most popular UNIX-like operating system in the world, is Apple's Mac OS X. It's possible to start a religious war over whether OS X is actually UNIX or not, but for our purposes (and under the terms of its license), it is. OS X has a fully functional BSD UNIX environment that is based on FreeBSD. It will compile and run most BSD software without modification, and it includes the majority of the BSD system utilities. Of course, at this point in time, OS X is only available for Macintosh hardware, although there is a long-standing rumor that Apple might port OS X to PC hardware—that is, recompile it so that it will run on the Intel/AMD architecture that most likely underlies your own computer.

Another version of BSD that is available for PC hardware is NetBSD. The main difference between FreeBSD and NetBSD is that FreeBSD focuses mostly on PC hardware, and thus is optimized to perform extremely well on it. NetBSD, on the other hand, runs on just about every platform under the sun, including things that aren't even computers in the traditional sense of the word—such as certain gaming consoles. FreeBSD has a larger user community than NetBSD; hence, it tends to be better documented and have a larger amount of ported software available.

OpenBSD is also available for PC hardware, as well as many other platforms, although not as many platforms as NetBSD. OpenBSD's main focus is on security, and some would argue (perhaps rightfully) that OpenBSD is the most secure general purpose operating system available. Like NetBSD, OpenBSD tends to be more difficult for beginners to work with than FreeBSD because it is not as well documented and doesn't have as much software pre-ported to it. Also, be aware that as of this writing, OpenBSD does not support SMP processing. This means that if you have a system with more than one CPU, you won't be able to take advantage of the second CPU with OpenBSD. (FreeBSD however, does support multiple processors.)

FreeBSD Compared to Windows 2000 and XP

In the 80s and early 90s, Microsoft primarily focused on the desktop market. Servers were pretty much the domain of UNIX vendors such as SUN, IBM and HP, and non-UNIX vendors such as Novell. However, with the introduction of Windows NT, Microsoft began to target the server market. Microsoft continued to push into the server market with new products such as Windows 2000, Windows XP, and technologies such as .NET and ASP scripting. In addition, various anti-UNIX campaigns on the part of Microsoft have made it clear that its intended target is UNIX. Among other things, Microsoft claims that UNIX is outdated, arcane, and not cost-effective. Is there any valid basis to these claims? Is UNIX really a technology in which its time has come and gone? After all, UNIX is more than 30 years old, which is a long time when you consider that the computer has only been a major business tool since the mid 1960s. Before UNIX is written off as an obsolete technology though, let's consider some of its benefits, as well as look at some of Microsoft's points.

Microsoft's claim that UNIX is not cost-effective might be true if we are talking about commercial UNIX vendors. Traditionally, commercial UNIX has been proprietary software that required expensive hardware to run. However, as PC hardware became more powerful, it began to be possible to run very serviceable servers on commodity PC systems, which traditionally has been the market that Microsoft has focused on. A PC-based server could be had for much less money than a proprietary UNIX server.

However, FreeBSD is focused on PC hardware. So this eliminates the expensive hardware argument for making UNIX not cost-effective. In addition, FreeBSD doesn't have any licensing fees. This eliminates a substantial cost that is associated with Windows. You can install FreeBSD on as many servers as you would like without paying a dime.

The number of simultaneous users who can be connected to the server is limited only by the capacity of your hardware. Once again, you don't have to pay a dime. With Windows, on the other hand, you have to pay a licensing fee for each server you want to run Windows on, as well as a fee for each user who needs to be connected to any given server. Basically, with the free UNIX systems such as FreeBSD, Microsoft's argument that UNIX is not cost-effective doesn't really work. In fact, FreeBSD could potentially save tens of thousands of dollars because of Microsoft's expensive licensing fees.

What about the idea that UNIX is an outdated technology? This idea doesn't really stand up either. For one, when UNIX was first invented, it was way ahead of its time. But also, UNIX's design philosophy allowed it to grow and meet future needs relatively easily because most of the functionality is handled by external programs that ship with the operating system. As far as the underlying technology of the operating system itself, UNIX had features in the 1970s that Microsoft didn't get around to adding to Windows until the mid 1990s.

Other than the fact that FreeBSD can potentially save thousands of dollars in licensing fees, it also has the potential to save a great deal of money in hardware costs because FreeBSD's resource requirements are relatively light compared to Windows. Depending on what you are doing with FreeBSD, even a 486 with 32MB of RAM might be suffi-cient. On the other hand, Microsoft states that the minimum requirements for Windows 2000 server are a Pentium 133 and 64MB of RAM. Realistically, for reasonably good performance, requirements for Windows 2000 are much higher than this.

As far as FreeBSD (and UNIX in general) being more difficult to learn than Windows is concerned, this is probably true. A lot of procedures performed from a graphical user interface in Windows need to be performed from the command line on FreeBSD—often by editing a text-based configuration file. However, the command-line interface does have several advantages over Windows graphical user interface.

- Once you've learned the command line, it can often be much faster than navigating through Windows graphical tools.
- Not having a graphical interface running means that the resource requirements of the operating system are much lower. It makes little sense to have a resource hun-gry graphical interface running on a headless server in a backroom somewhere that no one ever sees anyway.
- Not having the graphical interface also means that hardware requirements are lower. For example, you can get by with an old and small monitor instead of hav-ing to have an expensive high resolution monitor.

- You can administer FreeBSD from the command line remotely through any system that has a terminal emulator, even if it is not a UNIX system. With Windows, you need special software to do remote administration, and that software generally only runs on Windows.

The argument can also be made that FreeBSD is much more stable and secure than Windows. A properly designed graphical user interface can make system administration much more straightforward than in a command-line–based system; but because of the arcane nature of the Windows' system layout, its interface is hardly any more intuitive than that of FreeBSD. The really nasty part, too, is that the Windows' graphical interface leads people to *believe* that it's easier—with the result that a great many Windows servers in the world are configured improperly and insecurely, as well as administered by people who think it's still better than if they'd used Linux or FreeBSD.

System Requirements

The system requirements for FreeBSD depend on what you intend to do with the system. For a typical workstation setup that will run the X Window System (a graphical interface system similar to Windows or Macintosh, also referred to as X or X11), the following minimum system requirements are recommended:

- Pentium class processor
- 64MB of RAM
- At least 300MB of free hard disk space
- SVGA or better video card compatible with the X Window System (see Appendix A, "Resources for FreeBSD Users")
- Three-button mouse

It is possible to use the X Window System with a two-button mouse. However, unlike Microsoft Windows, X relies a great deal on the third mouse button. It is much easier to work in X with a three-button mouse.

If you have no intention of running a graphical environment, you can often get by with a lot less. In fact, if all you want is to set up an email server, router, or low end Web server, you can get by with even a 486.

Deciding How and Where to Install FreeBSD

There are two primary ways you can install FreeBSD on your system. Most people new to the operating system will probably want to opt for the dual boot method. With a dual boot system, you install FreeBSD alongside your existing Windows system. A program called a *boot manager* will be installed at the beginning of your hard disk. Each time you start your computer, you will be presented with a menu that allows you to choose whether you want to work in Windows or in FreeBSD. When you want to use Windows, you can simply select it from this menu, and the system will behave as if FreeBSD isn't even installed. In other words, your Windows system will work exactly the way it did before you installed FreeBSD.

The second way that FreeBSD can be installed is as the only operating system on the computer. If you only intend to work with FreeBSD on this system, you might want to opt for this method. If you choose to use this method on a system that already has Windows on it, you will delete your current system and start over with a new FreeBSD system. Because of this, it is important to back up any data you have on your system and want to keep. More about doing backups will be discussed later in this hour.

Backing Up Existing Systems

Before you can install FreeBSD, you will have to create a space for it on your hard disk, which will involve making some changes to the way your hard disk is currently set up. Although the program we will use to do this in the next hour can usually do this without causing you to lose data, it is still possible that a mistake could be made. Because of this, it is very important that you back up any important data that you want to keep.

Note that in general, you only need to back up your data. You don't need to back up programs or the Windows system itself because you will generally need to reinstall these anyway. Also, backing up all your programs and data would require a great deal of time and a huge amount of space on your backup media.

Do be sure to back up any registration keys for shareware and commercial software that you might have installed. If you reinstall these programs and then discover that you don't have those keys handy, you'll be reduced to limited functionality (or none at all).

There are several ways that you can back up data in Windows, and we aren't going to go into detail here. Of course, the simplest way is to just copy your data files onto your backup media (more on backup media later). You can save space by using a program such as WinZip to compress the files before copying them. Of course, several dedicated backup programs are also available for Windows.

As far as the media you use to back up your system is concerned, several choices are available—all of which have their advantages and disadvantages. We will next look at a few of the most popular methods.

Floppy Disks

If you only have a small amount of data to back up, floppy disks might work. The main advantage of floppy disks is that they are a very cheap way to back up small amounts of data, and virtually every computer already has a floppy drive, so you already have the hardware available to do the backup.

However, the disadvantages of using floppy disks for backups generally outweigh the advantages. For one thing, floppy disks are notoriously unreliable and prone to errors. In other words, you could back up your data only to find that when you try to restore it, the floppy disk was bad and the data is corrupt. Another problem with floppies is that they have a relatively low capacity. So if you have more than a small amount of data to back up, you could end up dealing with a lot of floppy disks. Not only is it very slow and time-consuming to back up and restore from a pile of floppies, but it also increases the chance that one of the disks will have errors. Floppy disks are generally the worst choice available for doing backups and should only be used if the amount of data to back up is small, and no other backup system is available. If you must use floppies, be sure to verify the contents of each disk after copying files to it.

Zip Disks

Iomega's Zip disks are a type of high-capacity floppy disks, having a capacity of either 100MB or 250MB. The main advantage of Zip disks is that they can be accessed like normal disks. In other words, you can load a document from it, make changes to it, and save it directly back on the Zip disk. Because of this, Zip disks are quite popular at University computer labs, for example. Because they can hold a relatively large amount of data, students can take the disks with them into and out of the computer lab, and they can be used like a normal disk. Zip disks are effective for backing up small amounts of data and are more reliable than floppy disks.

Zip disks have two primary drawbacks. The first is that the cost per megabyte is relatively high. For example, a 250MB Zip disk costs about 7.5 cents per megabyte as of this writing. Compare this to a rewritable CD, which costs about 0.35 cents per megabyte, and you can see that Zip disks are more than 20 times more expensive per megabyte than rewritable CDs. (Rewritable CDs do have some disadvantages that Zip disks don't have. We will look at those in the next section.)

The second primary drawback of Zip disks is that they are relatively slow. Although this isn't a huge issue for backing up and restoring data, it is an issue when attempting to use a Zip disk as a normal disk and accessing large documents from it.

Recordable and Rewritable CD-ROM

Recordable and rewritable CDs are perhaps the most popular backup media for small businesses and organizations that do not have to back up extremely large amounts of data. The cost of CD writers has come down greatly in recent years, making them afford-able to the average computer user. Recordable CDs are very cheap and can hold a rela-tively large amount of data (up to 700MB). For the average home or small business user, recordable CDs are probably the best backup option available.

Note that you can get recordable CDs (CD-Rs), which can only be written to one time, and rewritable CDs (CD-RWs), which can be erased and rewritten hundreds of times. For backup purposes, it is better to go with the recordable CDs because they are more reli-able than the rewritable CDs.

The primary drawback of recordable and rewritable CDs is that they cannot be written to like a regular disk. This means that you can't, for example, open a document from a rewritable CD, make changes, and then directly save it back on to the CD like you can with a Zip disk. Writing to a CD usually involves setting up a "burn" process with a number of files to write and then executing the "burn," which takes a fairly long time. What this means, really, is that CDs are not useful as an "on-demand" storage medium.

DVD-ROM

Recordable DVD-ROM drives are likely to replace recordable CD-ROM drives in the rel-atively near future. Like CD writers, the cost of DVD writers has come down greatly in recent years. Although they still cost significantly more than a CD writer, they are rea-sonably affordable (and a very good investment because they can write CDs and play DVDs as well). The DVD-R or DVD-RW media costs several times more than CD-R or CD-RW media, which means that they are far less "disposable" than CDs. DVDs can store up to 4.7GB of data per disk, making them effective for backing up even large amounts of data. However, for backing up *extremely* large amounts of data, DVD drives aren't quite a match for high-capacity tape drives.

Tape Drives

The oldest form of backup, it is still the most popular for backing up large amounts of data. Of course, the media has gone from huge reel-to-reel drives that held less than 100Mb of data, to Digital Audio Tape (DAT) cartridges smaller than a credit card that can hold more than 20GB of data. If you need to back up huge amounts of data, tape drives are still the best way to go. However, the cheaper tape drives can be unreliable, and the reliable ones are quite expensive (and often require a SCSI controller, which most computers don't have built-in anymore). The media isn't cheap either. Tape drives are best left for those people who have to back up huge amounts of data.

Summary

In this hour, we looked at what FreeBSD is and how it can be used. You saw that FreeBSD is a version of the UNIX operating system that is available free and can be installed on as many computers as you want without paying any licensing fees. We looked at some of the things that can be done with FreeBSD, including building a Web server, email server, file server, or an inexpensive UNIX workstation. We also compared FreeBSD to other operating systems including Linux, other versions of BSD, and Microsoft Windows. Finally, we introduced the two ways that FreeBSD can be installed and looked at the importance of backing up your system. We also examined several types of media that can be used for backing up your system before installing FreeBSD.

Q&A

Q Is FreeBSD a "true UNIX," or is it just "UNIX-like" as some people say?

A FreeBSD is a licensed implementation of the BSD code developed at UC Berkeley. Because that code is by definition "true UNIX," so is FreeBSD. So, in fact, is any operating system that uses such licensed Berkeley code.

Q Is there a way to run Windows programs within FreeBSD?

A There are ongoing projects whose goal is to allow users to run Windows programs in an "emulation mode" within FreeBSD, Linux, or other such operating system. These projects include WINE (an older emulator) and the Lindows project, whose main goal is to integrate Linux and Windows. These aren't mature or stable solutions, though, and your best bet is to bank on having to boot into Windows if you can't give up gaming.

Q What's the best media to use to back up my Windows system before partitioning my disk for dual-booting with FreeBSD?

A If you have a CD-R or CD-RW drive, this might be your best bet. You don't need to duplicate your entire hard drive and restore it later; in fact, it's often better to "nuke and pave" Windows and reinstall your software from time to time anyway. Just worry about backing up your personal documents, registration keys, and all files that aren't part of the operating system or any particular program.

Workshop

Throughout this book, the Workshop sections will test your knowledge of each hour's lesson with quiz questions, exercises, and activities. In this hour, we talked about pre-installation procedures, and so there will be no quiz yet. There are, however, some exercises to try.

Exercises

1. Go to your local electronics store or your favorite equipment supply Web site. Research the prices of optical media drives (CD-R, CD-RW, DVD-R), tape drives, and Zip drives. See if you can find which ones mention support for any operating systems besides Windows. If any mention UNIX, you're in luck. However, chances are that FreeBSD will work with almost any of them. Also look at the prices of the media for these drives; calculate how much it will cost you to back up all your important data using each method.

2. Find out what the terms are of the licenses under which some of the most popular open-source software on the Internet is developed and distributed: the Apache server (http://www.apache.org), BIND (http://www.isc.org/products/BIND/), Mozilla (http://www.mozilla.org). What do these projects' licenses have in common with the GPL? What do they have in common with the BSD license?

HOUR 2

Installing FreeBSD

Before you can actually use FreeBSD, you need to install it on your computer's hard disk. As long as you carefully follow the instructions in this hour, this is a fairly simple process that you should not have any problems with. In this hour, you will learn:

- How to begin the FreeBSD installation process
- How to partition your hard disk for FreeBSD
- How to install FreeBSD
- How to install some additional software
- How to properly shut down the system after installation is complete.

I suggest that you read this entire chapter before actually starting the installation. Also, make sure that you pick a time to do the installation when you will not be distracted. You will be making decisions about hard disk partitioning that could potentially cause you to lose existing data if you make the wrong decisions or press the wrong keys.

Beginning the FreeBSD Installation

As mentioned previously, the first thing you should do before installing FreeBSD is to make backups of anything important on your system that you want to save—even if you plan to use a program such as Partition Magic to repartition your drive. Although these programs normally do their job without damaging your data, mistakes can be made that could still cause you to lose everything on your disk. So it is always a good idea to make backups.

> If you plan to start with a blank hard disk and you want to install Windows and FreeBSD, make sure that you install Windows first. If you don't, Windows will make assumptions when you install it later and will wipe out the FreeBSD boot loader, which will leave you unable to boot into FreeBSD. Also, when you partition your hard disk to install Windows, make sure that you leave enough unpartitioned space for FreeBSD.

The CD included with this book is bootable, so place the CD in your CD-ROM drive and restart your system. If your system boots right back into Windows instead of starting the FreeBSD installation, you will need to change the order in which your system looks for bootable devices. This is done from your system's CMOS setup utility. Methods of accessing this utility vary on different systems, but usually it involves pressing a particular key or keys when the system is starting. The most common are the delete key or the escape key. Also, once you are in the CMOS, the methods for changing the boot order vary across systems. Basically, you are looking for an option that says something like "Boot device order." The important thing is to make sure that your system checks the CD-ROM drive first. When this has been configured, save the changes to the CMOS program and exit. The system will reboot, and you should see the FreeBSD installation program starting. Several messages will flash by your screen, and eventually you should see a screen that looks like Figure 2.1.

FIGURE 2.1

*The main menu of the
FreeBSD* sysinstall
*program, which allows
you to install and con-
figure FreeBSD.*

sysinstall

The sysinstall program is what is used to install FreeBSD onto your computer. At this
point, the only option you need be concerned about is Begin a standard
installation. However, don't select it yet because the next section gives some basic
pointers on navigating the program.

Navigating in sysinstall

The first thing to note about sysinstall is that you cannot use the mouse. You need to
use the keyboard to navigate through the program. The navigation is fairly intuitive.
Table 2.1 shows the keys used to navigate sysinstall.

TABLE 2.1   Keyboard Commands for Navigating sysinstall

Key	Action
Up Arrow	Moves up to the previous option in the menu.
Down Arrow	Moves down to the next option in the menu.
Left and Right Arrows	Toggles between the choices on the bottom of the menu. For example, on the main menu the left and right arrow keys toggle between Select and Exit Install.
Spacebar	In menus where multiple options can be selected, the spacebar toggles the currently highlighted option on and off.
Tab Key	Has the same effect as the left and right arrows in menus. Tabs between fields in screens where you need to fill in blanks.

To begin the installation, select the Begin a standard installation option from the
menu. You will be given a message about hard disk partitioning. Press Enter to continue,
and your screen will look like Figure 2.2.

FIGURE 2.2

Partitioning the hard disk in sysinstall.

Hard Disk Partitioning

Before you can install FreeBSD, you need to create a *partition* for it on your hard disk. A partition is sort of like a container on the hard disk that is separated from other containers. For example, you might have one partition for Windows and another for FreeBSD, as shown in Figure 2.3.

FIGURE 2.3

Partitions on a hard disk.

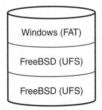

FreeBSD's Hard Disk Naming

At the top of Figure 2.2 (shown previously) notice where it says Disk name: ad0. This is how FreeBSD names physical disks in the system. The names start at 0 rather than 1. So, ad0 is the first hard disk in the system. ad means that this hard disk is an ATA hard disk. If you have a SCSI disk, it will be sd0 instead, but the concept is the same. ad0 or sd0 is the primary hard disk of the system. As you have probably guessed, ad1 or sd1 would be the second, and so on.

On this disk, there are currently no partitions. If we want to use the entire disk for FreeBSD, we can simply select A for Use entire disk. If, on the other hand, you already have another operating system such as Windows installed, you will want to select C for Create slice. You will then be asked the size that you want the slice to be. Simply enter the size and press Enter.

You will need to have at least some space available in order to create a slice for FreeBSD. This means that you must have some space available marked Unused. This space can then be assigned to FreeBSD.

Note that if you select the A option for Use entire disk, it will erase any existing partitions on your disk, including Windows partitions. Also note that if you delete the Windows partition from within this program, your Windows installation will be completely overwritten once the installation of FreeBSD starts.

2

Once you have finished creating the partition for FreeBSD, press Q to quit the program and move onto the next stage of the installation.

Boot Manager

You will then be given a screen that asks if you want to install the boot manager. Unless you already have another boot manager installed such as Linux's LILO, you will want to install the boot manager here. This will allow you to boot FreeBSD, as well as to boot Windows if you currently have that installed on your system and still want to be able to use it after FreeBSD is installed.

Creating BSD Partitions

Next, you will be given a message informing you that you need to create BSD partitions inside the fdisk partitions you created earlier. Press Enter here to get to the BSD partition table editor as shown in Figure 2.4.

Because this is the first time you have installed FreeBSD, I suggest that you choose the A option to select the auto defaults. After you have done so, your screen should look similar to Figure 2.5.

It's not important that you understand what all of these numbers mean right now. They will be explained later in the hour on hard disks and backup systems.

After you have finished editing the partitions, press q to exit the partition editor.

FIGURE 2.4

Creating BSD parti-
tions on the hard disk.

FIGURE 2.5

BSD partitions created
in the partition table.

Choosing the Distribution to Install

Next you will be asked to choose which distribution you want to install (see Figure 2.6).

FIGURE 2.6

Choosing which
distribution to install.

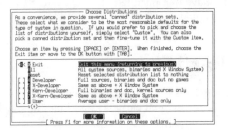

If you have a reasonable amount of free hard disk space (at least one gigabyte for a full installation of FreeBSD), I suggest that you select All by highlighting it with the arrow keys and then pressing the spacebar.

You will then be asked if you want to install the FreeBSD ports collection. I strongly suggest you select Yes here because this will allow you to install additional software very easily later on. We will see how to do this in a later hour.

Next, you will be taken back to the distribution menu (see Figure 2.7).

FIGURE 2.7

*The distribution menu.
Notice that all the sets
have been automati-
cally selected for you
because you selected*
All *previously.*

Arrow up to Exit and press Enter.

Choosing Installation Media

Next, you will be asked to choose which media you want to use to install FreeBSD (see
Figure 2.8).

FIGURE 2.8

*Choosing where to
install from.*

Because this is an introductory book, the only method we are going to cover here is
installing from the CD-ROM included with the book. Select the CD-ROM option and
press Enter.

After you have selected the media you want to install from, you will be given a message informing you that this is your last chance to back out before changes are made to your hard disk. If you are sure that you are ready to continue, select OK, and FreeBSD will begin copying files to your hard disk. Note that this process can take quite some time, and there is no sense in babysitting it. So feel free to do something else when the files are being copied.

> Up until the point when you are asked if you want to continue the installa-tion, no changes have actually been made to your hard disk. This is your last chance to back out. If you continue here, changes will be written to your hard disk.

Post Installation

After FreeBSD has finished copying files, several post installation tasks must be per-formed.

The first question you will be asked is if you want to configure any Ethernet or slip/ppp network devices. I suggest that you select No here unless you are sure that you know what you are doing. We will discuss configuring the network in detail in Hour 13.

There are some other advantages to not having the machine on the network right away. For example, the system will be relatively exposed, and if it isn't connected to the net-work, hackers can't get to it.

Next, you will be asked if you want this machine to function as a network gateway. Once again, I suggest that you select No here. The next question will ask you if you want to configure inetd and simple Internet services. Once again, select No here. These topics and their configuration will be discussed later on in this book.

Select No to the question about whether you want to allow anonymous FTP access to this machine. Anonymous FTP will be discussed in Hour 24, as well as how to enable it if you so desire.

At this point, you don't want to use this system as an NFS server, so you can select No to this question as well. NFS stands for Network File System, and it is a way for one UNIX server to access a filesystem located on a different server. NFS is not common in small business setups, and it is a topic that is beyond the scope of this book. You can also select No when asked if you want to configure this system as an NFS client.

The next question asks whether you want to change the default security profile. Unless you have very tight security requirements, I suggest that you select No here. You will then be given some information about the security level selected. When you have finished reading it, simply press Enter to continue.

Unless you have a foreign keyboard, you can also select No for the question about whether you want to customize the machine's console environment.

The next question will ask you if you want to set the system's time zone. It is probably a good idea to do this.

After you select Yes, you will be asked if your system's clock is set to GMT time. If you aren't sure, it probably isn't, so select No here.

You will then be given a list of regions to choose from to select your time zone (see Figure 2.9). Select the region that your time zone is in and press Enter.

FIGURE 2.9

Selecting a time zone region.

Next, you will be given a list of countries. Once again, select the country you live in from the list and press Enter. The final time zone list will ask you to enter the actual time zone. Do so and press Enter. You will then be asked if the abbreviation for the time zone looks reasonable or not. If it does, select Yes and the program will continue. If it doesn't, you can select No and try again.

You will then be asked if you want to enable Linux binary compatibility. I suggest that you select Yes here because the ability to run Linux applications is often very handy.

The next question is relatively straightforward. Simply select Yes if you have a USB mouse and No if you don't.

You will then be asked if you want to configure the mouse daemon. I suggest you select Cancel here because this daemon is not needed to use the mouse in the X Window System. In fact, it can interfere with the proper operation of the mouse in X.

When asked if you want to configure the X Window System, select No because we are going to configure this in a later hour. Configuring X can be a little tricky, so it is best left for later when we discuss it in detail.

Next, you will be asked if you want to browse the FreeBSD package collection. Select Yes here and then simply browse through the categories and see if you find anything that interests you. One thing I suggest you install is the bash shell located under the shells category because we will be using this shell in the next couple of hours.

You will then be asked if you want to create any additional users or groups (see Figure 2.10).

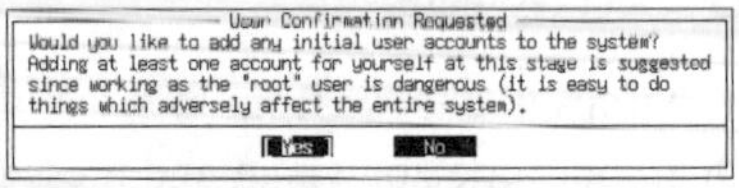

FIGURE 2.10

Dialog asking if you want to create any users or groups.

Select No here because we will be adding a new user for you in the next hour.

Next you will be asked to set the root user's password. After clicking OK, you will get a prompt like the following:

```
Changing local password for root.

New password:
```

Note that a good password should contain both letters and numbers and should not be a word found in the dictionary. It should be easy for you to remember to discourage writing it down, but it should be difficult for others to guess. It should also be at least eight characters long. After you have entered the password, you will be asked to confirm it. Simply retype it and press Enter.

You will then be asked if you want to visit the configuration menu to make any last minute changes. Select No, and the system will inform you that it is going to reboot. Select OK, and the system will reboot.

Make sure that you remove the CD-ROM just after the system has shut down and before it has started to reboot. If you don't, your computer will boot right back into the CD-ROM and, thus, back into the installation program. If this does happen, simply press the Restart button on your computer to restart it and then eject the CD-ROM as soon as your system starts to reboot.

Shutting Down the System After Reboot

As the system reboots, you will see a flurry of messages go by. (If you chose a dual boot system, you will see a menu first asking you to press a function key to select which operating system you want to start. Simply press the one labeled FreeBSD.) Finally you should get a prompt that simply says:

```
login:
```

Enter the name root here and press Enter. You will then be asked for the password that you gave during the installation. After you have entered it, you will be left with a prompt that looks like the following:

```
#:
```

This means that FreeBSD is waiting for you to give it something to do. In this case, we are simply going to tell it to shut down. The proper way to do this is to use the shutdown command. Because we want the system to halt (we want to turn it off as opposed to restarting it), we will type the command as follows:

```
shutdown -h now
```

The details of this command are not important right now, and they will be covered in a later hour. For now, simply know that this command tells FreeBSD to halt now. When you see the message Press any key to reboot, it is safe to turn off your computer.

It is not a good idea to log in as the root user except when absolutely necessary. Root has special privileges that can allow it to cause serious problems if used incorrectly. As mentioned before, we will create a normal user account in the next hour.

Never simply turn off a FreeBSD system without issuing the shutdown command first. Doing so could cause damage to files.

Summary

Congratulations! You now have successfully installed FreeBSD on your system. In this hour, we looked at how to partition your hard disk for FreeBSD. We then looked at the program used to install FreeBSD and did a walkthrough of the installation process. Finally, we saw how to properly shut down FreeBSD.

Q&A

This section is intended to answer some of the most common questions regarding FreeBSD installation.

Q I put the FreeBSD CD in my CD-ROM drive, but my system booted straight into Windows. What can I do?

A You need to select your CD-ROM drive as the first boot device in your system's CMOS setup utility. Restart your system and look for a message on how to get into the utility (the DELETE key is a common way). Press the key as soon as the system is starting up, and then look for an option to change the boot device order in the program that comes up.

Q After I restarted my system, it seems to hang and not load anything. What's wrong?

A Some systems will hang for a very long time if the CMOS is set to boot from the CD-ROM drive first, and there is no bootable CD in that drive. Eventually, the system will give up and boot from the hard disk, but to avoid the long delay, go back into your system's CMOS setup utility and change the primary boot device back to the original order. (Either primary hard disk first, or Floppy disk and then hard disk.)

Workshop

The quiz questions are provided for your further understanding of FreeBSD installation topics.

Quiz

1. What is the name of the FreeBSD installation program?

    A. `installation`

    B. `sysinstall`

    C. `setup`

    D. None of the above

2. Which of the following (if any) are good passwords?

    A. `october`

    B. `123abc`

    C. `xfgh`

    D. `fluffy`

3. What is the name of the command to halt FreeBSD?

    A. `shutdown`

    B. `stop`

    C. `down`

    D. `kill`

Quiz Answers

1. The correct answer is B.

2. None of these are good passwords. Answer A is a word that is found in the dictionary. Even worse, names of months (especially the current month) are some of the most common weak passwords in existence. Answer B contains sequential letters and numbers and thus is easy to guess. Answer C is too short. Answer D is likely the name of the user's cat, which is something that can easily be found out about him.

3. The correct answer is A.

HOUR 3

A Basic Tour of FreeBSD

FreeBSD, like most UNIX operating systems, has an extremely rich set of commands and utilities. This rich set of utilities allows users to do things with UNIX that most other operating systems cannot do. This power is one reason that UNIX has remained so popular, more than 30 years after it was originally written. Unfortunately, this rich set of utilities and commands can make FreeBSD a bit overwhelming and bewildering to the new user. This hour provides a gentle introduction to the FreeBSD command line interface and how to perform some basic operations.

In this hour, you will learn the following:

- The basics of the FreeBSD startup process
- Logging in to FreeBSD
- Your home directory and what it is for
- The rest of the directory structure
- Working with files and directories
- Logging out of the system
- The importance of proper system shutdown

The Basics of the FreeBSD Startup Process

When you first turn on your computer, a number of processes must occur before you can start using it. For example, your computer needs to check that all of its hardware is available and working properly, and load the instructions off the hard disk that tell it what to do next. A basic understanding of these processes is helpful for understanding how FreeBSD works, as well as for troubleshooting problems when things go wrong.

The POST

The first thing that happens when you turn on your computer is called the *Power On Self Test (POST)*. This is a program run by your computer's *BIOS (basic input/output system)*. During this stage of the startup process, the computer checks all of its hardware to make sure that everything is there and working. It counts the available RAM and performs some basic tests on it, determines the types and size of available media (hard disks, and so on), and assigns resources to plug-and-play devices. Note that this stage of the startup process has nothing to do with FreeBSD. This step is performed no matter what operating system you intend to start on your computer. At this point, your computer still doesn't know anything about what operating system it will be running.

The Bootstrap

After the POST has completed, your computer's BIOS looks for a device on your system that it can load an operating system from. The order in which devices are checked for an operating system can usually be configured in your system's BIOS setup menu. Oftentimes, the floppy drive is the first device that gets checked. This is why you get the "Non-systems disk or disk error" message if you have a floppy disk in your drive when you turn on your computer. Normally, the device that the system boots from will be the system's hard disk.

The Boot Manager

After the BIOS has found a bootable hard disk, it will read whatever is located at sector 0 on the hard disk. You can think of sector 0 as basically being the first thing on the hard disk. Sector 0 is also known as the *Master Boot Record* or *MBR*. This procedure begins what is called the *bootstrap*, which gets its name from the idea that the system is "pulling itself up by its bootstraps."

If you installed a dual boot system so that you can choose whether you want to work in Windows or FreeBSD each time you start your system, the FreeBSD boot manager program is what will be located in the MBR. You will know that this stage of the boot process has completed when you get a menu that looks similar to the following:

```
F1 DOS
F2 FreeBSD

Default: F2
```

The DOS entry is actually Windows. But it will show up as DOS with some versions of Windows. To select the operating system you want to start, simply press the function key corresponding to the entry in the menu. If you do nothing for a period of time, the entry listed next to Default will be started automatically. (The default will normally be whatever operating system you selected the last time you used your computer.) For the rest of this hour, I will, of course, assume that you selected FreeBSD from this menu.

> FreeBSD can also be booted from the Linux boot loaders: LILO and GRUB. However, configuring this is beyond the scope of this book. Please see the LILO or GRUB documentation for more information on how to add another boot option to either.

3

If you elected to install FreeBSD as the only operating system on the computer, you will not see this menu, but rather FreeBSD will start loading immediately.

The Kernel

There are actually a couple of startup stages between the boot manager and this stage, but we are going to skip them because they are not important at this point. They mostly exist for technical reasons. If you are interested in learning more about these stages and why they exist, there are more details of the bootstrap procedure in the FreeBSD Handbook available on the FreeBSD Web site at www.freebsd.org.

The next part of the startup process loads and starts the FreeBSD *kernel*. The kernel is a special piece of software that serves as the core of the operating system. It controls access to system resources such as RAM, hard disks, and so on, provides services (such as multitasking) that allow your computer to do more than one thing at the same time, ensures that two programs cannot interfere with each other by accessing resources not allocated to them, and, on a multiuser system such as FreeBSD, ensures that users cannot interfere with other users by controlling what parts of the system the users can access.

When the kernel has loaded, you will see a copyright notice that looks similar to the following:

```
Copyright 1992-2002 The FreeBSD Project
Copyright 1979, 1980, 1983, 1986, 1988, 1989, 1991, 1992, 1993, 1994
    The regents of the University of California. All rights reserved.
FreeBSD 4.7-RELEASE #0: Sun, Sept 14 02:04:15 CST 2002
    root@simba.lionresearch.org:/usr/obj/src/sys/SIMBA
```

The parts you want to take notice of here are the last two lines (lines 4 and 5). Line 4 contains important information about the version of FreeBSD you are running. In this case, we are running FreeBSD version 4.7 RELEASE (other possibilities are STABLE and CURRENT. I will explain these in a later hour). The date and time that follow the release indicate the date and time that this kernel was compiled. This might not mean much to you right now, but it will be important later on if you build a custom kernel for your system. (See Hour 10, "The FreeBSD Kernel and the Device Tree," for why you would want to do this and how to go about doing it.) Line 5 lists the name of the user who built the kernel, as well as the hostname of the system that the kernel was built on. The second part of the line lists the directory in which the object files for the kernel are located. If you are a C or C++ programmer and you know what object files are, great. If you don't know what object files are, don't worry. You can work with and administer FreeBSD just fine without ever having to worry about this.

After the copyright notice, you will see a flurry of messages go by the screen as FreeBSD detects and initializes the various hardware devices in your system. You don't need to understand what these mean at this point, but you might recognize some familiar hardware in the list. For example,

```
fd0: <1440-KB 3.5" drive> on fdc0 drive 0
```

is a 3.5 inch 1.44Mb floppy drive. The first part of the line (fd0) is the FreeBSD device name. It is similar to the designation "A: drive" in Windows. However, the FreeBSD system actually makes more sense because the designation tells you something about what the device is—fd stands for *floppy disk*. The number 0 indicates that it is the first floppy disk in the system. In FreeBSD, numbers almost always start at 0 rather than 1.

You might also see some lines that look something like this:

```
unknown: <PNP0501> can't assign resources
```

You needn't worry about these messages either. These are simply plug-and-play devices in your system that FreeBSD doesn't know anything about. With time, as FreeBSD supports more and more hardware, you should see fewer and fewer of these messages.

After the kernel has finished initializing hardware, it will *mount* the root file system. (More on mounting and unmounting file systems can be found in Hour 8, "Storage Systems and Backup Utilities.") Mounting the file system simply makes it available for use. You will see a message similar to the following when this process occurs:

```
Mounting root from ufs:/dev/ad0s1a
```

After this has happened, the kernel will invoke a program called init to handle the rest of the system startup. Messages coming from the kernel and messages coming from the `init` program can be distinguished by their color. Kernel messages are white, whereas messages from `init` are light gray in color.

init

One of the first things the `init` program does is check to make sure that the system was shut down properly the last time the computer was restarted. If it wasn't, `init` will run a program called `fsck`, which is basically the equivalent of the Windows Scandisk program. `fsck` will check and repair any file system damage resulting from improper shut down of the system.

After the file systems have been checked, `init` reads the system startup scripts and runs any programs that are set to run on system startup. These are similar to services in Windows or programs that have been placed in the Startup group in Windows.

After these programs have been started, `init` runs a program that initializes the console and provides you with a login prompt.

Logging In to FreeBSD

When the system startup process has finished, you will be left with a prompt that looks something like this:

```
FreeBSD/i386 (simba) (ttyp0)

login:
```

This prompt is asking you to enter the login name you gave to the user you created when you installed FreeBSD. (simba) is the hostname of this system. Your hostname if you just installed FreeBSD and didn't specify a different one during the install will probably be (amnesiac). (Note that the parenthesis are not part of the hostname.) You will learn how to change the hostname in a later Hour.

If you are coming from a Windows background, the first thing you might be wondering is why you have to login. FreeBSD is a multiuser system, meaning that many different users can use the system at the same time. FreeBSD was also designed to work in a networked environment. Because of this, security is a concern, so FreeBSD requires users to login with a username and password. This prevents unauthorized people from accessing files and such that they should not have access too. But even if you have a home system in which security is not an issue, there is still another good reason for users with separate logins. Each user can customize the system to his liking without affecting how the system works for someone else, which means no fighting over which wallpaper should go on the background, which sounds should be used for various events, and so on. Each user can set up the system the way they like it and not have to worry about changing the settings of other users.

> If you are the only person who uses the system, you might be tempted to just always work as the root user. This is not a good idea though because the root user has no restrictions and can do anything to any part of the system, including deleting important system files. Normal user accounts have built-in safety nets that prevent you from damaging the system (but not from damaging your own files). Because of this, it is always better to do most of your work with a normal user account and only login as root when you need to do something that can't be done as a normal user.

After you have entered your username at the login prompt and pressed Enter, FreeBSD will prompt you for a password. Enter the password you assigned to the user during the installation and press Enter again. Note that you will not see the password on the screen. Don't worry. FreeBSD is reading your password as you type it. It just isn't displaying anything on the screen in order to prevent someone who might be looking over your shoulder from getting your password. Assuming that you enter both the username and password correctly, you will see something similar to the following:

```
Last login: Fri Sept 20 02:04:15 on ttyp0
Copyright 1980, 1983, 1986, 1988, 1990, 1991, 1993, 1994
    The Regents of the University of California.  All rights reserved.

FreeBSD 5.0-RELEASE (GENERIC) #0: Fri Sept 20 03:15:25 CST 2002

bash$
```

If you made a mistake entering either the username or password, you will see the following instead:

```
Login incorrect
login:
```

Simply reenter the username and password and try again. When you have successfully logged in, you will see the bash$ prompt as described previously.

> Pay attention to the date listed for the "Last login" information after you have logged in. It can be a potential warning that someone else has used your account if you know that you didn't login at the time listed here. If this happens, change your password immediately and notify your system administrator (unless you are the system administrator). If you are the system administrator, see Hour 14 on network security for further information.

If you mistype your username or password a few times in a row, it will appear that the system has stopped responding because it will not give you the login prompt back. This is actually a security feature designed to help foil computer software that attempts to crack passwords by random guessing. Wait a few seconds, and the prompt will return. The delay will get progressively longer the more times you mistype your password.

Your Home Directory

After you have successfully logged in and you have the bash$ prompt, you will be located in your home directory. Your home directory is basically your personal space on the FreeBSD system. It is similar to the My Documents folder in Windows. All of your personal files are stored in your home directory, including your personal preference files for how FreeBSD is set up and any additional documents or directories you create. By default, no one else can write anything to your home directory. This means that no one else except you can create directories or files in your home directory. It also means that no one else can change or delete any directories or files in your home directory. This provides a measure of security because it prevents others from accidentally deleting your files.

By default, FreeBSD only prevents other users from deleting or changing files and directories that you have in your home directory. It does not stop other users from reading files stored in your home directory. If you have sensitive files that you want to make sure other users cannot read, you can change the file's settings to do this. This will be covered in Hour 4, "Basic UNIX Shell Use." Note however that the root user (system administrator) can read any file on the system. It is impossible to prevent the root user from reading any file. So keep in mind that even if you set a file so that only you can read it, anyone who has system administrator access to the system will still be able to read the file anyway.

The Rest of the Directory Structure

Your home directory is just one part of the entire FreeBSD directory structure. Outside of your home directory, FreeBSD has a complex, but well organized, set of directories. As a normal user, you cannot make any changes to any directories or files outside of your home directory (with certain exceptions, which are not important right now). However, you will access files located outside of your home directory structure on a very regular basis because this is where most of the programs you will be working with are located.

Like most modern operating systems, FreeBSD uses a hierarchal directory structure known as a *tree* structure. You are probably familiar with this term from Windows. If not, it gets its name from the fact that if visualized, the directory structure looks like an inverted tree with the highest level directory (the root directory) at the top (the root of the tree), and all other directories branching off the root directory. Figure 3.1 shows some levels of the FreeBSD directory tree. The levels given in the figure are explained next.

FIGURE 3.1

FreeBSD directory tree. Notice where your home directory is located on the tree.

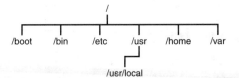

The directory at the top of the tree in Figure 3.1 is known as the root directory. It is represented by a single slash (/). All other directories are subdirectories of the root directory. An *absolute directory path* is written with each directory separated by a forward slash, going all the way back up to the root directory. For example, the directory /usr/bin indicates the directory bin, which is a subdirectory of the directory usr, which is a subdirectory of the root or top level directory /. Table 3.1 lists the purpose of the directories shown in the tree.

TABLE 3.1 Purpose of Directories Shown in the Tree of Figure 3.1

Directory	Purpose
/	The top-level root directory. Primarily serves as a container to hold the entire file system.
/boot	Containsfiles necessary for starting the system, including the kernel.
/bin	This directory contains programs that are part of FreeBSD, including the commands for creating and deleting directories, and so on.
/etc	Configuration scripts that control the behavior of the system. Also data files that store user information such as passwords.
/usr	Programs and directories generally accessed by normal users.
/usr/local	Programs and configuration files specific to the local system. This generally refers to third-party software installed that is not part of the base FreeBSD install.
/home/username	This is where users' home directories are stored, where username is the name of the user who owns the directory. I introduced the home directory earlier in this hour.
/var	This includes files that vary in size. Common things that are stored here include directories to hold print jobs waiting to be sent to the printer, Web server log files, and email directories.

Table 3.1 (and the tree in Figure 3.1) does not show all the directories, but it does show some of the more important ones to give you an idea of how the directory tree looks and works. If Table 3.1 is about as clear as mud to you right now, don't worry. Each of these directories will be explained in full when we deal with them later in the book.

Working with Files and Directories

Although various graphical interfaces are available for FreeBSD that provide Windows Explorer–like interfaces for managing files and directories, it is sometimes very useful to be able to manipulate files and directories from the command line. If you have never worked with a command line before, this might seem like a step backward in history to you. But actually, for many tasks, the command line can be much more powerful and quicker to work with than a graphical user interface—especially for doing things that involve manipulating a large number of similar files.

If you have worked with the command line in Windows, or with DOS, you will find that the FreeBSD command line is quite similar for most things, although some command names are different. If you have not worked a command line before, this section provides a gentle introduction to it.

> Even if you are an experienced Windows command-line user, you should at least skim this section because some commands will not behave the way you would expect them to behave in DOS. Particularly important is the section on FreeBSD wildcards, which behave quite differently from DOS wildcards.
>
> Wildcards that do absolutely nothing in DOS could potentially delete every file in a directory in FreeBSD!

The following sections go through some of the basic file and directory manipulation commands. Because most people learn best by actually doing rather than just reading, I suggest that you follow along by logging in to your FreeBSD system using the user you created during the installation and try these commands yourself.

Creating and Deleting Directories

The FreeBSD command for creating a new directory is `mkdir`. It is short for *make directory*. In its most basic form, simply follow the command name with the name of the directory that you want to create. For example,

```
bash$ mkdir mydir
bash$
```

This command creates a new directory in the current directory called `mydir`.

Rules for Directory Names

FreeBSD has very few rules for directory names. However, for the sake of making things easier to work with, there are certain conventions that I suggest you follow. Note that all these rules apply to filenames as well.

It is possible to create directory names that contain spaces, but in order to do so, you need to use quotation marks around the entire directory name. FreeBSD interprets a space as an argument separator for the command. In other words, if you type the command mkdir my dir, FreeBSD will interpret the space between my and dir as an argument separator. The result is that the command will create two new directories— one named my and the other named dir. For the command to have the desired effect of creating a directory called "my dir", you need to type it like this:

```
mkdir "my dir"
```

Because typing quotation marks around directory names is inconvenient and also error prone, I suggest that you avoid using directory names with spaces. One common solution is to use the underscore character instead of a space (for example, "my_dir"). This avoids the potential error of using spaces in directory names.

Directory names that contain spaces also pose a potential danger for making mistakes that can have unintended results. For example, suppose that you have a directory called documents from work, another directory just called documents, and a third one called work. You want to delete the directory called documents from work. As I said before, FreeBSD interprets a space as an argument separator unless it is quoted. The command to remove a directory is rmdir. If you forget to quote and type the command rmdir documents from work, FreeBSD will attempt to remove three directories named documents, from, and work. In this case, failure to quote will have disastrous results because this command will delete the documents directory and the work directory, while leaving the documents from work directory untouched—not what you intended to happen. Using the underscore character instead of the space avoids the danger of this happening.

Also, you cannot begin a directory or filename with a dash character (-) because FreeBSD interprets the dash to indicate that what follows is a parameter that modifies the behavior of the given command. You can have dashes in the middle of your filenames and directory names, however.

To delete the directory you just created, use the rmdir command. For example,

```
bash$ rmdir mydir
bash$
```

Note that `rmdir` can only remove directories that are empty. If there are any files or subdirectories within the directory, you will get the error message `directory is not empty`. Later in this hour, we will look at a command that can remove directories that are not empty.

Note that the `rmdir` command does not ask for confirmation before it goes to work. FreeBSD assumes that you know what you are doing and by default, commands almost never ask for confirmation before they go to work—even if you have told them to do something extremely destructive. If you are not sure what you are doing, there is a command line option to use with most commands. The option is `-i`. The _–i_ is short for _interactive_. This causes the command to ask you for confirmation before it actually does anything. This option can be very useful when you are not entirely sure that the command you are giving FreeBSD will have the intended effect. If it turns out that the command is going to do something other than what you intended, the `-i` option will let you know about it and give you the opportunity to bail out before it is too late.

Assuming that you are following along and you issued the preceding `rmdir` command, go ahead and re-create the directory using the `mkdir` command again because we will use it in the next section.

Listing Directory Contents

The `ls` command is used to list the contents of directories. Here is some sample output from the `ls` command:

```
bash$ ls
Mail          projects     proposal-draft        program1
tyfbsd         mail        program1.c
bash$
```

The main problem with this listing is that it gives you virtually no information about what kinds of things actually exist in the directory other than their names. But there is no way to tell whether the entry belongs to a file, subdirectory, and so on. Because of this, the `ls` command provides several options that can be used to get it to display more information on each entry. For example, the `-F` entry causes `ls` to give us more information about the type of each entry in the list:

```
bash$
Mail/         projects/    proposal-draft        program1*
tyfbsd@        mail/        program.c
bash$
```

The symbols behind some of the entries in the preceding listing tell us what kind of entry it is. Here is what they mean:

- /: The item is a directory.

- *: The item is an executable program or script.

- @: The item is a symbolic link to another location. This is similar to a shortcut in Windows.

Unlike Windows, executable files in FreeBSD are not required to have a .EXE or .COM extension. We will look at how FreeBSD determines whether a file should be executable or not later on.

In FreeBSD, files that begin with a leading period (.) will be hidden in the normal directory listing. Files beginning with periods are normally configuration files that control behavior of programs and your working environment. Because these files are rarely accessed, FreeBSD hides them in the normal directory listing to avoid cluttering up the listing with entries that are irrelevant most of the time. If you want to see the hidden files, use the -a option with the ls command. The -a is short for *all*:

```
bash$ ls -a
.          .forward      .mailrc      .profile      Mail
..         .hushlogin    .project     tyfbsd
.addressbook   .sh-history       .cshrc        .mail_aliases
bash$
```

It's not important that you know what all these files mean at this point, but you might be able to guess at the meanings from some of the names. For example, files here contain your user profile, control how your email should be delivered and whether it should be forwarded, and so on.

Two entries here deserve special mention. Those are the entries . and ... The single period represents the current directory, and the double period represents the parent directory of this directory—that is, the directory that this directory is a subdirectory of. With the exception of the root directory (/), all directories have a parent directory.

Another useful option to ls is the -l option. -l is short for *long*, and this gives you many more details about each entry in the list. For example,

```
bash$ ls -l
drwx——— 2 murban research    512 Feb 15 22:21 Mail
lrwxr-wr-w 1 murban research    15 Mar 20 06:55 tyfbsd ->
/home/murban/documents/books/tyfbsd
-rw-r—r— 1 murban research    782 Mar 15 01:22 proposal-draft
-rwx——— 1 murban research  15200 Mar 15 02:21 program
bash$
```

I'm not going to cover all the information given in this list at this point, but I will cover some of the more important information.

The first set of entries lists the type of the entry and its permissions. The first entry, Mail, starts with *d*, which means that the entry corresponds to a directory. The next nine spaces correspond to the permissions. There are three spaces for the owner of the file, three spaces for the group of the file, and three spaces for other, which includes everyone else. In this case, the owner has read, write, and execute permissions on this directory (rwx). The group and the user have no permissions. Who are the owner and group? Those are indicated by the third and fourth entries. In this case, the owner is murban and the group is research. (My group membership is research). In this case, this means that murban can do whatever he wants with this directory (read, write, execute), but no one else can do anything. I will explain permissions in more detail in a later hour.

The next entry after research indicates the size of the entry in bytes. After that comes the date and time that the entry was last modified. The last entry is, of course, the name of the file.

The second line deserves special mention. An entry that looks like this

```
lrwxr-wr-w 1 murban research     15 Mar 20 06:55 tyfbsd ->
/home/murban/documents/books/tyfbsd
```

indicates a symbolic link. As mentioned previously, symbolic links are like shortcuts in Windows. In this case, the entry tyfbsd is actually a shortcut to the directory /home/murban/documents/books/tyfbsd. The symbolic link allows me to get to this directory by just using tyfbsd instead of the much longer path.

Changing Directories

To move to a different directory, use the command cd, which is short for *change directory*. For example, to change to the directory tyfbsd, which is a subdirectory off the current directory, you would use the command cd tyfbsd. This is called a *relative path*. A relative path means that the directory given to the cd command is relative to the directory you are currently in. In other words, the command is relative to the directory you are currently in, and the tyfbsd directory is a subdirectory of the current directory. The alternative is an *absolute path*. An absolute path always begins at the root directory. Recall that the root directory is represented by / and is the top-level directory in the system. An example of using cd with an absolute directory would be cd /tyfbsd. This would change to a directory called tyfbsd located in the root directory.

You might recall from the previous section that the double period (..) represents the parent directory of the current directory. Because of this, you can use the double period to move up one directory level to the parent of the directory you are currently in. The command to do this would be cd ... If you want to move up two directory levels, you can use cd ../.., and so on. If you want to move to a directory called my_stuff—

which is located in the parent directory of the current directory—you could use the
command cd ../my_stuff.

> If you get lost in the FreeBSD directory structure, you can instantly return
> to your home directory by typing cd followed by pressing the Enter key.
> The cd command with no arguments will always take you back to your
> home directory no matter where you currently are in the directory tree.

The pwd Command

If you can't remember what directory you are currently in, the pwd command will list
it for you. pwd stands for *print working directory*. There is a way to make the current
working directory a part of your shell prompt so that the prompt always shows you
what directory you are currently in. We will look at how to do this in Hour 5, "Advanced
UNIX Shell Use."

Creating Files

There are several ways to create an empty file in FreeBSD. For our purposes right now,
we are going to use the touch command. If you are not already in it, change to the directory we created earlier called mydir using the cd command discussed previously. Now
enter the command **touch myfile**. This will simply create an empty file called myfile in
the current directory. Of course, empty files are not very useful, but this will allow you to
look at some basic file manipulation commands.

> The tilde character, ~, is shorthand for your home directory. It can be used
> anywhere that you want to refer to your home directory. For example, cd
> ~/documents will take you to the documents directory located within your
> home directory no matter where you currently are in the directory tree.

Moving Files

The command to move a file from one place to another is mv. Try the following
command:

```
mv myfile myfile1
```

This command will simply move myfile to a new file called myfile1. Of course, you
can also think of this as simply renaming the file. However, the behavior of mv will

depend on myfile1. If myfile1 does not already exist as an entry in the directory list, the behavior will be as previously mentioned. myfile will simply be renamed to myfile1. If myfile1 already exists in the directory and it is an existing file, myfile will overwrite myfile1. Note that FreeBSD will not ask for confirmation before overwriting the existing file. So once again, you might want to use the -i option to mv if you aren't completely sure of what you are doing. As with the rmdir command mentioned earlier, the -i will make the command interactive, so it will prompt before doing anything.

If myfile1 already exists in the current directory and is a subdirectory, the command will move myfile into the subdirectory myfile1 and myfile will keep its existing name. Thus, the result will be that the file is now located at myfile1/myfile. Note that if the file myfile already exists in the subdirectory myfile1, FreeBSD will overwrite the existing file—once again, without asking for confirmation first.

Copying Files

The command to copy a file from one location to another is cp. It behaves very much like the mv command except that it creates a copy of the file instead of moving it. Like the mv command, cp will create a copy of the file under a new name if the second name given to the cp command doesn't already exist. If the second name given is a directory, cp will make a copy of the file in the new directory, and the new file will maintain its original name. Also, like the mv command, cp will overwrite an already existing file with the same name without asking permission first. So once again, it might be a good idea to use the -i option if you are not 100% sure what you are doing.

The cp command can also be used to copy directories. By default, however, it will not go more than one level deep. If you want to recursively copy a directory and all of its subdirectories (in other words, you want to copy a directory and everything inside it), you can use the -R option to the cp command. Once again, you might also want to use -i to prevent cp from accidentally overwriting any files you didn't intend to overwrite.

You can get yourself in trouble with the -R option to cp. For example, a command such as cp -R ./* ./old will attempt to recursively copy everything in the current directory to a new directory called old, which is also located in the current directory. (I haven't introduced *wildcards* yet, but basically, * is a wildcard that means *everything*.) The problem with this is that the directory old will also be recursively copied into itself. The result is a recursive loop that will quickly fill up all the available space on the hard disk. Watch out for situations like this.

Deleting Files

The rm command is used to delete files. In its basic form, simply follow the rm command with the name of the file you want to delete. For example, rm myfile will delete myfile in the current directory. The rm command can also be used to delete a directory and everything underneath it by using the -r option. For example, rm -r mydir will remove all subdirectories and files located in mydir and then will remove mydir. Of course, it is possible to do a lot of damage with the -r option because once again, FreeBSD will not ask for confirmation before it carries out the command, so always double-check the command line before you press Enter to make sure that you are removing the right directory. Also always be sure that there is nothing you want to keep anywhere in any directory beneath the one you are deleting. If you are not totally sure, use the -i option along with the -r option. This will cause FreeBSD to ask you to confirm each thing it is going to delete.

Wildcard Basics

Like their card game counterparts, wildcards are used to match any character or sequence of characters. They can be used for such things as moving multiple files or deleting multiple files. There are many ways to write wildcards in FreeBSD, but here we will only look at the two most basic ways. These ways are the question mark (?) and the asterisk (*). The question mark stands for any single character, whereas the asterisk stands for zero or more characters. If you aren't familiar with the command line, this might seem as clear as mud at this point, so I will go through a few examples to make it more clear.

Suppose that we have the following list of files in a directory:

project1   project2   project3   myproject   proposal.draft

The command rm project? will remove the files project1, project2, and project3 because the question mark can stand for any single character. So in this case, the 1, the 2, and the 3 will be matched by the wildcard.

The command rm proj* would have the same effect as the previous command because it will match all files starting with "proj" and containing zero or more unknown characters following "proj."

The command rm pro* would also remove the same three files, but in addition, it would remove the proposal.draft file because it also begins with the sequence pro. This is an example in which wildcards could get you in trouble. The lesson is that you should always use the maximum number of characters you can before the * wildcard. Don't take unnecessary shortcuts just to avoid typing because as this example shows, you could end up deleting a file you didn't intend to delete.

As you might have guessed already, the command rm * will remove every file in the directory. Sometimes this might be your intention, but it also means that you need to double-check the command line whenever you are using the * wildcard. A simple typo can be disastrous. For example, suppose that you want to remove all the files beginning with "proj" but instead of typing rm proj*, you accidentally type rm proj *. Remember that FreeBSD interprets the space as an argument separator. So a typo as simple as putting a space between proj and the asterisk changes this command to delete the file proj and then delete every other file in the directory! As you can see, it is always very important to double-check your command line when working with wildcards because even simple typos can cause disaster.

One way you can see which files or directories will be affected by the wildcard you are intending to use is to use it with the ls command first. This will simply list all the entries that match the given wildcard.

DOS users beware! Wildcards in FreeBSD can behave much differently than you are used to. One major reason for this is that FreeBSD does not give any special meaning to a period in a filename as DOS does. As far as FreeBSD is concerned, the period is just another character. The result is that the command rm * will delete every file in the current directory in FreeBSD, whereas in DOS, the same command would usually have little to no effect.

Logging Out of the System

When you have finished using the system, it is important to log out—especially if you are using a computer that untrustworthy people have access to. Logging out returns the system to the login prompt so that no one else can use your account or access your private files. To log out of the system, simply type **exit** at the bash$ prompt. This will return the system to the login: prompt.

If you want to clear the screen before logging out so that no one else will be able to see what you were working on, simply type **clear** and press Enter before issuing the exit command.

Importance of Proper System Shutdown

When you have finished using your computer, it is important that you shut it down properly. Because FreeBSD often has several files open and is often doing several things at the same time, you can't simply turn off the power. Doing so could result in serious damage to your file system. Before you turn off your computer, you must issue one of the FreeBSD shutdown commands. This ensures that all running programs are stopped in an orderly fashion, all data has been successfully written to the disks, and all open files have been properly closed. There are several ways to shut down the system, but I'm only going to cover one of the commands here because this is the one you should almost always use. Note that you will need to be the root user to shut down the system. If you are still logged in under your normal user account, log out using the procedure discussed in the previous section. Then, at the login: prompt, enter the user name **root**, followed by whatever password you assigned to root during the system installation. Note that the command prompt will be different this time. Instead of bash$, you will have simply #. The different command prompt serves as a constant reminder that you are logged in as root and that you need to be especially careful about issuing commands. At the prompt, enter the command **shutdown -h now**, and press Enter. You will see several messages on the screen. When the following message

```
System halted
Please press any key to reboot
```

appears, you can safely turn off your computer. Or, if you want to reboot, you can simply press any key as it says, and the system will reboot.The syntax of the shutdown command as used previously contains the action that you want shutdown to perform, followed by when you want that action performed. In this case, -h means that we want shutdown to halt the system, and we want it done now. Another commonly used option to shutdown is -r rather than -h. -r tells shutdown that you want to reboot the system rather than halt it.

If you are sitting at the system you want to reboot, you can, of course, use the -h option and then press any key to reboot as the system instructs. However, if you are logged in to the system from a remote location, it is very important to remember that the network connection will be shut down before the system is halted. This means that from a remote location, you cannot reboot the system using the -h option because you will not get the chance to press any key to reboot the system. The result is that the system will remain offline until someone can physically reboot the system. If this all seems confusing to you at this point, simply remember this: If you are logged in to a system that you are not physically at and you want to reboot it, you must use the -r option and not the -h option.

If you come from a Windows or Macintosh background, the second parameter that `shutdown` takes (when you want it to perform the action) might
seem somewhat confusing to you. After all, why would you ever want to
issue a command that tells the system to shut itself down later? The main
reason for wanting to do this is the multiuser nature of FreeBSD. On a server
that can have multiple people using it, it is rather rude to simply shut down
the system with no warning, which in effect is "pulling the rug" out from
under the users, causing them to lose any unsaved changes they might have
in open files, and so on. Issuing a `shutdown` command with a delay will cause
broadcast messages to be sent to all users letting them know of the impend-
ing shutdown and what time it will occur. The messages will become more
frequent as the shutdown time gets closer. This allows users to make sure
that they have saved any open files and such before the shutdown actually
occurs. We will look at how to set a delayed shutdown in a later hour.

Workshop

The quiz questions are designed to test your understanding of the material covered in this
hour.

Quiz

1. The command to create a new directory in FreeBSD is

    A. `md`

    B. `createdir`

    C. `newdir`

    D. `mkdir`

    E. `makedir`

2. Which of the following directory names are legal? (Choose all applicable answers.)

    A. `mydir`

    B. `This is a directory`

    C. `"My Directory"`

    D. `_directory1`

    E. `-directory2`

3. The -a option to the `ls` command does which of the following?

    A. It causes all files to be listed.

    B. It shows files beginning with a period (.).

    C. All of the above.

    D. None of the above.

    E. The `ls` command does not have a -a option.

4. The command `rm *` will perform which of the following actions? (Choose the best answer.)

    A. It will delete a file that is named *.

    B. It will delete a file that contains the * character.

    C. It will delete all the files in the current directory.

    D. It will do nothing at all because * is an illegal filename.

    E. `rm` is not a valid FreeBSD command.

Quiz Answers

1. D is the correct answer. None of the other commands listed are valid FreeBSD commands.

2. A, C, and D are legal directory names. B is illegal because it contains spaces and is not quoted. E is illegal because directory names cannot begin with a dash unless quoted.

3. The correct answer is C.

4. The best answer is C. The * is a wildcard that will match all existing files in the directory.

Hour **4**

Basic UNIX Shell Use

The *shell* is the primary command line interface to FreeBSD. It is the principal means that the user has to communicate with the operating system. This hour covers the basics of working with the shell.

In this hour, you will learn the following:

- What the shell is and why you need it
- Different shells that are available
- Working with files and directories
- Getting help in the shell
- Process management
- Other basic shell commands

The Role of the Shell

The primary purpose of the shell is to provide an interface through which the user can interact with the kernel. (The kernel and its configuration will be covered in Hour 10, "The FreeBSD Kernel and the Device Tree.")

Basically, the kernel is the core of the operating system. It provides most of the functionality that the rest of the system needs in order to function. The user needs to be able to "talk" to the kernel in order to send commands to the operating system. However, the kernel doesn't speak a language that is anything like any human language.

Attempting to communicate with the kernel in its own language would be extremely complicated and frustrating. This is where the shell comes in. The shell is basically an interpreter that understands commands in something resembling common English and translates those commands into a language the kernel can understand. The shell also accepts messages from the kernel and displays them in a language the user can understand. The shell, in effect, isolates the user from the kernel (and some would say protects the user from the kernel). The result is that normally, the user never has to deal directly with the kernel and doesn't even have to care that it exists.

Figure 4.1 shows a diagram of how the kernel, shell, and system hardware relate to each other. The shell is an "abstraction layer"—it hides and protects the inner workings of the operating system from the user, in the way that the shell of a seed hides and protects its kernel from the outside world.

FIGURE 4.1

The shell, kernel, and system hardware, using the "seed" metaphor.

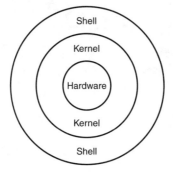

Windows or DOS command-line junkies will be familiar with this general concept because the FreeBSD shell is similar to the command line in Windows and DOS. (It is far less similar to the poorly named "DOS Shell" program that existed in some versions of MS DOS.)

Windows users who do not make use of the DOS command-line feature, and Macintosh users as well, will probably be less familiar with the concept. But in a very loose sense, you can think of the graphical desktop as being similar to FreeBSD's concept of the "shell" because it is also an abstraction layer, a user interface that isolates the user from having to deal directly with the kernel.

Different Shells Available

Unlike DOS/Windows, FreeBSD gives you a variety of different shells to choose from. The shells vary widely in the number of features they have, the ease of use for new users, and how they implement certain features. We aren't going to cover all the available shells here because there are far too many of them. However, we will cover some of the more popular ones.

The Bourne Shell

The Bourne shell (sh) is the oldest shell that is still widely used. It is named after its creator, Stephen Bourne. The Bourne shell is very primitive compared to more modern shells. It lacks advanced features like command history (the ability to recall previous commands) and command editing (the ability to edit a previously run command and run it again). FreeBSD does not include the original Bourne shell, but rather includes a shell known as the POSIX shell. The POSIX shell is an enhanced Bourne shell with complete backward compatibility with the original version, but that includes additional features such as history functions and command editing. If you don't specify otherwise, new user accounts will have POSIX as the default shell.

The C Shell

The C shell (csh) is so named because it was designed to have a syntax similar to the C programming language. It was developed by the University of California at Berkeley for the BSD version of UNIX. The C shell had many more features than the Bourne shell, including the ability to recall previous commands, the ability to edit and rerun previous commands, and the ability to automatically run a script of commands upon logging out of the system. (The Bourne shell could only run a script of commands upon logging in to the system.) Unfortunately, the C shell was not compatible with the Bourne shell and could not run scripts written for the Bourne shell.

The original C shell no longer ships with FreeBSD. Instead, it has been replaced by the tcsh shell, which is an enhanced version of the C shell with additional features. The tcsh shell is explained a little later on in this hour.

The default shell of the root user, or administrator, is csh—which in FreeBSD these days is the same thing as tcsh.

The Korn Shell

The Korn shell (ksh or pdksh—FreeBSD uses the latter) was AT&T's response to the C shell. The Korn shell is backward compatible with the Bourne shell, so it will run any script written for the Bourne shell. However, the Korn shell adds features such as command history and editing—features that were missing from the original Bourne shell. The Korn shell is one of the most popular shells for UNIX operating systems. However, new users will probably prefer the Bash shell (discussed next).

The Bash Shell

The Bash shell (bash) is short for *Bourne Again Shell*. This shell was developed by the Free Software Foundation; like the Korn shell, it is backward compatible with the Bourne shell. Also like the Korn shell, it includes history and command editing functions. However, Bash's history and command editing functions are more intuitive for new users than Korn's are. The Bash shell is also a very popular shell on UNIX systems today and is the standard default shell on all Linux distributions.

The Tcsh Shell

The Tcsh shell (tcsh) is an enhanced C shell. It adds features such as more intuitive command-line editing and history functions. In addition, it also includes command-line completion (the ability to automatically complete a command and save you some typing). One other feature of the Tcsh shell worth mentioning is its capability to recognize potentially dangerous commands and warn the user before carrying them out, thus giving the user a chance to abort the command. Tcsh is the default FreeBSD shell assigned to the root user. (But normal users are assigned the POSIX shell by default.)

Which Shell Should You Use?

For most tasks you will do, it is not particularly important which shell you decide to use. Copying and moving files, listing directories, and running programs, for example, will work the same in all the shells. In this chapter and the next one, we will be working primarily with the Bash shell because it is one of the most popular shells, one of the most powerful, and also one of the easiest for new users to work with.

One other reason to choose the Bash shell or some other Bourne compatible shell is that if you ever decide you want to do shell programming, these shells are a lot better candidates for shell programming than the C based shells are. You can, of course, use one shell for interactive use and a different one for programming use. But this can sometimes result in confusion because both shells handle certain tasks in different ways.

Getting Help in the Shell

As previously mentioned, FreeBSD has a very large number of commands available. It would be impossible to document what all of them do in this book. Fortunately, the commands come with documentation called *man pages* (short for "manual"). To access the man page for a command, simply type **man** followed by the name of the command. For example, to get help on the man command itself, you would type **man man**.

You can navigate the contents of a man page by using the Page Up and Page Down keys. You can also use the up and down arrow keys, as well as the space bar. The spacebar moves you forward one page.

Man Page Format

The first line of the man page generallytells you what category the man page is in (more on that in the next section), followed by the name of the man page and a number in parenthesis. For example, mv(1) indicates that the man page is for the mv command and that this page is in category 1 of the man pages.

man pages follow a fairly standard format that includes the following sections:

NAME—As its name suggests, this is simply the name of the command followed by a very short description of what it does.

SYNOPSIS—This section gives a short syntax for the command including the required and optional parameters it takes. Parameters included inside brackets are optional: Parameters not included in brackets are required.

DESCRIPTION—This is a longer description about what the command does and how the options are used.

OPTIONS—This section simply lists the options that the command accepts along with a description of what each option does.

USAGE—Not present in all man pages. When it is, it lists any special usage considerations that might apply in certain circumstances.

ENVIRONMENT—This section lists any environment settings that affect the behavior of this command. If you don't know what this means, don't worry. We will cover it in the next hour.

EXIT STATUS—Not present in all man pages. It lists the exit status values that the command will return based on whether the command executed successfully. Exit status is primarily only of interest to programmers writing automated scripts that need to make decisions based on whether commands execute successfully.

SEE ALSO—This is a list of other commands that have some relation to the command covered by this man page. It might also list man pages for configuration files that affect the operation of the current command.

NOTES—Any miscellaneous information that the man page author thought you might find useful.

There might also be a line at the bottom of the man page that tells when the man page was last modified, as well as what version of UNIX the command first appeared in. In addition, some commands contain an EXAMPLES section that gives some examples of how the command can be used.

Man Page Categories

The FreeBSD man pages are divided into several categories numbered 1 through 9. Table 4.1 lists the categories and what they contain.

TABLE 4.1 Manual Categories

Category	Description
1: User commands	This section contains information on the commands most commonly used by users such as commands for file manipulation, text searching, and so on. This is the category you will be most interested in.
2: System Calls	This category contains information on the FreeBSD API. You don't need to worry about any of it unless you are a programmer and you want to write software for FreeBSD.
3: Subroutines	This category documents library functions in the C header files. If you don't know what these are, don't worry about them. Once again, they are only of interest to programmers.
4: Devices	This section contains information on communicating with device drivers in FreeBSD. Again, you only need to worry about this if you are a programmer and you want to write software for FreeBSD.
5: File Formats	Next to the first category, this is probably where you will spend most of your time. It contains information on the file formats of various configuration files.
6: Games	Undoubtedly, this is the most important category in the man pages. It contains information on the games and other amusements that come with FreeBSD.

TABLE 4.1 continued

Category	Description
7: Miscellaneous	If it doesn't fit well anywhere else, it will be found here.
8: System Administration	This category contains information on commands used for administrative tasks, such as commands for checking and repairing file system damage
9: Kernel interfaces	More programmer stuff. Once again, you only need to worry about it if you want to write software for FreeBSD.

Specifying Which Category to Use

Some commands have more than one man page. For example, crontab is a command that allows you to program events to occur at certain times on a regular basis. crontab has an entry in category 1 that explains the crontab command itself and another entry in category 5 that explains the format of the crontab configuration file. By default, simply typing **man crontab** will give you the first crontab entry in the manual, which is the one in category 1 in this case. But what if you want to read the man page for the crontab configuration file? In this case, you have to specify on the command line which category of man pages you want to use. This is done by simply preceding the name of the command with a number corresponding to the category of man pages you want to use. For example, man 5 crontab will give you the man page for the crontab file format instead of the man page for the crontab command itself.

Searching the Man Pages

So what if you know what you want to do but are not sure of the command to do it? You can use the -k option to man to search the man pages for keywords. Unfortunately, the keywords are not always intuitive, so sometimes you have to get rather creative for what you search for. For example, suppose that you are looking for a command that will join two or more text files together and print them as one file. You could try using the command man -k join. This will often give you a lot of returns, but unfortunately, it won't give you any command that will do what you want to do. If however, you search for the word "concatenate", you will find the command cat, which does what you want.

Command Summaries

At other times, you might know the name of a command, but you are not sure what it does and just want a short summary instead of reading the entire man page. For example, suppose that you are poking around in the /usr/games directory, you find the command

4

pom, and you want to know what it does. You can type **man -f pom** to get a short, one line description. In this case, the result is

```
pom(6) - display the phase of the moon
```

As in the full man page, the number in parenthesis tells you what category of the man pages this command is in. As you might remember, category 6 is games.

You can also search for commands based on their summaries. The short descriptions of commands are stored in what is known as the *whatis* database. To search this database for a command that has to do with "mail," you might use the apropos mail command (equivalent to man -k mail):

```
# apropos mail
biff(1)                      - be notified if mail arrives and who it is from
forward(5)                   - mail forwarding instructions
from(1)                      - print names of those who have sent mail
mail(1)                      - send and receive mail
mail.local(8)                - store mail in a mailbox
mailaddr(7)                  - mail addressing description
mailq(1)                     - print the mail queue
smrsh(8)                     - restricted shell for sendmail
```

You can also use the whatis command to search only for whole-word matches. For instance, whatis mail (or man -f mail) would have returned a list like the one shown here, but without the smrsh entry.

The GNU Info System

As you might have already figured out, the man pages are rather obtuse and often seem to be written for users who probably don't need them. New users often don't find the man pages very useful. Because of this, the GNU project came up with the info system. The info system works similar to the man pages except that info pages are usually much more detailed and helpful to new users.

To read an info page, simply type **info** followed by the name of the command. Note that not all commands have info pages. If you request an info page for a command that does not have an info page, info will load the man page for that command instead.

Like the man page viewer, you can use the Page Up or Page Down keys, the arrow keys, and the spacebar to navigate through the info page. However, the info system also supports hyperlinks similar to links in Web pages. To use them, simply use the arrow keys to move the cursor over a link and then press the Enter key.

Searching for `info` Pages

To search the `info` pages, use the command option `-apropos` followed by an equals sign, and then the search term. For example,

```
info --apropos=concatenate
```

Special Features of Bash

As mentioned previously, we are going to focus primarily on the Bash shell in this hour because it is one of the easiest shells for new users to work with—yet it is also one of the most powerful shells available. We will look at some of the features available in Bash, including history editing and command line completion.

Bash can be installed from the FreeBSD installation CD, under the "shells" category in the packages. To run Bash, after it's installed, simply type **bash** at the command line. (You might have to log out and back in before the system recognizes it as a valid command.)

> To permanently switch your shell to Bash, use the `chsh` command ("change shell") and specify `/usr/local/bin/bash` on the Shell: line.

4

Command Line History

The `bash` shell store keeps a history of the commands you have typed. If you want to repeat a command, you can move back through the history of previous commands by using the Up arrow key. You can also move forward in the list by using the Down arrow key. When you have found the command you want to run again, you can simply press Enter to re-execute the command. If you want to edit the command first, you can use the left and right arrow keys, the backspace key, and the delete key to change it. The history file in which the commands are stored is `.bash_history`, which is located in your home directory.

Command Line Completion

Bash also has the capability to complete a command line for you. It can complete the name of a command as well as the name of a directory or file path. To access this feature, type the first few letters of the command or directory / file and then press the Tab key. If Bash currently doesn't have enough information to make the command or path unambiguous (that is, there is still more than one possible match), it will complete as much of the command or path as it can until it hits the ambiguous part. At this point, it will beep, and you can enter more text and then press Tab again. This process will continue until the command line is no longer ambiguous and it can complete the entire command.

If you've reached an ambiguous point and you press Tab again instead of entering another character, Bash will provide you with a list of the files or commands that are potential matches for what you have typed up to this point. You can then continue typing until the command or filename is no longer ambiguous and press the Tab key again. Bash will complete the command for you. You can then check to make sure that Bash chose the correct command, as well as make any changes to the command line that you need to make, such as adding a directory or filename onto it. When you have finished editing the command line, press the Enter key and the command will be executed.

File Permissions

Because FreeBSD is a multiuser operating system, it is important to have some way to protect unauthorized users from getting access to files that they shouldn't have access to. FreeBSD implements file permissions to do this

File permissions are divided into three categories, and are of three types. The three categories are:

Owner   These permissions determine what the owner of the file can do. By default, the owner is the person who created the file.

Group   These permissions determine what group members can do with the file. By default, the group the file belongs to will be the primary group that the owner belongs to. (See the next hour for more information on Users and Groups.)

Other   These permissions determine what everyone else can do with the file. Everyone else includes anyone who is not the owner and is not a member of the group that the file belongs to.

Displaying Permissions for a File or Directory

To display a directory listing including permissions, use the `-1` option to the `ls` command, so the command looks lie `ls -1`. The following shows some sample lines from the output:

```
-rw--r-r--  1 murban  murban    0 Oct 29 06:28 file1
-rw-r--r--  1 murban  murban    0 Oct 29 06:28 file2
drwxr-xr-x  2 murban  murban  512 Oct 29 06:28 mydir
```

The first part of each line gives the permissions. There are three types of permissions. They are:

r	Permission to read the file.
w	Permission to write to the file. This includes making changes to the file or deleting it.
x	Permission to execute the file. For normal files, this means that the file can be executed like a program. For directories, it means that the directory can be entered with the `cd` command.

In the directory listing, the permissions are given in the order of the previous table. If the permissions is not preset, a dash (-) will be used as a placeholder. In addition, permissions are listed in the order user, then group, then other.

In the previos listing, we can see that the first two entries are normal files, and that they have the following permissions:

- The user can read and write to the files, but can not execute them. This is indicated by the first rw-

- The group can read the file, but cannot write to the file or execute it. This is indicated by the second r--

- Other people can read the file, but cannot write to the file or execute it. This is indicated by the third r--

The third entry is a directory, as indicated by the d at the beginning of the line. In this case, we can see that the directory has the following permissions:

- The user can read the directory (list the entries with `ls`), write to the directory, and `cd` into the directory as indicated by the first rwx.

- The group can read the directory and and `cd` into the directory, but cannot write to the directory as indicated by the second r-x.

- Other people can read the directory and `cd` into the directory, but cannot write to the directory as indicated by the third r-x.

So what if we want to make it so that no one can read file1 except us? This is accomplised by using the `chmod` command. In this case, we can simply remove all of the permissions from the groupd and from other. A command like the following will work:

```
chmod go-r file1
```

This command basically says to subtract read permissions (indicated by the r) from the group and from other (indicated by the g and the o). If we now do a directory listing, the entry for file1 will look like this:

```
rw-------   1 murban   murban    0 Oct 29 06:28 file1
```

What if we want to give read permissions back to the group? As you might have guessed, the command to do this would be:

```
chmod g+r file1
```

There are some other ways that you can set file permissions using the chmod command, but they are beyond the scope of this book. Please see the man page for chmod if you are interested. Man pages were discussed earlier in this hour. Also, see Hour 5 for more information on users and groups.

> There are a couple of potential pitfalls you need to be aware of with file permissions. The main thing you need to keep in mind is that directory permissions can override file permissions. This means, for example, that if the group has write access to a directory, anyone in that group will be able to delete any file in that directory, even if they do not have write access to the file itself. (The write privilages on the directory allow them to make changes to the directory). Another thing to note is that if someone has execute privilages on a directory, but does not have read privilages on it, they will be able to go into the directory, but they will not be able to list the contents of the directory. However, they will still be able to read files in that directory provided that they know the name of the file.

Process Management

As we have mentioned in previous hours, FreeBSD is a multitasking operating system. This means that you can have several processes running at the same time. Many of them might be running in the background. You can use the ps command to see a list of processes that you are currently running. If you run ps with no options, it will give you a list of only the processes that are owned by you. Several useful options to ps can be used to change what it shows you. Table 4.2 shows some of the most common and useful ones.

TABLE 4.2   Common Options to the ps Command

Option	Action
a	Shows all processes that are running, including processes that do not belong to you.
u	Lists the username that the process belongs to.
w	Enables "wide" output. Basically, this wraps the output of a line to fit in your terminal window instead of just truncating the output as it would otherwise do.
x	Shows daemon processes as well as normal processes. In other words, shows processes running in the background that have no terminal attached to them.
U *username*	Lists processes belonging to the user *username* instead of to yourself.

Remember that FreeBSD is case sensitive, so u and U in the previous table are treated as different options. Here is some sample output from running the ps command with no options:

```
12572  tty0  S        0:00.01 /usr/local/bin/bash
12578  tty0  T        0:45:04 /usr/local/bin/mutt
12582  tty0  R        1:22:01 grep
```

Let's look at what this output means.

The first number in each line is the process ID number, also known as the *PID*. The PID is simply a number that FreeBSD (and sometimes you) use to refer to this process.

The second column contains the controlling terminal that started the process. If the process doesn't have a controlling terminal, such as a daemon process that was not started from a terminal, this column will contain ??. The third column contains the status of the process. In this case, the first line contains an S. This means that the process is sleeping, probably because it is waiting for some other event (such as the user to type something and give the process something to do). The second line contains a T in the status column. This means that the process is stopped. A stopped process is basically one that has been paused and can later be resumed. We will look at how to do this later on. The third process has an R in the status column. This means that the process is runnable. In a nutshell, this means that the process is in FreeBSD's queue to be run and is waiting for FreeBSD's scheduler to enable it to access the CPU.

There are more statuses as well. To see all the status codes and their meanings, see the man page for ps.

4

The third column is the amount of CPU time that the process has used. This can often give you a clue as to a process that has gone out of control and is misbehaving. For example, if people have been complaining that the system is slow, and you find a process in the ps output that has used an hour of CPU time and was only started 65 minutes ago, it is most likely the culprit and needs to be shut down and restarted.

The fourth column, of course, simply gives the name of the process.

Terminating a Process

Occasionally, a process in FreeBSD might stop responding. (No doubt, Windows users are familiar with this.) When this happens, you might have to force the process to quit, similar to the infamous Ctrl+Alt+Delete, End Task sequence in Windows. From the FreeBSD command line, this can be done with the `kill` command. The `kill` command is followed by the PID of the process you want to `kill` (which you can get from the output of the `ps` command).

For example, in the last section, one of the processes listed is `/usr/local/bin/mutt`. Mutt happens to be an email client that is available for FreeBSD. Assume that the `mutt` program, for whatever reason, has stopped responding to the user's commands. We see in the output from the `ps` command that the PID of the `mutt` program is `12578`. To `kill` this process, you can use the command `kill 12578`. After the command is issued, the `mutt` program should terminate and the command line should reappear. If the `kill` command doesn't work, you can use the `-9` option to force the misbehaving process to terminate (for example, `kill -9 12578`). The difference is that the normal `kill` command attempts to terminate the process gracefully by sending it a signal telling it to clean up after itself and exit. However, the process can ignore this request. In this case, the `kill -9` command will forcefully "squash" the process. This command is not a request, but rather a forceful termination that cannot be ignored.

> The `-9` option to the `kill` command should only be used if the normal `kill` command failed to terminate the process. `-9` basically "pulls the rug" out from under the process. As such, the process will not get a chance to do any pre-termination actions that it might normally do, such as delete temporary files it might have created, and so on.

What happens if you have a busy server with several thousand processes running? Obviously, you don't want to have to read the entire process list, looking for the PID of the correct process. In this case, you can use what is called a *pipe*. A pipe basically takes the output of one command and "pipes" it into another command for further processing or filtering. In this case, we can use the grep command to search the output of ps and display only the lines that match our search terms. For example, suppose that the mutt mail program is not responding. We could use the following command to find its PID number:

```
ps | grep "mutt"
```

The previous command will display only the lines of the ps output that contain the phrase mutt.

You can also kill a process by name using the killall command. For example, killall mutt will kill any process named mutt.

Use the killall command with care because it can have undesirable side effects. For example, if multiple copies of mutt are running, killall will terminate all of them instead of just the one that is misbehaving.

To kill processes belonging to users other than yourself, you must be logged in as the root user. Also remember that, by default, the ps command will only list processes belonging to you. So if you are the system administrator, and a user calls you to tell you that her mutt program has locked up for example, you will need to use either the -U option to the ps command with the user's login name or the -a option in order to find the PID for the offending process. Of course, you will also need to be the root user in order to kill the offending process.

Stopping a Process

If you want to stop a process that is currently running, you can use Ctrl+z. The system will respond with something like the following:

```
[1]+  Stopped                 mutt
```

You will then be returned to the command prompt, from which you can run more commands.

The 1 at the beginning of the line is the job number of the process. It is the number you will use when you want to start the job again.

Restarting a Process

Restarting a process is also known as bringing a job into the foreground. The command to do this is fg followed by the job number. For example, to bring the mutt program back into the foreground, you would type **fg 1**, which would place you back into mutt and allow you to work in it again.

> If you try to log out of the system while you still have stopped jobs, the system will respond with a message that says There are stopped jobs, and you will be returned to the command prompt. If you really want to log out of the system without handling the stopped jobs first, type **exit** again. You will be logged out and the stopped jobs will be terminated.

Moving a Process into the Background

The difference between stopping a process and moving a process into the background is that a stopped process has its execution suspended. A process running in the background, however, continues to run, but returns you to the command prompt so that you can do other things while the process runs in the background.

To move a process into the background, first stop it using the Ctrl+z key combination as described previously. Next, after the process has been stopped, use the bg command, followed by the job number to restart it in the background (for example, bg 1). Later, if you want to move it back into the foreground where you can work with it, simply type **fg 1** as before to resume a stopped job.

> You might be wondering when it would make sense to have a process running in the background where you couldn't interact with it. A good example of where this would be useful is the find command. For example, suppose that you have a lost file and you are searching a large file system (50Gb or so) for the file. This is going to take quite a bit of time, as in at least several minutes even on a very fast hard disk.
>
> If you leave the find command in the foreground, you will be unable to use your system for anything else during the time that the command is running. Basically, you will just have to wait until it is finished. In this case, you might want to have find direct its output to a text file for later viewing. (You can do this by following the find command with a redirect. For example, > MyLostFile.txt will send any output that find generates into a new file

called `MyLostFile.txt`; you can also append output to an existing file with the >> operator, as in >> `MyLostFile.txt`.) After you have started the `find` command, stop it with Ctrl+z, and then restart it in the background with `bg 1` (assuming that it was job #1 when you issued the stop command). You are now free to use your system for whatever you want while the `find` command grinds away in the background looking for your lost file.

Summary

In this hour, you learned about basic use of the UNIX shell in FreeBSD. You learned that the shell acts much like an interpreter, translating human commands into language that the kernel can understand and vice versa. You looked at the different shells available for FreeBSD and examined some of the benefits and drawbacks of each. You then learned how to get help in the shell using both the UNIX `man` pages and the GNU info pages. The next section covered some of the special features of bash, including command-line editing, command history, and command completion. Finally, you learned how to kill misbehaving processes, move processes into the background, suspend processes, and restore them to the foreground.

Q&A

Q Why does FreeBSD treat the C shell (`csh`) and Tcsh as the same thing when clearly they're not?

A The `tcsh` shell is completely backward compatible with `csh` and includes a lot more features. It's effectively just a more advanced version of the same shell. If you want to install the old-style C shell, you might want to check out the `44bsd-csh` port (`/usr/ports/shells/44bsd-csh`).

Q Some of these shell commands are unnecessarily long. How can I shorten them?

A Most shells allow you to set up *aliases*, which are short commands that you specify to stand for longer ones. FreeBSD comes with several aliases set up by default in Tcsh; for instance, the `ll` command is an alias for `ls -lA`. You can override this or set up more aliases in the `.cshrc` file in your home directory.

Q After I install a new program, if I type its name, the system tells me it's not found. How do I make it "see" the new program?

A Your shell needs to be restarted in order to re-read the programs in its path. Either log out and log back in, or type **rehash** to reread the path contents.

Workshop

The following section contains exercises and quiz questions designed to help you solidify your understanding of basic UNIX shell use.

Quiz

1. Which of the following is **not** a valid shell in FreeBSD?

    A. POSIX shell

    B. Corn shell

    C. Bash shell

    D. C shell

2. Which of the following options to the `man` command allows you to search the man pages?

    A. `-s`

    B. `-f`

    C. `-k`

    D. None of the these

3. Which of the following commands displays a list of processes running on the system?

    A. `ps`

    B. `plist`

    C. `process`

    D. `pl`

4. Which of the following commands will terminate a process running on the system?

    A. `term`

    B. `stop`

    C. `end`

    D. `kill`

5. Which of the following key sequences will stop a job that is currently running in the foreground?

    A. Alt+s

    B. Ctrl+s

    C. Ctrl+z

    D. Alt+z

6. Which of the following commands will move a stopped process into the background?

   A. Ctrl+b

   B. bg

   C. background

   D. None of these

7. To move a stopped or backgrounded process back into the foreground, you would use which of the following commands?

   A. restart

   B. Ctrl+f

   C. fg

   D. None of these

Quiz Answers

1. The correct answer is B. Note the spelling. There is a Korn shell, but not a Corn shell.

2. The correct answer is C.

3. The correct answer is A.

4. The correct answer is D.

5. The correct answer is C.

6. The correct answer is B.

7. The correct answer is C.

Exercises

1. Using the FreeBSD man pages, find out what the wc command does, along with what its various options are for.

2. Use the man pages to get a quick summary of what the df command does.

3. Use the ps command to display a list of all running processes on the system.

4. Use the ps command to display a list of all running processes on the system, but this time pipe the output to more so that you only see processes containing the phrase init.

5. At the command prompt, type the command **sleep 900** followed by pressing the Enter key. (This starts a command called sleep whose only function in this case is to tie up the terminal for 15 minutes or 900 seconds.) Stop the process.

6. Restart the `sleep` process in the foreground.

7. Stop the `sleep` process again and restart it in the background.

8. Kill the `sleep` process. (Hint: Use the `ps` command to find its PID.)

PART II

Basic FreeBSD Administration

Hour

HOUR 5

Users and Groups

Because FreeBSD supports multiple users, security is necessary in order to ensure privacy so that users cannot interfere with each other or have access to things they shouldn't be able to access. FreeBSD implements this security through a system of ownership (that works on individual users as well as groups) that allows collaboration on projects while still ensuring privacy and protection against unauthorized access.

In this hour, you will learn:

- How FreeBSD enables multiple users to use the same system
- Why it is beneficial to have more than one user—even if you are the only person using the system
- Why FreeBSD has groups and how to use them
- How to add new users to FreeBSD
- How to remove existing users from FreeBSD

Multiuser Capabilities of FreeBSD

FreeBSD is a multiuser operating system, which means that several users can use the operating system at the same time while doing different things. At first, this might be a difficult concept for Windows and Macintosh users to grasp. Those familiar with either of these systems might be tempted to think that Windows, for example, is a multiuser operating system because multiple people can be logged in to a Windows server and use a database that is running on it. However, this is not true multiuser capability. The only thing you are getting with this system is client-server functionality. You are not using the remote operating system itself but only the services that it provides. With FreeBSD, it is possible for several people to be accessing the operating system at the same time through remote terminals and have all the functionality as if they were sitting at the physical system.

You might think that this multiuser capability is not important if you are just running FreeBSD on a workstation or on a home system. But even then, it can be a very useful thing to have. For one thing, keeping individual users separate allows each user to have his own profile, meaning that you won't have to fight with other family members about what kind of wallpaper should be on the desktop, for example, or what sound scheme should be used. Each person can set up the system according to their personal preferences without affecting how the system looks and works for other users.

Another benefit is that you have assurance that other users cannot accidentally delete your files. And if you would like, you can make sure that other users cannot access or read your private files.

One other benefit of having multiple users is not so obvious. As we mentioned previously, FreeBSD can allow multiple users to use the system at the same time. As a demonstration, do the following steps:

1. Log in using your normal user account. At the command prompt, start a program such as the ee editor by typing **ee**.
2. Press ALT+F2. This should give you a new login prompt. Log in using the same username you logged in with the first time.
3. Issue a find command for any file you choose and have it search the entire hard disk. The only reason for this is to ensure that you supply FreeBSD with something to do that will take a while to complete.
4. Press ALT+F1, and you should be taken back to your original login prompt with the editor still running. Type some text in the editor window.
5. Press Alt+F2 again, and you should be taken back to the second window with the find command still running.

6. Press ALT+F1 again, and you will be taken back to the editor. Exit the editor so that you are back at the command prompt.

Type **who** at the command prompt, and the system will respond with something like the following:

```
simba    ttyp0    Jul  6 16:10    (localhost)
simba    ttyp1    Jul  6 18:31    (localhost)
```

The output of the who command shows that you are currently logged on twice. And the previous exercise demonstrated that you can switch between your two logins and perform tasks that are completely independent of each other. This is one way that you can use FreeBSD's multiuser capabilities to your advantage even if you are the only user of the system. If you start a task that is going to take a while and you want to keep on working while that task is completing, you can simply switch to another virtual terminal using the ALT+F*x* key combination (where *x* is one of the numbers on the function keys) to continue working while the other task runs in the other terminal.

Press ALT+F2 again to switch back to the second terminal. If the find command is still running, press CTRL+C to terminate it and then type **exit** at the command prompt to log out. (If you want to clear the screen first, use the clear command before issuing the exit command.)

> When you are finished working, make sure that you log out of **all** the virtual terminals you are logged in to. If you forget and leave one or more open, someone else could access your account through it. You can always use the who command to check how many times you are currently logged in to the system.

> By default, FreeBSD has seven virtual terminals that can be accessed with the function keys F1 through F8. F7 will usually be blank because it is reserved for the X Window System, so there will be no terminal running on it.

Adding Users to FreeBSD

The command to add new users to FreeBSD is adduser. The first time you run it, it will ask you a lot of questions. Don't worry. You won't have to answer all of these questions every time you run adduser. Listing 6.1 walks you through a typical adduser session when running it for the first time.

Listing 5.1 A Sample adduser Session

```
#adduser
Use option ''silent'' if you don't want to see all warnings and questions

Check /etc/shells
Check /etc/master.passwd
Check /etc/group
Enter your default shell: csh date ksh no sh tcsh [ksh]:
Your default shell is: ksh -> /usr/local/bin/ksh
Enter your default HOME partition: [/home]:
Copy dotfiles from: /usr/share/skel no [/usr/share/skel]:
Send message from file: /etc/adduser.messsage no
[/etc/adduser/message]:
Use password based authentication (y/n) [y]: y
Enable account password at creation (y/n) [y]: y
Use an empty password (y/n) [n]: n

Ok, let's go.
Don't worry about mistakes. I will give you the chance later to correct
[ic:ccc] any input.
Enter username [a-z0-9_-]: fbar
Enter full name []: Foo Bar
Enter shell csh date ksh no sh tcsh [ksh]:
Enter home directory (full path) [home/fbar]:
Uid [1002]:
Enter login class: default []:
Login group fbar [fbar]:
Login group is ''fbar''. Invite fbar into other groups: guest no
[no]:
Use password based authentication (y/n) [y]: y
Use an empty password (y/n) [n]: n
Enter password []:
Enter password again []:
Enable account password at creation (y/n) [y]: y

Name:       fbar
Password:   ****
Fullname:   Foo Bar
Uid:        1002
Gid:        1002
Class:
Groups:         fbar
HOME:       /home/fbar
Shell:          /usr/local/bin/ksh
OK? (y/n) [y]:

Added user ''fbar''
Send message to ''fbar'' and: no root second_mail_address [no]:
```

LISTING 5.1 continued

```
Foo Bar,

Your account ''fbar'' was created.
Have fun!

See also chpass(1), finger(1), passwd(1)

Add anything to default message (y/n) [n]:
Send message (y/n) [y]: n
Copy files from /usr/share/skel to /home/fbar
Add another user? (y/n) [y]: n
Goodbye!


#
```

Once again, don't panic because most of these questions you will only have to answer the first time you run the adduser program. After this, you can run it with the -silent option to prevent it from asking you many of these questions. Later, if you want to change the default options, you can run it without the -silent option to be asked the questions again.

Because a lot of this is probably rather intimidating to you at first, let's walk through it a step at a time, beginning with some general observations.

Many of the questions you are asked during this process have a default answer. The default answer is presented in brackets like this: []. To accept the default answer offered, simply press Enter without entering any text. For the vast majority of questions you are asked, it is probably best if you accept the default. Now, let's look at some of the questions in more detail:

```
Enter your default shell: bash csh date ksh no sh tcsh [ksh]:
```

By now, you are probably reasonably familiar with what a shell is, what it does, and the features of various different shells. This question will set the default shell that will be selected for any future users you create. Of course, you can override this during any new user creation by simply telling it to use a different shell. If you are managing a system with a lot of users who are not familiar with UNIX, the bash shell is probably the best choice you can make for new user shells. Users who are familiar with UNIX can always change their shell on their own if they don't like the default shell that you gave them.

Any shells that you want to have available to the adduser program, and available to users for that matter, must be listed in the /etc/shells file. Most shells that you install from ports will take care of this automatically for you and will install the correct information into the /etc/shells file for you.

```
Enter your default HOME partition: [/home]:
```

This is the default place where the users' home directories will be stored. There is usually no good reason to change this. One possible situation in which you might want to change it would be if users' home directories are located on a central home directory server. (Thus allowing them to have access to the same files and environment from any workstation.)

```
Copy dotfiles from: /usr/share/skel no [/usr/share/skell]:
```

The dotfiles referred to here are default configuration files that control how the user's personal shell environment will work. These are the files we talked about in Hour 5, "Advanced UNIX Shell Use," that you used to customize your shell environment. You should just press Enter here to accept the default unless you have created custom configuration files that you want for each user and that are stored somewhere else.

```
Send message from file: /etc/adduser.messsage no
[/etc/adduser/message]:
```

You can optionally have an email message sent to the new user after you create his account. If you decide to send the email, the file listed here will be used for the text of the email. You can leave this as the default and simply modify the /etc/adduser/message file so that it contains the message you want to send.

```
Use password based authentication (y/n) [y]: y
Enable account password at creation (y/n) [y]: y
Use an empty password (y/n) [n]: n
```

The first question specifies whether you want to use password authentication. The default is yes, and unless you have a very good reason, you should leave it alone. You should also answer yes to the second question. This is also the default, so you can just leave it alone as well.

The third question determines whether the password can be empty. You will usually want to select no here. Selecting yes allows new accounts to be created with no password, which means that they can be logged in to without using a password. This is almost always a bad idea.

The "Use empty password" question marks the end of the default questions. You won't have to answer these questions again if you specify the -silent option when starting adduser the next time. Of course, if you want to change the default options, you can simply run adduser without the -silent option and answer these questions again.

The rest of the questions are specific to the user you are creating. They will be asked each time you run adduser.

```
Enter username [a-z0-9_-]: fbar
```

This is, of course, the login name for the new user. It will also be the user's local email address. Login names can contain up to eight characters and can use the characters located inside the brackets—in other words, a-z, 0-9, the underscore (_), and the dash (-). The eight character limit might seem a bit odd, but there are historical reasons that it exists.

```
Enter full name []: Foo Bar
```

You can enter the user's full name here, or you can choose to leave it blank. The name entered here will be used for the From: field in email messages sent from the standard FreeBSD mail programs, so it is probably a good idea to fill this in.

```
Enter shell csh date ksh no sh tcsh [ksh]:
```

This sets the user's login shell. If left blank, it will be set to the default shell that you selected when you did the initial configuration of the adduser program.

```
Enter home directory (full path) [home/fbar]:
```

This will be where the user's personal files and such are stored. Once again, it is not a good idea to change this unless you have a central home directory server where all the home directories are stored or there are some other special circumstances that require you to change it.

```
Uid [1002]:
```

This is the user ID number that FreeBSD uses to keep track of processes and files owned by this user. It also determines what privileges this user has. Usually you will just want to accept the default that is offered because adduser will automatically use the first available ID in sequential order. You can change this number if you want, but you must be very careful not to assign duplicate user IDs. Although this is not explicitly forbidden, it will result in conflicts between users. Generally, normal user accounts should have UIDs ranging between 1,000 and 65,000. Numbers below 1,000 are reserved by convention for special system accounts.

Never create a user account with a UID of 0. The UID 0 is reserved for the
root user, which means that any user account you create with UID 0 will
have root privileges on the system!

```
Login group fbar [fbar]:
```

This will be the user's primary group. Until you know more about groups, it is best to
leave this as the default. By default, FreeBSD gives each user his own group. If you want
to give users access to other groups, you can make them members of secondary groups.
You will learn more about that later in this hour in the section on groups.

```
Login group is ''fbar''. Invite fbar into other groups: guest no
[no]:
```

I suggest that you leave this question alone for now and just accept the default. It is very
easy to add the user to other groups later on.

```
Use password based authentication (y/n) [y]: y
Use an empty password (y/n) [n]: n
```

Select y to the first question and n to the second question: Otherwise, you will end up
creating an account that can be logged in to without a password. This is almost never a
good idea. An example of where you might want something like this is with a guest
account that has restricted privileges, can only run a single program, and so on.

```
Enter password []:
Enter password again []:
```

There was a time when passwords were restricted to a maximum of eight characters.
However, this limit no longer applies these days.

The importance of creating strong passwords cannot be overemphasized. The security of
a system is only as strong as its weakest link, and weak passwords are often the weakest
link. All too often, users will choose passwords such as the name of their child, pet, city
of birth, and things that other people know or can easily find out about them. It's also
fairly common for people to write down their password on a Post-It note and then stick it
under their desk, keyboard, or even worse, directly on the side of the monitor. It is
important that you discourage this kind of behavior because bottoms of desks and keyboards are the first place someone who wants to steal a password will look. Here is a list
of guidelines for creating secure passwords:

- Passwords should be at least eight characters long.
- Use a mixture of upper- and lowercase letters, numbers, and at least one special
  character in passwords. This will help foil programs that try random words to crack
  a password through brute force methods.

- Don't use words that are in the dictionary because there are programs that will try random words to attempt to find a valid password.

- Don't use information that other people know or can easily find out about you.

- Use something that will be easy for you to remember, but difficult for others to guess. Things that are hard for you remember encourage the bad practice of writing the password down and storing it somewhere. Some ways of doing this include combining parts of two or more words that mean something to you but won't mean anything to anyone else and will not make sense when combined. Another possibility is substituting the character next to or above the real character in the word. In this case, you will end up with a password that is total nonsense but will still be easy to remember as long as you remember the substitution key you used.

- Make sure your users understand that no one from your company will ever call or email them and ask them for their password. Users receiving calls and email from people claiming to be from IT and asking the user for his password is a very common method of cracking systems. Many users will actually give the caller or sender the password.

After you have entered and verified the password, select y to answer the question about enabling the password at account creation. You will then be given a list of details about the account and asked if you are sure that they are all correct. Assuming that they are, select y. Next, you will be asked if you want to send the new user an email message. As mentioned before, the default message that will be sent is /etc/adduser/message. You can use this message to give the new user information about who to contact for help, system use policies, and so on.

After you have finished answering the questions about sending the message, the account will be created and you will be asked if you want to create another account. Simply answer yes or no, and you are done.

Removing a User Account

If you need to remove a user account from the system, use the rmuser command. An example is shown here:

```
rmuser fbar
Matching password entry:

fbar:DKNlIrd/dlQRj:1002:1002::0:0:Foo Bar:/home/fbar:/usr/local/bin/ksh

Is this the entry you wish to remove? Y
Remove user's home directory (/home/fbar)? Y
```

5

```
Updating password file, updating databases, done.
Updating group file: (removing group fbar - - personal group is empty) done.
Removing user's home directory (/home/fbar): done.
Removing files belonging to fbar from /tmp: done.
Removing files belonging to fbar from /var/tmp: done.
Removing files belonging to fbar from /var/tmp/vi.recover: done.
```

Most of this is fairly self-explanatory. The question about whether you want to remove the user's home directory deserves some further discussion, though. Why might you want to keep a user's home directory around? The main reason would be if someone left the company, but they had files in their directory relating to duties that a new employee was going to take on. In this case, you would want to preserve the old user's home directory while deleting his account. You could then change the ownership of the files to the new employee who will take on the duties.

Groups and Their Purpose

To provide more flexibility, FreeBSD also supports groups. Groups allow multiple users to have access to a file or directory while denying people who are not members of the group access to the file or directory. Here is an example of when this might be useful.

Suppose that you have a sales and a marketing department. The marketing department is working on some new flyers and other marketing materials. Five people are on the marketing team who all need to be able to read and write to the files. You also have a sales department with five people in it. The sales department should be able to read the new marketing flyers. However, they should not be able to make any changes to them. Furthermore, you have some experimental marketing ideas that your five marketing people are collaborating on for an experimental new marketing strategy. This needs to be strictly kept under wraps, and you don't want the sales people to have access to it yet. Also, suppose that the sales people has access to a file that contains customers' phone numbers. We don't want the marketing people to have access to this: Only the sales people should be able to access it.

The first thing we will want to do is create two groups. We can call one sales and the other market. Then we will add each of our users to the appropriate group.

Creating Groups

To create a new group, simply add an entry to the /etc/group file that contains the name of the group, a GID number, and a list of users who belong to the group. Here are two sample entries for the new groups we want to create:

```
sales:*:1005:john, joe, frank, dave, susan
market:*:1006:lynn,peter,dave,sara,alice
```

As with user ID numbers, group ID numbers for normal groups should be higher than 1,000. It is also important to make sure that there are no duplicate group ID numbers. Each field is separated by a colon. The first field contains the name of the group. The second field contains an asterisk, which is a place holder that primarily exists for historical reasons. The third field contains the group ID number, or GID, and the final field contains a list of all usernames who are members of that group. Notice that the user dave is a member of both groups. This is perfectly acceptable. In this example, suppose that Dave is the exception to the rule. He is a sales person who, for whatever reason, needs full access to the material reserved for marketing people.

After you have created the groups, you need to set the appropriate directory and file permissions and make sure that they are owned by the appropriate people.

> For the curious, the asterisk placeholder mentioned previously exists from a time when users could not be members of more than one group at any given time, so they had to change their group membership anytime they wanted to access a different group. This field used to hold the password for changing into the new group.

Changing the Group Ownership

The command to change the group owner of a file or directory is chgrp. For example, to change the customer-data file to be owned by the sales group, you would use the following command:

```
chgrp sales customer-data
```

The command always takes the name of the group that the file or directory should be changed to, followed by the name of the file or directory that you want to change.

> Only the owner of a file or the root user can change the group that the file belongs to. And the owner can only change the group to a group that he is a member of. Of course, the root user can change the group membership of a file to any group, regardless of whether root is the owner of the file or is a member of the group that the file is being changed to.

Repeat the previous command for each file or directory that you want to change the group ownership of. Also, repeat the same procedure for the market group.

5

If you want to change the group ownership of a directory and all the subdirectories and files underneath that subdirectory, you can use the -R option
to chgrp (for example, chgrp -R sales sales_files).

Setting the Permissions

After you have made sure that the files and directories have the proper owners, you will
want to set the permissions correctly. Let's walk through several sample files with their
requirements and how the permissions should be set.

The first file is the customer database that contains the phone numbers of customers.
Only the sales group should have access to this file. But only the sales manager should
be able to make any changes to the file. The rest of the sales department should have
read-only access. To accomplish this, the sales manager—we will say that it is dave in
this case—should do the following:

- Dave should be the owner of the file. If Dave is not currently the owner, he will
  have to ask a system administrator to change the ownership of the file so that he is
  the owner.
- The owner permissions should be set to read, write.
- The group permissions should be set to read.
- The other permissions (permissions for the rest of the world) should be set to nothing. In other words, those people who are not the owner and do not belong to the
  sales group should have no access to the file at all.

The numerical way of doing this would be

```
chmod 640 customer-data
```

Recall from Hour 5 that the first number represents the permissions for the owner, the
second number represents the permissions for the group, and the third number represents
the permissions for everybody else.

Only the owner of the file or the root user can change the access permissions of the file. Someone who is a member of the group that the file
belongs to, but is not the owner, cannot change permissions on the file.

Now let's look at the access permissions for the files that need to be readable and write-able by the market group, as well as readable by the sales group. In this case, let's assume that the owner is Alice:

- Alice should be the owner of the file. If she isn't, she will have to ask a system administrator to change the ownership of the file so that she is.
- The owner permissions should be set to read, write.
- The group permissions should be set to read, write.
- The other permissions should be set to read.

Once again, we can use the chmod command to accomplish this. In this case, the numerical sequence for setting these permissions would be

chmod 664

In this example, the limitations of the group system show up. The sales people are not members of the market group, so the group permissions don't cover them. Making them members of the market group would give them write access to the file, which is not what we want. So in this case, we are pretty much stuck with making the file readable by the entire world because this is the only way that we can give the sales people read access to the file in this scenario.

Because of situations like this, the *Access Control List (ACL)* system was developed and was implemented in FreeBSD beginning with version 5.0. Access control lists are a more advanced topic that are beyond the scope of this book. For coverage of advanced topics like this, check out a book such as *FreeBSD Unleashed* from Sams Publishing.

As with the chgrp command, the chmod command for changing file access permissions can be given the -R option to cause it to change the permissions on the directory, as well as any subdirectories and files located in that directory.

We mentioned this in Hour 5, but it bears repeating here. Directory permissions trump individual file permissions in some cases. For example, you can have a file set as read-only for the other permissions. However, if the directory the file is located in has write permissions for other, anyone who can log in to this system will be able to delete the file. Watch out for problems like this.

Primary Versus Secondary Groups

One final note on groups is that it is important to understand the difference between the primary and secondary group. A user can only be a member of one primary group. The primary group is the group that any files they create will belong to by default. However, a user can be a member of multiple secondary groups.

The primary group is the one that is listed in the /etc/passwd file along with the user's entry. Any other group that the user is a member of in /etc/group is considered to be a secondary group.

Summary

In this hour, you learned about the importance of users and groups in FreeBSD. You learned how to add users using the adduser command and change group membership with the /etc/group file. You also learned how to set file permissions and group permissions using the chmod and chgrp commands.

Workshop

The following quiz questions are designed to test your understanding of users and groups that were covered in this hour.

Quiz

1. The command to add a new user to FreeBSD is

    A. adduser

    B. newuser

    C. makeuser

    D. mkuser

    E. None of the above

2. When adding a new user to FreeBSD, the option to keep it from asking you about default settings is

    A. -shutup

    B. -noask

    C. -silent

    D. -dontbugme

    E. -usedefaults

3. The file that contains the names of groups and a list of their members is

   A. `/usr/group`

   B. `/etc/group`

   C. `/etc/groups`

   D. `/group`

   E. This information is not stored in a file

4. The command to change the group that a file belongs to is

   A. `newgroup`

   B. `diffgroup`

   C. `groupchange`

   D. `chgroup`

   E. None of the above

Quiz Answers

1. The correct answer is A.

2. The correct answer is C.

3. The correct answer is B. None of the other files exist.

4. The correct answer is E. Watch out for answer D. The correct command is `chgrp`, not `chgroup`.

5

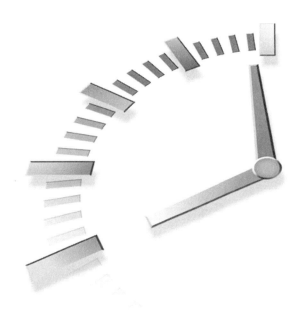

HOUR 6

Adding and Removing Third-Party Software

An operating system is not very useful by itself, and most people don't have a computer just for the sake of tinkering with an operating system. For the system to be useful, there have to be third-party applications that help you perform the kinds of tasks you want to perform. As of this writing, more than 7,000 applications exist for FreeBSD that can be downloaded free. In addition, FreeBSD will run most Linux applications. Some of the applications available for FreeBSD include word processors, spreadsheets, databases, Web browsers, MP3 players, image editing programs, video players, and more. This hour looks at how to locate and install software in FreeBSD, as well as how to remove software that you no longer want.

In this hour, you will learn the following:

- The two primary FreeBSD software packaging systems and the differences between them
- How to make sure that your list of available software is up to date
- How to install prebuilt binary software

- How to install software from source code
- How to remove installed software from the system
- How to manage existing applications
- How to work with Linux applications in FreeBSD

FreeBSD's Software Packaging Systems

FreeBSD has two different systems that can be used to install software. One of the systems works with prepackaged software that has already been built in to executable binary format. The other system downloads and builds the source code on-the-fly while installing the software. Both systems have their advantages and disadvantages.

The Differences Between Packages and Ports

As mentioned previously, packages are prebuilt binaries that you can install on your system. This is the type of software most users will be familiar with because it is similar to the way software is delivered for Windows or Macintosh. The main advantage of installing software from packages is that it can often be much quicker than installing from the alternative for two primary reasons. The first is that you avoid the time required to compile and build the software from source code. Although building the software from source does not require a lot of your time, it is a time-consuming process for the computer.

The other advantage of prebuilt packages is that it often requires far less download time. The reason is that building from source requires you to have all the libraries for the C and C++ compiler that the application requires. Any missing libraries have to be downloaded and installed before the application can be installed. In addition, some of these libraries will depend on other libraries, and so on. Although this process is usually automated in its entirety (FreeBSD automatically checks for missing dependencies and installs any that are missing), it can still eat up a lot of download time—especially if you do not have broadband access to the Internet.

However, installing from packages also has its disadvantages. The first one is that not all software is available in packages, so sometimes the only option is to build the software from the source code.

The other disadvantage is that you cannot customize the software or optimize it for your particular processor type. With packages, you are pretty much stuck with whatever options the package maker decided should exist in the software.

> If the idea of customizing software seems scary to you, don't worry. You don't need to know anything about programming in order to do this. All you have to do is tell the installer what options you want to build the source code with, and it will worry about how to actually include those options in the finished product. You will see how to do this later in this hour.

Discovering What's Available

The easiest way to find out what kind of software is available for FreeBSD is to browse around the ports page on the FreeBSD Web site. It is located at the address `www.freebsd.org/ports`.

Figure 6.1 shows the main ports page on the FreeBSD Web site.

FIGURE 6.1

A section of the main ports page on the FreeBSD Web site. Notice that the software is categorized according to its intended purpose.

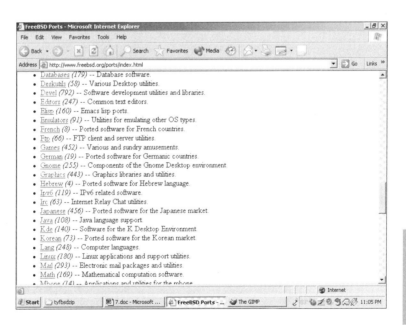

Clicking on any one of the categories will take you to a list of software available in that category. For example, Figure 6.2 shows a section of the Graphics category.

FIGURE 6.2

A section of the Graphics category on the ports page showing some of the graphics-related applications available for FreeBSD.

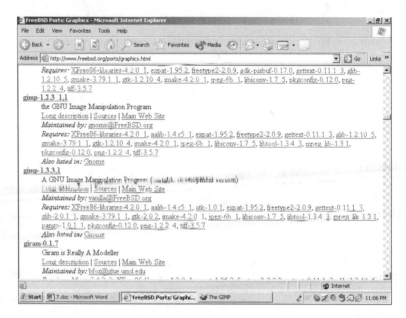

When you've found an application that interests you, simply remember what category it was under and then you can proceed with installing it. Previously, we mentioned that that two methods are available for installing FreeBSD applications. We will look at both of them, starting with the prebuilt package method. For our examples, we will assume that you are interested in the GIMP software. GIMP is a freely available image editing program that has features similar to Adobe Photoshop.

Installing Software from Prebuilt Packages

Prebuilt packages can be downloaded from the FreeBSD FTP server or one of its mirrors. If you've never worked with FTP before, the easiest way for you to do it will be from a Web browser. If you are working from the FreeBSD command line, you can use the Lynx Web browser, which is text based, but will work fine for our purposes here. To start the Lynx Web browser and point it to the main FreeBSD FTP server's package directory, enter the following command:

```
lynx  ftp://ftp.freebsd.org/pub/FreeBSD/ports/packages
```

Note that it is case sensitive, so the command must be typed exactly as shown; otherwise you will get an error.

After the connection has been made, you should see a screen that looks like Figure 6.3.

FIGURE 6.3

FIGURE 6.3

The Lynx Web browser connected to the FreeBSD package FTP server.

Use the arrow keys to navigate down the list until the graphics directory is highlighted and then press the Enter key. After the screen has reloaded, it should look similar to Figure 6.4.

FIGURE 6.4

Inside the graphics directory. The files ending in .tgz are the package files.

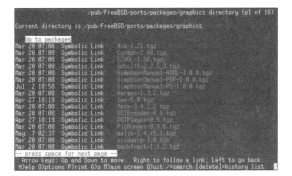

Once again, simply use the arrow keys to scroll down the list until you have found the GIMP package.

You can use the space bar to scroll forward in the list by an entire page.

The list of packages is in a semi-alphabetical format. All package names beginning with numbers are listed first. After this, all packages beginning with uppercase letters are listed in alphabetical order. This is followed by all packages beginning with lowercase letters listed in alphabetical order.

6

Figure 6.5 shows the screen with the GIMP package highlighted.

FIGURE 6.5

*The GIMP package is
highlighted and ready
to be downloaded.*

To download the package, simply press Enter. You will be asked where you want to save
the package. If you started Lynx from your home directory, that is fine for now. Simply
press Enter and the package will be downloaded (which could take anywhere from 30
seconds to an hour depending on the speed of your Internet connection). If you didn't
start Lynx from your home directory, add ~/ to the beginning of the path to indicate to
Lynx that you want to save the file in your home directory.

Installing the Downloaded Package

When the download has finished, you can exit the Lynx browser by pressing Q. You will
be asked if you are sure you want to quit. Press Y and you will be returned to the
FreeBSD command prompt. Type `ls` and you should see the newly downloaded package
in the directory list. At the time of this writing, the name of the package was `gimp-
1.2.3_1,1.tgz`. The name of your package might vary slightly depending on what the
current version of GIMP is when you read this.

The `pkg_add` command is used to install new software from packages. Usually, you will
have to be the root user to install software packages because they will want to install into
directories that normal users do not have write access to. To switch to the root user, you
can use the `su` command. Simply type **su** and then press Enter. You will be prompted for
root's password. After you have typed in the password and pressed Enter, you will have
root user privileges, but you will still be located in your same home directory.

In its simplest form, `pkg_add` can be invoked by simply supplying it with the name of the
package file you want to install. For example, to install the GIMP software we downloaded previously, we could simply type

```
pkg_add gimp-1.2.3_1,1.tgz
```

This assumes that you type the command from the directory where the package is currently stored. If you are not in the same directory, you need to supply the directory path to the pkg_add command of where the package is located.

When the package has finished installing, your command prompt will return and you are done. That's all there is to it—even easier than installing software in Windows. Unlike Windows, you will not be prompted for where you want to install the software, and so on because FreeBSD has a strictly enforced policy on where applications are supposed to install their files. Ultimately, this makes for much easier management in the long run because everything will be in a standard location instead of wherever the software programmer decided that the application should install its files.

If you want pkg_add to give you more detail about what it is doing when it installs the software, you can use the –v option, which is short for *verbose* (for example, pkg_add –v gimp-1.2.3_1,1.tgz).

Obtaining Information on Installed Packages

FreeBSD maintains a database of all the packages installed on your system. Among other things, this database contains a description of the package, as well as instructions that tell FreeBSD how to uninstall the package if you ever want to do so. You can get a list of packages currently installed on your system by using the pkg_info command. To display all the packages currently installed on your system, use the command pkg_info –a, the –a option being an abbreviation for *all*. If you just want information on a specific package, you can use the pkg_info command followed by the name of the package. For example, pkg_info gimp-1.2.3_1,1.tgz. If you don't know the exact name of the package you are looking for, you can use the grep command along with a pipe as you learned about in Hour 5, "Advanced UNIX Shell Use." For example,

```
pkg_info -a | grep gimp
```

This command will display all the packages that contain the expression gimp.

You can also use the pkg_info command to display information on a package that is currently not installed by simply supplying it with the location of the package. The location of the package can be either a local directory or an Internet address if the package is located on a remote FTP or Web server.

Installing Software from Ports

As mentioned previously, the alternative to installing software from prebuilt packages is to install the software from the source code. This system of installing software is known as the *ports* system. The ports contain information that tells FreeBSD how to build and

6

install the software from the original source code. Procedurally, installing software using this method is almost as simple as installing from packages. However, as mentioned before, it will probably take more time because of the requirement that FreeBSD build the software before it can be installed and the requirement that all necessary header files be installed so that the C / C++ compiler can build the software.

> The problem of missing libraries that need to be downloaded, built, and installed first will become less and less of a problem over time because many very common libraries are used by a large number of applications that you might want to install from the ports. However, these libraries only have to be installed once. So the next time you install an application that depends on the same library as a prerequisite, the library will already be installed on your system and the ports system will not have to install it a second time.

The FreeBSD Ports Tree

The ports tree is located in the directory /usr/ports. Like the ports Web site you looked at earlier, the ports directory is divided into categories containing different types of software. Under each category are subdirectories for each application that can be installed from the ports. In each of these subdirectories, there are more subdirectories and various files. You don't need anything more than a very basic understanding of what these files and subdirectories are for at this point, so I won't go in to detail about them. Basically, they contain instructions for the ports system on how to build the source code and where the completed products should be installed. They also contain dependency lists that list any prerequisite software that the software you are attempting to install depends on. If that software is not currently installed, the ports system will recursively install the missing dependencies.

Making Sure That Your Ports Tree Is Up-to-Date

Because the port structure is stored on your local hard disk, you will want to make sure that it is up-to-date. New applications are added to it on a regular basis, and new versions of existing applications are often released. To make sure that your ports system "knows" about this, you need to synchronize your ports with active ports tree on the FreeBSD project servers once in awhile. (The FreeBSD project servers are where new applications are added to the ports tree, and existing applications are updated to newer versions when they are released.) Synchronizing your ports tree is fairly easy to do and is done with a program called cvsup.

You should already have the cvsup program installed because it was one of the recommended packages during the hour in which you installed FreeBSD. If you don't already have it installed, you can install it from a package following the previously given instructions for installing packages. The cvsup utility can be found in the devel category of packages.

Once cvsup has been installed, you can use it to update your ports tree. Note that the following procedures require you to be the root user.

The first thing you need to do is create a cvsup configuration file. The easiest way to do this is to copy the sample ports supfile from /usr/share/examples/cvsup/ports-supfile to another location. /usr/local/etc is a reasonable place to put it. After you have done this, change to the /usr/local/etc directory. Now you need to edit the file to specify which server you want to update your ports from. Open ports-supfile in a text editor (see Hour 15, "Network Security," if you are not sure how to use any of the text editors), and look for the line that reads CHANGE_THIS.FreeBSD.org. Change the line to one of the cvsup mirrors that is close to you. A list of mirrors can be obtained at the following Web site:

http://www.freebsd.org/doc/en_US.ISO88591/books/handbook/cvsup.
html#CVSUP-MIRRORS

for the impatient, if you are in the United States, you can use cvsup1.FreeBSD.org through cvsup17.FreeBSD.org.

After you have saved the edited file, simply type the following command to start the cvsup process:

cvsup ports-supfile

If you are not in the same directory that ports-supfile is located in, you will need to supply the complete path for the file.

Depending on the speed of your Internet connection and how many ports have changed since you last updated, this process could take anywhere from a minute to an hour or so. The more often you update, the less time it will take since fewer changes will have been made and the system only updates those ports that changed since the last update was done.

6

If the connection attempt to the cvsup server times out or the cvsup program complains that the server is too busy, simply edit the ports-supfile again and change it to point to a different cvsup server.

Once the cvsup process has completed, you will be returned to the command line with a freshly updated ports tree. You are now ready to install software from the ports tree.

Installing a Port

Once again, the easiest way to find software that interests you is by browsing the FreeBSD ports on the FreeBSD Web site. When you have found something of interest, simply remember what directory it was located in. Then, as the root user, change to that directory in the /usr/ports directory. In this example, we will use the GIMP image editing program, which is located in the /usr/ports/graphics directory.

When you are in the graphics subdirectory, simply look for the directory of the port you want to install. You can do this by just using ls to list the directory. To prevent it from scrolling off the screen before you can read it, you might want to pipe the directory listing to more, like this:

```
ls | more
```

After you have found the directory location of the port you want, switch into that directory. To install the port, simply type **make**, and then press Enter. The ports system will then download and build the source code for the application, as well as recursively download, build, and install any prerequisites needed to build this application. During this process, you will see a lot of messages from the C/C++ compiler go past on your screen. After the build process has completed (which could take anywhere from a few minutes to several hours depending on the application you are installing, the speed of your Internet connection, and the speed of your computer), the command prompt will return. Now you can simply type **make install** to complete the installation of the port. As with packages, you will not be asked any questions about where you want to install the port because FreeBSD installs all software in standard locations.

Removing Installed Software

If you want to remove software installed from a package, use the pkg_delete command. In its basic form, the command is simply followed by the name of the package you want to delete. If you do not know the name of the package, use the pkg_info command discussed previously to find it.

pkg_delete will not remove the software if other software is currently installed that depends on the software you are trying to remove. If you want to force pkg_delete to remove the software anyway, you can use the -f option. However, this is usually not a good idea because it will probably cause some other applications that you currently have installed to stop working properly.

You can remove software that was installed from a port by either of the following two methods:

- Using the same procedure described previously for removing a package. This works because the ports system actually creates and then installs a package.
- Switching to the same directory you installed the port from by using the cd command and issuing the `make deinstall` command.

Updating Installed Software

When a new version of the software comes out, and you want to update to the newer version, simply follow the same procedures described previously. (Note that you will need to cvsup your ports tree if you want to install the new version from ports.) It is usually a good idea to remove the old version of the software using one of the methods described previously before you install the new version of the software.

Notes on Ports and Disk Space

When you build a port, the ports system downloads all the necessary source files to your hard disk. It then unzips those source archives and stores all the unzipped files in another directory. Building the application also creates new files. (These are called *object files* and they are created by the C/C++ compiler.) When the port has finished building, it does not remove these files. At first, you might wonder why. The reason is primarily in case you ever want to reinstall the application. If the ports system removed these files and you later want to reinstall, you would have to repeat the entire time-consuming downloading and building process. However, over time, if you install a large number of ports, the amount of disk space used by the source files and the object files can be quite substantial. Because of this, if you start to run low on disk space, you might want to delete some of these files and reclaim the space they are using. Note that the object and source files can be removed without affecting the functionality of the installed software in any way.

To remove object and other files left around by the port building procedure, switch to the directory in which you installed the port from and type **make clean**. This will remove all the work files created by the process of building the port, but it will not remove the original downloaded source archives. If you want to remove these as well, use the `make distclean` command.

Working with Linux Applications

Quite a few Linux applications are available in the FreeBSD ports tree. For the most part, working with these applications is no different from working with any other applications. They will install the same as any other application in the ports tree, and they will also run normally just like any other application.

The main caveat that you might run into when attempting to run a Linux application is that the Linux compatibility software is not loaded, or that you do not have the Linux runtime libraries installed.

If you did not install or enable Linux compatibility when you installed FreeBSD, you will need to do so before you can run any Linux applications in FreeBSD.

If you need to install the Linux runtime libraries, switch to the directory `/usr/ports/emulators/linux_base` and install it like any other port. (`make` followed by `make install` after the `make` process has finished.) After the runtime libraries have been installed, you will need to load the Linux compatibility module into the kernel. You can do this from the command prompt simply by typing **linux** and pressing Enter. However, if you will be running Linux applications on a regular basis, it is far more convenient to have the Linux module load automatically at system startup. To do this, open the file `/etc/rc.conf` in a text editor and add the following line:

linux_enable="YES"

Note that you will need to be the root user to make changes to this file. For more information on using a text editor in FreeBSD, see the section "Working with Text" in Hour 15.

> You can check to see if the Linux kernel module is loaded at any time by typing the `kldstat` command. If the module is loaded you will see a line that looks similar to the following:
>
> `7    1 0xc24db000 d000    linux.ko`

Summary

In this hour, you saw how to install new software in FreeBSD. You learned that you can find out about all the software that is available for FreeBSD by visiting the FreeBSD Web site. You also learned how to install software from packages using the `pkg_add` command, and how to install from ports using the `make` command.

Workshop

The quiz questions are designed to test your understanding of installing software in FreeBSD.

Quiz

1. The command to install new binary software in FreeBSD is

   A. `install`

   B. `pkgadd`

   C. `installpkg`

   D. `loadsoft`

   E. None of the above

2. The FreeBSD ports tree is

   A. A method of easily installing software from source code.

   B. A list of instructions necessary to build and install various applications.

   C. Not the same as the package system.

   D. All of the above.

3. The command to install a port that has already been built is

   A. `make`

   B. `make install`

   C. `install`

   D. `install port`

   E. None of the above

4. Which of the following commands removes an install package?

   A. `pkgrm`

   B. `pkg_delete`

   C. `pkg_remove`

   D. `trash_package`

   E. `delete_pkg`

6

Quiz Answers

1. The correct answer is E. Watch out for answer B. It is wrong because it lacks an underscore. The correct answer is `pkg_add`.

2. The correct answer is D.

3. The correct answer is B. Answer A is wrong because the command in answer A would build the port instead of install it. According to the question, the port is already built.

4. The correct answer is B.

Hour 7

System Configuration and Startup Scripts

Every computer is different; each machine in use in the world today has its own customized behavior set by its owner, which controls how it behaves, what services or programs it runs, and what it should do automatically when it's booted up. In the case of FreeBSD and other UNIX operating systems that have the capacity to be used as servers on the Internet, it's exceptionally important to be able to tune your system so that it's optimized either for serving clients over the network or for running as a desktop workstation.

For most users, the process by which FreeBSD starts up—probing for installed devices, bootstrapping its various disk partitions, launching the kernel, mounting filesystems, and doing all the little housecleaning duties necessary for an efficient multiuser operating system—is of little interest. However, if you want to configure your system to your taste, it's a good idea to have some understanding of what FreeBSD is doing when it spews all those mysterious lines onto your screen after you turn on the computer.

In this hour, you will learn:

- The steps by which FreeBSD raises itself to higher and higher levels of consciousness during boot
- What all those mysterious files in /etc are used for
- How to use /etc/rc.conf to configure your system
- What the inetd "super-server" is used for and how to configure it
- How to manage syslogd, the system logger

Understanding the FreeBSD Startup Process

When an operating system starts up after you power it on, it undergoes a rather remarkable transformation from a dormant set of ones and zeroes on a disk to a humming, vibrant creature with hundreds of interacting processes jostling with each other throughout memory and the disks. When you think about it, the capability of an operating system to "pull itself up by its own bootstraps"—or, as we term it colloquially, to "boot"—is quite a feat. It's comparable to a clutch in a car, allowing the engine (which must be running, even when the car is stopped) to gradually transfer power to the stopped wheels so that they can start turning without killing the engine.

The computer's hardware BIOS, or *basic input/output system*, knows next to nothing about the operating system. All it knows is where to find the hard disks that are in the system and how to execute a tiny piece of code that can be found on one of them. After it does that, the hardware's job is done. It's all up to that tiny piece of code on the startup disk to find larger pieces of code and execute them; those pieces of code continue executing larger and larger programs that know progressively more and more about what kind of operating system you're running and how to start it up. All operating systems boot in more or less the same way, but whatever the platform, booting is a ingeniously designed process—at heart a "hack," but well developed and understood by today's operating systems.

FreeBSD's boot process involves multiple stages, with each stage typically having a very limited function and scope and executing one crucial step before passing off control to the next stage. We will now examine each of these stages in order to see what they do. Chances are that you won't ever need to know the details of what happens when the system is starting up, but knowing them can't hurt.

Figure 7.1 shows a diagram of your startup disk. This disk contains multiple slices—each of which can contain a different bootable operating system; each FreeBSD slice contains multiple BSD partitions. Inside the "root" BSD partition is the kernel. Each of these levels must have a tiny piece of software that knows how to get into the next level.

FIGURE 7.1

A hard disk, its levels of partitions, and the boot blocks.

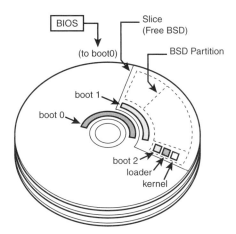

When you first power on the machine, the first thing it does is run the hardware checks and probes specified by the BIOS and the CMOS configuration. The hardware check and probe runs the memory check and the IDE or SCSI exploration that you see before the screen is cleared for the first time. This step is not OS specific; it happens the same way, no matter what you have installed on the machine. After it prints the table showing the hardware data it has collected, the BIOS reads the *Master Boot Record (MBR)* of the primary disk for the first preliminary boot block. It is the job of this and the next two boot blocks to find and run the `loader`, which configures and loads the kernel. Each of the boot blocks is sequentially a little more complex than the last; the first two are limited to 512 bytes in size (by the size of the MBR and the size of the boot sector of a slice), so they are both very simple. We will now look at each of the boot blocks in turn to see what their functions are.

- **Boot block 0 (boot0).** This preliminary boot block is what sits in the MBR and lists the available disk slices (the F-key commands that follow) from which you can choose what you want to boot. We will be talking more about disk slices (which most operating systems refer to as *partitions*) in the Hour 8's lesson, "Storage Systems and Backup Utilities."

```
F1 FreeBSD
F2 Linux
F3 ??

Default: F1
```

  You can press the appropriate F key to select the slice you want, or else just wait for several seconds—it will choose the default selection and continue.

7

- **Boot block 1 (boot1)**. This a very simple program that runs from the boot sector of the slice you selected in boot0, and its job is to use a stripped-down version of disklabel (what divides a slice up into BSD-style partitions, which we will cover in the next hour) to find and run boot2 in the appropriate partition. There is no user-interface portion to boot1.

- **Boot block 2 (boot2)**. Finally, we reach a boot block that has enough elbow room to have the necessary complexity to read files on the bootable filesystem in its BSD partition. The job of boot2 is to run a program called loader, which gives you a user interface that allows you to control the way the kernel loads. We will get to the kernel shortly.

- **loader**. You can find this program in the /boot directory. It reads the /boot/defaults/loader.conf and /boot/loader.conf configuration files, and loads the kernel and modules specified there. (The /boot/loader.conf file contains the overrides to /boot/defaults/loader.conf, in a similar fashion to the way /etc/rc.conf works, which we will cover later in this hour.)

  The loader counts down 10 seconds while it waits for a key press from you; if it doesn't get one, it boots the kernel in its default state. However, if you press Enter, it will put you into its command prompt interface in which you can control precisely your kernel boot procedure. You can boot in single-user mode (boot -s), boot an old kernel (boot kernel.old), boot from CD-ROM (boot -C), load and unload kernel modules one by one, view the contents of files (more), or perform a number of other tasks (see man boot for details). This should all be unnecessary most of the time. Usually, you will boot in the default configuration. Pressing ? at the ok prompt gives you a list of available commands, if you're curious. For further details on the options available at the loader command line, consult man loader.

This concludes the boot block phase of the bootstrapping process. We're now well on the way to bringing the system all the way up. The final phase of the boot process is where the complete FreeBSD system starts to come into play; where the kernel loads itself into memory, probes its available devices, and runs the "resource configuration" scripts that construct a working environment and start up the various system services.

- **kernel**. After loader transfers control, the kernel begins to probe all the devices it can find, and the results of each probe are echoed to the screen. This is the time when you will see many boot messages. These messages are logged in to the dmesg kernel buffer, which you can read with the dmesg command if you need to see what the kernel has to say about a certain device.

dmesg is a fairly rudimentary tool, listing the contents of the system message buffer that have accumulated since the system last booted. Simply enter **dmesg** to view the list of messages or enter **dmesg | less** to view the output in an interactive pager for easier access.

- **init**. After the kernel loads, it passes control to the init process, the final stage in the startup procedure. This is signaled by the Automatic reboot in progress message, which involves init running the Resource Configuration script (/etc/rc). This script first checks all the filesystem devices in /etc/fstab for consistency, using the fsck (*FileSystem Consistency checK*) program. If fsck finds no problems that it cannot correct on its own, it will mount all the filesystems (using mount -a -t nonfs) and continue running the rest of the startup processes. If fsck finds an unresolvable problem with the disks, it will exit to single-user mode for you to run fsck manually and repair the damage. Exit the single-user shell to continue rebooting into multiuser mode.

Finally, if all goes according to plan, you get a login prompt. This whole process usually takes no more than a minute.

Resource Configuration Scripts

After init has been started, the remaining startup tasks in the system—the ones that start up all the services and operating system processes—are handled by the Resource Configuration scripts. These scripts can all be found inside the /etc/rc.d directory, which usually means "Resource Configuration Directory" (depending on who you ask).

Anything in /etc/rc.d is a resource configuration script, a program that starts up parts of FreeBSD according to the system's configuration. Some are called recursively from other programs, some do nothing in the out-of-the-box configuration, and some will probably never even be run. You will generally never need to modify any of the files in /etc/rc.d.

A few other files are in /etc, however, that you will be modifying in order to configure your system. A list of some of the important resource configuration scripts that FreeBSD uses is shown in Table 7.1.

7

TABLE 7.1   Resource Configuration Scripts

Script Name	Description
/etc/rc	The main resource config script.
/etc/defaults/rc.conf	init reads in this file early to fill in its laundry list of tasks to do.
/etc/rc.conf	This is the file you edit to override defaults set in /etc/defaults/ rc.conf. This should be the **only** resource config file in /etc that you edit.
/etc/rc.d/diskless	init reads this script if you're doing a diskless boot via BOOTP.
/etc/rc.d/serial	Sets up terminals and other serial devices.
/etc/rc.d/pccard	Runs the PC-card daemon for laptops.
/etc/rc.d/network#	Scripts that set up TCP/IP networking.
/etc/rc.d/network_ipv6	Same as rc.network, except for IPv6 services.
/etc/rc.d/atm	Called from rc.network; sets up ATM devices for WAN machines.
/etc/rc.d/ipfw	Called from rc.network; configures an ipfw firewall.
/etc/rc.d/ip6fw	Called from rc.network6; configures an ip6fw firewall.
/etc/rc.d/devfs	Configures the device filesystem. See Hour 10, "The FreeBSD Kernel and the Device Tree," for more on this file.
/etc/rc.d/sysctl	Sets kernel variables specified in /etc/sysctl.conf.
/etc/rc.d/syscons	Sets up console settings.
/usr/local/etc/rc.d/	
/usr/local/X11R6/etc/rc.d/	Directory trees containing any new startup scripts you add (or are installed automatically by programs).

Modifying System Settings

The main resource configuration script, /etc/rc, is a completely automated "harness" that reads in a global configuration file and then executes a series of other scripts from /etc/rc.d in a specific order. Now that you know what the /etc/rc.d scripts do, we can look at how to configure the behavior of /etc/rc.

The /etc/defaults/rc.conf File

The /etc/rc program is a shell script that operates based on the states of dozens of different variables. If a certain variable (for instance, sendmail_enable) is set to YES, /etc/rc will run the /etc/rc.d script that starts Sendmail. If the variable is set to NO, it does not run the Sendmail script.

FreeBSD is installed with a file that defines all the default states for all the variables that have meaning to /etc/rc. This file is /etc/defaults/rc.conf. The first thing /etc/rc does is to read in this file so that it knows what default assumptions to use for all its configuration variables.

Let's look at a typical block in /etc/defaults/rc.conf, shown in Listing 7.1.

LISTING 7.1   Excerpt from /etc/defaults/rc.conf

```
# named. It may be possible to run named in a sandbox, man security for
# details.
#
named_enable="NO"              # Run named, the DNS server (or NO).
named_program="named"          # path to named, if you want a different one.
named_flags=""                 # Flags for named
#named_flags="-u bind -g bind" # Flags for named
```

By looking through /etc/defaults/rc.conf, you can find what /etc/rc will do unless you explicitly override it. In this case, you can see that the default behavior is to not run named at all.

The /etc/rc.conf File

How do you override the default settings in /etc/defaults/rc.conf? You do it with /etc/rc.conf, which is read into /etc/rc immediately after it reads in the defaults. FreeBSD can operate just fine without an /etc/rc.conf file present at all; it's just a plain text file that you can create manually in a text editor, with one variable per line. You only have to add the variables to this file that you want to override so that your desired value is used instead of the default value. After you make configuration changes with sysinstall, certain variables related to those changes are written out automatically by that program into /etc/rc.conf. You can see what's in yours by using more /etc/rc.conf.

Let's say that we do want to run named. In the simplest case, all we would have to do is edit /etc/rc.conf (the overrides file) and add the following line anywhere in the file:

```
named_enable="YES"
```

The rest of the named_* variables in /etc/defaults/rc.conf do not need to be copied into the overrides file; remember, every variable in the defaults file is loaded into memory by init, and they only matter if the "master switch" for that block has been turned to "YES". If it has, the variables will be used in the execution loop in /etc/rc to launch whatever process is controlled by the block we're working on (in this case, named).

7

You can use these other variables for fine-tuning, though, and you can override them just as easily. Let's say that your name server program was a customized version called mynamed. Let's also say that you created a bind user and group, intending that the name server should run as this user and group so that it won't be susceptible to as many security hacks. Well, to handle that, all you need to do (assuming that mynamed has the same behavior and command-line options as named) is add these two lines to /etc/rc.conf:

```
named_program="mynamed"
named_flags="-u bind -g bind"
```

From now on, when you boot the system and see named appear in the console messages after Doing additional network setup:, you know that it's applying your overrides over the defaults and running the name server automatically.

The most typical variables that appear in /etc/rc.conf are the TCP/IP configuration parameters because they will naturally be different for every system; FreeBSD can't very well specify them in the defaults, after all. Listing 7.2 shows a typical /etc/rc.conf just after a new FreeBSD installation.

LISTING 7.2 A Newly Installed /etc/rc.conf

```
# This file now contains just the overrides from /etc/defaults/rc.conf
# please make all changes to this file.

# Enable network daemons for user convenience.
# — sysinstall generated deltas — #
kern_securelevel="1"
kern_securelevel_enable="YES"
linux_enable="YES"
sendmail_enable="YES"
sshd_enable="YES"
portmap_enable="NO"
nfs_server_enable="NO"
inetd_enable="NO"
network_interfaces="fxp0 lo0"
ifconfig_fxp0="inet 10.6.7.101  netmask 255.0.0.0"
defaultrouter="10.6.1.1"
hostname="freebsd1.testnetwork.com"
usbd_enable="YES"
```

Some of these variables are in fact redundant with the defaults file; still, it can be useful to also have them in the overrides file because many of these features (such as the NFS server) now have a one-touch toggle control, as it were.

If you add a variable to /etc/rc.conf, make sure that another version of that variable isn't already in the file—or at least that it doesn't appear later on in the file. The variables are read sequentially, and the way the overrides work is simply that the last occurrence of each variable seen by the system is the one it uses. If you are always careful to add variables only to the end of rc.conf, you should be fine.

Many programs, when you install them, will have to install a way for themselves to start up at boot time; /etc/rc.conf is not, however, the place for them. That file is supposed to be touched only by you, the administrator, and by the sysinstall program when it makes changes to the core system. For user-installed programs (ports and packages) and for any scripts that /etc/rc and friends do not know about, another structure is in place for their startup scripts and configuration files: the /usr/local/etc hierarchy.

The /usr/local/etc and /usr/local/X11R6/etc Directories

Programs that you install yourself are considered to be *local*, meaning that they apply only to your particular machine and not to FreeBSD itself. Configuration files for your locally installed programs go into the /usr/local hierarchy in FreeBSD as one of its structural conventions. There is a /usr/local/etc/rc.d directory, which is equivalent in operation to /etc/rc.d—except that because the files in it apply to the programs that you have installed, rather than to the core system, you can edit these files yourself in order to change those programs' behavior.

init turns its attention to /usr/local/etc/rc.d after it has run through all the other /etc/rc.d scripts. Any executable file within the directory that ends in .sh will be executed in lexicographical order. Examples of files that will be installed in here include apache.sh, mysql-server.sh, and samba.sh. These scripts are custom built as part of the ports or packages (see Hour 6, "Adding and Removing Third-Party Software," for more about the ports and packages), and each one is tuned to take a start or stop argument. When init runs each script, it uses the start argument. Note that you can run these scripts yourself during runtime just as easily—for instance, to start a newly installed service without rebooting,

```
# /usr/local/etc/rc.d/apache.sh start
```

Some ports or packages will install with a secondary suffix of .sample (for example, samba.sh.sample) because the program that it's part of has to be properly configured before it can run successfully. Apache, for instance, will run immediately after

7

installation without any further modification to its `config` files (although you will no doubt be modifying them anyway), so it installs an `apache.sh` file, which could run the program cleanly if you rebooted it right then. But Samba (which we will discuss in Hour 24, "File Sharing") must be tuned first to run on your machine; if you ran the script right after installing it, it would fail to start the daemon. You need to rename the script to remove the `.sample` extension before it will be run on startup by `init`.

The `/usr/local/X11R6/etc` directory is analogous to `/usr/local/etc` except it is specifically tasked to X11-based (X Windows) programs: GNOME panels, graphical tools, games, window managers, and so on. This directory also has an `rc.d` subdirectory, and scripts in it are executed immediately after the ones in `/usr/local/etc/rc.d`.

> The local startup-script directories are configurable. Override this `rc.conf` line to add more directories if you need to:
>
> ```
> local_startup="/usr/local/etc/rc.d /usr/X11R6/etc/rc.d" # startup
> ➥script dirs.
> ```

The `inetd` Daemon and the `inetd.conf` Configuration File

Although a fair number of daemons in the base system have `.conf` files in the `/etc` directory, the most important (and sensitive) one you will have to deal with is `inetd`, the *super server*. We will take a brief look at `inetd` here and discuss how to configure it.

The job of `inetd` is to listen for connections on a specified set of network ports and fire off the appropriate server process when a request comes in. For instance, `inetd` is in charge of Telnet connections; if your system allows Telnet, you can open a connection to it and receive a login prompt without any `telnetd` process running on the server beforehand. Every time the system receives a connection request on Port 23, it creates a new `telnetd` process to handle the connection. Executable programs that run out of `inetd` (and other similar daemons) are in `/usr/libexec`. These programs are not generally part of your command path and are not supposed to be run from the command line; instead, they are spawned from within another process and passed certain resources (such as environment variables and network connections).

The use of inetd eliminates the need for a "master" telnetd process running as root, which is a situation that could be particularly dangerous if a security vulnerability were to be uncovered in telnetd. Many daemons (among them sshd, httpd [Apache], and sendmail) do run in this "stand-alone" mode rather than being called out of inetd. The master process (running as root) listens for the new connections and spawns new processes, owned by an unprivileged user, to handle each transaction. This allows for greater flexibility and speed in the program at the expense of a centralized security risk. inetd also runs as root, so it is just as dangerous if it is compromised. The more daemons that run as root, the more possibilities there are for security holes to be found.

Examining the /etc/inetd.conf file shows us that nearly all entries in it are disabled in the out-of-the-box configuration, assuming that you've selected the default security settings during setup. The only ones that are enabled are listed in Table 7.2.

TABLE 7.2 System Services Controlled by inetd That Are Enabled by Default

Service	Description	Port(s)/Resources Used
ftp	File Transfer Protocol	Port 21/TCP
telnet	Remote terminal	Port 23/TCP
comsat	"biff" server (notifies users of incoming mail)	Port 512/UDP
ntalk	command-line chat server	Port 518/TCP,UDP
ftp (IPv6)	File Transfer Protocol	IPv6
telnet (IPv6)	Remote terminal	IPv6

Other services that you might want to enable, depending on what you're using your system for, are shown in Table 7.3.

TABLE 7.3 Other Useful inetd Services

Service	Description	Port(s)/Resources Used
pop3	Post Office Protocol	Port 110/TCP
imap4	Interim Mail Access Protocol (server-side mail)	Port 143/TCP
smtp	Qmail (alternative to Sendmail SMTP server)	Port 25/TCP

7

TABLE 7.3   continued

Service	Description	Port(s)/Resources Used
netbios-ssn	Samba file sharing with Windows	Port 139/TCP
netbios-ns	Samba file sharing with Windows	Port 137/TCP
finger	Lookup user information	Port 79/TCP

To enable any one of these services, simply remove the comment (#) from the beginning of the line and then restart the inetd server, as follows:

```
# ps -waux | grep inetd
root    110  0.0  0.6  1032  752  ??  Ss   11:57PM  0:00.01 inetd
# kill -HUP 110
```

> If you have selected to run the system at security level 1 or higher (an
> install-time option—level 1 is the "Medium" security level mentioned in the
> installer), inetd will not be running. This is indicative of the risky nature of
> many services that run out of inetd. If you are running at this security level
> and want to run inetd, you can run it by entering inetd -wW. To enable it
> permanently, remove or toggle this line in /etc/rc.conf:
>
> inetd_enable="NO"

inetd is one of the areas of FreeBSD without a lot of automation built in or safety nets
to prevent bad configurations. If you must enable services in /etc/inetd.conf, be aware
that you're venturing into a nonstandard type of setup, and you should know what you're
getting into. For instance, the cvs services come with a dire warning about a security
hole that can be opened up with a misconfigured parameter. The Samba services (net-
bios-ssn and netbios-ns) expect to find the smbd and nmbd binaries in
/usr/local/sbin, but they won't be there unless you have installed Samba from the
ports or packages. (Running Samba from inetd instead of standalone is a nonstandard,
alternative configuration.)

Similarly, other services (such as pop3) try to run services installed into
/usr/local/libexec. But remember, this directory is inside /usr/local, meaning that
unless you explicitly installed a program there, it won't be there. Installing the popper
port/package will put the necessary binary into that directory, so you can enable the service in inetd. However, if you choose instead to install the qpopper port/package

(another POP3 server), the binary will be qpopper instead of popper, and you'll have to modify the line accordingly:

```
pop3    stream tcp    nowait root    /usr/local/libexec/qpopper    qpopper
```

Numerous other pitfalls await the unwary. Be sure not to modify the inetd services any more extensively than you really have to. The man inetd page provides a more extensive discussion of the syntax and technique of handling inetd.

> In order to be extra security conscious, you might choose to replace inetd with xinetd, available from the ports or packages (/usr/ports/security/xinetd). Beyond being a great deal more secure than inetd, it has a lot more configurability—it can employ sophisticated access control based on remote IP address, time of day, number of processes it's being asked to spawn, and so on. It's like inetd on steroids.

The System Logger (syslogd) and the syslog.conf File

System messages are logged to files in /var/log. The mechanism that does this is called syslogd, the system logger daemon. Its behaviors are set in /etc/syslog.conf, which defines various different log files for different services. Each service or *facility* that it knows about (which can be any of auth, authpriv, console, cron, daemon, ftp, kern, lpr, mail, mark, news, ntp, security, syslog, user, uucp, and local0 through local7) has a number of different *severity* levels for which you can control logging. These levels include emerg, alert, crit, err, warning, notice, info, and debug, listed in decreasing order of severity.

- emerg—Emergency! If this ultimate severity message level is triggered, every logged-in user receives a broadcast.
- alert—Something important on the system level has happened—something that must be corrected immediately—but only root really needs to be warned about it.
- crit—Critical error with one of the particular services or a piece of hardware. Print errors to all relevant log files and the console, but don't interrupt remotely logged-in users with warnings.
- err—Any generic "error" from any service. Messages are printed to the console and root's terminals.
- warning—A non-critical condition, but one that would be useful to find in a log file.

- notice—Special conditions worth mentioning, like startups/shutdowns of services.

- info—Informational messages; standard operating procedure.

- debug—These messages are only seen when debugging.

By default, syslog.conf defines several logging rules as follows:

```
*.err;kern.debug;auth.notice;mail.crit              /dev/console
*.notice;kern.debug;lpr.info;mail.crit;news.err /var/log/messages
security.*                                          /var/log/security
mail.info                                           /var/log/maillog
lpr.info                                            /var/log/lpd-errs
cron.*                                              /var/log/cron
*.err                                               root
*.notice;news.err                                   root
*.alert                                             root
*.emerg                                             *
```

We can interpret this to mean that all err messages from any service, debug messages from the kernel, authorization notice messages, and crit messages from mail programs will be printed out to the system console, and you will see them if you have a monitor hooked up to your FreeBSD machine. Similarly, all security-related messages go into the /var/log/security file, and all messages from mail programs at the info level go into /var/log/maillog. Almost everything else goes into /var/log/messages, the general system log file. (If you're used to Linux, this file is equivalent to what is usually called syslog.)

Certain types of messages are not merely written to log files, but are sent to a variety of other types of handling mechanisms. In the default syslog.conf, messages from any service at the err, notice, or alert level are printed to any terminal where root is logged in, and emerg messages are printed to the all users at all terminals. Table 7.4 shows the possible actions for syslogd messages and the syntax for each.

TABLE 7.4   Syntaxes for syslogd Actions

Syntax	Action Taken
/path/to/file	Messages are written to the specified file.
@some.hostname.com	Messages are forwarded to the syslogd at some.hostname.com using the syslog network service.
user1	Messages are printed to any terminal where user1 is logged in.
root,user1,user2	All specified users receive messages on all their terminals.
*	Messages are written to all logged in users.
| "mail root"	Messages are mailed to root.

After you make any changes to the /etc/syslogd.conf file, you can restart it by using ps to find out its process ID, and then sending it a kill -HUP signal.

```
# ps -waux | grep syslogd
root   79 0.0  0.1   964  484  ??  Ss   12Sep02   2:11.60 /usr/sbin/syslogd -s
# kill -HUP 79
```

Further details on how to configure syslogd can be found in the man syslogd and man syslog.conf pages.

Summary

In this rather technical hour, we covered the underlying structure that FreeBSD uses to get itself up and running from a cold start in which the only piece of running software is the BIOS. You learned how the hierarchy of partitioning levels in FreeBSD works, and saw how the sequence of boot blocks lead the system from one level to the next until the complete FreeBSD system is fully up and running.

You also saw how FreeBSD's resource configuration scripts work, as well as how to configure their operation. You saw how to enable and disable services that run out of the inetd super server and how to control the logging of system services using syslogd.

Most of what you have learned this hour will not be of direct use to you in the day-to-day operation of a FreeBSD machine; however, knowing the things that you know now will make understanding some concepts we will discuss later a lot easier. This will be particularly true in the next hour's lesson, in which we will be discussing disks and other types of storage systems.

Q&A

Q Most other operating systems only have one set of partitions; why does FreeBSD have this business of slices and BSD partitions?

A It's mostly because of compatibility. FreeBSD is designed to interoperate well with other operating systems. In the way FreeBSD disks are set up, only one of the four BIOS partitions that the BIOS is capable of addressing needs to be taken up with the FreeBSD operating system: The other three can be used for Linux, Windows, and so on. Within the single FreeBSD BIOS partition (also known as a *slice*), FreeBSD can have a larger number of sub-partitions (BSD partitions) available to itself, without using up more BIOS partitions that could otherwise be used by other operating systems.

7

Q **It takes my system two or three minutes to boot. It seems to get stuck on
sendmail or httpd. What's going on?**

A Both Sendmail and Apache (httpd) have to figure out your machine's hostname; to
do this, they need to do a reverse lookup against the *DNS (domain name server)*
configured in /etc/resolv.conf (which is written out by sysinstall). This
lookup will have to timeout for every configured name server before it fails and
allows the startup process to proceed. Network timeouts are often fairly long,
which is why networking is the most common cause of boot hang ups. One solution to this problem is to make sure that the name server listed first in
/etc/resolv.conf is reachable from your FreeBSD machine; this ensures that
Sendmail and Apache will be able to determine the machine's hostname and start
up without delay. If this is not possible, list 127.0.0.1 (localhost) as the first
name server and comment out the rest.

Q **My FreeBSD system doesn't have an /etc/rc.d directory; instead, it has a
bunch of files in /etc itself with names beginning with rc.. What gives?**

A Your system is probably a version of FreeBSD prior to 5.0. In FreeBSD 5.0, the
"next generation" resource configuration format was adopted, which is what uses
the /etc/rc.d directory. Don't worry—the operation of the resource configuration
scripts is almost exactly the same; it's mostly just an organizational issue.

Q **How do I create a task of my own to execute at boot time?**

A You can write a shell script and put it in /usr/local/etc/rc.d; that script will be
executed along with all the other scripts in that directory after the /etc/rc.d
scripts have been run. For best results, make sure that your script properly handles
the start and stop arguments, and also make sure that it's set to executable and
has a .sh extension. Alternatively, you can put commands into /etc/rc.local,
although that's a deprecated method no longer recommended.

Q **Whenever I log in as root, my terminal session keeps getting interrupted by all
these weird status messages that appear on the screen. How do I get them to
stop?**

A Edit /etc/syslogd.conf and comment out the lines that print to either
/dev/console or to root. Then restart syslogd as we discussed in this chapter.

Workshop

In this interactive section, you will be given a quiz and a few exercises in order to help solidify your understanding of the FreeBSD system startup process.

Quiz

1. What's the job of `boot0`, the first boot block?

    A. Load the kernel

    B. Run the BIOS self-test

    C. Find the bootable BIOS partitions and give you a list to choose from

    D. Find the BSD partition that has a bootable FreeBSD system and boot it

2. How do you boot into single-user mode?

    A. Hold down the S key during boot

    B. Enter **boot -s** at the loader prompt

    C. Press the S key at the `boot0` menu

    D. Reconfigure the BIOS and boot from the FreeBSD installation CD

3. What's `/etc/defaults/rc.conf` for?

    A It's your main configuration file; edit it to make changes to the system configuration

    B. Nothing; you can safely delete it

    C. It stores the default configuration options for all third-party applications that you install

    D. It defines default variables for `/etc/rc`; override it with `/etc/rc.conf`

4. Where do I find the automated startup scripts for third-party applications I install?

    A. `/usr/local/etc/rc.d`

    B. `/usr/etc/rc.d`

    C. `/etc/rc.d`

    D. `/rc.d`

5. How do I allow the system to accept Telnet connections?

    A. Run the `/usr/libexec/telnetd` program from the command line

    B. Enter **telnet_enable=YES** in `/etc/rc.conf`

    C. Uncomment the `telnet` line in `/etc/inetd.conf`

    D. Uncomment the `telnet` line in `/etc/inetd.conf` and restart the `inetd` process with `kill -HUP`

7

6. If I set a certain facility in `syslogd` to my username, what happens when that facility is triggered?

    A. Messages from that facility will be emailed to you.

    B. Messages from that facility will be printed to any console where you are logged in.

    C. Messages from that facility will be appended to `/var/log/syslog.<user-name>`.

    D. Messages from that facility will vanish into the ether.

Quiz Answers

1. The correct answer is D.

2. The correct answer is B.

3. The correct answer is D.

4. The correct answer is A.

5. The correct answer is D. Remember, your changed configuration doesn't take effect until you restart the daemon and force it to reread the config file.

6. The correct answer is B.

Exercises

1. Reconfigure `syslogd` so that all `warning` messages from all services are directed into a file called `/var/log/warn.log`.

2. Use `inetd` to disable Telnet connections. Now send out a message to anybody who might be using your machine: Telnet is no longer allowed; SSH is now the only way to access your machine via a remote terminal. It's not just a good idea, it's now the law—*your* law!

3. Use `/etc/rc.conf` to synchronize your system's time via NTP. Hint: use the `ntpdate_enable` statement. A good NTP server to use is `tick.usno.navy.mil`.

Hour 8

Storage Systems and Backup Utilities

Every operating system in use today is what was once referred to as a *Disk Operating System*, or *DOS*. The idea is that unlike some operating systems, which worked entirely from self-contained instructions on silicon chips (in ROM or firmware), a DOS allowed the user to swap in new instructions on *disks*—which at the time were either eight-inch floppy disks in flimsy plastic jackets, or else "hard disks" in sealed containers with much larger capacity. The disks could contain new programs to run, data for those programs to work with, or even other disk-based operating systems to run the programs. The key was versatility and expandability beyond what was sealed into a computer's case. Just swap in new disks to expand your computer's capacity as much as you like.

The situation today is about the same, except that the array of "disks" that we can use in our computers is vastly greater and more diverse. We now have optical discs (CDs, DVDs, magneto-optical media), customized proprietary media like Iomega's Zip and Imation's SuperDisk, tape drives, and network drives—to say nothing of the ubiquitous hard disk and the dependable 3.5-inch floppy.

The accepted spelling, by the way, is disk—except for optical media such as CDs and DVDs, for which the spelling generally remains disc, presumably in order to confuse people.

In this hour, you will learn how FreeBSD handles disks. Most storage media behave in similar ways, especially when you're reading from them; writing to them, however, can be tricky, depending on what kind of storage device you're using. You will learn:

- What a UNIX "Filesystem" is and how it relates to your computer's directory structure
- How to "mount" a disk, or attach its contents to the system for use
- How to simplify the process of mounting and unmounting disks
- How to work with tapes and tape drives
- How to work with optical discs and their drives
- How to back up your files to tape or other media

Understanding UNIX Filesystems

Think about your computer's directory structure—the way folder and files are organized throughout the system. If you're familiar with Windows, you probably have an image in mind that involves several disks sitting at the top level of the system—each with a letter assigned to it (C: for your hard disk, D: for your CD-ROM, A: for your floppy drive, and so on). In MS-DOS, the underlying structure beneath the Windows structure, you switch from one disk to another to work with each disk's files. The metaphor is rather like an "orchard" of trees, one tree per disk, but without the individual trees interacting or connecting at all. The Windows operating system itself overlays this structure with a "Desktop" metaphor that seems to exist above the "orchard" and tying all the trees together, but the fundamental separation of disks is still there.

Some operating systems use the term *volume* to refer to a disk—or, more specifically, a mountable *partition* of a disk. You will learn more about partitions later in this hour.

UNIX is different. In the UNIX directory structure, there's only a single large *tree* of folders, and all disks (or volumes) in the system are attached to the tree, or *mounted*, at

8

various points (as illustrated in Figure 8.1). The cd command (*Change Directory*) works the same in UNIX as it does in MS-DOS—except that in the latter, you can't use cd to move directly from a place on one disk to a place on another disk. You have to explicitly change disks first (by typing the drive letter you want). In UNIX, however, cd will take you anywhere in the system you want to go. You can change to /usr/home, for example, or /var/log; and in doing so, you might well have moved from one volume to another, or to an entirely different disk. But from your viewpoint, it's all the same; the commands and tools that you use in one part of the tree work just as well in any other part.

FIGURE 8.1

Diagrams of the FreeBSD (UNIX) and Windows filesystem structures, using the "tree" analogy.

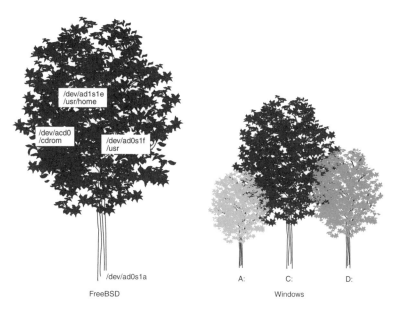

There are complications involved with having all your media sources (disks and volumes) mounted at various places throughout the system, with seamless movement allowed between them. For instance, the mv command will move files from one place to another *within a volume* by simply renaming the file and changing its path on the disk. But if you try to "move" a file from one volume to another, the system must first copy the file to the other volume, and then delete it from its original location. The end result is the same, but the process can take a lot longer, depending on how big the files are that you're trying to move and on the speed of the disks in question. Moving or copying files to or from a floppy disk (which might be mounted at /mnt/floppy, for example) is much, much slower than moving or copying files from one hard disk partition to another, which in turn is much slower than moving or copying files within the same partition.

Similarly, there can be different permissions on different volumes in the system, preventing you from moving files from one place to another where you might think you're just moving things around within "the computer." Remember, UNIX is a multiuser operating system, and not all users have the same capabilities as others. As we will see, there is also the ability to mount a disk or volume "read-only" or "read/write." Keeping disks logically separated, as in Windows, helps to reinforce the distinctions between their varying capabilities—but the UNIX way can make day-to-day operations a great deal simpler, particularly in systems that have only hard disks to worry about.

Partitions, Volumes, and Filesystems

A *filesystem*, which is a term we will be using throughout most of this hour, is equivalent to a volume—it refers to a single mountable disk, or a section of a disk that has been divided into several such sections, or *partitions*. It can also, however, refer to the entire system's directory structure, containing other filesystems attached at various *mount points*. We will refer to the "FreeBSD filesystem" (meaning the entire directory structure), but also to the "root filesystem" and the "/var filesystem" (meaning specific volumes attached at particular points).

Confusingly, a filesystem can also refer to the format in which a partition is written—UFS (the UNIX Filesystem), FFS (Berkeley Fast Filesystem), Ext2FS (Linux Extended Filesystem), NTFS (Windows NT Filesystem), and MSDOSFS (MS-DOS Filesystem) are all commonly used formats that FreeBSD understands or can be configured to understand. The native filesystem type that FreeBSD uses for its own disks is FFS, which is effectively synonymous with UFS, the traditional filesystem format used on BSD UNIX platforms for many years.

All operating systems provide the ability to *partition* any disk. The benefits of partitioning are that you can predefine certain segments of the disk to have maximum sizes that their contents cannot exceed. For instance, in Windows you might partition a hard disk so that your C: drive is for your operating system, D: is for your personal documents and files, and E: is reserved for file sharing. This way, file sharing activities cannot end up filling your entire disk with junk that other people upload to your computer. The only thing it can fill up is the E: partition.

UNIX benefits from partitions the same way. However, because there are no "drive letters" in UNIX, and because all mounted volumes are attached to the filesystem at certain points, the partitions are given names that match the mount points where they are attached. For instance, the /var partition (which contains variable files—files whose contents change continuously during normal operation, such as system logs) can be set to a certain size so that the log files within it don't grow to fill the entire disk—just the /var filesystem.

Figure 8.2 shows disks that have been partitioned and disks that have not, and how the terms *partition*, *volume*, and *filesystem* can be applied to them.

FIGURE 8.2

Various disks, partitioned and unpartitioned, showing how they fit into the FreeBSD filesystem.

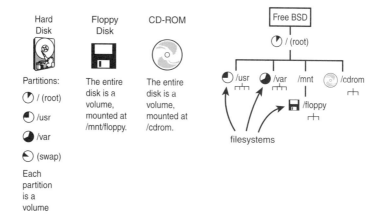

The FreeBSD Filesystem

Now that you know how a UNIX filesystem is structured, it's time to look at the actual files and folders inside FreeBSD's filesystem tree. FreeBSD's structure is very similar to other UNIX systems and to Linux. If you move to the top of the directory structure with the `cd /` command, and then use `ls` and `cd <directory>` to move around, you will see a structure similar to what appears in Figure 8.3.

FIGURE 8.3

The FreeBSD filesystem, showing part of the hierarchical structure beginning at /, or the root directory.

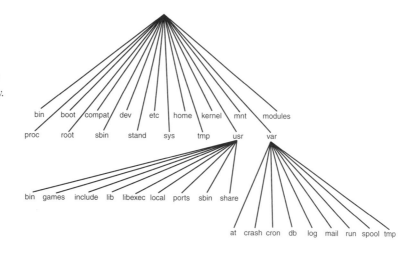

The directory names you see are short and cryptic—a far cry from the Program Files and Documents and Settings of Windows, and indeed from the Users, System, and Applications of Mac OS X. The meanings of these short names are often rooted in history and tradition, and many have lost their relevance. Table 8.1 lists the most important directories and explains what they are all used for. The symbols following each name are as they would appear in an `ls -F` listing, where / signifies a directory, @ a symbolic link to another item, and * an executable file.

TABLE 8.1   Key Elements of the FreeBSD Filesystem

Directory	Purpose
bin/	Statically linked binaries are contained here. These can be used even when you're doing an emergency boot and don't have access to any dynamically linked programs or any filesystems other than /.
boot/	This directory contains the *kernel*, which is the master executable of the system. The kernel manages all the devices and handles networking, along with a host of other tasks. See Hour 10, "The FreeBSD Kernel and the Device Tree," for more information. /boot also has configuration files and executables that are used during boot.
compat@	This is a symlink to directory structures that provide compatibility with other operating systems, such as Linux.
dev/	A special directory. Files in here are mostly *devices*, which are special file types that give programs an interface into any pieces of hardware that the kernel supports.
etc/	Long ago, this was merely a directory for random files that didn't fit elsewhere. It is now where most systemwide configuration files go, including your user (password) databases and startup scripts.
home@	Possibly a plain directory; possibly a symbolic link to /usr/home, depending on your installation. All regular users' home directories are contained here.
mnt/	An empty directory, provided for your convenience as a mount point if you need to mount another disk.
modules/	Loadable kernel modules are here.
proc/	The procfs, or process filesystem. This is an interface to the process table. Used for convenience by some programs, but not essential to the operation of the system. (It can safely be unmounted.)
root/	The root user's home directory. It's not in /home for security reasons, and so that it will be available during an emergency boot.

TABLE 8.1   continued

Directory	Purpose
sbin/	System binaries that are statically linked. These programs differ from the ones in /bin in that they generally alter the system's behavior, whereas the /bin programs are simply user tools.
stand/	Contains a set of hard-linked programs that provide a "mini-FreeBSD" environment during system installation and emergencies when running in standalone mode. The only program you will likely be interested in is sysinstall, which is covered in Hour 2, "Installing FreeBSD."
sys@	A link to the kernel sources if you installed them.
tmp/	Temporary files. Any user can write files into this directory.
usr/	The gateway to the rest of the system—dynamically linked programs, user files, and programs you installed yourself. It's often referred to in the UNIX world as "userland" (although that term also can mean "anything that's not directly handled by the kernel"). In upcoming hours, we will spend most of our time here.
var/	Variable files. These include runtime files used by programs, log files, spool directories, and other items that change with the normal operation of the system.

FreeBSD's structure is tightly controlled, and the clearest rule that distinguishes FreeBSD from other UNIX platforms (which can be much more chaotic in structure) is that "Anything installed by the administrator goes into /usr/local". Although other systems might allow user-installed programs the freedom to install files wherever they want, FreeBSD maintains strict structural guidelines in its ported programs and packages (see Hour 6, "Adding and Removing Third-Party Software"). Although a program might, by default, put its executables in /usr/bin, its libraries in /var/lib, and its configuration files into /etc, FreeBSD *patches* (modifies) the installation scripts so that the files would go into /usr/local/bin, /usr/local/lib, and /usr/local/etc, respectively. In fact, all configuration files for any software you might install will go into /usr/local/etc; and if the program installs a startup script to be launched on boot, the script is placed in /usr/local/etc/rc.d. Anything in that directory is run at boot time, after the scripts in the analogous /etc/rc.d (the base system's startup scripts) are run.

The advantage of a structure this carefully controlled is that a FreeBSD system is relatively easy to maintain and especially easy to re-create on a new machine (if you're upgrading to new hardware, for instance). You could theoretically copy the entire /usr/local directory tree from one machine to another, and everything would work as on the previous machine. This is the ideal toward which FreeBSD strives, though in practice it's not perfect.

To see which volumes are mounted and how much space is available on each, use the df (*Disk Free*) command.

```
# df
Filesystem  1K-blocks     Used    Avail  Capacity  Mounted on
/dev/ad0s1a    128990    74314    44358    63%      /
/dev/ad0s1f    257998       44   237316     0%      /tmp
/dev/ad0s1g   8027686  1990866  5394606    27%      /usr
/dev/ad0s1e    257998    30586   227694    14%      /var
procfs              4        4        0   100%      /proc
```

Mounting and Unmounting Various Media Formats

In FreeBSD, working with a disk isn't a simple matter of putting it into the slot, as it is in desktop operating systems like Windows or the Mac OS, which know how to automount volumes either when you insert them or when you try to access them. After you insert or install a disk, you then have to manually *mount* it in order for the system to be able to access it. When you're done using a removable disk, you have to *unmount* it before you can safely eject it.

Each type of disk or other media that you might want to add to your system has to be referred to by its *device name*—a short and often cryptic label that refers to the device in /dev that enables the kernel to talk to that piece of equipment. Table 8.2 shows typical storage devices and the device names that you must use to refer to them. The number sign (#) in each device name refers to the identification number of each device, which begins at zero. The first floppy drive in a system would be /dev/fd0, the second one would be /dev/fd1, and so on.

TABLE 8.2 Common Device Names for Storage Devices

Device Name	Used For
/dev/ad#	IDE/ATA hard disks
/dev/da#	SCSI hard disks (*Direct Access*)
/dev/fd#	IDE floppy drives
/dev/acd#	IDE CD-ROM and CD-RW drives
/dev/cd#	SCSI CD-ROM and CD-RW drives
/dev/sa#	SCSI tape drives (*Sequential Access*)
/dev/vpo#	Iomega Zip drives

When a disk is partitioned, the naming scheme gets a little more complicated. Let's say that you have an IDE disk that your system recognizes as /dev/ad0. (The boot messages, as well as the output of dmesg, will tell you what name the system has given it.)

> IDE/ATA disks are numbered from zero to three, supporting a total of four devices; the IDE architecture allows for two channels (primary and secondary), each with a *master* and a *slave* device. The sequence in which FreeBSD numbers these devices is—Primary master; primary slave; secondary master; secondary slave. So /dev/ad1 would be the primary slave, and /dev/ad2 is the secondary master.

FreeBSD disks can be divided into two levels of *partitions*: there are what Windows, Linux, and other operating systems call partitions, which FreeBSD refers to as *slices*. (These slices can be accessed directly by the system's BIOS, which is why they are often referred to as *BIOS partitions*.) Then, within each slice, you can create multiple *BSD partitions*, which you can then assign to different mount points. Experts can configure FreeBSD disks in a multitude of different ways—for example, configuring slices for FreeBSD, Linux, and Windows and subdividing the FreeBSD slice into /usr, /var, and / partitions. However, for your purposes, you will most likely be using the default configuration—in which a hard disk has a single FreeBSD slice and several BSD partitions underneath it, which are named with letters beginning with e. Figure 7.1, in the previous hour's lesson, illustrates these different levels of partitioning and how the sequential boot blocks interact with them.

Figure 8.4 shows a fully specified FreeBSD hard disk partition's device name. The first part (ad1) specifies the base device name. Next comes the slice name, whose numbers begin at 1 (s1). Finally, we have the BSD partition name (e).

FIGURE 8.4
Anatomy of a FreeBSD hard disk device name.

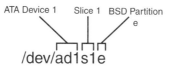

Unpartitioned disks have simpler names because all you have to specify is the base device name; there are no subpartitions to worry about. A floppy disk is simply /dev/fd0. However, there is one more complicating factor. This is the *dedicated* disk mode in which you must specify the c partition as a special code name to refer to the entire disk. Floppy disks don't generally need this, but many CD-ROM drives do. You will generally want to use `/dev/acd0c` instead of `/dev/acd0` to address a CD-ROM drive. If one name doesn't work, try the other.

Formatting Disks

Floppy disks and hard disks must be formatted before you can mount them. To format a floppy that has never been formatted before, use the `fdformat` command (noting, of course, that all its contents will be erased):

```
# fdformat /dev/fd0
Format 1440 floppy '/dev/fd0'? (y/n):y
```

After `fdformat` finishes formatting the disk, issue `disklabel` and `newfs` commands to complete preparing the disk for use with FreeBSD:

```
# disklabel -w -r /dev/fd0 fd1440
# newfs /dev/fd0
```

Hard disks are more difficult to format and label from the command line. There are many more options you might want to set, including possibly partitioning the disk (which is done with a utility called `fdisk`). To format a hard disk, it's best to use the `sysinstall` program. Refer back to Hour 2 for directions on how to use `sysinstall` to format and partition a hard disk.

CD-ROMs don't need to be formatted; if you have a CD or DVD burner, the process of writing data to the disc is coupled with the necessary formatting and labeling, and the resulting ISO 9660 filesystem type is compatible with all operating systems.

The `mount` Command

Mounting a disk is done with the `mount` command. In its most common form, using `mount` is a simple and straightforward procedure. All that's involved is picking a location somewhere in the directory tree to attach your disk, making sure that an empty directory is located there, and issuing the appropriate `mount` command.

FreeBSD ships with an empty `/mnt` directory, which is intended for use with disks that you mount temporarily or only once in a while. We will use that directory for some of our examples; however, you can mount any volume anywhere you like. For example, you can create a `/floppy` mount point on which to mount floppy disks. Just make sure to create the mount-point directory first:

```
# mkdir /floppy
```

Mount-point directories don't actually have to be empty. You can use directories that have files in them; however, once you've mounted a disk onto them, you will no longer be able to access those files until you unmount the disk.

Mounting a volume requires you to specify the device name of the disk (provided the disk is in the drive, in the case of removable disks) and the mount point, like so:

```
# mount /dev/fd0 /mnt
```

Done correctly, and assuming that no errors occur, there should be no output. You should be able to use the new filesystem immediately. Use the df command to see if it worked:

```
Filesystem  1K-blocks     Used    Avail Capacity  Mounted on
/dev/ad0s1a    128990    74314    44358    63%     /
/dev/ad0s1f   8027686  1990866  5394606    27%     /usr
/dev/ad0s1e    257998    30586   227694    14%     /var
procfs              4        4        0   100%     /proc
/dev/fd0         1424     1128      296    79%     /mnt
```

The last line shows the /dev/fd0 device, the floppy disk, mounted at /mnt. Success! You can now use ls /floppy to see the disk's contents and copy files back and forth to and from the disk's filesystem.

Mounting Non-UFS Filesystems

Using mount by itself will work with native FreeBSD disks—hard disk partitions, FreeBSD-formatted floppies, and so on. But as often as not, in this world of interoperability between operating systems, the disks you will want to mount are not in the native UFS/FFS format. Common disk types you will encounter include MS-DOS floppy disks (from Windows machines), Linux Ext2FS hard disks, and ISO 9660 CD-ROMs.

The mount command has a -t switch; this controls what filesystem type the disk in question is. If you read through man mount, particularly the "See Also" section at the end, you will see a list of commands of the form mount_XXX (where XXX is the name of a filesystem type—for example, msdosfs, mfs, ext2fs, smbfs, and so on). Each of these filesystem names can be used with the -t switch on mount; or, if you prefer, you can use these special mount_XXX variants. For example, the following two commands are equivalent:

```
# mount -t msdos /dev/fd0 /floppy
# mount_msdos /dev/fd0 /floppy
```

Similarly, to mount a CD-ROM, use the following:

```
# mount_cd9660 /dev/acd0c /cdrom
```

About NFS

NFS, the *Network Filesystem*, is a method for mounting volumes from across the network into your directory structure. The procedures for using NFS, including the syntax for mount_nfs, are covered in Hour 24, "File Sharing". However, for the purposes of this lesson, it is worthwhile to look briefly at how an NFS share should be mounted.

NFS shares (or available filesystems) are "exported" from UNIX machines on a network, such as a corporate LAN, and made available either freely to the entire network, or only to certain client machines. If your FreeBSD machine is one of the allowed clients, and if you know the NFS server's hostname and the names of the shares on it, you can connect freely to it and incorporate the directory structure of any of the shares into your own system. For example, if an NFS server on your network has the name spots with a shared resource called /usr/local/share/documents, you can mount it onto a directory on your machine called /docs with the following command:

```
# mount -t nfs spots:/usr/local/share/documents /docs
```

The following will also work:

```
# mount_nfs spots:/usr/local/share/documents /docs
```

The contents of the remote machine's documents share can now be browsed and worked with as though they were part of your local machine, albeit with a certain amount of lag time depending on how fast your network is.

The umount Command

Before you remove a disk from the system, you must unmount it from the filesystem. Unmounting a disk completes all pending write operations and makes sure that all processes trying to use the disk are complete. You can physically remove a floppy disk from its drive while it is still mounted, or even while a program is writing to it; however, this might damage the disk or throw the kernel into a frenzy of futile recovery attempts. CD-ROMs are harder to remove while in use (they have soft eject mechanisms that typically do not work unless the operating system has released control of the disk), but you can still cause mischief with a straightened paperclip.

The command for unmounting disks is umount (not "unmount"). To unmount the /mnt filesystem, issue the following command:

```
# umount /mnt
```

You can also use `umount /dev/fd0` to accomplish the same result or even `umount -a` to unmount everything except the root (/) filesystem.

> Unmounting filesystems is a much simpler procedure than mounting them, with only one major complicating factor: For a filesystem to be unmounted, it cannot be in use. This means that to unmount filesystems such as /usr and /var, you will probably have to be in single-user mode. This is what leads to the most common surprise that most users find when first experimenting with mount and umount: *You can't be inside a filesystem you're trying to unmount!* If you are, you'll get a "Device busy" error message. To be safe, be in the habit of entering `cd /` before you attempt to umount anything.
>
> Also be sure to check all your virtual terminals (Alt+F1, Alt+F2, and so on) to make sure that none of them are logged in and sitting inside a filesystem you want to unmount.

The `/etc/fstab` File

You might be asking whether there is a shortcut to all this mounting—a way to program "recipes" for all the mountable devices on a system. After all, Windows machines and Macintoshes don't need all this command-line mumbo jumbo in order to work seamlessly with disks, do they?

After you have figured out the commands needed to mount your second IDE hard drive, your NFS volume from across the network, your MS-DOS floppy, and your SCSI CD-ROM, do you really have to remember those commands every time you want to mount them? No, there is indeed a better way. That way is the `/etc/fstab` file.

Take a look at the file now, using `cat /etc/fstab`:

```
# Device            Mountpoint    FStype    Options      Dump    Pass#
/dev/ad0s1b         none          swap      sw           0       0
/dev/ad0s1a         /             ufs       rw           1       1
/dev/ad0s1f         /var          ufs       rw           2       2
/dev/ad0s1e         /usr          ufs       rw           2       2
/dev/acd0c          /cdrom        cd9660    ro,noauto    0       0
/dev/fd0            /floppy       msdos     rw,noauto    0       0
proc                /proc         procfs    rw           0       0
```

This file tells the system everything it needs to know about a given mount point: what device attaches to it, what filesystem type to expect, the mount options, and in what order it should perform filesystem checks when the system is booted. The `fstab` file is closely interrelated with the `mount` command; used in conjunction, the two tools can make filesystem management a relative breeze.

The main function of the `fstab` file is to give the system a profile of mounted devices that can all be activated at once at boot time. With all your mount points specified here, you can issue the command `mount -a` to mount them all. This is what happens during boot, when the system goes through its filesystem checks; the system runs `fsck -p` (to "preen" the filesystems, making sure that they are all marked "clean" and thus viable for use). It then runs `mount -a -t nonfs` to mount all but the NFS filesystems listed in `/etc/fstab`.

Beyond this function, though, is an even more convenient effect of having your mount configurations saved in a central file. After a mount point is specified in `/etc/fstab`, you no longer need to remember the `mount` command necessary to bring it online; now, the only thing you have to know is the name of the mount point:

```
# mount /floppy
```

This reads in all the necessary information from the `fstab` file. It knows that the device you want is `/dev/fd0`, that it's an MS-DOS filesystem, and that you want it mounted read/write (instead of read-only, which would be specified with `ro` rather than `rw`). Similarly, to mount a CD-ROM disc, enter the following:

```
# mount /cdrom
```

Now, it's starting to look almost user-friendly!

> The `noauto` option on the `/cdrom` and `/floppy` entries tells `mount` that these filesystems should not be mounted at boot time. As with NFS resources, there is no guarantee that a CD-ROM or floppy disk will be available when the system boots, so the `noauto` option prevents `mount` from spending pointless time trying to mount a disk that isn't there. It doesn't prevent you from easily mounting it later, however; the previous `mount` command is all you need.
>
> You can specify any of the `mount` options in the fourth column of the `fstab` file that are applicable to the filesystem in question. For instance, anything listed in `man mount` can be used, as well as anything in the filesystem's `man mount_*` page if it's a non-standard filesystem type.

The FreeBSD Automounter

NFS shares can be made a good deal more automatic with a nifty tool called amd, or the *Auto-Mount Daemon*. This daemon allows you to mount NFS shares (and other filesystem types, as a matter of fact) dynamically, simply by working in the directory in which the share would be mounted without ever having to bother with `mount` commands.

FreeBSD provides a basic way to set up amd. Simply add the following line to /etc/rc.conf:

```
amd_enable="YES"
```

When the system is booted with this option, amd runs with the options specified in the amd_flags setting, which are such that anything in the /host or /net directories—both of which are created automatically by amd—will auto-mount by name. You can also start it in the same way as it would be at boot time by issuing the following command:

```
# amd -a /.amd_mnt -l syslog /host /etc/amd.map /net /etc/amd.map
```

With amd running, cd into the /host directory and look around. It's empty.

```
# cd /host
# ls
#
```

However, try listing by name as if a directory were there with the same name as a known NFS server on the network (assume that the spots machine has an NFS share called /home, which might be a collection of users' home directories):

```
# ls spots
home
```

So, it seems that there's indeed a directory called spots in the /host directory, and inside it is a home directory—which contains everything that the spots:/home share has. You've just auto-mounted that share into the /host directory simply by listing it as a directory name. /host/spots/home is functionally the same thing as an NFS mount created manually by attaching spots:/home to that location using mount or mount_nfs. The df command will verify it:

```
# df
Filesystem      1K-blocks     Used    Avail Capacity  Mounted on
spots:/home     9924475    1642345  7488172     18%   /.amd_mnt/spots/host/home
```

> Notice that NFS shares mounted in this manner actually appear to be mounted inside a directory called .amd_mnt in the root directory. This directory doesn't actually exist; it's just a shorthand used by the amd daemon for bookkeeping purposes.

To specify a permanent location for a mountable NFS resource, simply make a symbolic link to the appropriate path within /host or /net:

```
# ln -s /home2 /host/spots/home
```

From now on, whenever you go into the /home2 directory, the spots:/home share will automatically mount and give you access to its files. When the share is no longer in use, it will automatically unmount.

> You can specify much more complex amd mount maps, which are more direct methods of mounting filesystems at particular points, with the /etc/amd.conf file. This file doesn't exist in the default FreeBSD installation; see man amd.conf for details on its format and capabilities.

System Backup Strategies and Utilities

Every operating system needs to have backup schemes available so that computers with critical data on them—no matter what platform—can be resurrected should their hardware fail, their security be breached, or the entire system be lost in a fire or a break-in. The risks are too many to be counted.

FreeBSD doesn't have as many options available for easy, seamless backups as Windows or even Linux do; this is one of the prices we pay for using an operating system that's not quite as "mainstream" as some. Proper backup solutions involve dedicated client-server software installations, a central server orchestrating daily transfers of data from all computers in a cluster, and a tape carousel that handles the incremental data from all involved machines. In a full-fledged corporate network, the best practices in business IT generally involve a tape carousel system that does full backups of all machines on a weekly basis, and incremental "delta" dumps (saving only the files that have changed since the last full backup) each day in between; the tapes are removed from the carousel and replaced each week (or, in some cases, daily) and moved to a secure off-site storage location. Thus, the entire network can (theoretically) be restored even if the main building should burn down.

Many corporate networks use software such as the Legato NetWorker for their centralized tape-backup solutions. However, this and other packages in its category might not be supported under FreeBSD (although /usr/ports/sysutils/nwclient is a working, if unsupported, Legato client). We will instead look at one or two more rudimentary backup methods—the ones FreeBSD supports natively.

Using tar

Although its use is not particularly easy, tar—the *Tape ARchiver*—is a ubiquitous UNIX tool whose purpose is to facilitate backing up large amounts of data to a tape or to a file that you can copy to a cheap removable disk such as a CD-R. The `tar` program will concatenate all the files in a directory structure together into a single long file, preserving the permissions, ownership, and timestamps of each one. Then you can use `gzip` to compress the file, potentially reducing its size by as much as an order of magnitude, depending on what kind of data you're backing up.

One way to use `tar` is to have it create a file from its input data. This is most useful if you don't have a tape drive, but must rely instead on removable disks for your permanent backups. Choose a starting point in your system—a top-level directory that contains most of the irreplaceable data in your system. (If you have such data in a lot of places in the system, you might have to do multiple backups.) The obvious place to do this, in FreeBSD, would be `/usr/local`, although your needs might vary. For instance, you might want to back up `/usr/home` as well to archive your users' home directories.

Check to see how big a complete backup of your selected starting point would be, using du (*Disk Usage*) with the `-s`, or summary, option:

```
# cd /usr/local/
# du -s
449212   .
```

This system's `/usr/local` tree only contains about 450 megabytes of data. This could fit onto a CD without even being compressed. However, the most important reason to check this number is not whether the resulting file will fit on a disk (though that is important); what you want to make sure of is that your hard disk will have enough room to hold the file during the backup process. Remember, you're effectively making a copy of `/usr/local`; so at least as much space as `/usr/local` requires needs to be available to you.

Pick a destination directory in a partition that has enough space to hold the output (use df to check); create a new directory if you like. Then run `tar` to create the tarfile output:

```
# tar cvf /usr/backup/usr.local.tar /usr/local
```

The c option tells `tar` to create a new file; v says to print verbose output; and f says to create an output file on disk, rather than writing to a tape (which is the native and traditional use for `tar`). You will see the name of each file printed to the screen as it is added to the archive file. After it is done, compress the resulting tarfile using `gzip` (which appends .gz to the filename, resulting in usr.local.tar.gz):

```
# gzip /usr/backup/usr.local.tar
```

You can use the z option to tell tar to gzip "on-the-fly"; the output will be compressed after the tar step, and you won't have to use gzip to compress it. Compressed tarfiles usually have extensions of .tar.gz or .tgz.

```
# tar cvfz /usr/backup/usr.local.tgz /usr/local
```

You can then copy this file (usr.local.tar.gz or usr.local.tgz) to a removable disk, another hard disk, or an NFS share—anything you like.

It might be helpful to keep the compressed tarfile around and not delete it after you've copied it to another medium; you can update changed files in it instead of deleting and re-creating it each time you make a backup, using the r (or *replace*) option:

```
# tar rvfz /usr/backup/usr.local.tgz /usr/local
```

Finally, you can find out what's in a tarfile using the t (or *table of contents*) option:

```
# tar tfz /usr/backup/usr.local.tgz
```

Using tar to create files is all well and good, but the program is really designed primarily for interacting with tape drives. However, with today's respective prices of tape drives, digital tapes, optical drives, and CD media, it's much more cost-effective to use tarfiles and CD-R (or even DVD) backups instead of tapes, and much more likely that you will have the necessary equipment. The media is less fragile, too.

Using burncd

If you have an ATAPI (IDE) CD-R or CD-RW drive, you will want to use the burncd program, which is part of the base FreeBSD system, to write your CDs. (Most optical drives sold today are ATAPI. If you have a SCSI drive, you will instead need to use cdrecord, found in the ports at /usr/ports/sysutils/cdrtools.) This tool is pretty simple to use, although it does involve a two-step process.

The first thing you must do is create an ISO disk image file, which is a bitwise copy of the data that will be written to the disc. You will need to install mkisofs in order to do this; it's in /usr/ports/sysutils/mkisofs (see Hour 7 for more on installing software from the ports or packages).

You have two options: You can make a direct copy of a live filesystem, or you can archive a compressed tarfile. The former is more useful if you want to have quick access to the backed up files after the disc is written; the latter is better if you have to cram more data onto the disc. Either way, the command to use is fairly simple:

```
# mkisofs -o /usr/backup/diskimage.iso /usr/backup
# mkisofs -o /usr/backup/diskimage.iso /usr/local
```

This creates a file called `diskimage.iso` in `/usr/backup`. If you are going to be using the CD on a Windows machine, you might want to add the `-J` option to enable Windows-style (*Joliet*) filesystem extensions, which enable long filenames that normally aren't supported in ISO 9660 filesystems. The `-R` option instead uses the *Rock Ridge* extensions, which are appropriate if the disc will only be used in UNIX systems.

After the ISO image is created, use `burncd` as follows to burn (or write) the CD:

```
# burncd -f /dev/acd0c data /usr/backup/diskimage.iso fixate
```

The `-f` option specifies the drive; `data` tells `burncd` which image file to use; and `fixate` closes the session so that the disc is completely burned and can be mounted. See `man` `burncd` for more useful options.

Recovery

Let's assume that you have a compressed tarfile burned onto a CD, which is the most complex and multi-step situation that we have discussed. You have accidentally deleted a critical directory (`/usr/local/oops`), and you must recover it from the archive.

First, mount the CD as we discussed earlier this hour:

```
# mount_cd9660 /dev/acd0c /cdrom
```

Next, extract the desired directory and its contents from the archived tarfile onto your hard disk:

```
# tar xvfz /cdrom/usr.local.tgz /usr/local/oops
```

If all goes well, your directory should be restored, good as new.

Creating "Seed" Files

One way you can ensure that your custom configuration will survive a catastrophic failure is to gather together the "seed" files, which you can use to customize a new system that you build from scratch. These files can be preserved offline by burning them onto a CD, or in the absence of writable optical media, a floppy disk. Here are the most important files to preserve:

- **/etc/rc.conf**—The main system configuration file.
- **/etc/master.passwd**—The master user database. All other user databases can be generated from this one.
- **/etc/mail/myconfig.mc**—The Sendmail "master config" file if you have a custom Sendmail configuration. (The filename will vary according to what you have named it.)
- **/etc/fstab**—Important for re-creating your disk structure.
- **/usr/local/etc/***—Individual config files for all the programs you've installed.

These are the most critical files—the ones that define your system and give it its identity. All told, they won't come to more than a few hundred kilobytes; those few hundred kilobytes can save weeks of painful tuning and trial-and-error when you rebuild the system.

You might even want to package these files together into a tarball (a tar/gzip archive) and mail it to yourself (at an account *not* on your FreeBSD machine) on a daily basis. Here's a sample one-line command to accomplish this:

```
# tar cvfz - /etc/rc.conf /etc/master.passwd /etc/fstab /usr/local/etc
➥| uuencode seedfiles.tar.gz | mail -s "Seed Files" me@myaccount.com
```

You can put this into a shell script in /etc/periodic/daily or into root's crontab file, as you prefer.

Summary

In this hour, we discussed the basic concepts behind UNIX filesystems, including the key differences between the UNIX directory structure and the Windows/DOS one that you might be used to. You learned how to mount disks onto the system and unmount them, as well as how to format new disks. You also learned how to simplify the mounting process. Armed with this knowledge, you then learned how to archive your critical data and create effective backups using only the built-in tools in FreeBSD.

A more in-depth look at these topics would go into much greater detail about potential backup methods. Backups are absolutely crucial to effective system administration, and many sophisticated tools are available that can be used with FreeBSD. So many exist, however, that to cover them all here would serve only to remove any certainty from what is already a rather convoluted process.

Q&A

Q Is a floppy disk a volume, a partition, or a filesystem? How about a hard disk?

A A floppy disk is generally all three because floppies are seldom partitioned. But a hard disk that has been partitioned has several volumes, also known as partitions, within it. Each volume is potentially a filesystem.

Q What's the difference between /bin and /sbin or between /usr/bin and /usr/sbin?

A Executable programs that have the capability to alter the system's operation are generally kept in the sbin directories, whereas executables that simply perform user functions live in the bin directories. For instance, /bin and /usr/bin contain tools such as ls, less, and top; but /sbin and /usr/sbin have tools such as mount, fsck, ifconfig, and others that can change the system configuration.

Q I don't plan to run a busy server or anything; my machine is just a workstation. Why should I bother partitioning my disk?

A You might not need to. The best argument for partitions is to divide the disk into regions for different purposes so that one area of functionality can't grow to fill the entire disk and interfere with other functions. But if your system won't be hosting busy Web services or a lot of users, you can probably get away with keeping your entire disk as one big partition.

Q I'm having trouble mounting disks with filesystems other than UFS. What can I do?

A Normally, support for filesystems such as MSDOSFS and SMBFS is not built in to the default kernel; those filesystems are available as loadable kernel modules, though, and they are automatically loaded into the kernel when called by the appropriate mount_XXX command. However, this might not be happening properly; use kldstat to see what kernel modules are loaded, and if necessary, use kldload to load the appropriate filesystem before mounting the disk (for example, kldload smbfs.ko).

Q I burned a CD from an ISO image created from a directory structure, but some of my files got lost in the process! How can I retrieve them?

A ISO 9660 doesn't support long filenames. The mkisofs tool will ignore files whose names are illegal under ISO 9660, unless you specify one of the extensions which enable long filenames (-J for Windows' "Joliet" extensions, or -R for UNIX "Rock Ridge" extensions). You can use -U -R to create a disc that's identical to what's on your hard disk, though this might not be readable on other machines.

Workshop

This interactive section is designed to solidify your understanding of storage devices with quiz questions and exercises which suggest further directions in which to take your exploration of the topic.

Quiz

1. What's the default filesystem type used by FreeBSD

    A. FFS

    B. EXT2FS

    C. MSDOSFS

    D. UFS

    E. NTFS

2. What's the device name for the first BSD partition in the second "slice" of an ATA/IDE hard disk installed as the secondary slave?

    A. `/dev/ad0s1a`

    B. `/dev/ad2s2c`

    C. `/dev/ad4s2e`

    D. `/dev/ad3s2e`

3. After a floppy disk is mounted (at `/floppy`), how do I change to where I can use the files in it?

    A. `A:`

    B. `cd A:`

    C. `/floppy`

    D. `cd /floppy`

4. What's the `/etc/fstab` file used for?

    A. Simplifying `mount` commands

    B. Specifying which filesystems to mount automatically at boot time

    C. Specifying default filesystem types for mount points

    D. Specifying the order in which filesystem checks should be done at boot time

    E. Specifying how frequently filesystems should be "dumped"

    F. All of the above

5. How do I mount a network filesystem using `amd`?

    A. `mount_amd hostname:/path/to/share`

    B. `mount_nfs /host/hostname/path/to/share`

    C. `amd hostname:/path/to/share`

    D. `cd /host/hostname/path/to/share ; ls hostname`

6. What `tar` option do I use to list the files archived in a tarfile?

    A. `x`

    B. `t`

    C. `c`

    D. `l`

Quiz Answers

1. The correct answer is either A or D. (They're pretty much synonymous these days.)

2. The correct answer is D.

3. The correct answer is D, though technically you can access and use the files in `/floppy` no matter where you are in the system.

4. The correct answer, as should come as no surprise, is F.

5. The correct answer is D.

The correct answer is B.

Exercises

1. What makes UNIX-style filesystems different from what you might know from Windows? One big difference is *fragmentation*, or how readily files get split into little chunks and written into widely disparate places all across the disk, leading to increased access time and decreased performance. Windows/MS-DOS filesystems can become badly fragmented over time, with as much as 20 or 30% of the files being split across the disk; but UNIX disks very seldom do. Why is that? You might want to read up on the UFS/FFS filesystem (and others, such as Ext2FS) and how it ensures that when it writes files onto the disk, it creates them in contiguous blocks by moving other files around on a continuous basis. This is why FreeBSD reports fragmentation figures of around 1% at boot time, but it never gets much higher than that.

2. What's a weakness of having the filesystem move files around the disk all the time? One downside is that if there's a power failure, the pending write operations vanish into the ether, and some files that were waiting to get rewritten might be lost. Some methods are available for protecting against this, however. *Journaling* is one technique that is becoming increasingly popular in advanced filesystems. FreeBSD has a similar technology called *Soft Updates*. Research these technologies online, if you are interested, and see how they each go about addressing the problem of making UNIX filesystems even more fault-tolerant than they already are.

HOUR 9

The FreeBSD Printing System

Printing is a fairly common thing that people want to do with their computers. Unfortunately, configuring a printer is also one of the more difficult things for someone new to FreeBSD to accomplish. With the instructions given in this hour, you will learn how to configure basic local printing services in FreeBSD. In this hour, you will learn:

- How FreeBSD handles printing
- How to install and configure a printer
- What Postscript is and why you should care
- What Ghostscript is and how to use print utilities
- How to manage printers and print jobs
- How to connect to a network printer

Before you begin trying to install your printer, you should be aware that there are certain printers called *Winprinters* that won't work with anything other than Windows. This is because much of the functionality has been moved to software, allowing the manufacturer to save on hardware costs. If your printer says that it requires a Windows operating system, chances are that it won't work with FreeBSD.

How FreeBSD Handles Printing

The FreeBSD printing system consists of two primary parts. The first is the print daemon, called lpd. A *daemon* is simply a program that runs in the background waiting to receive and handle requests. In this case, lpd runs in the background and waits to receive something to be printed. When it gets a job, it might do some pre-processing such as running it through filters or converting the data to a different format that the printer can understand. When this has been finished, the job is placed in the print queue, which is basically a holding area that stores jobs waiting to be printed. (Jobs are generally printed on a first come, first serve basis. However, you will learn how to change the priority of a print job later in this hour.)

When the printer is available to the queued print job, it will be *spooled* to the printer by the *spooler*. Why user a spooler instead of just send data directly to the printer? There are several reasons:

- The printer can be used by multiple users because data can be queued up and then sent to the printer when it is available. This means that the user can send a print job and forget about it.

- It allows you to send multiple print jobs to the printer without having to wait for currently printing jobs to finish.

- It allows you to print in the background because the program that sent the job to the printer can send it and then forget about it. This means, for example, that you can print a document from a text editor, and then exit the text editor and work on other things even if the document has not finished (or even started) printing.

- It has some fault tolerance. For example, if the printer jams and needs to be reset, the jobs in the queue should still print normally after the printer has been reset.

Configuring the Printer

At this point, we are going to assume that you have a relatively recent printer that is plugged in to your computer's parallel port. We aren't going to cover serial printers, which are relatively obsolete.

The first thing you will want to do is set the parallel port mode.

Configuring the Parallel Port

The lptcontrol program can be used to configure the mode of the parallel port. You will need to be logged in as the root user to do this. In its basic form, lptcontrol is run with an option that you wish to set on the port. The following options are supported:

Option	Description
-i	Sets interrupt driven mode
-p	Sets polled mode
-e	Sets extended mode
-s	Sets standard mode (that is, turns off extended mode)

The option you will probably be most interested here is -e. If your printer supports an extended mode such as ECP or EPP, and you have this configured in your BIOS, you will want to turn this option on with the lptcontrol command. The following command shows how this is done:

```
lptcontrol -e
```

Basically, extended modes allow additional features to simple printing, such as allowing the printer to communicate back to the computer and inform the computer of error conditions such as paper jams or if it runs out of ink. In standard printer mode (that is, no extended mode), data can only be sent one way from the computer to the printer. The printer has no way to communicate back with the computer.

By default, lptcontrol assumes the default printer port, which is /dev/lpt0 in FreeBSD. This will be the first parallel port on the system, which corresponds to LPT1 in Windows. If you have more than one parallel port, and this printer is not on the first one, you can use the -d option to specify a different port. For example, if you want to enable extended mode on the second parallel port, you could use the following command:

```
lptcontrol -e -d /dev/lpt1
```

Note that this setting will be lost when you reboot the system. If you want to have it maintained after each reboot, you need to add it to a system startup script. The best way to do this is to create a file in /usr/local/etc/rc.d that contains the command. Note that the file will need to be executable in order for the command to actually be run. (To do this, use the chmod command—for example, chmod 655 myprintscript.)

Now that you have configured the parallel port, you are ready to set up the printer's spool directory, which is the directory on the hard disk where the printer stores print jobs waiting to be printed and also spools them to the printer.

Configuring the Print Spool Directory

By convention, print spool directories are normally located in /var/spool/lpd. However, there is no rule that you have to put them here. Sometimes, you might want to put a spool directory somewhere else, such as if your /var partition doesn't have enough space. For this example, we are going to assume that you are placing the spool directory in /var/spool/lpd. If this is not the case, simply replace this directory path with whatever directory you are putting the spool directory in.

The first thing you need to do is decide on a name for the printer. You can call the printer anything you want. Later, you can also create aliases for the printer that allow you to access it using other names. Aliases are covered later in this hour under the section "The /etc/printcap File." If you have multiple printers in a large office environment, of course, it makes sense to name the printer something that either says something about what kind of printer it is, or where it is located. In this example, assume that we are configuring an HP Laserjet printer. So we will call it laserjet.

To create the spool directory for the printer, simply create a new directory in the /var/spool/lpd directory with whatever you have decided to name the printer. In this case, the following command will work:

mkdir /var/spool/lpt/laserjet

After you've created the directory, you will want to change the ownership and group membership so that they are both daemon and that only the user and group have any permissions on the spool directory. This will prevent users from snooping around the directory and looking at other people's print jobs or possibly even deleting other people's print jobs.

The following command will set the ownership, group membership, and permissions to their proper values:

chmod 770 daemon.daemon /var/spool/lpd/laserjet

After you've set up the directory, you need to configure a text filter for the daemon.

Configuring a Text Filter

We briefly mentioned filters earlier in the hour. Basically, they are where the majority of the printing work is actually done. All data being sent to the printer passes through a filter first. The filter can do such things as convert the data from one format into a different one that the printer can understand.

At a bare minimum, you will need a text filter. A *text filter*, as the name implies, is the filter used when the printer daemon receives simple plain text. Often times, the text filter is nothing more than a pass-through system that simply passes the raw data to the printer without doing anything to it. However, it can be as complex as a system that changes the data to a completely different format. (Later on, we will look at why you might need to change plain text to a completely different format.)

Text filters can either be written by you or installed as a program that someone else has written. Before you panic at the idea of writing your own filter, basic filters are easy to write. For example, if your printer can receive raw text data and print it fine without making any changes to it, the following filter can simply be written in a text editor and saved to a file. It might be all that you need:

```
#!/bin/sh
/bin/cat && exit 0
exit 2
```

The preceding program is what is known as a *shell script*. The details of writing shell scripts are beyond the scope of this book, but we will cover enough of the basics for you to understand what the preceding filter does.

The first line simply tells the shell which program it should use to interpret the rest of this file. In this case, it tells the shell that this file is a shell script and should be interpreted using the shell.

The second line executes the `cat` program. Basically, in its simplest form, `cat` takes whatever it receives on STDIN (which is normally the keyboard) and echoes it to STDOUT (which is normally the screen). How does this help us with printing? Because for printing, STDIN and STDOUT are redirected. In this case, STDIN is the print data being sent from the spooler, and STDOUT is the printer port that the printer is connected to. So in this case, the `cat` program simply takes whatever it receives from the print spooler and echoes it to the printer port.

The second part of the line, `&& exit 0`, is a shorthand notation of saying basically, "Perform the `exit 0` command if, and only if, the `/bin/cat` command completes successfully." If `cat` does complete successfully, the shell script will exit with a status of 0 (which indicates a successful execution of the command) and the third line of the script will not be executed because the exit command on line 2 will take effect.

If on the other hand, the cat command fails (for whatever reason, it can't send the data to the port or some other such error), the exit 0 command on line 2 will not be executed (because the "if and only if" test fails). In this case, line 3 will be executed, which causes the shell script to exit with a status of 2. (Why exit status 2? Because lpd reads the exit status of the filter. A status code of 2 indicates that the filter failed with an unrecoverable error, and therefore informs lpd that it should not attempt to print the job again.)

The filter can be named anything you want. In this case, we will assume that it is named if-text. By convention, print filters are stored in /usr/local/libexec. When you have saved the file, you need to make it executable so that the lpd program can run it. The following command is an example:

```
chmod 555 /usr/local/libexec/if-text
```

A simple filter such as this should work fine for printing plain text on most non-Postscript printers. However, Postscript printers can't handle plain text. If you have a Postscript printer, you will need a slightly more complex setup that can convert the plain text into Postscript. This is covered in the following section.

Formatting Plain Text for Postscript Printers

Postscript is a programming language for formatting text and graphics. It is device independent so that any printer that understands PostScript can print a PostScript document with no special drivers. PostScript is so common in the UNIX world that most UNIX applications can print PostScript output. Because of this, PostScript can be a very useful thing for your printer to have. However, one problem with PostScript printers is that they generally expect that everything they receive will be in PostScript format. As a result, you can't send plain text data directly to a PostScript printer. Plain text must first be run through a filter that can convert the plain text to PostScript.

The program a2ps, which is available in the print directory of the FreeBSD ports collection, is designed to do just that. After you have installed a2ps, you need to write a filter that can recognize if it is receiving PostScript or plain text, and then take the appropriate action. (Either send the data directly to the printer if it is already in PostScript format, or convert the data to PostScript and then send it to the printer if it is plain text.) Listing 9.1 is a sample filter that will do this.

LISTING 9.1   A Sample Text Filter for PostScript Printers

```
#!/bin/sh
# Simple filter for PostScript printers

read header
ps_test=`expr "$header" : '(../)'`
if [ "$header" = "%!" ]
then
    # File is PostScript. Print pass through.
    echo "$header" && cat && printf "\004" && exit 0
    exit 2
else
    # File is plain text. Convert it first.
    (echo "%header"; cat) | /usr/local/bin/a2ps && printf "\004" && exit 0
    exit 2
fi
```

9

Like the previous filter, this file should be saved in /usr/local/libexec. The name if-
ps might be a good choice. Also, remember once again to set the file to executable so
that lpd can run it. You can use the following command to do this:

chmod 555 /usr/local/libexec/if-ps

We aren't going to go into detail about what this script does, but in a nutshell, it checks
to see if the first two characters of the file are %!. (PostScript files start with these two
characters.) If they are, the filter assumes that the file is PostScript, and it gets passed
directly to the printer. If they are not, the filter assumes the file is plain text, and the data
is passed through the a2ps program to be converted to PostScript before being sent to the
printer.

Of course, if you don't have a PostScript printer, you might have the opposite problem.
In other words, you need to print a PostScript document on a printer that doesn't under-
stand PostScript. In this case, you can use a program called Ghostscript, which converts
PostScript into a format that your printer can understand.

Configuring a Ghostscript Filter

As mentioned previously, most UNIX applications can output PostScript. Although some
UNIX applications contain print drivers for various printers, most of them do not.
Instead, they just output PostScript. Use the Ghostscript program, which is available in
the FreeBSD ports collection under the print directory, for converting the PostScript
output.

Ghostscript supports a lot of printers. A list (which might not be complete) of supported printers is available at www.cs.wisc.edu/~ghost/doc/printer.htm.

The filter script for this is similar to the script for printing plain text on a PostScript printer—except that this time, the operations are reversed. This time, if the filter receives plain text, the text should be passed straight through without any formatting. On the other hand, if the filter receives PostScript, it should be sent to the Ghostscript program for conversion into an understandable format for your printer.

The following script, taken from the FreeBSD handbook, works for an HP Deskjet 500 (which cannot print PostScript directly).

```
#!/bin/sh
    #
    #  ifhp - Print Ghostscript-simulated PostScript on a DeskJet 500
    #  Installed in /usr/local/libexec/hpif

    #
    #  Treat LF as CR+LF:
    #
    printf "\033&k2G" || exit 2

    #
    #  Read first two characters of the file
    #
    read first_line
    first_two_chars=`expr "$first_line" : '\(..\)'`

    if [ "$first_two_chars" = "%!" ]; then
        #
        #  It is PostScript; use Ghostscript to scan-convert and print it.
        #
        #  Note that PostScript files are actually interpreted programs,
        #  and those programs are allowed to write to stdout, which will
        #  mess up the printed output.  So, we redirect stdout to stderr
        #  and then make descriptor 3 go to stdout, and have Ghostscript
        #  write its output there.  Exercise for the clever reader:
        #  capture the stderr output from Ghostscript and mail it back to
        #  the user originating the print job.
        #
        exec 3>&1 1>&2
        /usr/local/bin/gs -dSAFER -dNOPAUSE -q -sDEVICE=djet500 \
            -sOutputFile=/dev/fd/3 - && exit 0

        #
        /usr/local/bin/gs -dSAFER -dNOPAUSE -q -sDEVICE=djet500
        ➥-sOutputFile=- - \
            && exit 0
    else
```

```
      #
      #  Plain text or HP/PCL, so just print it directly; print a form feed
      #  at the end to eject the last page.
      #
      echo $first_line && cat && printf "\033&l0H" &&
  exit 0
  fi

  exit 2
```

Like the script for converting plain text into PostScript, this script basically reads the first two characters of the file to see if they are %!. If they are, the script assumes that the file is a PostScript file and uses Ghostscript to print it. If they are not, the script assumes that the file is plain text and passes it directly to the printer.

As with the other filters, this filter should be saved in the `/usr/local/libexec` directory and made executable so that lpd can run it (for example, `chmod 555 /usr/local/libexec/if-gs.sh`).

After you have finished creating and installing a text filter (and any applications it might need such as Ghostscript or a2ps), you need to configure the `/etc/printcap` file.

The `/etc/printcap` File

The `/etc/printcap` file is the main printer configuration file. It is where the printer is defined, along with information about which filter it uses, where its spool directory is located, and so on.

The format of this file is relatively simple. Here is a sample entry, and a discussion of what each part means follows:

```
simba|lp|local line printer:\
#        :sh:\
         :lp=/dev/lpt0:sd=/var/spool/lpd/simba:lf=/var/log/lpd-errs:
  :if=/usr/local/libexec/if-ps:
```

The first line simply gives the name of the printer and any aliases that we want to associate with it. In this case, the printer is named simba and has the alias of lp. One of the printers defined in the `/etc/printcap` file should always have the alias lp because this will make it the default printer. The alias is a long description of the printer.

The pound sign beginning the second line means that the line is commented out. In other words, it will be ignored. If the line is uncommented, the printer will print a header page (also known as a cover page) for each job that contains the name of the user and name of the file printed. You might want to uncomment this line if you have a lot of users printing to the same printer in order to make it easier for users to find their job in the pile.

The third line gives lpd information about where the printer and its associated spool files are. lp means that the printer is a local printer (as opposed to a network printer), /dev/lpt0 means that the printer is on the first parallel port in the system, sd=/var/spool/lpd/simba will be the printer's spool directory (make sure that the directory actually exists and that lpd can read and write to it), and lf=/var/log/lpd-errs is the file that any errors that occur will be logged to.

The fourth line is the input filter, which is the text filter that you configured in the previous section. In this case, it is using the filter that converts normal text to PostScript and passes plain PostScript through with no modifications.

Starting lpd

After you have finished configuring the /etc/printcap file, you are ready to start the print daemon. To do this, you can simply type the command **lpd** as the root user. To have the print daemon started automatically on each system startup, add the following line to the /etc/rc.conf file:

```
lpd_enable="YES"
```

Command Line Printing

lpr sends a file to the print spooler. For example,

```
lpr filename
```

This command will print the file with the name *filename* to the default printer. (Remember that the printer with the alias lp in /etc/printcap is considered to be the default printer. Users can, however, override the system default to configure a different printer to be their default. We will look at how to do this later on.)

If you want to print multiple files, you can specify more than one on the command line. For example,

```
lpr file1 file2 file3
```

If you want to print to a printer other than the one configured as the default, you can use the -P option followed by the name of the printer you want to print to, such as lpr -P simba file1. In this case, the file will be printed to the printer named simba.

lpr has several other options, which are listed in Table 9.1.

TABLE 9.1 Options Supported by the `lpr` Command

Option	Description
-l	Uses a filter that will print control codes and suppress the page breaks. This means that the normally invisible characters that control things in the printer, such as carriage returns, will actually be printed on the paper.
-p	Formats the file with `pr` before sending it to the printer. `pr` formats pages to have 66 lines per page, along with a header at the top containing the date and time the file was created. It also contains the page number and five blank lines at the bottom of the page (probably useful mostly for old dot matrix printers).
-P	Specifies a printer to print to other than the default one.
-h	Suppresses the printing of header pages. If header pages are suppressed already by default, (in `/etc/printcap`), this option has no effect.
-m	Causes `lpd` to send you an email notifying you when your print job has completed. It's useful for busy network printers located on other floors and such.
-r	Removes the file after it has been spooled. It should probably not be used because it removes the file before it has actually printed.
-s	Creates a symbolic link in the spool directory that is then used to print the file. It is useful if the file is too big to copy into the spool directory. The problem with this is that if you use this with the original file, you can't modify or delete the file until after it has finished printing.
-#n	*n* is the number of copies that you want to print of each file.
-J name	*name* is the name of the job that should be printed on the header page (if header pages are enabled). If this option is omitted, the name of the job will be the name of the first file that was sent.
-T	This is the title that `pr` should use at the top of each page. It has no effect unless the -p option is also used.
-I n	*n* is the number of columns that each line of printed output should be indented by.
-w n	*n* is the page width in columns. It has no effect unless the -p option is also used.

Checking the Status of Jobs

The `lpq` command can be used to check the status of jobs that are currently in the print queue. If it is run with no options, it will show the status of jobs for the default printer. Similar to the `lpr` command, `lpq` can use the -P option followed by the name of a printer to show the queue for a printer other than the default one. Here is an example of `lpq` output:

```
bash$ lpq -P simba
simba is ready and printing
Rank      Owner    Job    Files                    Total Size
Active    mike     5      /home/murban/myfile.txt  2500 bytes
2nd       jane     6      /home/jane/file1.txt     3000 bytes
3rd       jane     7      /home/jane/file2.txt     4000 bytes
4th       mike     8      . . .                    3500 bytes
```

The first line tells what the printer is currently doing. In this case, it is ready and currently printing a job. Other messages you might see here include messages if the printer is jammed, and so on.

Four jobs are listed in the queue. The first one is currently active, which means that it is printing. It is owned by the user mike, and the file being printed is /home/murban/myfile.txt. The size of the file in bytes is also given.

The rest of the jobs are in the queue waiting to be printed, and will be printed in the order of their rank.

Notice that the last job doesn't list the name of the file being printed and just has three periods instead. This simply means that the path of the file was too long to fit in the list, so it simply wasn't listed.

If you want to see the status of only one particular job or only the status of jobs owned by one particular user, you can follow the lpq command with the job number or the name of the user you want information for.

Two other useful options for the command are -l, which will cause information about the file being printed to be displayed even if it would cause the output to break across multiple lines (that is, the filename is long) and -a, which will display information on all local queues for all printers.

Removing Jobs from the Queue

The lprm command is used to remove print jobs from the queue. If you run it without any command line arguments, it will remove whatever job is currently printing. (This is assuming that the job belongs to you. You can't remove jobs of other users unless you are the root user.)

If you run lprm followed by a job number, it will remove whatever job number you specify. (The job number can be obtained by examining the queue with lpq as described earlier.) For example,

```
bash$ lprm 2
dfA002simba.lion.org dequeued
cfA002simba.lion.org dequeued
bash$
```

Two files were removed from the queue even though you only listed one job because one of the files is a control file. However, although two files were removed, only one print job was actually removed.

The system can sometimes take a few seconds to respond after typing the lprm command, and it might seem that the system has hung up. Chances are it hasn't; it just takes a few seconds for this command to complete sometimes.

A few options to lprm can be useful. Like most of the other printer commands we have discussed up to this point, lprm supports the -P option to specify a printer other than the default one. Another useful option is simply a dash (-) by itself. This will remove all the jobs from the queue that belong to you (lprm -).

If you are logged in as the root user, you can also supply the name of a user after the lprm command. This will remove all the jobs belonging to that user.

Note that if you cancel a currently printing job , it will not stop printing right away because any pages already in the printer's buffer memory will still print. Depending on how much memory is in your printer and what kinds of things are in the document (images take up more memory than text, for example), this could mean that several more pages will print even after you have canceled the job.

Controlling the Printers

The lpc command is used to control printers and print queues connected to the server. Note that only the root user (with certain exceptions covered later on) can access most of the lpc functions. lpc is used to disable print queues, enable print queues, reset printers, check the status of print queues, and change the order of the jobs in the queue.

There are two ways that you can start lpc. The first is with the name of a command as a command line argument. If you start lpc this way, the given command will be run, and lpc will exit. See the man page for lpc for details on the commands that can be given from the command line.

The second way that lpc can be started is in interactive mode. If you start it with no command line arguments, this is the mode you will be placed in. When in interactive mode, lpc will display a prompt that looks like the following:

```
lpc>
```

If you type ? or help at this prompt, you will be given a list of commands that lpc understands.

Queue Status

When in lpc, you can check the status of print queues by using the status command. It needs to be followed by either the keyword all, which will display the status of all queues, or by the name of a specific printer that you want to get the status of. Some sample output of the status for a default printer follows:

```
lpc> status lp
lp:
        queuing is enabled
        printing is enabled
        2 entries in spool area
        waiting for lp to become ready (offline?)
lpc>
```

In this case, the queue is enabled, printing is enabled, and two entries are in the print spool waiting to be printed. However, the printer is not ready to print, and lpc suggests the possible reason might be that it is offline.

Disabling the Queue

There are times when you might want to disable the print queue to prevent it from allowing users to queue jobs on the printer. For example, the printer might be down for maintenance. There are two ways that you can disable the print queue from lpc.

The first way is with the command disable. In this case, the queue will be stopped, but printing will still be allowed. This means that any jobs still in the queue will be printed (assuming that the printer can print them), but no new jobs will be accepted. If a user tries to print to a printer where the queue is down, he will get a message similar to lpr: Printer queue is disabled. Similar to the other lpc command we have discussed, disable requires either the keyword all to disable all queues on the system or the name of a printer that you want to disable the queue on.

The other command that can be used to disable the queue is down. Once again, it needs to be followed by either the keyword all or the name of a specific printer.

Unlike the disable command, the down command disables the queue and also disables printing as soon as the current job has finished printing. This means that any jobs left in the queue will not be printed.

You can also give an optional status message with the down command. For example,

```
lpc> down lp Printer is trashed.
```

This status message is stored in a file named status that is located in this printer's spool directory and will be displayed when a user uses the lpq command to examine the printer's queue.

Enabling the Queue and Restarting the Printer

To enable a queue that is down, you can use the enable command followed by the keyword all or the name of a specific printer whose queue you want to enable. Note however, that this command will only enable the queue. If printing is disabled, it will not enable printing. This means that jobs will be accepted and queued for printing, but they will not actually be printed.

The up command will re-enable the queue and also re-enable the printer. But it will not get rid of the status message if you provided one. Use the restart command to do this and clear the status message.

Restarting the Daemon

Occasionally, for whatever reason, you might need to restart the print daemon for a printer (perhaps the daemon has hung). The restart command can do this. Once again, it needs either the keyword all or the name of a specific printer that you want to restart.

> At the time of this writing, the restart command sometimes kills the daemon but doesn't restart it again even though its status message claims that the daemon has been restarted. To verify that the daemon actually did restart, use the lpq command to check the status of the printer. If it contains the line Warning: no daemon present, it means that the daemon was not actually restarted. Simply run the restart command from lpc again to take care of this.

Cleaning the Queue

Occasionally, because of printer problems and such, the print queue directory can accumulate some garbage. (Files that cannot be printed and such because information is missing and they are not complete jobs.) To clean out the queue directory, you can use the clean command from lpc. As you have probably guessed by now, it requires either the keyword all or the name of a specific printer.

Changing the Priority of Print Jobs

To change the priority of jobs in the print queue, use the topq command. It requires the name of the printer followed by a list of job numbers that you want to move to the top of the queue. For example, topq 5 3 8 2 will move the jobs 5, 3, 8, and 2 to the top of the queue, respectively. Only the root user can change the priority of print jobs.

Abbreviating Commands

Commands in `lpc` can be abbreviated to their shortest nonambiguous form when you type them. For example, `status` can be abbreviated to `stat`, and `lpc` will know what you mean. It cannot, however, be abbreviated to `sta` because it is ambiguous with the command `start`.

Summary

In this hour, you learned how to configure a basic printer in FreeBSD. There is a lot of advanced material that we didn't cover here, such as network printers. More in-depth coverage of advanced printing topics can be found in *FreeBSD Unleashed* from Sams Publishing, and also in the FreeBSD handbook.

Workshop

This section is designed to answer common questions that come up about printing, as well as to solidify your understanding of printing with quiz questions.

Q&A

Q My printer doesn't receive data, and jobs just keep sitting in the queue. What could be wrong?

A Make sure that the printer isn't disabled by checking the queue with `lpq`. Also make sure that there is no warning about the queue being disabled. If there is, you will need to restart the queue using the `restart` command in `lpc`.

Q The printer seems to be getting data (the data light is flashing), but it never prints. How can I correct this?

A This is commonly caused by trying to send non-PostScript data to a printer that only understands PostScript. The printer is expecting control codes that it is not getting. Make sure that you are using a filter such as the one discussed earlier in this hour to convert non-PostScript data into PostScript.

Q Printer prints out a lots of garbage, especially when trying to print images. Why is this happening?

A This often happens when you try to send a PostScript document to a printer that can't handle PostScript. See the section in this hour on "Configuring a Ghostscript filter" for information on how to correct this.

Q The printer is very slow. How can I speed it up?

A You might be able to fix this problem by setting the printer to polled mode with the lptcontrol program. This can be done with the command lptcontrol -P. Don't forget that you need to add this to a startup file if you want it to take effect on each system boot.

Quiz

9

1. The file that contains printer definitions is

    A. /etc/printers

    B. /etc/print.conf

    C. /etc/printcap

    D. /etc/printdef

2. One printer should always be aliased to which of the following?

    A. lpc

    B. lpd

    C. lpr

    D. lp

3. Which of the following programs can be used to look at printer queues?

    A. lpd

    B. lpr

    C. lpc

    D. lpq

4. Which of the following commands controls printers and their queues?

    A. lpd

    B. lpc

    C. lptcontrol

    D. None of the above

5. Which of the following commands removes a job from the queue?

    A. lpremove

    B. lpr

    C. lprm

    D. lpdelete

Answers

1. The correct answer is C.

2. The correct answer is D. All the other options are names of printer commands and not printers.

3. The correct answer is D.

4. The correct answer is B. Watch out for answer C, which is the name of the program that configures the printer port, not the name of the program that controls printers and print queues.

5. The correct answer is C. Answers A and D do not exist. Answer B sends a job to the queue.

HOUR 10

The FreeBSD Kernel and Device Tree

We have talked briefly about the role of the kernel in previous hours of the book. In this hour, we will look at the kernel in greater depth. In addition, you will see how to build a new kernel and the reasons why you might want to do so.

In this hour, you will learn:

- What the kernel is and why you need it
- Why you might want to build a new kernel
- How to work with the kernel configuration file
- How to build and install the new kernel
- What you need to know about the device tree

The Kernel and Its Purpose

The kernel is a special piece of software that serves as the core of the operating system. Among other things, it controls how users interact with the hardware and how resources are allocated for software. In addition, the kernel implements network communications so that the computer can communicate with other computers over the LAN or the Internet. When a running program misbehaves, it is the kernel's job to keep it from interfering with the operation of other programs, or from crashing the system. Figure 10.1 shows a simple diagram of how the kernel relates to the hardware and other running software.

FIGURE 10.1

The kernel isolates software and users from the hardware and thus controls access to system resources.

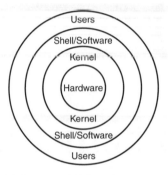

We mentioned that the kernel isolates software from the hardware. This is not always entirely true because in some special cases, software other then the kernel can access the hardware directly. This is primarily for performance reasons. Some examples are programs used for rendering high-end animation and so on. In this case, it is too much of a performance hit to make the program go through the kernel to access the video hardware, so it will usually access it directly.

Why Build a Custom Kernel?

These days, it is far less common to have to build a custom kernel. In the past, the main reason for doing so was for device support. Usually, one built a custom kernel because the default kernel didn't have support for a device in her system (a sound card, for example). These days however, sound card support—as well as support for most other devices—can be dynamically loaded as a kernel module. (Rather than being built directly into the kernel, the module can be loaded into the kernel dynamically at boot time.)

However, there are still times when you might want to build a custom kernel. There are generally four possible reasons for doing this:

- You've cvsupped to a newer version of FreeBSD, and you need to rebuild the kernel to sync with the newer version.
- You need to apply a patch to the kernel to fix a bug or security issue.
- You want to remove support for devices you don't have to give the kernel a smaller footprint.
- You want to add support for a device in your kernel, and you don't want to or can't use a dynamically loadable module.

The idea of rebuilding the core of the operating system from source is understandably rather intimidating to new users. However, the process is not nearly as complicated as it sounds, nor does it require any programming knowledge. Anyone can build a custom FreeBSD kernel by following the instructions given in this hour.

10

The Kernel Configuration File

Based on what you have learned about FreeBSD configuration up to this point, you are probably guessing that kernel configuration is handled by a plain text file. And you are absolutely right. The kernel configuration file is located in the directory /usr/src/sys/i386/conf. The name of the configuration file that is used to build the default kernel (the one you are running after a fresh FreeBSD install, for example) is GENERIC. You won't want to edit this file directly. Instead, make a copy of it. You can give the copy whatever name you want, but it usually makes since to give it a meaningful name. One common naming system is to give the kernel the same name as the system's hostname on a network. If you aren't on a network, you can be as creative as you want, or you can simply call it MYKERNEL or something. For example,

```
cp GENERIC MYKERNEL
```

Note that you will need to be logged in as root to make the copy of the file, as well as to make changes to it (which we will discuss shortly).

Editing the Configuration File

Once you have made a copy of the file, open the copy you made in a text editor. At the top of the file, after several comments that begin with the pound sign (#), you will see the following lines:

```
machine      i386
cpu      I486_CPU
cpu      I586_CPU
cpu      I686_CPU
```

The first line specifies the machine type, and it will never change unless you are compiling a kernel for an Alpha system, which is currently the only other platform that FreeBSD supports with a production stable version. A discussion of Alpha support is beyond the scope of this book. Assuming that you are using an Intel x86 or compatible system (AMD or Cyrix), you will never need to change this line.

The next three lines provide support for different generations of processors. Because the GENERIC kernel will run on everything from a 486 up to the latest Pentium 4 and AMD Athlon processors, the default kernel has support compiled in for all of them. In the custom kernel, you will want to remove support for all the processors that you don't have. For example, if you have a Pentium 3 or Pentium 4, you can remove all of the cpu lines except the I686_CPU line. Instead of actually deleting the lines, you can place a pound sign (#) in front of them. # indicates to the kernel building system that the rest of the line should be considered a comment. Comments are ignored by the system and not processed. So any line that starts with a # will not be included in the kernel, accomplishing the same thing as deleting the line altogether.

> There is the possibility for confusion here because of different naming schemes among CPU vendors. Keep the following guidelines in mind: The original Pentium processor is an I586. The Pentium 2 through Pentium 4 processors are I686. Cyrix processors are even more confusing because the Cyrix 686 is actually an I586 as far as FreeBSD is concerned. AMD K6 processors are also I586, but AMD Athlon processors are I686. If you install a kernel that does not include support for your CPU type, you will be left with a system that cannot start. In the event that this happens to you, see the section near the end of this hour titled "Recovering from Botched Kernel Builds."

There are several more lines that are important and you might want to change:

```
ident       GENERIC
```

This is simply the name of the kernel. It is what will show up when the kernel starts. The name listed here should be the same as the name you gave the new file you created.

```
maxusers    32
```

This option is rather poorly named and can cause a great deal of confusion. It has absolutely nothing to do with the maximum number of users who are allowed on the system. It actually controls the number of resources available in important system parameters. The number it sets will be approximately equal to the number of resources required by the number of users listed here. If you set maxusers to 1, FreeBSD will automatically manage the number of resources available.

```
device          npx0     at nexus? port IO_NPX irq 13
```

Why does the configuration file even give this option to you? Who knows. But basically, this option provides floating point support. You cannot remove this device because the kernel cannot boot without it.

```
#makeoptions    DEBUG=-g             #Build kernel with gdb(1) debug symbols
```

By default, this option is commented out. Normal users will probably want to leave it that way. The debug symbols will greatly increase the size of the kernel. You only need the debug symbols for troubleshooting consistent kernel problems. You should leave this option commented out unless you are experiencing regular kernel panics. Then building a kernel with debug symbols can help you track down the problem.

```
options         MATH_EMULATE         #Support for x87 emulation
```

Unless you have a relatively ancient 386 system without a math coprocessor, or you have a 486SX, you can comment this line out. This option allows FreeBSD to emulate floating point math for systems that do not have a coprocessor.

> FreeBSD's floating point math routines are not very accurate. Because of this, if you do not have a math coprocessor (all Pentium and higher CPUs do have one), you should change this option to GPL_MATH_EMULATE. The GPL math routines are more accurate than the default FreeBSD ones.

You can generally ignore the rest of the options lines.

The device lines are where you will want to make most of the changes to the kernel configuration. Here you can remove support for devices that you don't have, as well as add support for devices that you do have, which are not supported in the default kernel. For example, you can remove support for network cards you do not have. Several devices listed here are commented out and thus not included in the default kernel. If you have one of these devices and need to enable it, you can do so by removing # from in front of the device.

Several additional devices can be enabled that are not listed here. We will look at how to get a complete list of all possible devices later on in this hour. An example of a device that is not listed here but is fairly common is a device to support sound cards. To add support for most common sound cards, you would add the following line:

```
device          pcm
```

The NOTES File

In the same directory as the kernel configuration files, you will also find a file called NOTES. The NOTES file contains a list of all possible options and devices, along with comments that explain what they do. The NOTES file also contains device hints, which will be discussed later in this hour.

Typing the command make lint from the directory will cause a kernel configuration file called LINT to be created in the directory. This file contains every possible device as well as every possible option. You should not actually try to build a kernel with the LINT file though. For one thing, if the kernel did build, it would be huge. Also, the kernel probably would not be able to boot because certain devices and options are mutually exclusive and will cause conflicts if used together. Probably, a kernel will not even compile if you use LINT as the configuration file.

Building the New Kernel

Afteryou have finished editing your custom kernel configuration file and have saved it, you are ready to build the new kernel. Change back to the /usr/src directory and use the following command:

```
make buildkernel KERNCONF=MYKERNEL
```

MYKERNEL should, of course, be replaced with the actual name of the custom kernel configuration file that you used.

After you have entered the command, FreeBSD will first check the kernel configuration file to make sure that it is valid. If you have any illegal options or formatting errors in the file, FreeBSD will let you know about them and then the process will stop so that you can go back and fix the problems. After you have fixed any problems, simply run the make buildkernel KERNCONF=MYKERNEL command again.

Assuming that no problems are found with your configuration file, FreeBSD will begin building the new kernel. You will see a lot of messages go by on the screen from the C compiler during this process. Don't worry about what these messages mean. On a reasonably fast system, the process of building the new kernel will probably take around 15 minutes or so. Of course, extremely fast systems could take much less time, and extremely slow systems could take much longer. After the process has completed, you will be returned to the command prompt.

Installing the New Kernel

After the build process is complete and you have the command prompt back, the new kernel has been built, but it is not yet actually installed. Installing the new kernel is the focus of this section.

> After you install the new kernel, you will need to reboot the system for the new kernel to actually be loaded and start running the system. It is important to make sure that you have physical access to the system at this point. It is possible to build and install a new kernel remotely, and then also reboot the system remotely. However, if you botch the kernel configuration file and the new kernel cannot boot, the system will be rendered unusable until you can get to the physical system and straighten out the problem from there. Unless you are absolutely sure that the new kernel will boot, it is always best to wait until you can get physical access to the system before you install the new kernel and reboot the system.

10

To install the new kernel once the build process has finished, use the following command:

```
make installkernel KERNCONF=MYKERNEL
```

Once again, *MYKERNEL* should be replaced with whatever name you gave your custom kernel configuration file. The install process will cause two main things to happen:

- The new kernel will be copied into /boot and given the name kernel.
- The old kernel will be copied to /boot/kernel.old, giving you a rescue kernel that is known to be good. If the new kernel cannot boot, you can fall back on this rescue kernel to allow you to reboot the system and then fix whatever problem is preventing the new kernel from booting.

> Whenever you install a new kernel, whatever kernel is currently installed will be copied to /boot/kernel.org. This means that if you botch the kernel configuration and create a kernel that can't boot, the next time you install a kernel, the broken kernel will be copied to kernel.old. If the new kernel you created won't boot, you will be out of luck since now both kernel and kernel.old are broken. Because of this, if you do have to boot kernel.old and fix a problem with your new kernel, it is a good idea to copy kernel.old to some other name (kernel1.old for example). This ensures that you will still have a bootable kernel even if your second kernel won't boot. At that point, you can boot kernel1.old. More on how to boot a rescue kernel will be explained later in this chapter.

After the install process has completed, you can reboot your system to boot the new kernel. If all goes well, you should see your custom kernel name listed when the system reboots, as well as the time that you created the new kernel. If something goes wrong, the following section can help.

Recovering from Botched Kernel Builds

Several things can go wrong while attempting to build a new kernel. Here are some of the possible problems and how to remedy them.

"Kernel panic!" Message After Reboot

The is one of the most serious problems. Basically, the kernel builds and installs fine, but then "panics" after you reboot.

Depending on what is wrong, you might get an error message on reboot that says "Kernel panic!" followed by a short description of the error. At that point, the system might automatically reboot, or it might simply halt. However, just because the kernel is panicking doesn't mean that you have to panic as well. You have the backup kernel that was created for you when you installed the new kernel, and you can use it to boot the system so that you can fix whatever is preventing the new kernel from booting.

To boot from the old kernel, restart the system if it hasn't automatically done so already. At the prompt where it is counting down from 10, press any key to interrupt the boot process. Then, at the prompt, type the following:

`boot /boot/kernel.old`

If you need to boot some other kernel, simply replace `kernel.old` with the name of whatever kernel you need to boot, for example `kernel1.old`. After the kernel has finished booting, start over with the kernel configuration instructions you learned at the beginning of the hour.

System Hangs After Reboot

Another problem that could occur is that the kernel simply hangs during the boot process instead of panicking. In this case, you can reboot the system and follow the same procedures given previously to boot an alternative kernel.

Another possibility is that the kernel might not be hung at all, but is attempting to probe for a device that you don't have. In this case, the kernel might wait for a long time before continuing to boot. The messages on the screen should give you some help in figuring out which device is causing the problems.

Kernel Build Fails with "* Error code" Message

Another thing that can go wrong is that the build process bails out with an error message. One of the most common is "* Error code 1". If this happens, it means that something is wrong with the kernel source code itself. In this case, try to use the last compiler message to see if you can find out which module was being compiled when the error occurred. Unless you are a programmer, the best thing you can probably do is post the error message along with the last few lines to the FreeBSD-questions mailing list and ask for help. Before you do this though, if you have cvsupped to a newer source tree, make sure that you check the freebsd-stable mailing list for any warnings that the kernel compile might be broken at the present time. If so, wait until the all clear is posted to the list, cvsup the source tree again, and start over.

Another possible compiler error message you might see are signal 11 errors. This is an internal compiler error that is often more difficult to track down. It can be the result of flaky hardware—with bad RAM being a common culprit. Make a note of where the signal 11 error occurred, and then attempt to rebuild the kernel. If the signal 11 occurs again in a different spot than it did the first time, hardware problems are almost certainly the culprit.

Certain System Utilities Stop Working

One other problem you could run into is that certain system utilities such as ps stop working with the new kernel. This is usually caused by your kernel being out of sync with the rest of the system. This can occur if you have cvsupped your source code tree to a newer version of FreeBSD but have not rebuilt the system. In this case, your kernel will have been built with the newer sources, but the rest of your system will have been built with older ones. You will need to rebuild the rest of your system so that it is sychchronized with the new kernel. Instructions on how to do this can be found in Hour 11, "Updating FreeBSD."

Summary

In this hour, you learned more about what the kernel does and why you might want to build a custom one. You learned that like most things in FreeBSD, the kernel configuration is controlled by a text file. You saw how to build and install a new kernel and how to recover if something goes wrong.

Workshop

The following quiz questions are designed to test your understanding of kernels and kernel configuration that were covered in this hour.

Quiz

1. The kernel provides all of the following functions except

    A. Controlling access to system resources

    B. Providing basic networking services

    C. Providing an interface for the user to interact with the system

    D. Providing support for multiple users to use the system

2. Kernel configuration files are located in which directory?

    A. /usr/src/sys/i386/conf

    B. /etc/kernel.conf

    C. /boot/kernel

    D. /usr/src/kern

3. You can load the backup kernel by interrupting the system startup and entering the following command:

    A. start /boot/kernel.old

    B. load /boot/kernel.old

    C. boot /boot/kernel.old

    D. kernel = /boot/kernel.old

4. The command to build the new kernel is

    A. make kernel kernconf=MYKERNEL

    B. make buildkernel kernconf=MYKERNEL

    C. make MYKERNEL build

    D. None of the above

5. Why is it important to make sure that you have physical access to the system when installing a new kernel?

Quiz Answers

1. The correct answer is C. The interface between the user and the system is provided by the shell that runs on top of the kernel.

2. The correct answer is A. Answers B and D do not exist. Answer C is the name of the actual kernel, not the name of the configuration file.

3. The correct answer is C. All the other answers are invalid commands.

4. The correct answer is D. Answers A and C do not exist. Answer B would be correct if it were KERNCONF instead of kernconf. Remember that FreeBSD is case sensitive.

5. It is important to make sure that you have physical access to the system in case the new kernel cannot boot. In that case, you will not be able to restart the system from a remote location. You will need physical access to the system to restart it and boot an alternate kernel.

10

Hour **11**

Updating FreeBSD

Like all other operating systems, new versions and updates of FreeBSD are released on a periodic basis. These updates and new versions are necessary for several reasons. Some of these reasons include

- Patching security problems that are found.
- Keeping up with advances in technology.
- Adding support for new hardware.

Minor upgrades to FreeBSD are released fairly often (usually around every three months or so). Major versions (for example, FreeBSD 5.0 versus FreeBSD 6.0) are released, on average, once every year or so. With FreeBSD, you can update your system as often as you wish without ever having to buy another CD. Updates can be downloaded from the Internet. In this hour, you will learn

- Why there are two different FreeBSD source trees, their differences, and how to decide which one to use.
- How to prepare your system for an upgrade.
- How to update your FreeBSD sources using the cvsup program.

- How to use "make world" to rebuild your system from the updated sources.
- How to recover if something goes wrong.

The Two FreeBSD Source Trees

With Windows and Macintosh, you generally only have one choice for updating your system. You simply go to the store and purchase the new upgrade to Windows or MacOS and then install it on top of the existing version. (Or in some cases, you download a patch from the Internet or use an automatic update program such as that included with more recent versions of Windows.)

With FreeBSD however, you always have to upgrade options available to you. One of the options is called *STABLE* and the other option is called *CURRENT*.

What Is a Source Tree?

A *source tree* is the set of source code files that make up the operating system. Source code files are just plain text files that contain the programming code written by the FreeBSD programmers. These source code files are read by the FreeBSD C compiler and converted into machine code that can be read by the computer. Ultimately, the entire operating system is built out of the source code from one of the source trees.

The Difference Between STABLE and CURRENT

STABLE and CURRENT are the two different source trees of FreeBSD that you can use to upgrade your system.

CURRENT

CURRENT was a very poor choice of names for one of the trees because it is rather misleading. CURRENT is **not** the current released version of FreeBSD. Rather, it is the tree in which programmers are actively developing the next version of FreeBSD. Basically, CURRENT can be thought of as the development version of FreeBSD. The CURRENT source tree is constantly changing as new features are added, broken code is fixed, and so on.

It is not uncommon for the CURRENT tree to be broken. In other words, it cannot actually be used to build a working operating system. It is also not uncommon for someone to accidentally check broken code into the CURRENT tree. This means that CURRENT can literally be usable one minute, broken the next minute, and a few minutes later, it is usable again after someone figures out that broken code was checked into the tree.

CURRENT is also a testbed for new features that will eventually end up in the production version of FreeBSD. Often, these features are buggy in CURRENT. Also, they are often poorly documented at best, and completely undocumented at worst.

As you might have guessed by now, CURRENT is not intended to be used by the average FreeBSD user. Rather, it is intended to be used by programmers and developers. CURRENT should definitely not be used on a production system because of its potential instability with new features that have not been tested well. If you want to play with the latest gizmos and gadgets in FreeBSD, and thus you want to run CURRENT, it is very important that you are subscribed to the FreeBSD-CURRENT mailing list. This list will contain announcements of when CURRENT is broken, as well as advance warning of new features being added that will likely cause things to break or become very unstable. Most readers of this book will probably want to shy away from CURRENT and look at STABLE instead.

STABLE

The STABLE tree is where patches and upgrades are made to the current production version of FreeBSD. Although it does change on a regular basis as patches are made and such, it does not change as often as CURRENT. Of course, people do make mistakes, so it is still possible that the STABLE tree can be broken at any given time. But it is far less likely to be broken because any code that gets checked into STABLE has been thoroughly tested and debugged in CURRENT. STABLE usually contains the latest security patches and bug fixes since the last RELEASE was made.

That brings up another issue. There are two other versions of FreeBSD that can be run. One of them is RELEASE and the other is SNAPSHOT.

RELEASE Versions of FreeBSD

A RELEASE is an official FreeBSD version that has been released as an ISO, and thus is available on CD-ROM or DVD-ROM. It can also be installed over a network via FTP. As mentioned previously, minor RELEASES are generally made every few months, and major RELEASES are generally made on a yearly or semi-yearly basis. Unlike a RELEASE, STABLE and CURRENT versions of FreeBSD cannot be directly installed from a CD or via FTP. If you want to run a STABLE version, you first need to install a RELEASE version and then update to STABLE using the procedures that will be described in this hour.

11

What was said previously about not being able to install STABLE or CURRENT directly is not entirely true. It is possible to create a custom RELEASE based on either STABLE or CURRENT. The custom RELEASE can then be used to make a CD-ROM that will allow STABLE or CURRENT to be installed directly. However, creating a custom RELEASE is an advanced topic that is beyond the scope of this book.

One thing that is important to note about RELEASE is that it will not have all the latest security patches and such installed. In other words, a fresh install from a CD-ROM could have security holes that were not discovered until after the RELEASE was made. STABLE will have the patches.

SNAPSHOT Versions of FreeBSD

Occasionally, during the FreeBSD development process, when the CURRENT tree is relatively stable, a SNAPSHOT of CURRENT will be made. This snapshot can be downloaded as an ISO and burned on to a CD-ROM. It can often also be purchased from various sources on CD-ROM. This allows you to install CURRENT directly, as well as gives you a version of CURRENT that is about as stable as CURRENT can be.

Current SNAPSHOTS that are released on CD-ROM are usually relatively stable. However, they should still not be considered suitable for production servers because they are still development versions of FreeBSD that have not been extensively tested.

Updating Your Source Tree

After you have decided which version of FreeBSD you want to update to (which is probably STABLE), you need to prepare your system for the update. The first thing you need to do is cvsup your existing FreeBSD source tree so that it matches the source tree of either STABLE or CURRENT. For the rest of this hour, we are going to assume that you are updating to STABLE.

What Is `cvsup`?

`cvsup` is a client program that works with the CVS system. CVS is basically a system for managing the source code of programming projects. The `cvsup` program will connect to one of the FreeBSD servers that contains the most recent source code for STABLE, and it will compare each source code file on your system with the same file on the server. If your file is different, it will be updated to match the file on the server. In addition, if any files are on the server that do not exist on your system, they will be created on your system.

Using CVSup

The CVSup program is not installed by default with FreeBSD. However, if you have worked through Hour 6, "Adding and Removing Third-Party Software," and have updated your ports tree, you already installed CVSup. The CVSup program used here is the same one used to update the ports tree.

If you have not already installed CVSup, it is available as a port in the `/usr/ports/net` directory. It can also be downloaded as a prebuilt binary package. If you do not know how to install the CVSup program or how to download a package or build a port, see Hour 7, which contains instructions for installing new software in FreeBSD.

Once CVSup has been installed, make a copy of the sample `supfile`, which is located in `/usr/share/examples/cvsup`. A reasonable place to copy the file to is `/usr/local/etc`.

> An easier way to build a supfile is to use the `cvsupit` pseudo-port, located at `/usr/ports/net/cvsupit`. Type **make** and then **make install**, and you will be guided through a menu-driven interface in which you select your desired source tree, CVSup server, and other options. The port will then create `/etc/cvsupfile` based on your options and even offer to run CVSup for you for the first time. (After that, though, you're on your own.)

Editing the CVSup Configuration File

Open the configuration file in your favorite text editor. You won't have to edit very much of it because the default options will usually work. However, there are a few things you need to change.

The first thing you need to do is specify which version of FreeBSD you want to update to. This is done with the `*default tag=` line in the file. What follows the equals sign determines which version of FreeBSD your source code will be updated to.

You will probably want to update to the latest version of STABLE. If 5.0 is the current RELEASE, the tag you want to use is `RELENG_5`. So the line should look like this:

```
*default tag=RELENG_5
```

This will synchronize your source code with the STABLE tree. Unlike periodic packaged updates that you might be familiar with for Windows or Macintosh, updating to STABLE can be done at any time. Announcements are not made when STABLE is updated because it is updated on a very regular basis (often daily). This does not mean that you have to update your system every day because most of the updates done to STABLE are minor bug fixes that won't affect most people anyway.

When security problems are found with FreeBSD, announcements will be made on the FreeBSD-Security mailing list. It is a good idea for all FreeBSD users to be subscribed to this list. Often, the suggested solution to fix the problem will be to update to FreeBSD STABLE. This is about the closest you will get to an announcement that STABLE has been updated.

Subscribe to the mailing list by sending a message to `majordomo@freebsd.org`, with the body being the single line:

```
subscribe freebsd-stable
```

It is also possible to specify that you want to update to a specific RELEASE. This is more like the traditional upgrade system you are used to with Windows or Macintosh. These source trees are fixed and are not changing like STABLE.

Tags for specific versions of FreeBSD contain the word "RELEASE" in them. For example, the line to specify that you want to update your source to 5.0 RELEASE is

```
*default tag=RELENG_5_0_0_RELEASE
```

Note also that a third number is in this one. If the most recent RELEASE of FreeBSD is 5.0.1, this would be `RELENG_5_0_1`. If the most recent RELEASE is FreeBSD 5.1, it would be `RELENG_5_1_0`, and so on. Basically, the third number has to be present to specify that you want to update to a specific RELEASE, even if the third number is 0. The RELEASE suffix is also required.

To obtain a current list of the RELEASES that you can update to through CVSup, see the following Web page:

```
http://www.freebsd.org/doc/en_US.ISO8859-1/books/handbook/cvs-tags.html
```

Updating to the latest RELEASE version does not ensure that the latest security patches will be installed on your system. As mentioned previously, security problems that were discovered after the RELEASE was made will not be incorporated into the RELEASE, but will be inserted into STABLE. The RELEASE is fixed and does not change after it has been made.

The best policy is to use tag names such as RELENG_5_0 or RELENG_4_6; this will give you the most recent STABLE sources on those branches, finalized to a specified point-release level. For example, a system synchronized to RELENG_4_5 might have a version string of 4.5-RELEASE-p17.

A special tag can also be used that is a simple period (.) The line *default tag=. indicates that the CURRENT tree should be used for the update. As stated before, this is probably not the tree that most users will want to update with, so you probably won't want to use the period with the tag.

You will notice that you can cvsup to older versions of FreeBSD. For example, at the time of this writing, RELENG_4_3 is still available and is still being maintained to a certain extent. (Security patches and critical fixes will be applied to it.) Although FreeBSD will let you do it without complaining, cvsupping backwards to a lower version number than you are currently running is generally a bad idea because it could cause things to break and the system to not work correctly.

The other line you will want to change is the *default host= line. This line controls where FreeBSD will obtain the new source code from. A list of available servers can be found at the bottom of the following Web page:

```
http://www.freebsd.org/doc/en_US.ISO8859-1/books/handbook/cvsup.html
```

Normally, you will want to choose the server closest to you. However, if it is too busy and is rejecting your connection attempts, you can choose a different one.

The other relevant line in the file is src-all. Make sure that this line is not commented out. This will cause all source files to be obtained, which is normally what you will want if you are doing an update.

After you have finished editing the file, save the file and exit the text editor.

11

Running CVSup

To start the cvsup process, make sure that you have an Internet connection available, and issue a command similar to the following:

```
cvsup supfile
```

supfile is the name of the configuration file that you just finished editing. If you did not name the file supfile, replace this part of the command with whatever name you gave the file.

This will start the cvsup process. The client will try to connect to the CVSup server specified in your supfile; if the server is overloaded, as happens from time to time or with certain servers, it will pause and try again several minutes later, with the spacing between subsequent attempts growing larger and larger each time. You might want to cancel the process (press Ctrl+C) and edit the supfile to specify a different CVSup server (just try a higher number, for example cvsup9.freebsd.org).

Depending on the speed of your Internet connection and on how many changes have been made to the source tree since the last time you cvsupped, the process could take anywhere from a minute or two, to a few hours. CVSup only updates the files that have changed since the last time you ran cvsup. Because of this, updates are usually fairly quick since you do not have to download an entirely new version of FreeBSD. You only have to download those parts that have changed.

After the cvsup process has finished, you will be returned to the command prompt. At this point, you have a freshly updated source tree. However, the updates have not yet been installed. We will get to actually installing the updates later in this hour. However, you should do several things before installing the updates.

The UPDATING File

The first thing you should do after the cvsup process has completed is read the file /usr/src/UPDATING. This file will contain important information about any special considerations that you need to watch out for when updating using the source code you just downloaded. It includes information on potential problems and any special procedures that you need to follow to avoid them. If anything in UPDATING contradicts something you read here, you should follow the instructions for that particular thing in UPDATING rather than the ones given in this book.

The /etc/make.conf File

The /etc/make.conf file contains settings that the C compiler will use when rebuilding the system from the source code you just downloaded. Another file, called /etc/defaults/make.conf, contains the default options that the C compiler will use. However, you do not want to make any changes to the /etc/defaults/make.conf file. Instead, make the changes to /etc/make.conf (creating it yourself if it does not already exist, as is the case in the default installation). This file will override the defaults given in /etc/defaults/make.conf. For most people, adding the following two lines to /etc/make.conf should suffice:

```
CFLAGS= -O -pipe
NOPROFILE= TRUE
```

Note that the option after CFLAGS is a capital letter *O* and not a zero. This option tells the C compiler to apply certain optimizations when it compiles the code. The second line tells the compiler not to build profiled binaries. Profiled binaries are useful for debugging, but they also increase the size of the binary and reduce performance. So most users will probably want the NOPROFILE option set to TRUE.

After you have made these changes, save and exit the /etc/make.conf file.

Updating Important Files

In some cases, certain configuration files might need to be updated before the system upgrade is actually performed because certain new versions of FreeBSD might expect, for example, certain user accounts or groups to exist for system purposes. If these groups and accounts did not exist in earlier versions of FreeBSD, the update process can fail.

The easiest way to upgrade these files is to use the program called mergemaster.sh. Start it with the -p option so that it only updates files that are important to the pre-upgrade. You don't want to update the rest of the files yet. For example,

```
mergemaster.sh -p
```

It's very important to back up your /etc directory before running mergemaster. Simply copy it to a new location, for example by entering **cp -R /etc /etc.old**. This way, if you accidentally overwrite a file in /etc, you can retrieve the old one with a minimum of pain.

Dealing with mergemaster is probably the most difficult part of the updating process. Basically, mergemaster compares the configuration file on your system with the new configuration file included with the updated source that you download. If the two files are different, mergemaster will let you know, show you the differences, and ask you what to do about them. After you have scrolled to the bottom of the mergemaster list, you will be given a menu of options:

```
Use 'd' to delete  the temporary /etc/group
Use 'i' to install the temporary /etc/group
Use 'm' to merge the old and new versions
Use 'v' to view the differences between the old and new versions again

Default is to leave the temporary file to deal with by hand

How should I deal with this? [Leave it for later]
```

The default option is to not make any changes to the file, and leave the new file in the directory /var/tmp/temproot. This way, you can examine the original file and the new file later on and decide which, if any, changes you want to incorporate.

Here are what the other options do:

- d—Deletes the new version of the file out of /var/tmp/temproot and leaves the current version that you are using untouched.

- i—Copies the new version of the file from /var/tmp/temproot. Note that this replaces the current version you are using, so any customizations you made to the file will be lost.

- m—Invokes a program that allows you to merge the two files visually by selecting which version of each line or group of lines you want (either the old one or the new one). It is generally easier to simply make a note of which files have changes and then go through them manually and decide which changes you want to incorporate.

  If you do decide to use the built-in merge utility invoked here (sdiff), you can get help at its command line by entering a question mark (?). This will show you the available commands for selecting the left version (old) or the right version (new).

- v—Simply repeats the output and shows you the changes again.

Note that /etc/group, /etc/passwd, and /etc/master.passwd will always be flagged by mergemaster because of users and groups that you have added to your system, which makes these files different from the ones included with the source you downloaded. You should **never** choose the i option on these files because this will overwrite your existing files, which will cause your group and user databases to be lost. This, of course, can be disastrous, especially if you have a lot of users.

Rebuilding the System

Now you are ready to rebuild the system. The best way to do this is to break it down into two steps so that the majority of it can be done without dropping into single user mode. This means that the system can continue to function normally throughout most of the build process.

Removing the Old Object Files

The first thing to do is remove any old object files from previous builds. This is done by changing to the /usr/obj directory and using the following command:

```
chflags -R noschg *
rm -rf *
```

The second command is one that you are familiar with, but the first one requires some additional explanation. This command removes the immutable flag from any files that might have it set. This flag protects files from accidental deletion or modification despite what the normal file permissions are set to. Even root cannot delete a file that has the immutable flag set until the immutable flag has been removed.

The process of removing the object files can take several minutes. (There are a lot of them). When it is done, you are ready to start the actual build process.

Building the World

The first thing you want to do is start a log file that will log all compiler messages generated during the build process. This can be useful for troubleshooting problems later on if need be. The log can be started with the following command:

```
script /var/tmp/mw.out
```

11

The system should respond with `"Script started, output file is /var/tmp/mw.out"`. Of course, you can use a different location for the output file if you want to.

Once the script has been started, make sure that you are in the `/usr/src` directory and type the following command to start the build process:

`make buildworld`

This will invoke the C compiler and other necessary programs that will rebuild the entire operating system from the source code that you downloaded. (Hence, that's why it is called "making the world.")

This process will take quite some time, even on a fast system. On a slower system, it could take several hours. Feel free to go do something else while the make process is running because there is no need to watch it. It won't ask you any questions or anything.

> Recall that, in an earlier hour, you learned how to switch to another virtual terminal using the ALT keys plus the function keys. Feel free to switch to another terminal and continue working while the build process is running. It is safe to continue using the system during this process because no system files are actually being updated at this point. They are only being built and placed in a temporary location for later installation.

If the `buildworld` process is interrupted—for example if you were running it from a remote terminal, and then you lost access, killing the process—nothing has been lost or corrupted. Go back into `/usr/src` and type make buildworld again. This might delete all the object files that had been compiled thus far, though, so don't be too disappointed if you aren't able to save any time this way.

Installing the New World

After the build process has finished, you need to install the new world. Before you do this, however, you should reboot the system into single user mode because during this process virtually every file in the system will be updated. If these files are in use during this process, it could cause problems.

To get into single user mode, you can use the following command:

`shutdown now`

This will kick everybody off the system and bring it down to single user mode. You might be asked to specify which shell you want to use. Simply press Enter to accept the default.

Change to the /usr/src directory and run the following command to start the install process:

```
make installworld
```

This process will take a few minutes, but it won't take nearly as long as the make buildworld process. When it is finished, you will be returned to the command prompt. However, you aren't quite finished yet. You need to run mergemaster again to update the rest of the configuration files. The first time you ran mergemaster, you only updated files that were potentially essential in order for the world to build correctly. To run mergemaster and update the rest of the files, use the following command:

```
mergemaster -v
```

The -v option causes mergemaster to be more verbose about what it is doing. In the future when you run mergemaster, you might want to leave out the -v option, but the first couple of times you run it, use the -v option to help you become more familiar with how the command works.

Once again, watch for any changes that you know you made to files because these will show up in mergemaster's output. It is important that you do not select the i option in these cases because this will cause all of your customizations in the configuration file to be overwritten. Also, make sure that you especially watch out for changes made to the /etc/group, /etc/passwd, and /etc/master.passwd files.

> If you wish, you can combine the make buildworld and the make installworld processes into the single command, make world. This command will perform the build and then automatically perform the install afterward. However, if you decide to do this, you should drop the system in to single user mode before issuing the make world command. This, of course, means that your system will be tied up in single user mode a lot longer than if you separate the two processes.

Building the New Kernel

You need to do one more thing before you reboot the system: You need to build a new kernel to go along with the FreeBSD update you just installed. Kernel building was covered in the previous hour, so we are not going to go over it again here. If you need instructions for building a new kernel, see Hour 10, "The FreeBSD Kernel and the Device Tree."

After you have finished building the new kernel, you can reboot your system with `shutdown -r now`. This should bring the system back up into multiuser mode running a newly updated version of FreeBSD.

Troubleshooting

Several things can go wrong during this process. Here are some of the most common problems you might run into and some possible solutions:

- **My `make buildworld` process failed!**

    One problem that can occur is that the `make buildworld` fails with a compiler error, often citing "`* Error code 1`". If this happens, it usually means that the compiler ran into a problem related to the source files themselves. This probably means that you were unlucky enough to `cvsup` when the source tree was broken and could not be built. Check the FreeBSD-STABLE mailing list archives for any recent posts about the build being broken. Run `cvsup` again at a later time. Note that `cvsup` will not take nearly as long next time because not much will have changed since the last time you did it—other than the few changes necessary to fix whatever was broken. At this point, no changes have actually been made to your system, so the functionality of the existing system has not been affected in any way by the failed build.

- **I got a bunch of "signal 11" errors while compiling.**

    Another possible compiler error is signal 11 errors. These errors are usually caused by faulty hardware. RAM is often the culprit. Clean out the `/usr/obj` directory as described earlier in this hour and start the build again. If you get another signal 11 error and it occurs at a different point in the process than the first one did, it is almost a sure sign of hardware problems—most likely RAM issues.

- **The `top` and `ps` programs don't work anymore!**

    So what happens if you finish making the world, reboot, and certain utilities such as `ps` have stopped working? Did you remember to build a new kernel after you installed the world? The most common cause of problems like this is the kernel being out of sync with the rest of the world.

Summary

In this hour, you learned about the different update paths available for FreeBSD and how to decide which one you should use. You learned how to update your system source tree to the latest version from a FreeBSD server. You also learned how to rebuild your entire system from the new sources and update the configuration files. In addition, you learned how to recover if something goes wrong during the build process.

Q&A

Q I have a FreeBSD 4.6 system. I want to keep it updated to the most recent security-patched version, but I don't want to upgrade all the way to 5.0. (My system is too critical to risk changing everything.) What branch tag name do I use?

A Use `RELENG_4_6`. This will keep synchronized to the most recent 4.6 code, which has security patches and critical fixes applied to it and new point-release tags assigned to it regularly. However, it never has new features put into it or anything changed around which might affect system behavior in any significant way.

Q How do I synchronize my ports tree to either the 5.0 branch or the 4.6 branch?

A You don't. Ports only have one "branch," and one place you can synchronize them is the "top-of-tree" point, specified with the dot (`.`). Because all the ports are changing all the time, there is no way to "freeze" them the way they were at a particular point during the history of FreeBSD; nor does it make sense to do so. Each port is maintained independently. It's up to each port's developer and maintainer to keep it patched and up to you to keep it synchronized with your system's ports tree.

Q I accidentally told `mergemaster` to leave one of the installed files alone when I really wanted to install the new version. What do I do?

A Simply run `mergemaster` again, and say "yes" when it asks if you want to use the existing `/var/tmp/temproot`. It will then ask you only about those files that are left over from the previous run.

Q Now I managed to overwrite one of my personally customized files with the generic one in `mergemaster`!

A You did make a backup of `/etc` before you ran `mergemaster`, didn't you? If so, just copy the file out of there back into `/etc`.

11

Workshop

In this interactive section, you will be given a quiz and a few exercises in order to help solidify your understanding of the procedure by which to upgrade your FreeBSD system.

Quiz

1. The program used to update FreeBSD sources is

    A. `update`

    B. `cvsup`

    C. `pkg_add`

    D. `make`

2. The `mergemaster` program

    A. Compares differences in configuration files

    B. Merges changes from the new system source code into your current system

    C. Downloads new source code from FreeBSD servers

    D. None of the above

3. Which of the following trees is intended for production use and has the latest security patches applied to it?

    A. CURRENT

    B. RELEASE

    C. STABLE

    D. SNAPSHOT

Quiz Answers

1. The correct answer is B. Answer A does not exist. C is the command used to install software packages. D is the command used to build software from sources (but it does not update the sources).

2. The correct answer is A.

3. The correct answer is C. Answer A is the development version of FreeBSD, and it should not be used on production systems. B is a stable released version of FreeBSD, but it will not always have the latest security patches applied. D is a snapshot of the development version, so it still is not suitable for production systems.

Exercises

1. Explore some of the many uses of CVSup. Notice that you can install a CVSup server on your FreeBSD machine; you can use this to create an efficient mirroring system, so that you can back up your machine's contents to another machine nightly. See `http://www.cvsup.org` for details.

2. Create a `periodic` script (see `man periodic`) that will synchronize your source tree—either nightly or weekly—to the latest versions of your source branch. This way, theoretically, you will always have the most recent sources immediately available if you want to upgrade your system on a moment's notice.

11

PART III
Networking

Hour

Hour **12**

Introduction to Networks

These days, it's hard to imagine a computer without a network to connect it to. There's only so much you can do with a machine that doesn't have access to the Internet or to other machines on its own local network. Word processing and image editing is fine in its own right, but a computer in this day and age isn't worth the desk space it takes up if you can't use it to read email, surf the Web, and share files between neighboring computers.

Fortunately, FreeBSD is one of those operating systems that was designed from the ground up for networking. As you will see in this hour and the next, everything in FreeBSD is designed under the assumption that the computer will be networked and accessible by multiple users at once. Unlike Windows, which started life as a standalone operating system for single-user computers, FreeBSD is one of those operating systems that helped build the Internet, and it continues to form much of its backbone. Because of its UNIX heritage, FreeBSD is just as comfortable *serving* Internet traffic as it is requesting it.

The first topics we must cover in this hour are general networking concepts. TCP/IP networking isn't like USB, where you can just plug in a cable and you're off and running. To network properly, you will need to know something about the underlying technology. That's what we will discuss first. You will learn:

- What the OSI networking model is and how it applies to the Internet
- What people mean when they talk about the TCP/IP "Stack"
- What the different components used in networking are, and how they are used
- What an IP address is and how it applies to routing
- How IP addresses, netmasks, and network addresses are related

The OSI Networking Model

Most modern networking, including the Internet, is done via a system known as the *Transmission Control Protocol/Internet Protocol (TCP/IP)*. This name refers to a combination of the two most common protocols, or methods of communication, that adhere to a structured "stack" of protocol layers known as the *Open Software Interconnect (OSI)* model. OSI dictates how computers and networking components can be broken down into a number of conceptual *layers* so that data can be exchanged between them.

There are seven layers in the typical OSI model, ranging from the *application* layers at the top (where they interact with you, the user) all the way down to the *data link* and *physical* layers at the bottom (where the specialized hardware, such as Ethernet cards, talk to each other and trade raw data). Figure 12.1 shows how a typical OSI or TCP/IP stack in a computer is structured.

FIGURE 12.1

OSI stack layering diagram, showing how a TCP/IP-based application transmits data from one user to another.

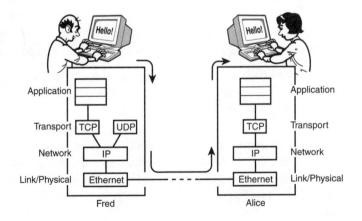

The bottom layers of an OSI stack represent hardware that is specifically tuned to communicating data onto a wire, such as Ethernet and Token Ring cards; but the components down at the bottom are not capable of knowing where that data is supposed to go other than onto the wire. All they do is send out the ones and zeros, and they rely on those ones and zeros to know where they are supposed to go next.

Fortunately, they do. The next layers up in the stack wrap the data (which is broken up into *packets*, or chunks of data usually around a kilobyte in size) with *headers*, which are blocks of preliminary data that can only be read by software at the corresponding layer in another computer's OSI stack. For instance, the *network* layer of one computer's OSI stack puts an IP header onto a packet and sends it down to the *link* layer, where the Ethernet card (and its *PHY*, the chip that handles the physical communications) sends it out onto the wire destined for another computer's Ethernet address—the lowest level of addressing in the OSI scheme. The data is received by the target computer, but the link layer of the stack can't do anything with it beyond receiving it—so it passes it up the stack to its own network layer, which reads the IP header and decodes such useful information from it as the IP address that the packet came from, as well as the IP address that it's supposed to go to.

If the receiving computer's own IP address doesn't match the destination IP address of the packet, it usually means that the receiving computer is a *router*—a computer whose specialized job is to take packets that are destined for IP addresses of computers on other remote networks and forward them on through the Internet until they get to their destination. We will talk a little more about routers later in this hour.

12

The upper layers of the OSI stack work in a similar way. The topmost layers interact with the user, who thinks of his software as interacting with similar software (or a similar user) on the other end of a connection. He inputs data, which is sent down the stack by the application and wrapped in a TCP header by the *transport* layer—transport protocols such as TCP, UDP, and ICMP are all used by different kinds of applications—and then passed down to the network layer, which adds an IP header. Finally, the packet reaches the link layer, gets transmitted out of the computer, is passed from destination machine to destination machine, and finally reaches the intended target. Here, the packet is handed up from layer to layer, one header stripped off at each level, until it reaches the application and the user and appears (for instance) as an Instant Message reading `"Hello! Want to go to lunch?"`.

Why bother with all these layers? Why can't the applications simply talk directly to each other? Well, that's what the Internet is all about. As you can see in Figure 12.2, the Internet is made up of a huge number of smaller networks all hooked together by means of routers. Each router manages a network of its own, in a hierarchical manner; the networks that each router manages get larger and larger as you progress toward the middle of the Internet, and smaller and smaller as you approach the endpoints, which are single computers. A large router at a telecommunications company at the "backbone" of the Internet can have thousands of smaller routers sending traffic up to it. This is necessary so that widely separated *Local Area Networks* (*LANs*, which we will discuss shortly) can know how to send traffic to each other. The layers of the OSI model enable data packets to contain the information they need to navigate from one part of the Internet to another without having to know anything about the route along the way. The routers themselves handle it all so that the sending and receiving computers don't have to.

FIGURE 12.2

The Internet consists of thousands of different routers— each managing a network all its own.

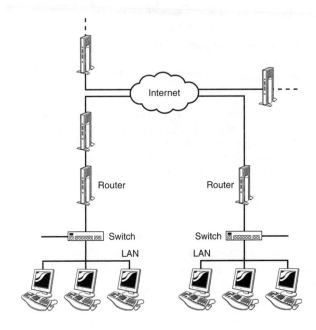

A LAN consists of a relatively small number of computers hooked together by means of a high-speed but non-routable communication mechanism such as Ethernet. A corporate network is an example of a LAN; computers within such a network can communicate very rapidly with each other. But such a network is not feasible beyond a certain size for the simple reasons that Ethernet cables can only be so long before they start to lose their signal strength and that a LAN is typically managed by a single company or person, whereas the Internet is managed collectively by thousands of different companies.

Traffic from a computer on a LAN to a computer on another LAN is passed to a router, which knows where to find other routers along the way to the traffic's destination. The traffic goes from router to router, using *Wide Area Network (WAN)* connections such as high-speed serial links (T1, T3, OC-3, and so on) until it reaches the router that manages the LAN where the destination computer is located; it is then transmitted from the router over the LAN via Ethernet. This way, network traffic can travel between many different kinds of networks, managed by different companies or people, using the transmission method that is the most efficient at each level.

Basic Networking Components

Many different kinds of networking equipment can be found in the path from one computer on the Internet to another. Each type of component is designed to connect computers at a different level of the TCP/IP stack or to perform a certain function or layout in a networking topology.

Cables

Ethernet cables can carry traffic from one Ethernet card to another on a LAN at very high speeds—10Mbps, 100Mbps, or even 1Gbps in the newest (and most expensive) kind of LAN, Gigabit Ethernet. The cables, regardless of speed, can be had very cheaply; you can even make them yourself. The downside is that Ethernet can't be used over long distances. Because the signals aren't serialized or transmitted by equipment designed to support long-distance transmission, signals degrade with cable length.

The most commonly used cabling these days is via *Unshielded Twisted Pair (UTP)* cables, also known as Category-5 or *Cat-5*. Other types of Ethernet cables have been in common use over the years, such as *ThickNet* and *ThinNet*, using altogether different physical types of cable, such as the coaxial cable that plugs in to a TV; but by far the most common configuration today is the RJ-45 phone-style jack on a UTP cable. This same style of cable can be used on 10Mbps (10base-T) networks, 100base-TX, and 1000base-T (Gigabit) networks, interchangeably.

Straight-through and Crossover Cables

Only one complication exists in UTP cabling, and that is the difference between *straight-through* and *crossover* cables. The difference between them lies in whether the positions

12

of two pairs of wires in the cable are reversed from one end to the other, and it's important to understand the different circumstances under which each are used.

Devices with RJ-45 connectors can be thought of as either *computer-type* or *hub-type* devices. Computers, routers, bandwidth managers, and other *endpoint* devices are considered computer-type devices, and hubs and switches are hub-type devices. The RJ-45 jacks on computer-type devices are all wired equivalently to each other, and hub-type devices are also all wired the same. Ethernet cables are wired to connect computer-type devices to hub-type devices.

To connect a computer to a hub, you need a straight-through cable. The same is true for connecting a computer to a switch or a router to a hub. These are all connections between *unlike* devices. However, to connect a hub to a hub or a hub to a switch, you need a crossover cable. You also need one to connect a computer to a computer; for instance, to play in two-player death-match mode. The rule to remember is this: Use straight-through cables between unlike devices, and crossover cables between like devices.

The tricky part is with the *uplink* port on hubs. This special port is wired as if it's a computer-type device, so you can connect a hub's uplink port to a standard port on another hub with a straight-through cable. This became necessary in large networks—in which a very long straight-through cable would be connected to a large enterprisewide hub or switch (in the server room, for example), and wound through walls and conduits to emerge in another room. This cable couldn't be connected directly to a standard port on a smaller hub; it had to be fitted to an adapter and a short crossover cable before it could talk to the smaller hub. Replacing the Ethernet cable with a long crossover cable was impractical, to say the least. Hence the uplink port was born: a port that allowed a hub to be connected directly to another hub for which swapping out the cable for a crossover was not a viable option. Remember, though, that connecting two hubs' uplink ports together requires a crossover cable—which is a configuration that rather defeats the purpose, in any case.

How do you tell whether an Ethernet cable is a straight-through or a crossover cable? It's pretty easy: Hold up the two ends of the cable next to each other. If the color sequences of the wires match, it's a straight-through cable. If some of the wires appear out of place, it's a crossover cable.

The pinout (pin wiring diagram) for a straight-through cable is shown in Figure 12.3.

And to make a crossover cable, reverse the positions of pair 3 (wires 1/2) and pair 2 (wires 3/6), as shown when crimping the second end (see Figure 12.4).

FIGURE 12.3

Straight-through cable wiring diagram.

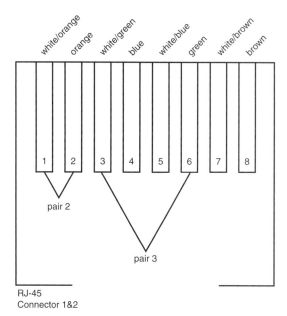

Straight-thru

FIGURE 12.4

Crossover cable wiring diagram.

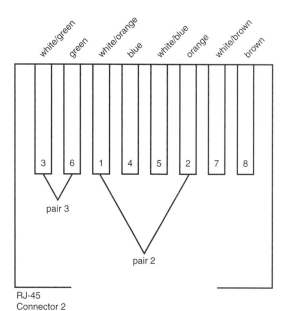

Crossover

12

Hubs

One end of the cable connects to your computer's Ethernet card; that much is clear. However, the other end needs to connect to something, too; far more often than not, what it connects to is a hub.

Hubs are devices with multiple RJ-45 ports, usually between 4 and 24, to which you can connect as many Ethernet cables as there are ports. These cables can connect to computers, other hubs, switches, or other network components as necessary. Hubs range in cost from about $40 to several hundred dollars—depending on quality, number of ports, and the capability to operate simultaneously with 10base-T and 100base-TX devices. Many hubs can only do one or the other of the two popular speeds, and an auto-sensing hub (often referred to as *N-Way*) can cost significantly more. Hubs range in size from small boxes no larger than your hand to full 19-inch rack-mountable units, and all require a power source. Some hubs are even *managed*, meaning that you can telnet to them and configure each port's capabilities through a command-line interface. These hubs are naturally much more expensive than standalone hubs.

Hubs can be small standalone devices, as shown in Figure 12.5, or they can be sized to fit into a 19-inch networking rack.

FIGURE 12.5

Small five-port hub, with one Uplink port.

A hub is effectively a repeater, with all traffic appearing simultaneously on all ports, so a computer connected to one port on a hub will be able to see traffic to and from any other computer on the same hub. One port on a hub is usually reserved for uplink—a link to another hub, a switch, or a router higher up in the network hierarchy, as laid out in

Figure 12.2; this uplink port is usually wired so that a crossover cable is not needed between the hub and its next upstream device. This port and one of the standard ports on the hub can also be wired so that they're mutually exclusive—a *five-port* hub, such as the one in Figure 12.5, might have six RJ-45 jacks but only give you the option of hooking five computers together (ignoring the uplink port), or four computers to an upstream device (ignoring the fifth standard port). This might be hard-wired, it might be controllable with a push-button or a DIP switch, or all the ports might be simultaneously usable. These are just some of the possible variations between different hubs.

Another matter that complicates the way hubs and other devices communicate with each other is that of half- and full-duplex. The difference is essentially that in half-duplex mode, a host can only be "listening" or "talking" at one time; whereas in full-duplex mode, twice as many wires are used, enabling the host to "listen" and "talk" at the same time. Thus, a 100Mbps Fast Ethernet link in full-duplex mode can transport up to 100Mbps on each direction simultaneously, whereas the same link in half-duplex mode can only do an aggregate total of 100Mbps in both directions.

Switches

Now that you know the nature and purpose of hubs, we can move on to switches. A *switch* looks like a hub that's a lot more expensive and usually has fewer ports. It has multiple RJ-45 ports, it ranges from hand-sized to rack-sized (as shown in Figure 12.6), and the same companies that make hubs make switches, so it's easy to mistake one for the other on store shelves. They even operate somewhat similarly—you can plug multiple devices in to a switch, and a switch used in place of a hub in a network would usually give you what appears to be the same result. The difference between switches and hubs, however, is subtle, yet crucial.

FIGURE 12.6
*Rack-mounted
eight-port switch.*

On a hub, all ports share the same internal wiring; all computers connected to the hub, as well as computers connected to other hubs connected to the first hub, exist on what's known as a *collision domain*—in which a signal sent to one computer gets sent to all computers within the domain. It's up to each computer's Ethernet card to determine whether the signal is destined for it or not; and if it isn't, to throw it away.

A switch's internal wiring is much more complex. Each port comprises its own collision domain, and hosts connected to one port can't see any traffic destined for hosts on any of the other ports. Switches incorporate the software necessary to read each packet's Ethernet header and determine which port has the host that should get the packet, which means that a switch operates at the next highest layer up from a hub, at the network level, where it can see each packet's IP destination address as well as the hardware Ethernet address where it is headed.

Because each port on a switch has its own collision domain, this means that switched network traffic will be able to take fuller advantage of the available network bandwidth. An eight-port, 100base-TX hub with all ports in use has to divide the available 100Mbps between the eight ports. If all eight ports are simultaneously trying to do bandwidth-intensive tasks and their aggregate bandwidth demand is greater than 100Mbps, *collisions*—cases in which two ports try to transmit or receive traffic at exactly the same time—will become much more common, resulting in retransmissions at the physical link level and performance degraded well below what each host would logically see as a share of the available 100Mbps. Switches alleviate this problem. Whereas a 100Mbps hub has 100Mbps of internal wiring in total, an eight-port switch has 800Mpbs worth of wiring—the full bandwidth duplicated for every port. This is why switches tend to have fewer ports than switches, and switches with many ports are quite expensive.

Switches usually have no uplink ports, although occasionally (as with some two-port switches, which serve purely as a filter to keep out irrelevant traffic) one or both ports will have a push-button to select whether the port should need a straight-through or crossover cable. As a general rule, treat ports on a switch as hub-type devices, and use crossover cables to connect one switch to another, or a straight-through cable to connect a switch to a hub's uplink port.

Bridges

A *bridge* is a device that acts somewhat like a switch, but in a rather more complex way. Bridges are like switches that connect different kinds of *link-layer* networks together instead of just different networks of the same type. You could use a bridge to connect an Ethernet network to a Token Ring network, for instance, or one Ethernet network to another one that normally would need a router to direct traffic from one side to another. Bridges aren't generally useful except in very complex network topologies, so we won't cover them more fully here.

Routers

A *router* is the most complex (and expensive) of all networking devices. You have already seen the role that routers play in the OSI stack and in the Internet. But what exactly *is* a router?

Most routers are rack-mounted devices such as the one in Figure 12.7. The largest manu-facturer of routers is Cisco, and most networks are managed by at least one Cisco router. However, a router can be made from a FreeBSD computer (or any operating system that supports routing, including all UNIX systems and even most Windows platforms). Most routers have either one or two LAN-side ports, RJ-45 jacks, or AUI ports that require transceivers to convert the interface to twisted-pair. On the other side of the router is a serial cable that connects to the DSU/CSU or other such high-speed serial converter—beyond which you have WAN traffic.

FIGURE 12.7

A Cisco router with a serial (WAN-side) and Ethernet (LAN-side) interface.

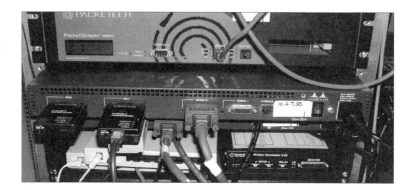

Routers have full operating systems and maintain tables that keep track of where entire networks can be found. Most networks have only one router, specifying which network numbers indicate your LAN and which ones should be forwarded upstream into the WAN. You can have any number of routers in your network, though—each one managing a subnetwork and subservient to the topmost router.

What's more, routers use a variety of protocols to communicate with each other and plot out the best way for a packet to get from one place to another. When you send out a packet, it travels from router to router, further and further upstream by whatever route each router thinks is the best available, until it reaches a router that knows where *down-stream* to find the destination network for your packet, and off it goes down through the downstream route until it reaches the destination LAN and, ultimately, the destination host. Routing is the backbone of the Internet and possibly the most complex part of the way TCP/IP networking operates.

The IP Address System and Subnets

If you've ever done anything on the Internet at all, you're probably familiar with IP addresses—at least enough to know what they look like. An IP address is typically used

12

as a way to refer to a specific computer on the Internet, though its meaning is actually a lot more flexible than "one IP address per machine." Most generally, it's a logical designation whose purpose is to locate a machine on the Internet so that IP routers can direct traffic between it and any other machine.

An *IP address* is a string of 32 bits in the IP header, which specifies either what machine a packet came from or where it is destined (both addresses are present in the header). The 32 bits can be thought of also as four 8-bit bytes, each of which is expressed as a number from 0 to 255—hence, our familiar four-part dotted-decimal notation (of the form 111.112.113.114).

Typically, a single IP address is bound to a single Ethernet card; this is only by convention, though. The only constraint is that no two Ethernet cards on the same network can share the same IP address. You can bind multiple IP addresses to the same card, though, and every card needs to have at least one unique IP address to function. You might choose to install two Ethernet cards in your system in order to have access to two different networks at once, for example, or one address might be bound to an Ethernet card, whereas another refers to your wireless 802.11 card. It all depends on how your network is set up.

You can find out the IP addresses of any Ethernet card and other network interfaces in your system using the ifconfig utility, shown in Listing 12.1. The -a option shows all devices, or you can specify a specific interface (such as x10) to single out just that one. The inet line shows a configured IP address; the x10 interface in this example shows multiple IP addresses bound to a single card.

LISTING 12.1 Typical Output of ifconfig

```
# ifconfig -a
x10: flags=8843<UP,BROADCAST,RUNNING,SIMPLEX,MULTICAST> mtu 1500
        inet 64.41.131.102 netmask 0xffffff00 broadcast 64.41.131.255
        inet6 fe80::201:2ff:fe55:1256%x10 prefixlen 64 scopeid 0x1
        inet 209.154.215.246 netmask 0xffffffff broadcast 209.154.215.246
        ether 00:01:02:55:12:56
        media: autoselect (100baseTX) status: active
        supported media: autoselect 100baseTX <full-duplex> 100baseTX
➥10baseT/UTP <full-duplex> 10baseT/UTP 100baseTX <hw-loopback>
lp0: flags=8810<POINTOPOINT,SIMPLEX,MULTICAST> mtu 1500
gif0: flags=8010<POINTOPOINT,MULTICAST> mtu 1280
gif1: flags=8010<POINTOPOINT,MULTICAST> mtu 1280
gif2: flags=8010<POINTOPOINT,MULTICAST> mtu 1280
gif3: flags=8010<POINTOPOINT,MULTICAST> mtu 1280
lo0: flags=8049<UP,LOOPBACK,RUNNING,MULTICAST> mtu 16384
        inet6 fe80::1%lo0 prefixlen 64 scopeid 0x7
        inet6 ::1 prefixlen 128
```

LISTING 12.1   continued

```
        inet 127.0.0.1 netmask 0xff000000
ppp0: flags=8010<POINTOPOINT,MULTICAST> mtu 1500
sl0: flags=c010<POINTOPOINT,LINK2,MULTICAST> mtu 552
faith0: flags=8000<MULTICAST> mtu 1500
```

There are a few "special" IP addresses to keep in mind. First is the *network* address. This is an IP address in which one or more of its bytes are zero, such as `64.41.131.0`. If the final byte is a zero, the address is a synonym for the entire `64.41.131` network and is generally used only when configuring routers. More important is if one or more of the trailing bytes are 255 (all bits set to 1). This is the *broadcast* address for the network; for example, `64.41.131.255` matches all hosts on the `64.41.131` network, and `64.41.255.255` matches all hosts on the `64.41` network.

A "Class A" network has only the first eight bits of the network specified in its assigned number; there are 16.7 million potential IP addresses in a Class A network, such as `64.0.0.0`. "Class B" networks have 65,534 available addresses because sixteen bits (two numbers) of the address are specified. "Class C" (24-bit) networks are the most common, with 254 available addresses; this is the kind of network that the output of `ifconfig` showed.

Subnets and the Network Mask

Netmasks, which travel hand-in-hand with IP addresses when configuring TCP/IP on a machine, are one of the most misunderstood parts of the whole structure, and yet potentially one of the most elegant when understood properly.

The purpose of the network mask (or *netmask*) is simply to tell a router or host whether a packet is supposed to go to the network it's on or go upstream to the next router. When a router receives a packet and has to decide what to do with it, it checks the packet's destination IP address against its own netmask.

The netmask, a 32-bit string like an IP address, is usually of the form `255.255.255.0`. Let's say that we have a router managing the `64.41.131` network, with a netmask of `255.255.255.0`. The router receives a packet addressed for `64.41.131.45`. This is matched against the netmask in an "and" fashion, meaning that the smaller of each pair of numbers in the comparison is taken:

```
        064.041.131.045
AND     255.255.255.000
–  –  –  –  –  –  –  –  –
        064.041.131.000     (Match!)
```

The result matches as far as 64.41.131, which is the address of the network our router manages. This packet is passed on to the network. Another packet now comes in, destined for 64.41.189.45; this match against the netmask fails, and the router passes the packet upstream to the next router.

```
        064.041.189.045
AND     255.255.255.000
————————————
        064.041.189.000     (No match!)
```

This mechanism allows you to set up subnets within your network. Assume that you have a Class B address range to work with (64.41.xxx.xxx). Your network's main router, R1, manages this entire range, but you can put a router (R2) inside this network to manage two Class C address ranges: 64.41.131.xxx and 64.41.132.xxx. Hosts in the 64.41.131 network can be plugged in to the same hub as hosts in the 64.41.132 network, as shown in Figure 12.8, but they won't speak directly to each other if their netmasks are set to 255.255.255.0, a Class C mask. Destination IP addresses in sent packets won't match the senders' netmasks. However, if a sender host (H1) in 64.41.131 sets its netmask to a Class B mask (255.255.0.0), the addresses *would* match, and the sender would be able to send the packet directly to H2—a host on 64.41.132. However, note that H2 wouldn't be able to send its replies directly back to H1 because its netmask prevents it! It has to send the reply back via R2, which has multiple network addresses and subnets bound to its internal interface. You'd need to set H2's netmask to 255.255.0.0 for it to talk directly to H1 without going through the router.

FIGURE **12.8**

A network with subnets, demonstrating the packet path between two hosts whose netmasks don't permit them to communicate directly.

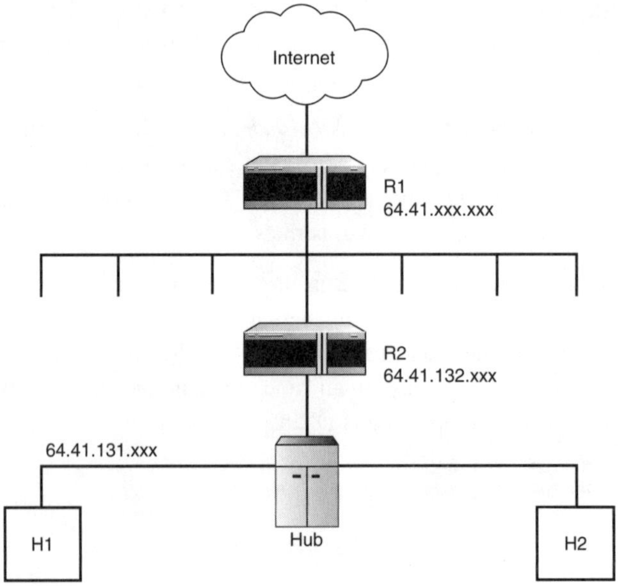

Another notation used in specifying networks that incorporates the netmask is *CIDR*, or *Classless Inter-Domain Routing*, which takes the form of the network address, a slash, and the number of bits that make up the mask. For example, a mask of 255.255.255.0 on our 64.41.131 network would be written as 64.41.131/24 because the mask consists of three 8-bit bytes with all bits set to 1, or 24 bits. The 255.255.255.192 example, likewise, would correspond to a notation of 64.41.131/26. This notation is seen in routing tables and other places where succinctness is useful.

Summary

This hour's lesson covered the fundamentals of TCP/IP as seen from the point of view of the computer. It has laid the groundwork for a deeper understanding of how TCP/IP configuration works and how applications use the Internet's communications protocols so that when you encounter them later, you will have a better chance of knowing how the software is interacting. The Internet is the great leveler of operating systems—in which Windows, Macintosh, and UNIX computers all come together to accomplish the same tasks—and you now know the common language that they all speak.

Q&A

Q How many layers are there in the OSI stack, and how are they arranged?

A Seven. Top to bottom, the layers progress from human-centric data directed from a user to another user (or from a host to another host), down to machine-centric data directed from one specialized piece of hardware to another.

Q What is the difference between a hub and a switch?

A In a hub, all connected devices are wired together in one big *collision domain* so that each machine's Ethernet card sees all traffic that any of the rest of them sends or receives, and all connected machines must share the same aggregate bandwidth. A switch's ports each comprise their own collision domains, though, so no machine can see traffic destined for another on a different port.

Q How can I tell a hub and a switch apart?

A Most hubs and switches will be clearly marked as to what they are. However, there are other ways in which you can tell. For instance, hubs can only communicate in half-duplex mode, whereas switches will negotiate to full-duplex mode if they can. If you connect a machine to a device, look at the output of `ifconfig`, and see that your link is up in full-duplex mode, you know it's a switch; otherwise, it's probably a hub.

12

Q What is the purpose of a router?

A Routers convert LAN traffic into WAN signals that can be sent to remote networks over high-speed serial connections. A router keeps a table of upstream routers to which to send packets to whose destination it doesn't know the route.

Workshop

This section is designed to flesh out your understanding of TCP/IP networking with quiz questions and exercises, leading you to further areas of study if you are so inclined.

Quiz

1. What is the most common type of Ethernet cable today?

    A. UTP with RJ-45 jack

    B. DIX/AUI serial transceiver

    C. ThinNet coaxial with BNC connector

    D. ThickNet coaxial with "vampire tap" connector

2. How big is the average TCP/IP packet on the network?

    A. 50 bytes

    B. 1 kilobyte

    C. 2048 bytes

    D. 32 kilobytes

3. In an 8-port 100base-TX switch, with eight connected machines all using the network actively, how much bandwidth is available to each machine?

    A. 8 Mbps

    B. 12.5 Mbps

    C. 50 Mbps

    D. 100 Mbps

4. What is the subnet mask for a network whose address is 241.155.4?

    A. 255.0.0.0

    B. 255.255.0.0

    C. 255.255.255.0

    D. 255.255.255.255

5. What "class" of network is this?

    A. Class A.

    B. Class B.

    C. Class C.

    D. Class D.

Quiz Answers

1. The correct answer is A.

2. The correct answer is B, though it depends on your network's Maximum Transmission Unit (MTU) size. This value is usually set to 1500 for local-area networks or 536 for WAN links.

3. The correct answer is D. Hubs must divide their available bandwidth among all connected machines, but switches are internally multiplexed so that each machine gets the full amount.

4. The correct answer is B.

5. The correct answer is C.

Exercises

1. Explore how Network Address Translation (NAT) works. This technique allows you to create a network behind a router in which all the machines have unique IP addresses that only really have meaning within the network—when they communicate with machines out on the Internet, their traffic appears to come from a virtual address that is assigned by the NAT-capable router. For instance, you can create an entire Class A network inside your basement and put 16 million computers in it, each with their own IP addresses; with NAT, those computers could all appear to be coming from the single IP address that your dial-up provider assigned you. This technique is vitally important to enterprises and anybody concerned with security; with NAT, no external hacker can directly target any single machine on the network. Look into it!

2. A Virtual Private Network, or VPN, is a method for creating a secure, encrypted "tunnel" into a network that's otherwise protected by a firewall (which might include NAT). This enables employees to access the corporate network from home, among other applications. How does VPN work? How does a client authenticate with a VPN server and create a secure tunnel? How is traffic redirected on your client machine so that it reaches the correct router?

12

3. CIDR isn't the only technique for specifying subnet masks other than those aligned with the "Class" divisions—nor is it the most flexible. There's another technique, called Variable Length Subnet Masks, or VLSM. This notation allows you to specify masks with as much specificity as you like; a good summary of VLSM, which is also worth reading in order to further your understanding of how masks in general work, can be found at `http://www.lirmm.fr/~ajm/Docs/IP-VLSM.html`.

Hour **13**

Connecting FreeBSD to an Existing Network

Now that you know what networking is all about, the arcane numbers that you must enter into a computer's "TCP/IP Settings" window should make a little bit more sense. Even though operating systems these days are getting so that you don't have to configure as many of these numbers as you would have in earlier years (DHCP, for instance, makes most network configuration automatic), we can't take for granted that everything will always set itself up on its own. The next topic to cover will be configuring your FreeBSD machine for networking.

This chapter assumes that you'll be connecting your machine to a local area network (LAN) using an Ethernet card. If you don't have an Ethernet card and are instead planning to configure your machine to use a dial-up Internet connection with PPP and a modem, you can skip to the next hour.

In this hour you will learn:

- Which kinds of Ethernet or 802.11 cards you can use to hook up your machine

- How to use `sysinstall` to input your machine's TCP/IP settings
- How to determine whether your machine is configured correctly for TCP/IP

The Network Interface Device

The first thing to make sure that your machine is equipped with is a network interface device. In most desktop PCs, this device is an Ethernet card with an RJ-45 jack on it—the most common modern type of Ethernet connector. Almost all cards today are 10/100 cards, meaning that they support both 10Mbps and 100Mbps speeds. Some are even Gigabit cards, although those are more expensive. Some cards have multiple types of connectors on them, such as the card shown in Figure 13.1, which has (from left to right) an RJ-45 jack, a DB-15 serial connector, and a BNC coaxial connector. Most cards today only have an RJ-45 jack. Modern machines frequently come with Ethernet capabilities built on to the motherboard, and an RJ-45 connector will be visible on the back of the machine among the other connectors.

FIGURE 13.1

An Ethernet card with multiple connectors.

Network interface devices aren't always Ethernet, however. Some computers, especially laptops, have wireless 802.11 cards either built-in or added via a PCMCIA slot. 802.11 is a "wireless Ethernet" standard, known variously as Wi-Fi and AirPort; and even though there is no connector to plug in, the operating system still treats the 802.11 card as though it were another Ethernet card. The antenna connected to the card serves the same purpose in the configuration as the UTP cable does in a traditional Ethernet network.

Your computer might have more than one Ethernet card, or it might have both a standard Ethernet card and an 802.11 card. FreeBSD can operate with as many cards as you care to cram into the box. Each one will get its own IP address, as we discussed in the last hour.

FreeBSD comes with support for the vast majority of modern Ethernet cards, both wired and wireless, that are in use today. Table 13.1 shows a listing of the modern Ethernet cards available in the default (GENERIC) kernel configuration. Ethernet cards have become a commodity in recent years, and almost every card made is 100% compatible with existing standards, as well as being quite cheap. Chances are that whatever card you have, it will work with FreeBSD without any additional configuration. Just plug it in and turn it on.

TABLE 13.1   Ethernet Cards Supported in the Default (GENERIC) FreeBSD Kernel

PCI Cards	
de	DEC/Intel DC21x4x ("Tulip")
em	Intel PRO/1000 adapter Gigabit Ethernet Card
txp	3Com 3cR990 ("Typhoon")
vx	3Com 3c590, 3c595 ("Vortex")
PCI/MII Cards	
fxp	Intel EtherExpress Pro/100B (82557, 82558)
tx	SMC 9432TX (83c170 "EPIC")
dc	DEC/Intel 21143 and various workalikes
pcn	AMD Am79C79x PCI 10/100 NICs
rl	RealTek 8129/8139
sf	Adaptec AIC-6915 ("Starfire")
sis	Silicon Integrated Systems SiS 900/SiS 7016
ste	Sundance ST201 (D-Link DFE-550TX)
tl	Texas Instruments ThunderLAN
vr	VIA Rhine, Rhine II
wb	Winbond W89C840F
xl	3Com 3c90x ("Boomerang", "Cyclone")
Wireless (802.11) PCMCIA Cards	
wi	Lucent WaveLAN 802.11
an	Aironet 4500/4800 802.11
awi	BayStack 660 and others

13

Unlike Linux, FreeBSD has different device names for each of the drivers it uses for network interface cards. Although Linux uses simply eth0, eth1, and so on for its Ethernet cards, FreeBSD will name a pair of Intel EtherExpress cards fxp0 and fxp1, and a RealTek card will become rl0. It's not as easy to tell that fxp0 is an Ethernet card as it is with Linux's eth0 designation.

Note, also, that Linux and FreeBSD number their PCI cards in different "directions"; Linux's device numbers rise as you move *toward* the motherboard, whereas in FreeBSD the numbers rise moving *away from* the motherboard. If you have a machine with two PCI Ethernet cards, the one with the 0 on the end of its name will be closest to the motherboard on the PCI chain in FreeBSD, or the on-board Ethernet if there is one. In Linux, however, the device with the 0 will be the one at the *end* of the PCI chain, farthest from the motherboard.

Most Ethernet cards sold today for PC hardware are PCI-based, which means that the PCI controller handles all the addressing automatically and you don't need to do any of the IRQ/DMA/memory address gyrations associated with older ISA cards. If all you have is an ISA card, do yourself a favor and spend the 30 dollars to get a new PCI card from Intel or 3Com. You will save yourself a great deal of entirely unnecessary pain.

If you have a PCI Ethernet card, you can simply delete all the ISA cards from the kernel configuration during installation (in "visual config" mode). If your card is ISA, however, you will need to know your card's chipset and manufacturer, so you know which one to keep and which ones to delete.

How will you know whether FreeBSD recognizes your installed Ethernet card? Simply enter the dmesg command. This command prints out the kernel message buffer that has been building since your machine last booted, and the messages it has will contain all the device discovery lines that you saw go by during the boot process. Look through the lines describing each device. If you see something like this,

```
xl0: <3Com 3c905C-TX Fast Etherlink XL> port 0xd800-0xd87f
➥mem 0xf6800000-0xf680007f irq 12 at device 2.0 on pci1
xl0: Ethernet address: 00:e0:18:29:92:a0
```

This means that your system found an Ethernet card that it can use.

Configuring Network Settings with `sysinstall`

The simplest way to configure your Ethernet card, and probably the most familiar looking to anyone who's gone through this process on a Windows machine or Macintosh, is with `sysinstall`. The first time you ask `sysinstall` to do anything that requires a network connection (a net installation of the system, browsing packages, or various other tasks), it will bring up the network configuration window in which you can set the TCP/IP options for your Ethernet card visually.

An easy way to get to this screen—if you're already up and running multiuser and not in the initial system installation process—is to run `/stand/sysinstall`, select Configure from the main menu, and scroll down to the Media option. In this submenu, select FTP and some FTP server (it doesn't matter which), and you'll see a dialog box that says Running Multiuser, Assume that the Network Is Already Configured? Choose No to enter the network configuration screens. The next thing that appears is the Network Interface selection screen, shown in Figure 13.2.

FIGURE 13.2

Selecting your network interface card in the sysinstall *program.*

You're presented with a list of the interfaces that FreeBSD has found in your system. You'll probably see a number of choices that don't make a lot of sense—aside from choices such as `lp0` (the parallel port) and various PPP or SLIP options on your serial ports, you'll see things like `gif0` and `faith0`. These are IPv6 devices; you can ignore them. The option you want is probably at the top. The one we're using in this example is `fxp1`, an Intel EtherExpress Pro/100B PCI card.

When you select your Ethernet card, you're given two dialog boxes: a choice to let the system try to configure the card automatically using IPv6 and then another choice to let it try using DHCP. Say No to both choices. You'll then be presented with the visual Network Configuration screen, as shown in Figure 13.3.

13

FIGURE 13.3

The visual Network Configuration screen in the sysinstall *program.*

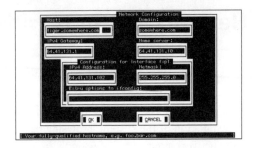

Each field in this screen has a short description at the bottom of the window, but we can explain it a little further here.

- *Host*—This is the hostname, which is just the first part of the machine's fully qualified domain name. For instance, if your machine is www.somewhere.com, the Host: field should be set to www.

- *Domain*—This is the rest of the domain name, or somewhere.com. This can be a composite or multi-level domain for networks with named subnets, such as cslab.ivyleague.edu if your machine is called, for instance, lysine.cslab.ivyleague.edu.

- *IPv4 Gateway*—This is the IP address of your gateway router. Use the next-hop router closest to your machine. This router will be responsible for transmitting any traffic between your machine and any other machines in the world. Ask your network administrator what this number should be if you don't know it.

- *Name server*—The IP address of the most reliable domain name server (DNS) in your network. You should use the DNS provided by your enterprise, ISP, or university network if at all possible; remote name servers are useful as backups, but they won't necessarily be set up to service non-local requests reliably.

- *IPv4 Address*—This is the IP address you're assigning to your Ethernet card. It needs to be on the same subnet as your IPv4 Gateway as matched against your netmask, as we discussed in Hour 12, "Introduction to Networks." Ask your administrator for an unused IP address to put in here, if you don't have one already; you can't just type in any old address and hope it will work. If you enter an address that is already in use elsewhere on the network, one or both machines trying to use that address will lose their network connectivity.

- *Netmask*—This is used to determine whether a packet's destination is on the local network or not. Set the field to 255.255.255.0 for a Class C network, 255.255.0.0 for Class B, and so on, as discussed in Hour 12.

- *Extra options to* `ifconfig`—You most likely won't need to put anything in here unless you're a power user looking to tweak the performance of your interface card. Anything put in here will be added to the `ifconfig` command line that `sysinstall` issues in the background.

> These network settings are the same as in any operating system. If you are unsure what to put in any of these fields in `sysinstall`, check to see if there is a Windows machine nearby on your network that you can peek into. If you open up the TCP/IP settings (usually called Properties under Network, available in the Control Panel, depending on your version of Windows), you will be able to find out what the settings such as the netmask, the gateway, and the name server should be. Don't copy the Windows machine's IP address to your machine, though.

After you've set all these options, select OK; the network settings will be applied to the card on-the-fly, and whatever you were doing in `sysinstall` will continue. If you're following the steps of this example, `sysinstall` will connect to your selected FTP server. If this isn't successful, there's likely a problem with the network settings you entered, and you'll have to go back in and troubleshoot. Consult your network administrator, if you have one available, for assistance.

This process works in much the same way if you're doing a first-time installation of FreeBSD; you will be presented with this same configuration screen early in the install process, and if you're doing a network installation, it will use the settings to pull down the system distribution.

Testing Network Connectivity with `ping`

After you've finished your network configurations, you will want a quick way to make sure that the settings are correct. The easiest solution is the `ping` program—a simple ICMP-based tool that checks for echoes from a specified host and reports the round-trip time it takes each packet to get to the host and back.

The use of `ping` is pretty simple. You can run it against either an IP address or a hostname; it will run until you interrupt it with Ctrl+C:

```
# ping fred
PING fred (114.235.123.11): 56 data bytes
64 bytes from 114.235.123.11: icmp_seq=0 ttl=243 time=485.344 ms
64 bytes from 114.235.123.11: icmp_seq=1 ttl=243 time=351.589 ms
^C
—- fred ping statistics —-
```

13

```
2 packets transmitted, 2 packets received, 0% packet loss
round-trip min/avg/max/stddev = 351.589/418.466/485.344/66.877 ms
```

This is a healthy TCP/IP configuration—the specified host replied to the ping. However, if the host isn't reachable, the ICMP packets will timeout and report the failure to connect. If this happens, something's wrong with your configuration (or, of course, the remote host might actually be down—make sure to try multiple target hosts, including some that you know *must* be online, such as www.microsoft.com).

```
# ping 64.41.131.133
PING 64.41.131.133 (64.41.131.133): 56 data bytes
ping: sendto: Host is down
ping: sendto: Host is down
ping: sendto: Host is down
ping: sendto: Host is down
^C
—· 64.41.131.133 ping statistics —·
10 packets transmitted, 0 packets received, 100% packet loss
```

Summary

In this hour, we briefly ran through the most basic and straightforward way to set up your FreeBSD machine for the Internet. A full discussion of this topic would have gone into greater depth on such topics as manually configuring your IP settings with ifconfig, your gateway routes with netstat, and your name server settings with the /etc/resolv.conf file. You would also have seen how to start the network manually using /etc/netstart, and how to do automatic TCP/IP configuration through DHCP. Those topics, however, are beyond the scope of this brief discussion. For the vast majority of FreeBSD users, connecting your machine to the Internet is a simple, straightforward process without much that can go wrong.

Q&A

Q My Ethernet card isn't listed among the cards that FreeBSD supports, or I don't know what the heck my card is. What do I do?

A Don't panic! There are a number of things you can try. First of all, just read the output of dmesg. Chances are that you'll see something among the device discovery lines which tells you what your Ethernet card is. If you don't, however, and you're sure that your card is seated properly in its slot and is working, try using it in a Windows machine. Windows might be able to tell you what the card is by what driver it picks. You can then look in `/usr/src/sys/i386/conf/NOTES` to see if a driver is there for that card; if so, you can compile it into the kernel as you saw in Hour 10, "The FreeBSD Kernel and the Device Tree."

Something else to try is to look at the chipset on the card itself (the largest chips on it), which might have a manufacturer name or a model number on it. This chipset information is what's really important to the kernel; if you see a driver that matches it in the kernel configuration, or a driver for a major Ethernet card using the same chipset, try it—it might work.

Q What should I do if I have an old ISA Ethernet card?

A If FreeBSD supports your card, you might have to set its IRQ and memory address to values not used by anything else in the system. Unfortunately, this can usually only be done with a DOS utility that comes with the card, which writes the values out to the card's firmware. You can use the full-screen visual installation mode of FreeBSD's installer to tell you whether your card's IRQ or memory address conflict with any other drivers in the system.

Q After running `sysinstall`, I can't get network connectivity to anything. What's wrong?

A Any number of things could be wrong with your chosen TCP/IP settings; talk to your network administrator to make sure that the correct values are entered into `sysinstall`.

If you're your own network administrator, check all the usual suspects—the cabling (make sure that you have "link" lights on your Ethernet card and that the "activity" light is flashing to indicate that traffic is reaching it); connectivity to other machines on the same network segment; the presence of an IP address and `status: active` in the output of `ifconfig <device>`. If you can plug another machine in to the same hub or switch that the FreeBSD machine is connected to, it's a local problem with your TCP/IP configuration settings. Make sure that you're not using an IP address already in use elsewhere on the network and that your subnet mask is correct!

Q I can ping machines by their IP address, but not by their names. How can I fix this?

A Your DNS (name server) setting is probably incorrect. Try pinging the name server machine itself to make sure it is running. If not, see if there's another name server you can use. Also, make sure you've specified your name server by IP address, not by hostname!

13

Workshop

This interactive section is designed to solidify and deepen your understanding of how TCP/IP settings work, through quiz questions and exercises which test your knowledge of the topic.

Quiz

1. What is the most common type of Ethernet card in use in desktop computers today?

    A. ISA

    B. PCI

    C. PCMCIA

2. How much should you expect to pay for a good 10/100 PCI Ethernet card?

    A. $30

    B. $70

    C. $100

    D. $300

3. Your hostname is `klepto.cluster.somewhere.com`. What should you put in the `Host:` field?

    A. `klepto`

    B. `klepto.cluster`

    C. `klepto.cluster.somewhere.com`

    D. nothing

4. What networking protocol does the `ping` tool use?

    A. TCP

    B. UDP

    C. ICMP

    D. NetBIOS

5. Suppose that you have a machine with an on-board Ethernet chipset and two PCI Ethernet cards installed. If the installed cards are both 3Com 3c905 cards, what's the device name for the second one?

    A. `/dev/xl0`

    B. `/dev/xl1`

    C. `/dev/xl2`

    D. `/dev/eth0`

Quiz Answers

1. The correct answer is B. Laptops, however, typically use PCMCIA cards.

2. The correct answer is A. Unless you're buying a 3Com card, which is usually much more expensive for some reason.

3. The correct answer is A.

4. The correct answer is C.

5. The correct answer is B, though if the motherboard's built-in Ethernet chipset is also a 3Com 3c905, the second installed card would be /dev/xl2.

Exercises

1. After running sysinstall, look at your /etc/rc.conf file and examine the changes that have been made. Are they correct? How would you configure another Ethernet card that you choose to install—without using sysinstall? Remember that the only persistent configuration that sysinstall does is to write these settings into /etc/rc.conf. This means that you can do everything sysinstall does simply by manually adding lines to rc.conf and rebooting.

2. How can you change your network settings without rebooting? It's actually quite easy. After making your changes in /etc/rc.conf, use the /etc/netstart script to automatically read them in and apply them. Note, however, that /etc/netstart does not reset your default gateway router; the proper sequence is to first issue a route delete default command, and *then* run /etc/netstart.

13

Hour **14**

Dial-Up Network Connections

Although broadband Internet connections are becoming increasingly common and more widely available, a regular phone line and modem are still a widely used method of connecting to the Internet. This hour looks at how to configure a dial-up network connection to the Internet.

This hour's lesson only applies to readers who want to connect to the Internet using a dial-up connection over a phone line. Readers wishing to connect to the Internet using DSL or cable modems, or who are simply connecting to an existing Ethernet network, should follow the procedures in Hour 13, "Connecting FreeBSD to an Existing Network."

In this hour, you will learn how to do the following:

- Select an ISP for use with FreeBSD.
- Configure a dial-up Internet connection using User PPP.

Selecting an Internet Service Provider

When selecting an *Internet service provider (ISP)* for use with FreeBSD, there are more considerations to be made than when selecting a provider for Windows or Macintosh. Many ISPs have never heard of FreeBSD, Linux, or other operating systems; or if they have, they don't have official support for them. Whereas Windows and Mac users often have access to step-by-step tutorials and customized installation procedures, with FreeBSD you will have to shoulder more of the burden of setup and configuration yourself. If you can find an ISP that officially supports FreeBSD, that's a major plus. However, such ISPs are few and far between.

The good news is that because FreeBSD is an operating system that supports all the standard networking protocols, there should be no difficulty connecting even to an ISP that doesn't officially support the platform. In this hour, you will learn what you need to know in order to make that process a seamless one. However, you will probably be on your own as far as tech support goes when things don't work correctly.

In general, it is best to avoid so-called online services such as AOL and MSN. Getting these services to work with FreeBSD can be extremely difficult (and in some cases impossible) because these services often require special software that is only available for Windows or Macintosh. NetZero also will not work with FreeBSD at this time because their service requires special software.

Some general questions to ask your ISP include the following:

- **Can I get unlimited and unmetered access?** Almost all ISPs have unlimited access these days, so this is rarely a concern. However, check and make sure. You don't want to run in to a situation in which you use up your monthly allotment of 150 hours and end up getting charged a high hourly rate for each hour beyond that limit that you use.

- **What is your subscriber to phone line ratio?** This number, also referred to as the "user-to-modem ratio," tells you how many customers the ISP has in total versus how many are typically dialed in at once. If the ISP has a lot of customers and not enough phone lines, you will end up getting a lot of busy signals when trying to connect. A typical ratio in the ISP industry is 6:1; higher ratios (such as 10:1) can be problematic.

- **How much upstream bandwidth do you have?** This is how big the ISP's connection is to the Internet backbone. ISPs that have a large number of subscribers and not a lot of upstream bandwidth can result in slow connections. For small-town ISPs, make sure that at least a T1 line or two is available. (A T1 line is 1.5Mbps.) For large corporate ISPs with many thousands of subscribers, multiple T3 (45Mbps) or larger lines are a necessity.

- **What kind of value added features do you offer?** Many ISPs will throw in additional email addresses or space on their Web server for a personal Web site at no additional charge. If you want these features, find out if they are available, whether you get charged extra, and if so, how much.

After you have found a suitable ISP, make sure that you have the following information available from them:

- The phone number you need to dial for connecting to the Internet.
- Your login name and password.
- The type of authentication that your ISP uses. Normally this will either be CHAP or PAP, although some older systems still might use a shell login. (Don't worry about what this means at this point; we will cover the various authentication methods later in this hour.) If the person you talk to doesn't know what authentication is being used, FreeBSD and your ISP's server can probably negotiate a compatible authentication on-the-fly, so it probably won't be a big deal.
- Whether you have a static or dynamic IP address. Chances are you will have a dynamic IP address. But if you have a static one, make sure that you know what the address is.
- The IP addresses of your ISP's primary and secondary *Domain Name System (DNS)* servers. These servers are used by your Web browser and such for looking up the addresses of Web sites.

Modem Information

The next thing you need to obtain is information about your modem. Generally, the only thing you will need to know is what communications port your modem is on. If you do not know, and you have Windows installed, you can check the "Modems" tab in the Phone and Modem Options control panel and find the communication ports for any installed modems.

The following shows Windows COM ports and their FreeBSD equivalents:

Windows	FreeBSD
COM1	cuaa0
COM2	cuaa1
COM3	cuaa2
COM4	cuaa3

14

> FreeBSD requires a "real" hardware-based modem. In many cheaper modems (which are often the kind installed in systems from the factory these days), much of the modem functionality has been moved to software to save some money on the cost of building the modem. Unfortunately, these modems, often known as *WinModems*, generally only work with Windows. If you have a WinModem, you are probably out of luck and will have to purchase a different modem if you want to use a dial-up connection with FreeBSD.
>
> If you're adventurous, you might want to look into the `ltmdm` port (`/usr/ports/comms/ltmdm`); it's a third-party Linux driver for the Lucent WinModem chipset combined with a FreeBSD "shim." It might be worth a try if you have no other options.

Configuring the Dial-up Internet Connection

After you have all the required information, you are ready to configure the connection. Your Internet connection will use a method called the *Point-to-Point Protocol (PPP)*. This is the most common protocol of communication in use today that allows Internet format traffic to be passed over a dial-up phone line.

Setting Up the DNS Servers

The first thing to do is tell FreeBSD what the addresses of your ISP's DNS servers are. This is configured in the file `/etc/resolv.conf`. Here is an example of what it looks like:

```
domain myisp.com
nameserver 111.111.11.1
nameserver 222.222.22.2
```

Note that you will need to be logged in as root to edit this file.

The first line contains the domain name of your ISP. For example, if you use EarthLink (a popular national provider) as your ISP, the domain you would list here would be `earthlink.net`.

The second and third lines contain the primary and secondary DNS servers for your ISP. Replace `111.111.11.1` and `222.222.22.2` with the primary and secondary addresses given to you by your ISP, respectively. After you have done this, save the file and exit the editor.

When you have finished editing the /etc/resolv.conf file, you are ready to configure the connection. FreeBSD can connect to the Internet through a dial-up connection in two ways. The method that we will cover in this book is known as *kernel PPP*. It is slightly more efficient than the alternative, which is known as *user PPP*.

Configuring the Options File for Kernel PPP

Most of the configuration for kernel PPP is done in the file /etc/ppp/options. Here is what a sample file might look like:

```
/dev/cuaa0 115200
crtscts
modem
connect "/usr/sbin/chat -f /etc/ppp/chat.script"
noipdefault
silent
domain myisp.com
defaultroute
user foobar
name foobar
```

Here is what each line means.

> **/dev/cuaa0 115200**—This line indicates the device that your modem is on. You should have figured this out back when you gathered the information about your modem. In this case, as we pointed out earlier, cuaa0 corresponds to COM1 in Windows. The second part of the line (115200) indicates the serial communication rate of the computer with the modem. Unless you have a very old system, 115200 should probably work fine. If you encounter weird problems, you might try reducing this to 57600.

> **crtscts**—This line turns on hardware flow control for the modem. Hardware flow control is required in order for high speed communication to work reliably; this line is therefore required.

> **modem**—This line tells FreeBSD that it should use the modem control lines.

> **connect "/usr/sbin/chat -f /etc/ppp/chat.script"**—This line specifies the "modem script" to run when connecting. It calls the chat program, which is a simple way for FreeBSD to communicate with the modem. The second part of the line (/etc/ppp/chat.script) tells the chat program the name of the modem script that it should read and execute. We haven't created this script yet, but it is what will contain the phone number for the modem to dial, as well as other options.

> **noipdefault**—This line means that your ISP has not assigned you a static IP address and that you are using a dynamic IP address. Most dial-up users will have a dynamic

14

IP address, so this line should be included. If your ISP has given you a static IP address, include a line such as the following in place of the `noipdefault` line:

    111.111.111.11:222.222.222.22

The number `111.111.111.11` should be replaced with the static IP address that your ISP has assigned to you. The number `222.222.222.22` should be replaced with the gateway address that your ISP gave you. If your ISP did not give you a gateway address, leave the second number off but make sure that the first number still has the colon at the end.

`silent`—This line tells the system to wait for Link Control Protocol (LCP) packets when initiating a connection. This is a useful performance tweak, though its meaning is esoteric.

`domain myisp.com`—The domain name of your ISP should go here. (For example, if your ISP is EarthLink, replace `myisp.com` with `earthlink.net`.)

`defaultroute`—This means that a default route will be added to the routing table while the Internet connection is up. The route provides a way for you to send and receive traffic from the Internet.

`user foobar`—This corresponds to a profile that we will create later in a different file that contains the login name and password for your ISP. `foobar` corresponds to the username that we will list in the other file.

`name foobar`—The `name` option sets the name of the local machine to `foobar` for the purposes of authentication using the `pap-secrets` and `chap-secrets` files, which we will cover shortly.

Once you have saved the `options` file, you next need to create the `chat.script` file that was referenced in the options file. Like the `options` file, `chat.script` should be located in the `/etc/ppp` directory.

Creating the Chat Script

As stated previously, the `chat.script` file is what contains instructions telling FreeBSD how to connect to your ISP. Its primary function is to dial the phone number. Here is a sample `chat.script` file. In `/etc/ppp`, create a new file called `chat.script` in a text editor and enter the following text all on a single line:

```
ABORT BUSY ABORT 'NO CARRIER' "" AT OK ATDT5551212 CONNECT ""
```

The syntax of this script is quite bizarre, but fortunately you probably won't need to alter it very much (if at all). Translated to English, here is what the script is telling the modem:

- If the modem responds with either BUSY (the number dialed was busy) or NO CARRIER (the connection was lost), the script ABORTs.
- The script sends the AT command to the modem, which is sort for *ATTENTION*. It then waits for the modem to respond with OK.
- After the modem has responded with OK, the script dials the phone number 5551212. This number should, of course, be replaced by the phone number that your ISP gave you. The ATD stands for *ATTENTION DIAL*, and the T tells the modem to use Touch-Tone dialing. If you have an ancient phone system that doesn't support Touch-Tone, you can use ATDP instead, which tells the modem to use pulse or rotary style dialing.
- The script waits for the modem to respond with CONNECT.

Save the chat.script file and exit the editor. There is at least one more file we need to create—possibly two more files. These files contain the PAP or CHAP authentication information needed for you to log in to your ISP.

pap-secrets and chap-secrets

The /etc/ppp/pap-secrets and /etc/ppp/chap-secrets files contain authentication information for *Password Authentication Protocol (PAP)* and *Challenge-Handshake Authentication Protocol (CHAP)* authentication, respectively. If your ISP told you which form of authentication it uses, you only need to create the file corresponding to that type of authentication. If you do not know which form of authentication your ISP uses, you will need to create both files.

Both files only need to contain a single line, which has the following format:

```
loginname * password
```

In the previous sample options file, the login name we gave to the name line was foobar, so this line in chap-secrets or pap-secrets should read

```
foobar * password
```

Of course, you will want to replace *password* with whatever your login password is for your ISP. The asterisk separating the username and password means that this entry is good for any host.

When you have finished entering this line, save one or both of the files (pap-secrets and chap-secrets) and exit the text editor.

14

Because the pap-secrets and chap-secrets files contain your password for your ISP, they should be readable only by the root user. This can be accomplished by setting the file permissions as follows: chmod 600 pap-secrets or chmod 600 chap-secrets. Failing to do this will allow anyone with an account on the system to obtain the ISP password!

Starting the Internet Connection

You should now be ready to start the Internet connection. To do so, as the root user, enter **pppd** at the command prompt. Your modem should dial and connect to the Internet. To disconnect from the Internet, simply kill the pppd program. The killall pppd command will do the trick. If it doesn't work, the section "Troubleshooting the Connection" at the end of this hour can help.

Dial-on-Demand

If you want your system to automatically connect to the Internet anytime an Internet resource is requested and the connection is not already up (you enter a Web page address in a Web browser, for example), you can set up dial-on-demand. To do this, you can just add two more options to the /etc/ppp/options file. Here are the relevant options:

demand—This option turns on the dial-on-demand function.

idle n—This option determines how long the connection should be allowed to be idle (that is, no incoming or outgoing traffic) before FreeBSD hangs up the modem. *n* is a value given in seconds.

Note that you will still need to start the pppd program after you turn on your computer in order for this to work. If you want to have the pppd program loaded automatically each time you start your system, create a file called ppp in the directory /usr/local/etc/rc.d that contains the single line pppd. This will cause the pppd program to be loaded automatically each time the computer is started.

Persistent Connections

If you want to have FreeBSD automatically redial the connection anytime it is lost, you can add a line to /etc/ppp/options that says persist. Basically, this will cause your Internet connection to always be on; thus, it will also cause your phone line to always be tied up.

Keeping your system connected to the Internet all the time, even when you are not using it, could cause your ISP to cancel your account even if you have unlimited access. Or they might ask you to purchase what is known as a dedicated line, which will cost you a great deal more than a standard Internet connection.

A further concern is that a system that's online at all times is also more vulnerable to being hacked. Beware—an always-on connection carries with it significant risks!

Automatically Running Commands on Connect and Disconnect

Two files called /etc/ppp/ip-up and /etc/ppp/ip-down allow you to automatically have commands run on each connect and disconnect from the Internet, respectively. Simply place a list of commands that you want to run in these files. A simple example of an ip-up script would be as follows:

```
apachectl start
echo "My network connection is up! Web server started."
```

An example of where this can be especially useful is for laptop users who want to read and respond to email offline and then have all the email they wrote automatically sent the next time they connect to their ISP. This can be done using the Fetchmail program, available in the ports (/usr/ports/mail/fetchmail).

Troubleshooting the Connection

Several things can cause your Internet connection not to work correctly. Some of the most common problems and potential solutions for them are listed as follows.

The Modem Never Dials

- Make sure that you have selected the proper communications device for your modem.
- Try reducing the speed in the first line of the options file from 115200 to 57600.
- Check your modem handbook and see if it is expecting some kind of special initialization string. If so, you can supply this in the chat.script file; if your modem's initialization string, for example, is AT&F, you can add the string AT&F OK into the script right after the ATZ OK part.

14

- Make sure that your modem is not a WinModem. Check your computer's documentation to see if you can determine the modem manufacturer and chipset; if it's a Lucent WinModem, you may be able to make it work with the `ltmdm` port, as discussed earlier; you may be better off, though, picking up a real, standard UART-based modem instead.

The Modem Dials but Never Establishes a Connection

- Make sure that you are using the correct login name and password. Also, don't confuse your FreeBSD login name and password with your Internet login name and password. They are not the same.

- Make sure that you are using the correct authentication type that your ISP expects. When in doubt, create both the `pap-secrets` and `chap-secrets` file to ensure that your system is ready to handle whichever authentication your ISP requests.

- If you have a static IP address, make sure that you are using the correct one in `/etc/ppp/options`.

- Check your modem handbook and see if it needs a special initialization string. If so, you can supply it in the `chat.script` file; if your modem's initialization string, for example, is `AT&F`, you can add the string `AT&F OK` into the script right after the `ATZ OK` part.

- If you have Windows or another system available, see if you can establish a connection from there. If not, and if calls to tech support have failed to resolve the issue, it might be worth contacting your phone company to see if something is wrong with your phone line that is causing an excessive amount of line noise. Another symptom of excessive line noise is disconnections that happen on a regular basis for no apparent reason.

  If you use the same phone line for voice calls that you do for dialing up, a noisy line can cause static in your voice calls as well; that's one way you can tell the quality of your lines.

The Modem Establishes a Connection, but You Can't Access Any Web Sites, and so on After the Connection Has Been Made

- Make sure that you have the correct DNS servers for your ISP listed in `/etc/resolv.conf`.

- Check the `/etc/host.conf` file and make sure it contains a line that says `hosts` followed by a line that says `bind`, as follows:

```
# $FreeBSD: src/etc/host.conf,v 1.6 1999/08/27 23:23:41 peter Exp $
# First try the /etc/hosts file
hosts
# Now try the nameserver next.
bind
```

- If you have a static IP address, make sure that you are using the correct one in `/etc/ppp/options`.

- If your ISP gave you a gateway address, make sure that you have it listed following the colon after your IP address and make sure that it is the correct address.

Dial-on-demand Sometimes Dials the Modem Even when You Aren't Trying to Use the Internet

- This means that some program running the background is probably trying to connect to the Internet. More than likely, one or more parts of the email system are the culprit. Information on how to stop this behavior can be found in Hour 23.

The Internet Connection Never Drops Even Though You Have an Idle Value Set in the `options` File and You Are Not Using the Internet

- This is usually caused by the same culprits that cause the previous problem. More than likely, some part of the email system is polling a mail server at your ISP on a regular basis—thus causing the connection to stay up. Information on how to stop this behavior can be found in Hour 23.

Summary

This hour's lesson covered the basic knowledge you will need to have when connecting a FreeBSD machine to the Internet via a modem. FreeBSD isn't anywhere nearly as easy to set up for PPP connections as Windows or the Mac are, nor is it for certain that the ISP with which you have your account will be able to help you troubleshoot your connection. However, PPP is PPP no matter what the platform; with a little bit of experimentation and tweaking, your FreeBSD machine will be able to harness PPP every bit as effectively as the more popular platforms can.

14

Q&A

Q My ISP says it will support Linux, but not FreeBSD. What do I do?

A Consider yourself lucky. Most ISPs won't even go so far as to offer a helping hand to Linux users; what they usually don't realize, though, is that Linux and FreeBSD behave almost the same way when it comes to PPP. The details of implementation might vary, but at least you know that the ISP doesn't rely on Windows-based software in order for you to connect. That's all you really need to worry about.

Q Why is it called "kernel PPP"?

A FreeBSD actually supports two kinds of PPP connections: kernel PPP and user PPP. This hour talked about kernel PPP because it's more straightforward, and support for PPP is built in to the FreeBSD kernel by default; however, if you're using a FreeBSD machine in which PPP support has been removed from the kernel, you can also use user PPP to make dial-up connections. See the man ppp page for details.

Q How do I set redialing options for Dial-on-Demand or persistent connections?

A This only applies if you're using user PPP. If you are, you can use the set redial option to create a "recipe" for redialing behavior. See the man ppp page for more information.

Workshop

In this interactive section, you will be given a quiz and a few exercises in order to help solidify your understanding of dial-up networking in FreeBSD.

Quiz

1. DNS server addresses should be listed in which file?

   A. /etc/nameservers

   B. /etc/dns

   C. /etc/resolv.conf

   D. /etc/ppp/resolv.conf

   E. /etc/ppp/nameservers

2. Which of the following files contains most of the information needed for connecting to the ISP?

    A. `/etc/internet.conf`

    B. `/etc/ppp.conf`

    C. `/etc/ppp/options`

    D. `/etc/ppp/internet.conf`

    E. None of the above

3. Which of the following files contain username and password authentication information for the ISP?

    A. `/etc/passwd`

    B. `/etc/ppp/pap-secrets`

    C. `/etc/ppp/passwords`

    D. `/etc/ppp/passwd`

    E. There is no file with this information

Quiz Answers

1. The correct answer is C.

2. The correct answer is C.

3. The correct answer B. Watch out for answer A. This file does exist, but it contains information for the local FreeBSD system, not for the Internet connection.

Exercises

1. Try setting up user PPP instead of kernel PPP. Then, experiment with the `ppp -auto` mode and with creating a redial recipe—for example, try setting it up so that PPP will redial ten times, starting with a minute between dial attempts and increasing the interval between attempts by thirty seconds each time.

2. Set up an `ip-up` script that starts a Web server, starts your mail program, and downloads a certain Web page. Create an `ip-down` script that shuts down the Web server, kills your Web browser and mail program, and prints a message to all logged-in users that tells them the network is down. What's wrong with this last one? Nobody else will see it, unless they're logged in on the local network via an Ethernet card.

14

HOUR **15**

Network Security

A long time ago (relatively speaking—a long time in computer years), you didn't have to worry much about the security of your computer system. Basically, your computer was as secure as the building it was housed in. If someone couldn't get into the building, he couldn't get access to your computer and whatever information was stored on it.

However, this all changed, of course, with the advent of networks, and with the advent of the Internet in particular. These days, your computer can be locked in a vault and still be vulnerable to outside intruders if it has a network connection. If it has an Internet connection, it can be vulnerable to attack by someone on the other side of the world. Because of this, network security is more important now then ever before.

In this hour, you will learn:

- How to ensure that passwords are secure
- How to control remote logins and increase the security of allowing them
- How to configure a basic firewall
- How to make sure that the console is secure

Ensuring Password Integrity

One of the most common methods that hackers use to access a system is to simply obtain a valid username and password combination and then log in with it. This method works because most companies don't adequately educate their employees about the importance of password security and the methods that hackers will often use to steal passwords. Some of the most common problems with passwords, as well as methods that hackers use to steal passwords, are discussed next.

Weak Passwords

Weak passwords meet one or more of the following criteria:

- They are too short.
- They are easily guessed.
- They are words that can be found in a dictionary.

Of course, the problems with passwords that are too short is that there is a better chance of getting a correct one simply through random guessing. It's relatively easy for a hacker to obtain or write a program that can automate this process and simply try random passwords until it hits one that works.

A similar problem exists with using words that can be found in the dictionary as passwords. Password cracking programs exist that simply go through the dictionary and try words until it hits one that works.

Probably the most common password weakness is passwords that are easily guessed. In its most extreme form, this includes such things as using the word "password" as the password (you'd be surprised how many people actually want to do this), using the login name as the password, or using the current month or season as the password.

Not quite as bad, but still very insecure (and very common), is using such things as the name of a child or pet, city of birth, or other information that a lot of other people know about you, or can find out relatively easily. *Dumpster diving*, a technique that gets its name because it sometimes literally involves diving into dumpsters outside of an office building and looking for discarded documents that contain personal information about someone, is sometimes employed by hackers to look for information that might be used as a password.

It's also best not to discount the issue of "social engineering"—convincing people, whether for good or evil purposes, to just hand over their passwords and sensitive data. Many security systems in use today and planned for the future is founded on the concept

15

of "trusted systems"—in which the environment is assumed to be secure, and in which people are encouraged to be very free with their information. If the impression of security is false in any way, this can be the gravest risk of all.

Writing Down Passwords

Another fairly common security problem that a lot of people engage in is writing down their password and placing it somewhere that hackers are very likely to look for it. No, hackers are not dumb. The first place they are going to look for a password is the bottom of the keyboard or the bottom of the desk, which is where a lot of people seem to "hide" their passwords—no smarter a practice than keeping the key to the house under the doormat. Even worse, and amazingly, quite common, is people who write their password on a Post-It note and then stick it on the frame of their monitor. Passwords should not be written down. Having said this, I know that a lot of people are going to ignore it and write down their password anyway. So if you must write down your password, at least keep it in your wallet or something where it is difficult for someone to steal it. Of course, if you do this, and your wallet gets stolen, you will want to change your password immediately.

Try embedding passwords into other pieces of information, such as addresses, where it will be impossible to tell what's a password and what's not. You don't necessarily have to outwit all the wily hackers in the world; you just need to be smarter about passwords than the average hacker target is.

What Makes a Good Password?

Now that we have talked about all the things that make a bad password, what makes a good one? Generally, a good password should have the following characteristics:

- It should be at least six characters long.
- It should contain a mixture of upper- and lowercase letters.
- It should contain at least one number.
- It should contain at least one character that is not alphanumeric ($, !, and so on).

Of course, as mentioned before, a good password should not be a word from the dictionary, it should not be something that can be easily guessed, and it should not be something that can be easily found out about you. However, it is also important that the password is something you can remember. Picking a password that is too complex will tempt you to write it down somewhere, and you want to avoid that.

One commonly-used technique for developing a password is to choose a favorite sentence or song title, and use the first letters from each of the words in it. Then, replace the letter *S* with $, and *A* with @, and so on.

Be Aware of Suspicious Activity

It's been said that all good server administrators are a little bit paranoid, but that is probably a good thing when it comes to security. Be on the lookout for any suspicious phone calls or suspicious activity in or around the office. Also make sure that other employees are educated about this. Report any suspicious activity to the proper person. Here are a couple of common "social engineering" tactics that you should be very suspicious of.

The first is someone claiming to be from the computer or IT department who calls and claims to be testing user accounts, upgrading accounts, adding new features to your account, and so on, and asks you for your username and password. NEVER give out your username and password to someone calling and claiming to be a system administrator or IT personnel. Remember that the system administrator can log in as you without needing your password by using the su command. Therefore, there is no reason that a system administrator should ever ask you for your password so that he can do anything. Basically, he doesn't need it.

The second thing to be aware of is anyone in or around the office who claims he is conducting a survey regarding almost anything (favorite foods, most common pet names, and so on). Even kids are a risk here. In fact, they are often more of a risk because people don't suspect them and because they will sometimes claim that they are doing it for a school project or something. This is a somewhat common method for hackers to obtain personal information that they can later search through for potential passwords.

Remote Login Issues

Of course, allowing remote logins to your server through a network significantly increases security risks. However, sometimes it is necessary for users to be able to log in to the server remotely. If you do need to allow remote logins, there are some things you can do to make them as secure as possible. We will look at each of these next.

Telnet

Telnet is a very primitive method of allowing remote logins to a server. It really should be considered obsolete even though it is still commonly used. Telnet's primary security problem is that it does nothing to encrypt the transmission of the password when the user logs in remotely. Because of this, anyone sniffing the network traffic going to your server can obtain a login name and password combination relatively easily.

Because of the inherent security problems with telnet, we aren't going to discuss its configuration here other than to say that it should be considered obsolete and should not be used. To make sure that telnet is indeed disabled (it is by default on modern versions of FreeBSD), look at the file /etc/inetd.conf and make sure that any references to telnetd are commented out.

rlogin

rlogin is another older protocol used for logging in to a system remotely. Like telnet, it is gradually being phased out in favor of SSH because it has the same basic problems. Although rlogin does have the advantage of not needing to transmit a password over the network (sometimes), it still doesn't encrypt network traffic. Once again, because of this, we are not going to cover rlogin here.

SSH

SSH stands for *Secure Shell*, and it is the primary reason that Telnet and rlogin are rapidly becoming obsolete. SSH provides remote login services like Telnet. However, unlike Telnet, SSH encrypts the connection so that someone sniffing your network traffic cannot read the password. To enable remote logins through SSH on FreeBSD, add the following line to your /etc/rc.conf file:

sshd_enable="YES"

Of course, this change will not take effect until the system has been restarted.

To log in to the system from another FreeBSD box (or any other UNIX box that has SSH installed), simply issue a command such as the following:

ssh lion.simba.org

SSH will then prompt you for a password.

Note that SSH assumes that your login name on the remote system is the same as your login name on the system you are using SSH from. If this is not the case, you need to specify the login name on the command line. You can do this by specifying the login name, followed by an @ sign, and then the hostname of the system you want to log in to. For example,

ssh foobar@lion.simba.org

Where foobar is, of course, substitute the login name that you use on the remote system.

Note that the telnet client that ships with Windows does not understand SSH and therefore cannot log in to an SSH server. However, several alternatives are available, including Putty, QVT/Term, and TeraTerm Pro (if you install the SSH plug-in) that can handle SSH connections. All these programs are available from the Telnet category at www.tucows.com. Macintosh users will probably want to check out MacSSH, also available from the Macintosh section of www.tucows.com in the Telnet category.

Configuring a Basic Firewall

A firewall is a system that is designed to control access to and from a computer or network. Its two primary tasks are to prevent unauthorized outside users from accessing the computer or network (or parts of it), as well as to prevent internal users from going outside of the network. In other words, it can prevent internal users from accessing the Internet, certain Internet services, or parts of the Internet.

Figure 15.1 shows an illustration of where a firewall is in relation to the internal network (LAN) and the rest of the world (Internet) A DMZ ("demilitarized zone") is also present; this is a third port on the firewall machine that leads to machines that are physically on the same LAN as the rest of the machines, but logically (and relative to the firewall) are part of the outside Internet. This is where Web servers, mail servers, and so on would live.

FIGURE 15.1

A diagram of a gateway machine providing firewall services.

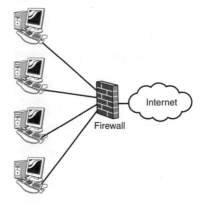

Creating Firewall Rules

When you initially configure the firewall, make sure that you have access to the console of the system where it is running. It's easy to lock yourself out of your own network if you accidentally set a firewall rule that denies access to yourself. By default, the firewall will deny everything when first enabled. Of course, if you lock yourself out, you will not be able to access anything again until you have physical access to the system console.

Before you enable the firewall, you will want to create a configuration file for it that contains the rules you want the firewall to enforce. There are two basic firewall designs you can use:

- Deny everything that is not specifically allowed. This is the most secure fashion of building a firewall.
- Allow everything that is not specifically denied. This is less secure, but can be effective if you only want to block a couple of ports or IP address/hosts from accessing the network.

To create a set of firewall rules, we will create a text file to hold them. This file can be called whatever you want and stored wherever you want, but here we are going to assume that the file you are using is /usr/local/etc/firewall.conf.

Basically, a firewall rule takes the following information in the following order:

1. **What to do.** This can be either the keyword allow or the keyword deny, which determines what should be done with the rule that follows.
2. **What type of traffic the rule applies to.** This can be a network protocol such as tcp, udp, or icmp. It can also be the keyword all; in which case, the rule applies to all types of network traffic.
3. **Where the traffic comes from.** This can be a specific IP address, hostname, or domain name. It can also be the keyword any; in which case, it applies to traffic coming from any host.
4. **Where the traffic is going.** This can be the hostname or IP address of a system on your network that the rule applies to. It can also be the keyword any; in which case, the rule will apply to all systems on your network.
5. **An optional port number.** If it exists, the rule will only apply to that network port. If it does not exist, the rule will apply to all ports.

Here is an example of a set of firewall rules that could go in this file.

```
add allow tcp from any to www.simba.org 80
add allow all from lion.simba.org to www.simba.org
add 65000 deny all from any to any
```

The last rule was specifically assigned a number because this way you can dynamically add firewall rules without having to reset the entire firewall. The next paragraph explains why this is an issue.

Note that the rules are read in sequential order. In other words, the first rule the firewall comes to that matches the traffic being sent or received is the one that will be applied. If this seems confusing, the following rule set might clear things up:

```
add deny all from any to any
add allow tcp from any to www.simba.org 80
add allow all from lion.simba.org to www.simba.org
```

Even though the same rules are present in this set that were present in the previous one, the results of this rule set will be very different from the intended results for it. This is because the first rule will match all traffic; therefore, the next two rules will be ignored and the first rule will be applied. Of course, this means that because the first rule applies to all traffic (which includes lion.simba.org), the traffic will be denied—even though the second two rules allow it. As you can see, it is very important in which order you list the rules in the set.

The first rule set that was given previously is an example of the "deny everything that is not specifically allowed" strategy. The following gives an example of how the "allow everything that is not specifically denied" strategy would work.

```
add deny all from nasty.hacker.org to any
add deny all from any to www.simba.org 80
add 65000 allow all from any to any
```

In this case, everything is allowed except for traffic that comes from nasty.hacker.org, which is denied access to all systems that are behind this firewall. In addition, all traffic from any system is denied to `www.simba.org` if it is directed toward port 80. (Port 80 is normally where a Web server could be running. In other words, this rule would have the effect of blocking any attempts to access the Web server port.)

It is a good idea to set your firewall rule file so that it can only be accessed by the root user. There is a small security risk involved in letting other users know what firewall rules your system is using. For example, if a hacker can obtain an IP address that your firewall allows to access the network, he can potentially spoof the IP address and thus fool your firewall into thinking that the traffic is coming from an authorized system when, in fact, it is not.

Enabling the Firewall

After you have saved the firewall configuration file, you need to configure the `/etc/rc.conf` file to enable it. This can be done by adding the following two lines:

```
firewall_enable="YES"
firewall_type="/usr/local/etc/firewall.conf"
```

After you have added these two lines, reboot the system. Remember to make sure that you have access to the console in case you accidentally mess up the rule file in such a way that causes you to lock yourself out of your own system once it has rebooted and the firewall has started. If the firewall starts correctly, you should see something similar to the following as the system starts back up.

```
Kernel firewall module loaded
Flushed all rules.
00100 allow tcp from any to www.simba.org 80
00200 allow all from lion.simba.org to www.simba.org
65000 deny all from any to any
Firewall rules loaded, starting divert daemons:.
```

Note that this section has only covered the configuration of a very basic firewall. Several more configuration options can be used in the firewall configuration. For full information on configuring the firewall, see the ipfw man page and also the online handbook at www.freebsd.org/handbook.

Securing the Console

Securing the physical server console itself involves both physical security and security settings on the software. Ideally, your server should be locked in a room that only trusted administrators have access to. However, this is not always feasible in a small office. By default, however, FreeBSD allows root access to the console in single user mode without providing a password. If the server cannot be physically secured, it is important to change this. This is done by editing the file /etc/ttys. Look for the line that says

```
console none        unknown off secure
```

Change it so that it reads

```
console none        unknown off insecure
```

This will prevent FreeBSD from allowing someone to boot in to single user mode without supplying a password. Make sure that you don't get confused by the terminology, which admittedly is a bit confusing. When the console is set to insecure, it actually makes the console more secure as far as accessing the root account. Basically, insecure versus secure refers to the physical security of the console. Setting it to insecure increases some security options in FreeBSD to compensate for the lack of physical console security.

> Note that even after securing the console, it is possible for someone with physical access to it to boot from a floppy disk or CD-ROM and get root access to the system without entering a password. To protect against this, make sure that you configure your computer's CMOS setup utility to disable booting from the floppy drive and CD-ROM drive. This is still no guarantee of security, though, because someone with physical access can change the BIOS settings back.
>
> Bear in mind, simply, that without a guarantee of physical access, total security is not possible.

Security Holes in FreeBSD

FreeBSD is one of the more secure operating systems available. However, it is inevitable that, at times, security problems will be found that can allow an attacker to compromise your system. Because of this, it is important that you keep your system updated and that you are subscribed to the `freebsd-security` mailing list, which will contain announcements regarding security holes that have been discovered. To subscribe to this list, send a message to `majordomo@freebsd.org`, with the contents being the single line:

```
subscribe freebsd-security
```

Also, it is important to note that a RELEASE version of FreeBSD that you just installed might have security problems out of the box, which is why it is important to `cvsup` your system to STABLE. However, remember that `cvsup`ping your system to STABLE will only fix security problems related to FreeBSD itself. Most security breaches related to software do not happen because of FreeBSD, but rather because of a problem with third-party software running on FreeBSD that has a security issue. Note that this third-party software will not be updated by the `cvsup` process. A security hole in Apache, for example, requires that you update or patch Apache to fix the problem.

Summary

This hour looked at some basics of securing your FreeBSD system. However, a lot of security related issues were not covered. These include issues such as security problems caused by CGI scripts running in Web servers. For more information on basic security issues, check out the `security` man page.

Q&A

Q I've heard of some institutions (government agencies, research facilities, and so on) that require "one-time passwords". How do I use those?

A FreeBSD has a mechanism called S/Key that allows users to generate one-time passwords, which only work once each, in response to a "challenge phrase" issued by the login program. Look into the man skey page for details on how this works.

Q How do I secure email services for my users?

A POP3 and IMAP traffic, both of which are common forms of mail delivery for users, can be encrypted using a daemon called stunnel (available in the ports at /usr/ports/security/stunnel). This daemon creates a secure "tunnel" (hence the name) through which regular POP3 and IMAP traffic is piped, after being encrypted in the same way that SSH traffic is encrypted. Most modern email programs support secure POP3 and IMAP (look for the "SSL" switch), so installing stunnel is an extremely good idea.

Q Some secure services, like Apache 2.0 and stunnel, talk about my needing a "security certificate." What's that about?

A You will need to generate a certificate that proves you are who you say you are if you want remote users to be able to trust the encrypted content that your server sends. (This is an integral part of network security.) Use the openssl program to generate a certificate; usage of the program is very complex, but the syntax you will want in order to generate a certificate request (which you can then submit to a signing authority, such as VeriSign) is

```
openssl req -new -nodes -out req.pem -keyout /etc/certs/cert.pem
```

This assumes that you have created a directory called /etc/certs to hold your certificates.

Workshop

The quiz questions and exercises listed in this interactive section are provided for your further understanding of the current hour's topics.

Quiz

1. Which of the following is the best password to use?

    A. ChangeMe

    B. 12345

    C. nospmoht

    D. N3v1R$4yD13

2. What program should you be using to connect to your FreeBSD system remotely?

   A. Telnet

   B. FTP

   C. SSH

   D. POP3

   E. rlogin

3. What's the best way to stay on top of security holes that are discovered in FreeBSD?

   A. Subscribe to the `freebsd-security` mailing list

   B. Keep your ports updated to the most recent versions

   C. Don't run any services that you don't absolutely need

   D. All of the above

   E. Cover your eyes and hope for the best

4. What's the one form of security compromise that you absolutely can't defend against through software?

   A. Password sniffing

   B. Denial-of-Service (DOS) attack

   C. Root compromise

   D. "Dictionary" attacks

   E. A guy with a screwdriver

Quiz Answers

1. The correct answer is D. Believe it or not, all the rest can be guessed relatively easily by commonly available software.

2. The correct answer is C.

3. The correct answer is B.

4. The correct answer is D. If you're on the Internet, you *must* be on guard!

5. The correct answer is E.

Exercises

1. Install `tcpflow` (available in the ports in `/usr/ports/net/tcpflow`); use it to see if any cleartext traffic is being sent to and from your machine, aside from Web traffic and SMTP (which generally requires no passwords). What potential problems can you foresee facing an administrator as a result of using this program? Why might you choose to use `tcpdump` (which only prints out packet headers, rather than the entire packet) instead? Hint: It's an ethical question.

2. Design a scheme by which to generate random passwords for new users. One example is to use `md5 -s` to create a hash string from a bunch of randomly pressed input characters; you can take the first seven letters from that hash output and use it as a random initial password for each user.

3. Use the `pkg_version` utility to determine which of your installed ports are out of date. Make sure to synchronize your ports tree first!

PART IV

FreeBSD as a Workstation

Hour

HOUR 16

Command-Line Applications

Command-line applications might seem like a rather archaic way to work in today's world of graphical user interfaces. However, they can still be quite powerful and definitely have some advantages. For one thing, they can be run on virtually any computer because they don't require very many system resources. The other advantage is that they can be run remotely from any terminal emulator with some kind of network access to the FreeBSD system that your application is on. For example, this means that you can take your Windows or Macintosh laptop to the other side of the world, connect to the Internet, log in to your FreeBSD system that is 5,000 miles away, and work with applications on it without requiring any special software.

In this hour, you will learn:

- How to work with the various text editors included with FreeBSD
- How to work with text-based email applications
- How to work with other miscellaneous applications

Working with Text

A text editor is one of the most basic applications necessary for any computer system. Virtually all operating systems come with at least one or often several text editors. For example, Windows comes with Notepad and the older text mode Edit program. In FreeBSD, because so much of the system configuration is handled by text-based configuration files, the ability to work with a text editor is especially important.

By default, FreeBSD installs two fully featured text editors. The first is the vi text editor. vi is one of the oldest UNIX text editors still in widespread use. It is also one of the most powerful. Unfortunately, it also has a reputation for being rather arcane and difficult to learn. Because of this, FreeBSD also provides another editor called ee (short for *Easy Editor*) that is installed by default. This editor is much easier to learn for new users, so it is the editor we will cover first. However, we will also cover vi because it is the "universal UNIX text editor." No matter what version of UNIX you ever have to work on, you can be assured that vi will be installed on it. In fact, vi might sometimes be the only editor installed on some UNIX systems. So having at least a basic ability to work with vi can be very handy for anyone who works with FreeBSD or any other form of UNIX.

The ee Editor

To start the ee editor, simply type **ee** at the command prompt. This will start the editor with no file loaded into it. If you want to start ee with a file, simply follow the command with the name of the file—for example, ee myfile. If the file myfile exists, it will be loaded into ee. If the file doesn't already exist, a new file with that name will be created.

Figure 16.1 shows the ee editor with a blank file loaded into it.

FIGURE 16.1

The ee text editor. Notice the handy cheat sheet at the top that shows you keyboard shortcuts.

The ^ symbol in front of the menu options is called the *caret*. It represents the CTRL key. To access the menu options, you press the CTRL key along with the key that follows the caret symbol. Table 16.1 lists some of the less obvious menu options and what they do.

TABLE 16.1 Some ee Menu Options and Their Associated Action

Key Combo	Action
Ctrl+o	This will bring up a prompt where you can enter an ASCII code for a character. This is primarily useful for entering certain foreign characters that do not have keys on the keyboard.
Ctrl+c	This changes the menu at the top to display a new list of commands. You will also get a prompt at the bottom of the screen where you can enter the name of the command you want to use. To exit the prompt without entering a command, just press Enter.
Ctrl+x	This option is somewhat confusing as it will not actually bring up a prompt for you to search for something. Instead, it will repeat the previous search that was done. To initiate a search that allows you to enter something to search for, use Ctrl+y.

Note the ^g and ^v that are listed as Previous Page and Next Page. On most systems, you can also use the Page Up and Page Down keys to accomplish the same thing. However, if you are logged in to a system remotely, the Page Up and Page Down keys might not work correctly. In this case, the CTRL key substitutes should work.

You can also bring up a menu window by pressing the Esc key. This will bring up a window such as the one in Figure 16.2

16

FIGURE 16.2

The ee menu window.

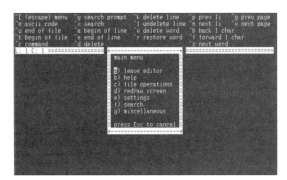

To navigate the menu, you can either press the letter corresponding to the option you want, or you can use the arrow keys to move the cursor over the letter and press the Enter key.

Configuring ee

As we have mentioned before, most FreeBSD configuration is handled by text-based configuration files. ee is no exception. However, ee provides a menu-based interface to most of the configuration options, so you don't have to edit the configuration file directly if you don't want to.

The configuration file is located in your home directory and has the name .ee.init. It will be automatically created for you the first time you customize the settings of ee. Remember that files beginning with a period are hidden in the normal directory listing, so you will not see this file unless you use ls -a.

To access the setup options, you can press Esc to bring up the main menu, and then you can press e to access the settings menu. Figure 16.3 shows what it looks like.

Figure 16.3

The ee configuration settings (modes) menu.

Most of the options can be toggled on or off by pressing the corresponding letter or using the arrow keys to highlight them and then pressing the Enter key. Table 15.2 shows what these options mean.

TABLE 16.2 Configuration Options in *ee*

Option	Action
Tabs to spaces	This option converts tab characters into the equivalent number of normal spaces. This is mostly useful for Python programmers and such where whitespace is used to delimit code blocks.

TABLE 16.2 continued

Option	Action
Case-sensitive search	It's off by default. If you turn it on, only terms that match the case of your search will be returned. For example, searching for "unix" will not find the word "Unix."
Margins observed	It's off by default. This controls whether the editor word wraps. When it is on, the editor will automatically move to a new line when it reaches the value set in the right margin. When off, you will need to press the Enter key anytime you want a new line.
Auto paragraph format	It's off by default. When on, the editor will attempt to automatically reformat the paragraph when you insert text in to the middle of it. This means that it will behave similar to a word processor.
Eightbit characters	It's on by default. It allows extended characters to be displayed. Extended characters are generally foreign characters that cannot be generated from a typical U.S. English keyboard.
Info window	On by default. This causes the top part of the window to display the menu shown in the previous figures. If you turn it off, no menu will be displayed. You should leave this on unless you are very familiar with the various key commands.
Emacs key bindings	On by default. Basically, this means that the ee CTRL key sequences behave like Emacs. If you don't know what Emacs is, don't worry about it. Just leave this option as it is set by default.
Right margin	This is the column number that the right margin is at. By default, it is the width of a standard 80 character text-based terminal. As stated before, this setting is ignored unless the Margins Observed option is changed to yes.
16-bit characters	This controls how 16-bit characters are handled internally. Unless you are working with a Chinese character set or something, you shouldn't have to worry about this option.

The final option allows you to save the editor configuration. When you select this option, you will be asked whether you want to save the editor configuration to the current directory or to your home directory. Saving to your home directory will cause the settings to be the default editor settings. Saving to the current directory will cause these settings to apply only when the editor is started from the directory you are currently in. This will override the default settings that are supplied by the configuration file in your home directory. If no .init.ee file is found in your home directory, the settings from your .init.ee file in your home directory will be used.

The vi Editor

As mentioned previously, the vi editor is one of the earliest editors created for UNIX that is still in use. Virtually all flavors of UNIX come with the vi editor installed by default. Sometimes, vi might be the only editor you have available, so it pays to know at least the basics of how to use vi.

Unfortunately, vi has a reputation for being very difficult to use. For one, virtually all commands in vi are carried out by a series of keystrokes that are not very intuitive. So why is vi so popular? The main reason is that it is very powerful once you have learned the various keystrokes. It can also be very fast because the commands are set up so that the most commonly used ones can be accessed without your fingers having to leave the home row of keys.

The vi editor can be started by typing **vi** followed by the name of a file you want to edit. If the file doesn't already exist, an empty buffer with that filename will be created. You can also start vi with no filename; in which case, it will be opened with an unnamed buffer. Figure 16.4 shows the vi editor opened with a blank file.

FIGURE 16.4

The vi editor window.

The first thing you will notice if you try to type in the editor window is that nothing happens, or it simply beeps at you. This is because vi is currently in *command mode*. You can use either the o, a, or i key to switch vi into text entry mode. Each of these keys performs a slightly different action before entering text entry mode:

Key	Action
o	Opens a new line and then places the cursor at the beginning of the new line to start entering text.
a	Appends text starting after the character the cursor is currently positioned on.
i	Inserts text before the character the cursor is currently positioned on.

In addition, you can use A to begin inserting text at the end of the current line (note the case difference) and O to insert a line above the current line and begin inserting text there.

To get back into command mode, press the Es key.

> To enter any text into the editor, you must be in text entry mode (which can be entered using the o, a, i, O, and A keys as described previously). To enter any commands in vi for tasks such as saving files, you must be in command mode (which can be entered by pressing the Esc key).

16

Navigating in vi

In most cases, you will be able to use the arrow keys to navigate in vi. However, in some cases, the arrow keys may not work when logged in remotely. Of course, you also will not be able to use the arrow keys if you are logged in from a terminal that doesn't have any arrow keys. In this case, you will need to enter command mode (press Escape) and use the following keys to navigate:

Key	Action
h	Moves the cursor left one character.
j	Moves the cursor down one character.
k	Moves the cursor up one character.
l	Moves the cursor right one character.

If you cannot remember which keys move in which direction, the following memory aids might help:

- The h key is the farthest to the left, and it moves the cursor left.
- The j key looks a bit like a downward pointing arrow, and it moves the cursor down.
- The l key is the farthest to the right, and it moves the cursor to the right.
- The k key, which is the only key left, moves the cursor up.

Many more movement keys are available in vi. See the man page for vi for a complete list.

Searching in vi

To search for text in vi, gointo command mode and then press the slash key (/). Directly following the slash (don't press Enter first) enter the string you want to search for and then press Enter. To repeat the same search, simply press the slash key again, but do not follow it with any search string. The n key also has the same effect as pressing the /.

Saving Files and Exiting vi

Table 16.3 shows a list of the commands that can be used to save files and exit vi.

TABLE 16.3 Saving Files in vi and Exiting the Editor

Keys	Action
ZZ	Saves changes to the current file and then exits.
:w	Saves changes to the current file.
:wq	Saves changes to the current file and then exits. Has the same effect as ZZ.
:w!	Saves changes to the current file, overwriting an already existing file of the same name.
:wq!	Saves changes to the current file, overwriting an already existing file of the same name, and then quits.
:q	Exits the editor. If unsaved changes are in the file, vi complains and refuses to quit.
:q!	Forces vi to quit, even if there are unsaved changes.
:e!	Loses any changes that you have made, and reloads the file from disk in its most recently saved state.

Commands that have an exclamation point following them will force the requested action to take place and will not ask for confirmation before carrying out the action. For example, q! will quit vi even if the changes to the file have not been saved, and you will not be asked whether you want to save the changes.

An improved version of vi called vim is available in the ports collection. It adds additional features to vi. Some of the improvements include color syntax highlighting for source code if you are a programmer, the multiple undo levels, and so on.

Email Applications

Several text-based email applications are available for FreeBSD. Once again, these applications have some advantages over graphical interface email programs, including the fact that they require very few resources because they do not need a window system, and they can be run remotely from any terminal emulation program that has some kind of access to the FreeBSD system.

The Pine email client was originally written by the University of Washington as an easy to use email program for new users. Pine is a recursive acronym that stands for *Pine Is Not Elm*—Elm being an older mail client that was one of the first menu driven email clients for UNIX, but was not a shining example of user friendliness. Pine remains one of the easiest and most user-friendly email programs available for UNIX, and it is available in the FreeBSD ports collection for you to install.

To start pine, simply type **pine** and press Enter. Figure 16.5 shows the pine main menu.

FIGURE **16.5**

The main menu of the Pine email program.

When you first start Pine, you will be in your inbox. Note the status line across the top. The right side of the line tells you what folder you are currently in as well as how many messages are in it. Menu options can be selected either by pressing the letter corresponding to the menu entry you would like, or by using the up and down arrow keys to highlight the entry you want and then pressing Enter. Note that options on the menu at the bottom of the screen can only be selected by pressing the highlighted letter on your keyboard. You can't use the arrow keys to select items from this menu.

Pine's menu options are fairly self-explanatory. One thing to note is that as in the ee editor, menu options beginning with the caret symbol (^) indicate that to access that option, you hold down the CTRL key and press the letter that follows the caret. For example, from within the Compose Message screen, you use Ctrl+x to send the message you are currently editing.

Pine is one of the easiest email programs to use, and because of this, it is one of the most popular. It is, unfortunately, plagued by a history of potential security problems. Although all the known security issues with Pine have been fixed as of this writing, many security experts believe there are likely many more security problems that have not yet been found. FreeBSD will likely warn you of this when you install the Pine port. Because of these potential security issues with Pine, it is important that you keep up with the latest versions of Pine. If security is a serious concern, you might want to look into the `mutt` client, available in the `mail` category of the ports collection. `mutt` is much more secure, and also quite powerful. However, `mutt` is not nearly as easy to use as Pine, so your users might form a mutiny if you take Pine away from them and force them to use `mutt`.

The message editor that comes with Pine is called `pico`, and can be used as a standalone editor. In the tradition of Pine, the Pico editor is one of the easiest text based editors available for FreeBSD. To use Pico, you must, of course, have Pine installed. Once Pine is installed, you can access the Pico editor by simply typing **pico** followed by the name of the file you want to edit. (Or type `pico` by itself to open a blank buffer with no filename.)

The Lynx Web Browser

Lynx is a text-based Web browser for FreeBSD and other versions of UNIX. Of course, a text-based browser comes with the limitation of not being able to display inline graphics, and so on. Still, Lynx can be a fast way to browse the Web, especially on a slow connection because Lynx won't load any graphics. Lynx is available in FreeBSD ports collection. Figure 16.6 shows the Lynx Web browser with the FreeBSD home page loaded.

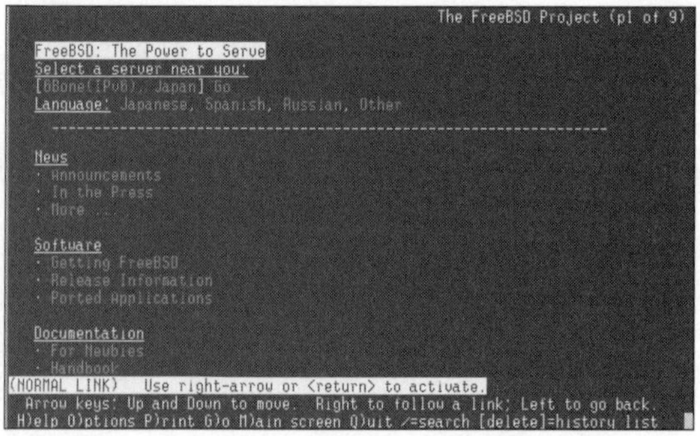

FIGURE 16.6

The Lynx Web browser displaying the FreeBSD home page.

To start the Lynx browser, type **lynx** at the command prompt, optionally followed by the address of a Web site that you want to load. (The Lynx home page will be loaded if you don't specify an address). You can navigate in Lynx by using the arrow keys to move between links. When a link you want to follow is highlighted, press the Enter key or the right arrow key to select the link. The left arrow key moves backward to previous pages that were visited. To enter a new address to visit, use the g key and type the new address. To quit, press q.

Unfortunately, it is becoming more and more difficult to use text-based browsers such as Lynx on the Web. Some of this has to do with the fact that Lynx doesn't support frames or JavaScript, and so on, but a lot of it also has to do with poor site design practices on the part of Web designers (not using proper markup tags, and so on).

16

Summary

In this hour, you learned how to work with some common FreeBSD command-line applications including text editors, email clients, and Web browsers. Note that all these programs have far more options available than we have the space to cover here. For more information on the various options available for the various programs, see their manual pages.

Q&A

Q Aren't these programs old and outdated? After all, in Windows and Macintosh, everything has a graphical user interface. Why would I want to use these programs?

A There are several reasons. One is that these applications can run almost anywhere, and can run on very cheap hardware. For example, if you are just setting up an email server, you can spend $10 on a used small monitor instead of $200 on an expensive monitor that can do fancy graphics. Also, these applications can be run remotely from any computer that supports a terminal emulator, including Windows, Macintosh, another version of UNIX, or even a dumb terminal that is not a computer at all. The applications also work reasonably well even over slow network connections because there are not large graphics and complex user interface features to transfer.

Q Why should I learn vi since its commands seem so arcane?

A There are a couple of good reasons for learning vi. One reason is that it is pretty much a universal editor that will be found on all UNIX systems and often might be the only editor available. Because of this, basic knowledge of vi can get you out of a bind if you ever need a text editor on a UNIX system in which nothing else is available. Another reason for learning vi is that it is a very powerful and quick editor. After you have learned the various keystrokes, they become second nature. Not having to take your hands off the keyboard to use a mouse can greatly enhance productivity. Many people who initially start out hating vi learn to greatly appreciate its power after having worked with it for a while, so give it shot.

Q Are there other editors available besides the ones you mentioned here?

A Yes. To see what is available, look through the Editors category in the ports collection. In particular, you might be interested in the emacs editor. Emacs is very powerful, but also very complex, so it is beyond the scope of this book.

Workshop

The following exercises are intended to help you become more comfortable with the various programs we talked about in this hour, as well as help you to become more comfortable about finding additional information on your own.

Quiz

1. The command for entering command mode in vi is

    A. Control key

    B. Alt key

    C. Escape key

    D. Enter key

2. Which of the following keys can be used to enter text entry mode in vi?

    A. t

    B. p

    C. h

    D. o

3. When in command mode, which of the following key sequences will quickly save and exit vi?

    A. SS

    B. ZZ

    C. zz

    D. ss

4. Which key can follow most `vi` command names to force the action to occur?

    A. *

    B. %

    C. !

    D. &

Quiz Answers

1. The correct answer is C.

2. The correct answer is D.

3. The correct answer is B. Remember that case is important.

4. The correct answer is C.

Exercises

1. Open a new file in the `vi` editor called `test.txt`. Insert some text in to it. Then save the file and exit the editor.

2. You have a file open in `vi`, and you want to cut a line of text and paste it in to a different area of the file. What is the command sequence to do this? (Hint: Use the man page for `vi`).

3. You want to change the default home page of the Lynx Web browser. There is an environment variable that you can set to do this. What is its name? (Hint: Once again, use the man pages to help you answer this exercise).

Exercise Answers

2. Use yy to cut the current line of text; then move to the area you want to paste it in to and use p.

3. The correct environment variable is WWW_HOME.

Hour 17

Configuring the X Window System

The X Window System (X, or X11) provides a graphical user interface for FreeBSD. X works along with a program called a *window manager*, which determines how the windows look, how the mouse buttons behave, what menus are available, how the interface is configured, and so on. Window managers range from very simple managers that provide basic windowing functionality to very complex ones that can either emulate the look and feel of Microsoft Windows or Macintosh or create a completely custom look and feel. Figures 17.1 and 17.2 show two of the available Window managers for FreeBSD.

Hour 18, "The KDE Desktop Environment," will cover KDE in detail, and Hour 19, "Window Managers and Desktop Environments," will cover the various window managers available, as well as some of the differences between a window manager and a desktop environment. This hour covers how to configure the X Window System in general.

In this hour, you will learn:

- What X is
- How to configure X using the `xf86config` program

FIGURE 17.1

The twm *window manager is one of the oldest window managers for X. It provides basic windowing functionality.*

FIGURE 17.2

The KDE window manager (part of the KDE desktop environment) provides a very user-friendly interface that rivals Windows and Macintosh in ease of use and features.

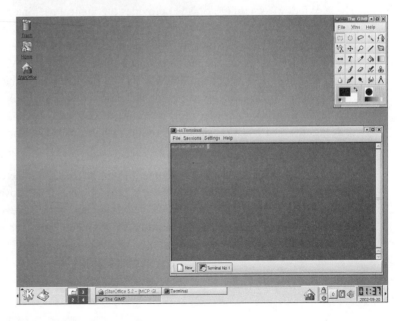

More About X

X is an accepted standard for a UNIX windowing system. Several distributions of X are available. The one included with FreeBSD is called XFree86, which is a freely available version of X intended for x86 (Intel and compatible) computers. The XFree86 project is developed by volunteers, and the programming source code for the system is available to those who want it. XFree86 runs on most UNIX operating systems including FreeBSD, Linux, Solaris, AIX, and so on. In addition, it runs on some non-UNIX systems such as OS/2. Some work has been done on a Microsoft Windows port of XFree86.

> Although the 86 in XFree86 stands for the x86 hardware architecture, and this is what it was originally designed to run on, XFree86 has since been ported to several other platforms including the PowerPC platform (Mac OS X, AIX), and the Sparc platform (Solaris).

17

Some technical things are important to note here. First of all, X and XFree86 only provide a windowing framework for UNIX. They do not provide any functionality. Figure 16.3 shows the X Window system running by itself.

FIGURE 17.3

The X Window System running by itself. Notice that the windows have no frames, no control buttons, and so on. In addition, they cannot be moved around.

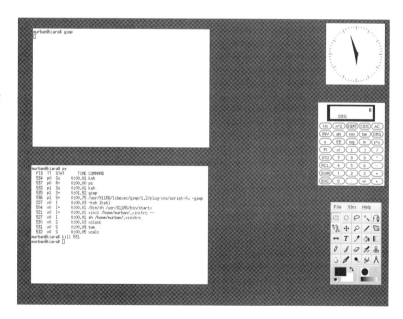

As you can see from the figure, X is not very useful by itself. To have a windowing system that is actually useful, a program called a *window manager* must be used along with

X. Figure 17.4 shows the same applications as Figure 17.3 does; this time they are running with KDE (which we will talk about more in Hour 18).

FIGURE 17.4

FIGURE 17.4

X running with KDE. The windows now have borders, control buttons, and can be moved around. There is also a menu at the bottom of the screen.

Although it is important to know about the basic differences between X and the window manager, you usually don't need to worry about them because they are transparent except when you are making configuration changes. On a general level, you can think of X as providing FreeBSD with a similar functionality to that of Microsoft Windows.

Configuring X

Before you can use X (and before you need to worry about window managers), you need to configure it for use with your system. Configuring X involves telling the system about such things as what kind of video card your computer has, what kind of monitor it has, what resolution you want to use on your monitor, and the maximum number of colors you want to use.

Most XFree86 configuration is controlled by the file /etc/X11/XF86Config. As with most configuration in FreeBSD, this file is a human readable plain text file that can be edited by hand. However, there is also a configuration program called xf86config that

will ask you a series of questions and then automatically generate the
/etc/X11/XF86Config file for you based on your responses.

> Remember that FreeBSD is case sensitive. Thus, xf86config and XF86Config
> are not the same thing. Be careful not to confuse the two. xf86config is the
> program you run to assist you with configuring X Windows. XF86Config is
> the actual configuration file that controls how X behaves.

Required Information

Before you run xf86config, you will need to gather the following information:

- What type of video card you have
- The amount of video memory it has
- The maximum refresh rates that your monitor can support
- What kind of mouse you have (USB, PS/2, and so on)

Information on the video card, and sometimes also on the refresh rate your monitor is
using, can often be obtained from the Windows control panel. Your monitor's manual
should also contain information on refresh rates.

You should also be able to obtain information on the type of mouse your system has
from the Windows control panel. However, here are some other pointers on determining
which type of mouse you have (examples are shown in Figure 17.5):

- If your mouse has a small, round connector, it is probably a PS/2 mouse.
- If your mouse has a flat, rectangular connector, it is probably a USB mouse.
- If your mouse has a large D-shaped connector with nine holes in it, it is a serial
  mouse.

> It's very important that you pay close attention to the maximum refresh
> rates that your monitor can support. There is a small chance that if you use
> values your monitor cannot support, you could actually damage your moni-
> tor. Most monitors have a built-in protection circuit that causes it to shut
> itself down if it receives a refresh rate higher than it can handle. Some older
> monitors won't do this, however.

FIGURE **17.5**

Common types of mouse connectors.

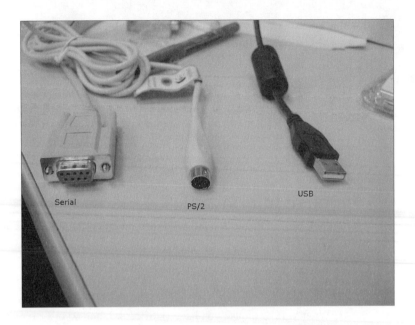

Chances are you have a PS/2 mouse or a USB mouse. Serial mice are becoming more and more obsolete these days.

Using xf86config

To use the xf86config program, you must be logged in as root. Once you have become root, simply type **xf86config** at the command prompt to start the program. You will be given a short message explaining what the program does and asked to press Enter to continue, or Ctrl+C to abort. Go ahead and press Enter. Your screen will then look something like the following:

```
First specify a mouse protocol type. Choose one from the following list:

 1.  Microsoft compatible (2-button protocol)
 2.  Mouse Systems (3-button protocol)
 3.  Bus Mouse
 4.  PS/2 Mouse
 5.  Logitech Mouse (serial, old type, Logitech protocol)
 6.  Logitech MouseMan (Microsoft compatible)
 7.  MM Series
 8.  MM HitTablet
 9.  Microsoft IntelliMouse
```

```
If you have a two-button mouse, it is most likely of type 1, and if you have
a three-button mouse, it can probably support both protocol 1 and 2. There are
two main varieties of the latter type: mice with a switch to select the
protocol, and mice that default to 1 and require a button to be held at
boot-time to select protocol 2. Some mice can be convinced to do 2 by sending
a special sequence to the serial port (see the ClearDTR/ClearRTS options).
```

```
Enter a protocol number:
```

Here, you are simply being asked what kind of mouse you have. Note that if you have a
Microsoft mouse with a PS/2 connector on it, you should select the PS/2 mouse option
and not the Microsoft option. The Microsoft options are only for Microsoft serial mice.
The same also applies for the Logitech mice. If you have a PS/2 mouse from Logitech,
select the PS/2 mouse option. The rule to remember is that you should select PS/2 if you
have a PS/2-style mouse of any brand; all PS/2 mice are more or less the same, and you
only need to worry about the specific manufacturer-named drivers for older, more proprietary kinds of mice.

For laptops that have built-in pointing devices (track points, track pads, and so on), these
almost always have PS/2 as well.

You will then be asked the following question:

```
If your mouse has only two buttons, it is recommended that you enable
Emulate3Buttons.
```

```
Please answer the following question with either 'y' or 'n'.
Do you want to enable Emulate3Buttons?
```

Unlike Microsoft Windows, which tends to make use of only the left and right mouse
button, X makes use of all three. (The middle button is generally used to paste text that
has been copied to the clipboard.) If you only have a two-button mouse, X can emulate a
three-button mouse by clicking both the left and right buttons at the same time. In practice, this often doesn't work very well, so you might simply want to purchase a three-
button mouse. Simply answer y here if you have a two-button mouse, and n if you have a
three-button mouse.

```
Now give the full device name that the mouse is connected to, for example
/dev/tty00. Just pressing enter will use the default, /dev/mouse.
```

```
Mouse device:
```

Here, you need to specify which device your mouse is on. If you have a PS/2 mouse, the
device will almost always be /dev/psm0. The suggested default of /dev/mouse only
works if you have created a symbolic link to the actual device that your mouse is on. If
you haven't done this, you will need to specify the actual device that your mouse is on.

17

For serial mice using the COM1 or COM2 port, use `/dev/cuaa0` or `/dev/cuaa1`, respectively. A USB mouse will be `/dev/ums0`.

```
Please select one of the following keyboard types that is the better
description of your keyboard. If nothing really matches,
choose 1 (Generic 101-key PC)

 1  Generic 101-key PC
 2  Generic 102-key (Intl) PC
 3  Generic 104-key PC
 4  Generic 105-key (Intl) PC
 5  Dell 101-key PC
 6  Everex STEPnote
 7  Keytronic FlexPro
 8  Microsoft Natural
 9  Northgate OmniKey 101
10  Winbook Model XP5
11  Japanese 106-key
12  PC-98xx Series
13  Brazilian ABNT2

Enter a number to choose the keyboard.
```

Here you need to select the type of keyboard that you have. For most modern systems, you will want to select `Generic 104-key PC`. If your keyboard doesn't have the Windows buttons, located next to the Alt keys, you might only have a 101 key keyboard; in which case, you should select this option instead. Note that special options exist for ergonomic keyboards such as the Microsoft Natural Keyboard. PC-98 is a Japanese standard that is not used in the United States.

```
 1  U.S. English
 2  U.S. English w/ISO9995-3
 3  Belgian
 4  Bulgarian
 5  Canadian
 6  Czechoslovakian
 7  German
 8  Swiss German
 9  Danish
10  Spanish
11  Finnish
12  French
13  Swiss French
14  United Kingdom
15  Hungarian
16  Italian
17  Japanese
18  Norwegian

Enter a number to choose the country.
Press enter for the next page
```

Choose the country layout for your keyboard here. There are more entries than will fit on one screen, so you can press Enter to see more of them. When you have reached the end of the list, pressing Enter again will cycle back to the beginning of the list.

The next question asks you to enter a variant name for the layout. Simply press Enter here to accept the default.

```
Please answer the following question with either 'y' or 'n'.
Do you want to select additional XKB options (group switcher,

group indicator, etc.)?
```

Unless you are familiar with X and UNIX programs, you will probably want to select n here. If you select y, you will be given the opportunity to remap certain keys on your keyboard and perform various other advanced setup operations. For example, if you are an Emacs guru, you might want to swap the Caps Lock key and the Ctrl key. (Emacs uses the Ctrl key a lot, and many people find that the Caps Lock position is more convenient.)

The next message you get will inform you that you are moving to the monitor configuration section of the program. Press Enter to continue on to the next question.

```
You must indicate the horizontal sync range of your monitor. You can either
select one of the predefined ranges below that correspond to industry-
standard monitor types, or give a specific range.

It is VERY IMPORTANT that you do not specify a monitor type with a horizontal
sync range that is beyond the capabilities of your monitor. If in doubt,
choose a conservative setting.

    hsync in kHz; monitor type with characteristic modes
 1  31.5; Standard VGA, 640x480 @ 60 Hz
 2  31.5 - 35.1; Super VGA, 800x600 @ 56 Hz
 3  31.5, 35.5; 8514 Compatible, 1024x768 @ 87 Hz interlaced (no 800x600)
 4  31.5, 35.15, 35.5; Super VGA, 1024x768 @ 87 Hz interlaced, 800x600 @ 56 Hz
 5  31.5 - 37.9; Extended Super VGA, 800x600 @ 60 Hz, 640x480 @ 72 Hz
 6  31.5 - 48.5; Non-Interlaced SVGA, 1024x768 @ 60 Hz, 800x600 @ 72 Hz
 7  31.5 - 57.0; High Frequency SVGA, 1024x768 @ 70 Hz
 8  31.5 - 64.3; Monitor that can do 1280x1024 @ 60 Hz
 9  31.5 - 79.0; Monitor that can do 1280x1024 @ 74 Hz
10  31.5 - 82.0; Monitor that can do 1280x1024 @ 76 Hz
11  Enter your own horizontal sync range

Enter your choice (1-11):
```

This question is where the refresh rates discussed at the beginning of the hour come in. Once again, you can probably get this information from your monitor manual.

The options given to you are pretty generic and probably won't take full advantage of your monitor's capabilities. If you know that your monitor can display the listed resolutions at higher refresh rates than those listed, you will probably want to choose the option that allows you to specify your own horizontal sync range. If you do, you will be asked to input your monitor's horizontal and vertical sync ranges:

```
Please enter the horizontal sync range of your monitor, in the format used
in the table of monitor types above. You can either specify one or more
continuous ranges (e.g. 15-25, 30-50), or one or more fixed sync frequencies.

Horizontal sync range:
```

Make sure that you enter the horizontal sync range here and not the vertical sync range. After entering the horizontal sync range, you will be asked about the vertical sync range:

```
You must indicate the vertical sync range of your monitor. You can either
select one of the predefined ranges below that correspond to industry-
standard monitor types, or give a specific range. For interlaced modes,
the number that counts is the high one (e.g. 87 Hz rather than 43 Hz).

1   50-70
2   50-90
3   50-100
4   40-150
5   Enter your own vertical sync range

Enter your choice:
```

If one of the ranges given matches the range of your monitor, select that one. If not, select the last option and then enter the ranges manually.

You will then be asked to provide an identification/description string. Just press Enter here and accept the default.

The monitor configuration is now complete, and you must configure the video card. You will be given a message about this and also be asked the question about whether you want to look at the card database. Select y here, and you will be given a list like the following:

```
0   2 the Max MAXColor S3 Trio64V+            S3 Trio64V+
 1  2-the-Max MAXColor 6000                   ET6000
 2  3DLabs Oxygen GMX                         PERMEDIA 2
 3  928Movie                                  S3 928
 4  AGX (generic)                             AGX-014/15/16
 5  ALG-5434(E)                               CL-GD5434
 6  AOpen PA2010                              Voodo Banshee
 7  ASUS 3Dexplorer                           RIVA128
 8  ASUS PCI-AV264CT                          ati
 9  ASUS PCI-V264CT                           ati
10  ASUS Video Magic PCI V864                 S3 864
11  ASUS Video Magic PCI VT64                 S3 Trio64
12  AT25                                      Alliance AT3D
```

```
13   AT3D                                          Alliance AT3D
14   ATI 3D Pro Turbo                              ati
15   ATI 3D Pro Turbo PC2TV                        ati
16   ATI 3D Xpression                              ati
17   ATI 3D Xpression+                             ati

Enter a number to choose the corresponding card definition.
Press enter for the next page, q to continue configuration.
```

Far too many cards are in the database to fit on one screen, so press Enter to scroll through the list. When you find your card, enter the card number and then press Enter to continue.

> If you can't find your card in the list, all is not lost. See if you can find out from the manual or manufacturer what chipset your card uses. The chipset, which defines the internal workings of the video card, and with which FreeBSD must communicate, is often developed by a certain company (for instance, ATI or Nvidia) and licensed to other video card manufacturers. If you can determine the maker of the chipset, you might be able to use a similar card that has that same chipset, even if your card doesn't appear in the list. For example, many generic video cards use the S3 chipset.

17

After you have selected a card definition, you will be given some information about the card and asked to press Enter to continue. Go ahead and press Enter, and you will then be asked about how much memory your video card has.

```
How much video memory do you have on your video card:

1   256K
2   512K
3   1024K
4   2048K
5   4096K
6   Other

Enter your choice:
```

Almost all modern video cards have more than 4,096KB of memory, so chances are that you will want to select the Other option from this list and manually enter the amount of video memory you have.

It is important to note that you need to enter the amount of memory in kilobytes and also that computers deal with binary numbers. (Binary numbers are base-2 numbers instead of base-10 numbers.) In binary arithmetic, 1 megabyte is not exactly 1,000 kilobytes. It is actually 1,024 kilobytes. Thus, 2 megabytes is 2,048, 4 megabytes is 4,096, and so on. So, for example, if your video card has 32 megabytes of memory, the number you actually want to enter here is 32,768 (32M * (1024K/M) = 32768K).

Once again, you will be asked to enter a definition/identification string. I suggest that you just leave it blank and accept the default.

After this has been completed, you will need to configure the video modes that you want your card to use. This will look like the following:

```
For each depth, a list of modes (resolutions) is defined. The default
resolution that the server will start-up with will be the first listed
mode that can be supported by the monitor and card.
Currently it is set to:

"640x480" "800x600" "1024x768" "1280x1024" for 8-bit
"640x480" "800x600" "1024x768" "1280x1024" for 16-bit
"640x480" "800x600" "1024x768" "1280x1024" for 24-bit

Modes that cannot be supported due to monitor or clock constraints will
be automatically skipped by the server.

    1   Change the modes for 8-bit (256 colors)
    2   Change the modes for 16-bit (32K/64K colors)
    3   Change the modes for 24-bit (24-bit color)
    4   The modes are OK, continue.

Enter your choice:
```

By default, X will start in 640x480 mode and display only 256 colors. This is less than desirable, so I suggest that you change it unless this is all your monitor and video card can support.

Of course, as a general rule, the more colors you can display, the better off you are. If you can display 24-bit color (and unless you have an ancient video card, you probably can), the first thing that you might want to do here is get rid of the 8-bit and 16-bit modes. To do this for the 8-bit mode, select option number 1 to change the modes for 8-bit. You will then be given a screen like the following:

```
Select modes from the following list:

    1   "640x400"
    2   "640x480"
    3   "800x600"
    4   "1024x768"
    5   "1280x1024"
    6   "320x200"
```

```
7   "320x240"
8   "400x300"
9   "1152x864"
a   "1600x1200"
b   "1800x1400"
c   "512x384"
```

```
Please type the digits corresponding to the modes that you want to select.
For example, 432 selects "1024x768" "800x600" "640x480", with a
default mode of 1024x768.
```

```
Which modes?
```

Simply pressing Enter here, and thus not selecting any resolutions for this color depth, will completely remove this color depth.

You will then be asked if you want a virtual screen that is larger than the physical screen. If you select y here, it means that you will be able to get to other areas of the screen by dragging the mouse pointer off the end of the screen in the direction you want the screen to scroll. This can be very useful if you're accustomed to working with a lot of windows at once; but some might find it annoying because you can't see the entire screen at the same time. Of course, because you completely removed the 8-bit mode, you will want to select n here anyway because you will not be using 8-bit.

After you have answeredthe virtual screen question, you will be taken back to the screen on which you can change the color depths and resolutions. Notice that the 8-bit line is gone. Repeat the previous procedure to get rid of the 16-bit line.

Assuming that you can display 24-bit color, you will probably want to rearrange the resolutions. By default, X Windows will start in 640x480. It's difficult to work with X Windows in a resolution this low. You will probably want 1024x768 or better.

After you have selected 3 to change the modes for 24-bit color, you will be given the following screen:

```
Select modes from the following list:
```

```
1   "640x400"
2   "640x480"
3   "800x600"
4   "1024x768"
5   "1280x1024"
6   "320x200"
7   "320x240"
8   "400x300"
9   "1152x864"
a   "1600x1200"
b   "1800x1400"
c   "512x384"
```

17

```
Please type the digits corresponding to the modes that you want to select.
For example, 432 selects "1024x768" "800x600" "640x480", with a
default mode of 1024x768.

Which modes?
```

If you only want to display 1024x768, you can simply type 4 and press Enter. However, X allows you to cycle through resolutions using a key combination (more on that in a later hour), so you can select multiple resolutions if you think you might ever want to use others. The resolutions are cycled through in the order you list them. So, for example, if you enter 4532 here, the default resolution will be 1024x768. This is what X Windows will start in. However, you will also be able to cycle through these resolutions in the order listed: 1280x1024, 800x600, 640x480. After you have typed the numbers for all of the resolutions you want to cycle through, press Enter. Once again, you will be asked the question about the virtual screen, and I suggest that you select n.

```
Please specify which color depth you want to use by default:

   1   1 bit (monochrome)
   2   4 bits (16 colors)
   3   8 bits (256 colors)
   4   16 bits (65536 colors)
   5   24 bits (16 million colors)

Enter a number to choose the default depth.
```

This question determines which color depth X will start in by default. As a general rule, the more colors you have available, the better, so you will probably want to select the highest color depth that your video card can support here. The only exception to this would be if you have software that requires a certain color depth to run.

```
I am going to write the XF86Config file now. Make sure you don't accidentally
overwrite a previously configured one.

Shall I write it to /etc/X11/XF86Config?
```

You have finished answering all the questions, and the program is now ready to write the configuration file. The option you are given is the default location that XFree86 will look for the configuration file, so I suggest that you type y here. If you type n, you will be given some additional questions about alternative places to write the file. Note that this will overwrite the existing configuration file.

After the configuration file has been written, you will be given a message telling you how to change resolutions in X (only applicable if you selected multiple resolutions), as well as how to exit X if it doesn't start up correctly (Ctrl+Alt+Backspace).

Starting X

When you have exited xf86config and you are back at the command prompt, you are
ready to start X. First of all, log back in under your normal user account, or type **exit** if
you used su to become root. When you are back at your normal user prompt, type the
following command to start X:

startx

Your screen will go blank for a few moments, and pretty soon you should see a check-
ered background with a large X on it. This means that the X Window System is starting
up. After a few more seconds, you should see a screen that looks like Figure 17.6.

FIGURE **17.6**

*The default X environ-
ment running the* twm
window manager.

The first thing you might notice about X is that it looks very ugly. Don't worry about
this. As we mentioned earlier, different window managers can change the look and feel
of X. By default, FreeBSD uses the twm window manager, which is very simple and is
one of the first window mangers created for X. In the next hour, you will learn how to
change the default window manager to something more user friendly and a lot more aes-
thetically pleasing.

If, instead of getting an X screen, your monitor goes blank and stays that way or your
power light starts blinking and the monitor appears to have turned off or gone into suspend mode, it probably means that you selected a refresh rate that is higher than your

monitor can support. Use the Ctrl+Alt+Backspace key combination mentioned earlier to exit X and restart the xf86config program—this time making sure that you enter refresh rates that your monitor can handle.

> If your screen appears garbled or if you hear a high pitched whine coming from your monitor, **immediately** press the Ctrl+Alt+Backspace key combination to kill the X Window System. Either one of these is a sign that your monitor is trying to run a refresh rate that it can't handle. A high pitched whine especially indicates that your monitor is about ready to destroy itself. If you leave it in this state much longer, it might even start smoking.

To exit from X and return to the command prompt, hold down the left mouse button on a blank area of the desktop. A menu will pop up, and one of the options will be Exit. Move the mouse pointer over this option and release the mouse button. X should exit, and you should be returned to the command prompt.

Summary

In this hour, you learned that the X Window System is a system that provides a graphical user interface to FreeBSD similar to that of Windows. You also learned the basic differences between X and a window manager, and learned that they work together to provide you with a working environment that can actually be used productively. You saw that X configuration is handled by the file XF86Config, and that you can use the xf86config program to build this configuration file for you. Finally, you learned how to start X and exit from the default twm window manager.

Q&A

Q Where can I obtain a complete list of the video cards that XFree86 supports?

A An up-to-date list of supported video hardware can be obtained from the XFree86 projects Web site at the following address:

http://www.xfree86.org/current/Status.html

Q What is the difference between X and a window manager?

A X provides a framework for running a graphical user interface on FreeBSD. The window manager runs on top of X and is what provides the actual functionality for the user.

Q What is the difference between a window manager and a desktop environment?

A We will cover this more in Hour 19, but in a nutshell, a desktop environment generally provides more features than a window manager—such as integrated file managers, drag and drop, desktop icons, and often an integrated suite of applications. Window managers, on the other hand, usually just provide basic window management functionality—such as simple menus, the ability to move and resize windows, and controls such as minimize, maximize, and close.

Q What is the difference between `XF86Config` and `xf86config`?

A `XF86Config` is the actual text-based configuration file that controls various attributes of the X Window System, whereas `xf86config` is the program that provides a set of questions for you to answer and helps you build the `XF86Config` file.

Workshop

The following section is designed to test your knowledge of the material covered in this hour with quiz questions, and to provide some exercises for further exploration of the subject of the X Window System.

Quiz

1. What is the name and location of the X main configuration file?

   A. `/etc/XF86Config`

   B. `/etc/xf86config`

   C. `/etc/x11/XF86Config`

   D. None of the above

2. Which program helps you configure X?

   A. `XF86Config`

   B. `Xconfig`

   C. `xf86config`

   D. `startx`

3. The program used to start X is

   A. `xstart`

   B. `xwindows`

   C. `startx`

   D. None of the above

4. Which of the following key combinations can be used to immediately terminate the X session?

    A. Ctrl+Alt+Delete

    B. Ctrl+Alt+Backspace

    C. Ctrl+Alt+End

    D. Ctrl+Alt+Escape

Quiz Answers

1. The correct answer is D. If you said C, remember that FreeBSD is case sensitive. The path should contain X11, not x11.

2. The correct answer is C. Answer A is the name of the configuration program. Answer D is the name of the program used to start X. Answer B does not exist.

3. The correct answer is C.

4. The correct answer is B.

Exercises

1. If you need to make simple changes to your X configuration, it is often easier to edit the XF86Config file by hand instead of going through the entire xf86config question set again. Using the more or less command, browse the /etc/X11/XF86Config file and look at its various sections. Look for lines that correspond to the information you entered in xf86config. Also, browse the man page for XF86Config to become familiar with the basic format and layout of the XF86Config file.

2. Experiment with virtual screens. If you set the virtual screen size to something large, you can play with it for a while and see if you find it useful or annoying. You can always go back and reset the virtual screen setting so that your display doesn't scroll around. Note that certain window managers support "virtual desktops," which are somewhat like virtual screens, but different in that you explicitly select one of as many as eight or nine window layouts that are kept in memory, instead of manually scrolling around one large desktop.

Hour **18**

The K Desktop Environment (KDE)

In the previous hour, you learned how to configure the X Window System to work with your hardware. In this hour, you will learn how to actually work with the X Window System using KDE (the K Desktop Environment).

In this hour, you will learn:

- What a desktop environment is
- How to make KDE your default desktop
- How to navigate in KDE
- About the applets (mini-applications) available in KDE
- How to manage files in KDE
- How to customize your KDE desktop

What Is a Desktop Environment?

A desktop environment can be thought of as a window manager that has some additional features. Whereas a window manager generally provides basic functions such as simple menuing systems, the ability to move and resize windows, and window controls such as minimize, maximize, and close, a desktop environment provides much more. Desktop environments provide additional features such as desktop icons, integrated file management, and a set of miniature applications. In addition, software applications written for the desktop environment tend to integrate well with the desktop, as well as being capable of taking on the configuration options of the desktop (color schemes and so on).

The desktop environment is what has brought the UNIX desktops into the same ballpark of usability as Windows and the Macintosh. With desktop environments such as KDE, users can easily work with FreeBSD, customize their own settings, and so on. It's quite literally a power user's dream. However, meager application availability and a certain tendency for the developers of desktop environments to focus on customizability rather than ease-of-use continues to hamper the UNIX desktop, even with such environments as KDE at our disposal.

Installing KDE

During the installation, you were given the option of installing KDE and making it your default desktop. If you elected to use this option, there is nothing else you have to do. If you didn't, you will need to install KDE first. The latest version of KDE is available as a port in the directory /usr/ports/x11. (At the time of this writing, it is /usr/ports/x11/kde3.) Refer to Hour 6, "Adding and Removing Third Party Software," for information and details on installing software from ports.

 KDE is a very large download. On a 56KB modem connection, it will take several hours. Also, it takes a long time for KDE to build from a source: once again, several hours. Of course, because FreeBSD is a multitasking operating system, you can be working on other tasks while KDE is downloading and building.

Making KDE Your Default Window Manager

If you did not set KDE as your default window manager during the FreeBSD installation, you can do so now (after you have downloaded and installed it, of course). The file that controls your default X options is .xinitrc, which is located in your home directory.

Note that because the filename begins with a period, the file will be "hidden" and not appear in the normal directory listing (unless you use the -a flag for ls). Edit the .xinitrc file in a text editor. If the file doesn't already exist, simply create it by opening a new file in the text editor named .xinitrc. If it does already exist, you might want to make a backup copy before making any changes. For example,

```
cp .xinitrc .xinitrc.back
```

In the original .xinitrc file (not the backup you created), add the following line:

```
startkde
```

Any other lines that exist in this file should be removed.

After you have finished editing the file, save it and exit the text editor.

Starting KDE

When you have exited the text editor, you can start KDE by typing **startx** at the command line. The screen should go blank for a few seconds, and after KDE has finished loading, you should see a screen that looks similar to Figure 18.1.

FIGURE 18.1
The default KDE desktop.

18

Navigating the KDE Desktop

If you have used Windows in the past, it will be fairly easy for you to get used to KDE. Notice some of the similarities. On the desktop, you have a trash can, which serves the same purpose as the Windows recycle bin. There is also a folder on the desktop labeled Home. This is your home directory. Its closest equivalent in Windows is probably the My Documents folder.

Click on the Home folder on the desktop. Note that unlike Windows, you only have to single click. In a few moments, a window should open showing you the contents of your home directory (see Figure 18.2).

FIGURE 18.2

The KDE file manager, showing the home directory of a user.

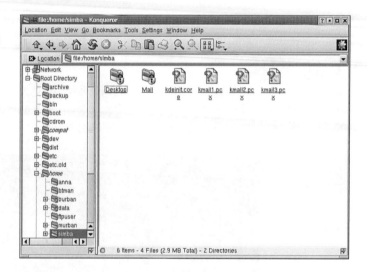

We will cover the details of file management with the KDE file manager later on. For now, click on the X in the upper right corner of the window to close the file manager.

The bar along the bottom of the screen is similar to the Windows taskbar. The large K on the left side is the equivalent of the Windows Start button. Clicking on the K will bring up a menu similar to that shown in Figure 18.3.

Entries in the menu that have an arrow on their right side have sub-menus under them. Simply move the mouse pointer over one of these entries, and the sub-menu will pop up to the right.

FIGURE **18.3**

The KDE Start menu.

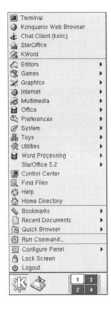

The icon on the bar next to the large K that looks like a desktop with a light over it will instantly show the desktop if you click on it. Any windows currently covering the desktop will be minimized.

Virtual Desktops

Next to that on the bar is the control panel that allows you to select which of the four virtual desktops you want to see. This might be a new concept for Windows users. Virtual desktops allow you to have different sets of windows open on entirely different screens, with each layout suspended in memory; you can quickly switch between as many as six or nine different window layouts by clicking on one of the virtual desktop icons. This concept differs from "virtual screens" (which you saw in the last hour's lesson) in that these are discrete window layouts, each of which uses the full screen and no more; whereas the "virtual screen" concept in X involves a single large screen that's "larger" than your monitor, which you navigate by scrolling.

If you want a certain window to be visible on all the virtual desktops, you can "pin" it to the desktop using the little icon on the left side of the window's title bar that looks like a bulletin board pin. The pinned window will not be visible on all the virtual desktops. If you want to move a window from one virtual desktop to a different one, pin it to the desktop, click on the virtual desktop that you want to move it to, and then unpin it by clicking on the pin icon again.

18

Window Controls

The window controls in KDE behave very similar to the same controls in Microsoft Windows. Figure 18.4 shows a standard window in KDE.

FIGURE **18.4**

A standard window in KDE: in this case, showing the file manager.

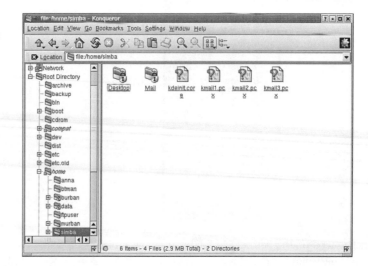

The title bar of the standard window has five buttons. From left to right, they perform the following functions:

- **Window menu**. From this menu, you can access various window functions such as shading the window (rolling it up), moving it to a different virtual desktop, and so on. You can also control various options about how the window looks from this menu.

- **Pin**. We talked about this earlier. Pinning the window to the desktop makes it visible on all the virtual desktops instead of just the current one.

- **Minimize**. This minimizes the window and hides it. The window can be restored by clicking on its entry in the bar at the bottom of the screen.

- **Maximize/restore**. This expands the window to cover the entire screen. If the window is already maximized, the button restores it to its original size.

- **Close**. This button closes the window and terminates any applications that are running in it.

If you want to shade (roll up) the window, you can also do this by double-clicking on the title bar. To unshade it, double-click on the title bar again.

The Window Menu

The Window menu can be accessed in one of two ways. The first way is by clicking on the Window Menu button, as described previously. The second way is by right-clicking on the window's title bar. Both of these methods have the same effect and bring up the same menu. Figure 18.5 shows the Window menu.

FIGURE 18.5

The Window control menu in KDE.

The options in the menu perform the following operations:

- **Move**. Clicking this option causes any mouse movement to move the window. You can also use the arrow keys on the keyboard to move the window. Pressing the mouse button or the Enter key drops the window in the new location.

- **Size**. Clicking this option causes any mouse movement to resize the window. You can also use the arrow keys on the keyboard to resize the window. Pressing the mouse button or the Enter key keeps the new size that you have selected.

- **Minimize**. Minimizes the window to the taskbar.

- **Maximize**. Expands the window to fill the entire screen.

- **Shade**. Rolls up the window

- **Always on Top**. This is a toggle. When active, there is a check mark by it, and the window will always stay on top even when it is not the active window. This means that the active window can be hidden behind this window. Click on it again to deactivate the Always on Top functionality.

- **Store settings**. Simply saves the current settings.

The other options need a little bit more explanation. The Decoration option allows you to select several different schemes for how the window controls look. For example, the B II scheme causes the windows and title bars to closely resemble BeOS (see Figure 18.6).

FIGURE 18.6

A KDE window using
BeOS-like decorations
from the B II *scheme.*

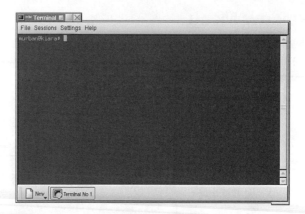

Note that changing the window decorations also changes the functionality of the buttons and possibly the location of the buttons.

The To Desktop option allows you to move the window to a different virtual desktop. As mentioned previously, this can also be accomplished by pinning the window, switching to a different virtual desktop, and then unpinning it there.

Moving and Resizing Windows

As you probably guessed, windows can be moved by holding down the left mouse button on the title bar and dragging the window to a new location, and then releasing the mouse button to drop the window at the new location.

Move the mouse pointer over the border of the window, hold down the left button, and drag the mouse to resize the window. Let go of the button when the window has been resized to where you want it. If you want to be able to resize horizontally and vertically at the same time, hold down the button over one of the window corners. Note also that the mouse pointer looks different when you are over the border of a window and indicates in which directions you can resize the window.

Restoring Windows

As with Microsoft Windows, KDE maintains a taskbar at the bottom of the screen that has a list of windows currently open. (It only lists the window open on the current virtual desktop.) You can restore a minimized window simply by clicking on a taskbar entry. In addition, right-clicking on the taskbar entry brings up a list of other options you can perform on the window, such as moving it to a different virtual desktop, shading or unshading it, and closing it.

The Desktop Menu

Right-clicking on a blank spot on the desktop will bring up a menu with several options (see Figure 18.7).

FIGURE **18.7**

The Desktop menu in KDE can be activated by right-clicking on a blank area of the desktop.

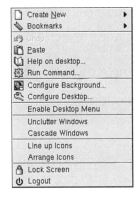

Here is what the options in the menu do:

- **Create new**. This option allows you to create new links on the desktop, which are basically the same thing as shortcuts in Windows. You can also create new directories on the desktop, open a new text file in the text editor for editing, and so on.

- **Bookmarks**. This option provides quick access to your bookmarked Web sites. Bookmarks in Netscape and KDE's built-in Web browser are automatically imported into this menu.

- **Paste**. Pastes a copied item onto the desktop (a file, for example).

- **Help on desktop**. Brings up the KDE help center, which can be browsed like a Web page.

- **Configure background**. Allows you to change the background color or image of the desktop. We will cover more on this later on.

- **Configure desktop**. Allows you to customize various features on the desktop. We will talk more about this later on.

- **Enable desktop menu/Disable desktop menu**. This is a toggle. When enabled, a menu bar is displayed across the top of the desktop that enables you quick access to bookmarks, open windows, help functions, and so on. Clicking this option again turns off the desktop menu.

- **Unclutter windows**. This option attempts to arrange the windows on your desktop in an orderly manner.

18

- **Cascade windows**. Performs the same function as the Microsoft Windows equivalent. It arranges the windows on the desktop in a cascading style.

- **Line up icons**. This option lines up the icons in an orderly fashion. They will be lined up in whatever order they are closest to now.

- **Arrange icons**. This option arranges the icons down the left side of the screen.

- **Lock screen**. This option blanks the screen and locks the desktop. To unlock it, you need to enter your password.

- **Logout**. This option logs you out of the KDE desktop. However, you will still be logged in to FreeBSD.

KDE Applets

Applets are basically miniature applications bundled with KDE. Many of them can be accessed from the Utilities menu off of the K menu. For example, there is a calculator here, as well as an address book. The calculator is pretty self-explanatory, but the address book is a neat little utility that eases the use of KMail, the KDE email program, by integrating contact addresses into it and other KDE applications such as the Konqueror Web browser. We will look at the address book next.

The Address Book

Figure 18.8 shows the KDE address book. The first time you start it, you will be given a couple of messages telling you that it is creating your personal address files and such. You will only see these messages the first time.

FIGURE **18.8**

The KDE address book.

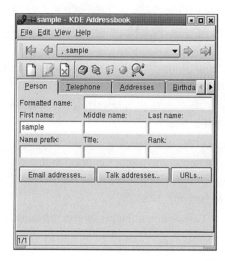

Because no entries are currently in the address book, most of the options are grayed out. To add an entry, you can either click on the first icon in the icon bar that looks like a piece of paper, or you can click on the Edit menu, and then Add Entry.

To search for an entry, click on the magnifying glass icon. This will bring up a search box like the one shown in Figure 18.9.

FIGURE 18.9

Searching for an entry in the KDE address book.

Choose which key you want to search by (last name, first name, and so on.) Then enter the search term in the ...Matches... box. You can use wildcards here if you want to match multiple entries or if you aren't sure of exactly what you are looking for. For example, if you are searching by last name, and you enter **a*** here, all people whose last name begins with a will be matched. If you enter **a????**, all people whose last name begins with a and contains four additional characters after it will be matched.

Note that the address book also allows you to search by *regular expressions*. Regular expressions, also known as *regexps*, are a mechanism for constructing complex, variable-based searches. A full discussion of how regexps work is beyond the scope of this book. However, a brief glance at some of the features of a regexp is shown here:

.	Matches any character
[abc]	Matches any of a, b, or c
[a-z]	Matches any characters in the range a-z
*	Matches any number of consecutive times (including zero)
+	Matches one or more consecutive times
?	Matches either once or not at all
{n}	Matches *n* consecutive times

18

So, for example, the regexp [a-zA-Z0-9]{3} would match any string of three consecutive alphanumeric characters.

Text Editors

If, up to this point, you have been struggling with the command-line text editors like vi and ee, you will be happy to know that now that you have X Windows running, you don't have to anymore. KDE comes with a couple of text editors similar to Notepad in Windows, but with many more features. The two editors available are simply named Text Editor and Advanced Editor. They look almost identical. Figure 18.10 shows the advanced editor.

You will only see these messages the first time.

FIGURE 18.10

The KDE advanced editor.

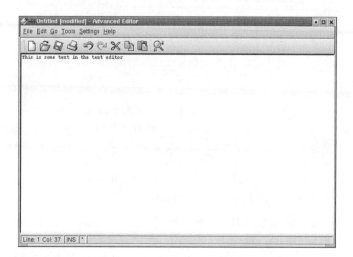

The main difference between the Text Editor and the Advanced Editor is that the Advanced Editor has more flexible searching functionality, as well as the capability to insert comments and indent text. Both editors have the capability to spell-check what you write. The basic features of the editors behave very similarly to most Windows or Macintosh text editing applications you are probably familiar with, so we aren't going to cover them here. Advanced features, such as commenting and paragraph formatting, are beyond the scope of this book.

If you want to use one of the KDE text editors to edit a system configuration file, be aware that you need to be logged in as the root user (either by logging in directly as root, or by logging in as a regular user and using su to gain root capabilities) and have started X Windows as the root user. If you start X while logged in directly as root, you will need to have an .xinitrc file in root's home directory (/root) in order to make KDE the default desktop. You can simply copy the one out of your home directory into root's directory.

Now that we have brought up the subject of text editors, it would be a good time to mention some tips about cutting and pasting text in X. All the KDE applets, and many other applications as well, can cut and paste text as you are used to doing it in Windows. In other words, select the desired text, click Edit, Copy and then move to the application you want to paste the text to and click Edit, Paste. However, not all applications support this. In this case, you can copy text by selecting it while holding down the left mouse button. You can then paste it by clicking the middle mouse button. This works for pasting text into terminal windows, in which you are running a command-line session, for example.

18

File Management in KDE

The KDE file manager looks and behaves very much like the Windows Explorer. To access the file manager, click on the Home folder on your desktop. This will bring up the file manager displaying the contents of your home directory (see Figure 18.11).

FIGURE 18.11

The KDE file manager displaying a home directory.

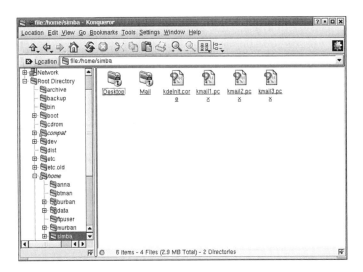

Moving and Copying Files and Folders

To move or copy a file or folder in the KDE file manager, move the mouse pointer over the file or folder you want to move or copy. Hold down the left mouse button and drag it to the location you would like to put it. When you release the mouse button, a menu will pop up asking what you want to do with the file. The options are Move, Copy, and Link. The first two options don't need any explaining: However, the third one might need a little bit. Basically, a Link is a pointer to the actual file. It allows you to access the file from somewhere other than where it is located without actually making a copy of it. You can think of a link as being the same thing as a shortcut in Windows.

If you change your mind and decide that you don't want to do anything with the file, simply click anywhere that is not on the pop-up menu and the operation will be canceled.

You can also move or copy a file or folder by right-clicking on it and then clicking Cut or Copy in the pop-up menu. You can then navigate to where you want to move or copy the file, right-click on a blank area of the file manager, and click Paste.

Deleting Files or Folders

You can delete files or folders in the KDE file manager in four ways. The first is by dragging them to the trash can on the desktop. In this case, as in Windows and Macintosh, they are not really gone until you have emptied the trash. You can empty the trash by right-clicking on the trash can and clicking Empty Trash Bin.

The other three ways that you can delete a file or folder are by right-clicking on the file or folder and then selecting one of the menu options. The three menu options that allow you to delete a file or folder are as follows:

- **Move to Trash**. This option has the same effect as dragging the file to the trash can. Once again, the file is not really gone until you have emptied the trash.

- **Delete**. This option simply deletes the file. It is not moved to the trash bin. In other words, as soon as you have deleted the file, it is gone for good; so make sure that you really want to get rid of the file before selecting this option.

- **Shred**. This option deletes the file, and then writes over the area on the disk where the file was located several times. This basically ensures that the file is extremely difficult to recover—even with special software designed to recover deleted files.

Changing File Attributes

To change the attributes of a file, right-click on it and then select Properties from the pop-up menu. In the box that pops up, click on the Permissions tab, which will bring up a dialog box like the one in Figure 18.12.

FIGURE 18.12

The Permissions dialog box.

All the permissions were covered in Hour 4, "Basic UNIX Shell Use," with the exception of the SetUID and SetGID ones. Basically, if these boxes are checked and this is a binary file that can be executed, it will be run as the user who owns the file no matter who actually runs the file. This also means that it will have all the permissions and access rights of the owner instead of the user who actually ran the file. Unless you fully understand the implications of doing this, you should leave these two options alone.

SetUID and SetGID can be a serious security hole if used improperly because they can allow a user to run programs as another user. There are very few times when this is actually necessary, so you will almost never need to use these options in the Permission dialog box of KDE's file manager.

Searching for Files

Inevitably, you will save a file and then not remember where you put it when you come back for it later. To help you find it, you can select Find Files from the K menu. This will bring up the window shown in Figure 18.13.

In the Named box, simply type in the name of the file that you are looking for. If you don't know the file's whole name, you can use wildcards. For example, my* will find all files beginning with my. By default, the program starts looking in your home directory and also checks all directories under your home directory. You can change the directory that the search starts at by clicking the Browse button. In addition, if you don't want to

look in the directories underneath the starting directory, uncheck the Include
Subdirectories box. If you want to narrow down the search further—for example, you
know you created the file in the last two days—you can use the tabs across the top to
specify advanced search criteria such as a date range.

FIGURE **18.13**

*KDE's Find Files
utility can help you
find lost files.*

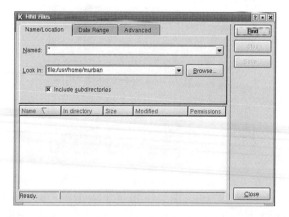

When you are ready to start searching, simply click the Find button. Depending on how
much of the disk you are searching, the find could take some time (especially if you
started at the root directory and told it to search all subdirectories.) A list of files that
match the search criteria will be provided in the box below the Include Subdirectories
button.

Customizing Your KDE Desktop

You can do several things to customize your desktop. The most common such customiza-
tion is a desktop background image; KDE supports this as well as the capability to
rearrange your menu bar or add new icons for commonly-accessed programs. We will
start by looking at how to change the background.

Changing the Desktop Background

To change the desktop background, right-click on a blank area of the desktop and then
select Configure Background from the pop-up menu. This brings up the window shown
in Figure 18.14.

If you want to, you can create different backgrounds for each of the virtual desktops.
Otherwise, you can check the Common Background box so that they will all be the
same.

FIGURE 18.14

Customizing the desktop background.

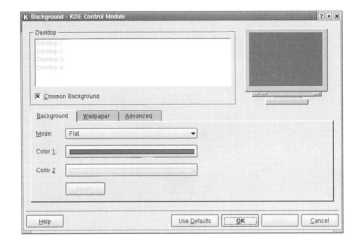

Under Mode, you can select various color gradients, or you can select that you want a pattern on the background. If you select that you want a pattern, the Setup button will become available, and you can select the pattern that you want from there.

Of course, you can also click on the Wallpaper tab to select an image that you want to display on the background. If you choose to display an image on the background, it will, of course, cover any color gradient and such that you have selected.

Adding Desktop Icons

One thing you might want to do is add icons to your desktop to quickly access your most commonly used programs. The easiest way to do this is to simply find the program in the K menu, and then hold down the left mouse button while dragging the entry out to the desktop. When you release the mouse button, you will be asked whether you want to copy, move, or link it. Select the option to link it, and a new shortcut to the program will be created on the desktop.

Customizing the Menu Bar

You can customize the Menu bar at the bottom of the screen by right-clicking a blank area of it and then selecting Settings from the pop-up menu. This will bring up the window shown in Figure 18.15.

Here, you can select such things as the Buttons tab, and then select an option so that the icons on the Menu bar show up with a colored and textured tile behind them.

FIGURE 18.15

Dialog box for customizing the Menu bar.

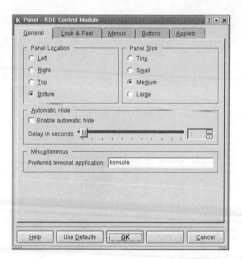

Customizing the Clock

The clock on the Menu bar can be customized by right-clicking on it and selecting Preferences. You can change the type of the clock from analog to digital or *fuzzy*. The fuzzy clock gives you an approximation of what time it is, and the accuracy can be controlled in the preference. Accuracy can range anywhere from "5 to 3," to "Middle of week."

You can also adjust the date and time by right-clicking on the clock and selecting this option from the menu. However, you will be asked for the root password in order to actually be able to set a new date and time.

Summary

In this hour, we took a whirlwind tour of the KDE desktop environment. You learned the basics of how to make KDE your default desktop, and the basics of navigating in KDE. You also learned about some of the KDE applets and about file management in KDE. Finally, we looked at some basic ways of customizing the KDE desktop.

Q&A

Q I thought I was running programs in several windows, but they've all disappeared!

A Check to make sure that they haven't been placed into one of the virtual desktops that you're not currently using. Virtual desktops might be convenient for getting stuff out of the way, but they also do a good job of hiding things you're looking for.

Q Where can I get more KDE tools and applications?

A KDE on FreeBSD is an ongoing project, and as of this writing, it is not quite stable for everyday use in a lot of respects. Check the KDE/FreeBSD Web site at `http://freebsd.kde.org`; it contains news, listings of packages, how-to guides, and most of the information you will need to know in order to get the most out of KDE on FreeBSD. The fact is that most KDE applications are written specifically for Linux, and efforts to port them to FreeBSD are ongoing. The built-in KDE applications that work well—KMail, Konqueror, and so on—are discussed in Hour 20, "Productivity in the X Window System."

Be sure to read the FAQ at the site for helpful tips and guidance as to where the project is going.

Q How can I learn more about the features of KDE?

A You can select the Help option from the K menu, which will bring up KDE's help system. The help system can be browsed like a Web site.

Q I don't like KDE. Are there alternatives?

A Yes, there are several alternatives to KDE. The most well-known and well-developed full-featured desktop environment is GNOME, although there are others with similar scope and maturity. GNOME can be installed in the standard FreeBSD installation program (`sysinstall`), but other less comprehensive window managers must be installed individually from the packages or ports. We will look at some of them in the next hour.

Workshop

In this interactive section, we will deepen your understanding of KDE through quiz questions and some exercises which will point you in the direction of new things to try.

Quiz

1. The file that stores your personal information about X Windows, including the default window manager that you want, is

   A. `.profile`

   B. `.xwindows`

   C. `.xinitrc`

   D. `.xprefrc`

2. Which of the following statements should be placed into the personal X Windows file mentioned in question 1 to start the KDE desktop environment?

   A. `kde`

   B. `kdestart`

   C. `kstart`

   D. `startkde`

3. What option can I use to completely delete a file I want thrown away and that I specifically want to be unrecoverable?

   A. Empty Trash Bin

   B. Delete

   C. Move to Trash

   D. Shred

4. What special character is used in regular expressions to signify "match the preceding character any number of consecutive times"?

   A. `?`

   B. `+`

   C. `*`

   D. `.`

5. Where are KDE applets usually found?

   A. In the K menu

   B. In the Trash Bin

   C. In the taskbar

   D. The last place you look

Quiz Answers

1. The correct answer is C. If answer A rang a bell, it is because it is the personal configuration file for the shell. Answers B and D do not exist.

2. The correct answer is D.

3. The correct answer is D. The others all leave the file's occupied space on the disk untouched, and the file can be recovered with "undelete" utilities.

4. The correct answer is C.

5. The correct answer is A; although D is also true, by definition.

HOUR 19

Window Managers and Desktop Environments

Although KDE is one of the most popular desktop environments available for FreeBSD, it is by no means the only one available. There are several alternatives ranging from the very simple to the very complex. In this hour, we will look briefly at some of these alternatives.

In this hour, you will learn:

- The difference between window managers and desktop environments
- About some of the alternatives available to KDE
- How to install alternative window managers
- How to change your default window manager

The Difference Between Window Managers and Desktop Environments

In the last hour, you learned about and worked with the KDE desktop environment. Desktop environments like KDE usually have more features than bare window managers. For example, KDE comes bundled with several small applications, control panels for changing the background, and so on. In addition, desktop environments often have better integration with applications than window managers. (Applications are often written for specific desktop environments, as you will see in the Hour 20, "Productivity in the X Window System.") In addition, they usually support features such as drag-and-drop, which window managers often don't support.

However, running a bare window manager such as twm on top of X Windows, instead of a full-featured desktop environment, also has its advantages. The primary one is that such window managers are usually much smaller and much less resource intensive then desktop environments. This means that they tend to be faster and take up far less memory while running. This makes them useful on older systems with limited processing power or low memory, as well as lower-end laptops. In addition, it makes them useful on servers in which the graphical interface is rarely used anyway.

Another advantage that window managers have over desktop environments is that they are often simpler to use for the end user, especially if you are setting up a specialized workstation of a particular purpose. With a window manager—such as Blackbox, for example—you can create a simple menu listing only the applications that are relevant to the purpose of the workstation. Thus, the only thing the end user has to worry about is selecting the application that she wants from the menu.

Figure 19.1 shows the KDE desktop environment and Figure 19.2 shows the Blackbox window manager.

One more common thing that advocates of window managers say is that window managers tend to do a better job of staying out of your way and just letting you work.

Now that we have said all this, it should also be noted that the line between window managers and desktop environments has blurred quite a bit these days. Some window managers, such as WindowMaker, have many of the features of desktop environments— dockable applets, integrated applications written specifically for it, and the like. Other window managers, most of which are less full-featured but with certain design aspects that many users find attractive (such as a specific "look and feel" or just the right kind of configurability) are Enlightenment, Qvwm, IceWM, and dozens more, which can all be found in the ports at /usr/ports/x11-wm. Each window manager has a Web site where you can find screenshots and descriptions that you can peruse before deciding to experiment with a new window manager.

FIGURE 19.1

The KDE desktop, which you are familiar with from the previous hour.

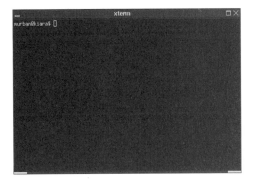

FIGURE 19.2

The Blackbox window manager. Notice that there are no icons as there are in KDE. In addition, the menu bar is gone.

19

Alternative (Non-KDE) Windowing Environments

In this section, we will look at a few of the alternatives available to KDE. Even if you like KDE, I encourage you to give a few of these a try just so you can get a feel for the variety that is out there.

WindowMaker

WindowMaker is a very popular window manager that is available for FreeBSD. It is basically a clone of the desktop designed for the now defunct NextSTEP system. Although NextSTEP itself now survives only as the framework for Apple's Mac OS X, adherents to the design philosophy of the platform in its early conception often find WindowMaker to be an attractive implementation of those design goals. Figure 19.3 shows WindowMaker in action.

FIGURE 19.3

The WindowMaker window manager. The bar on the right is called the dock.

One of WindowMaker's most useful features is the dock located on the right side of the screen. Many miniature applications are available for download that are designed to run in the dock. They range from clocks to calendars to miniature CD players. Four of these dockable applications are shown in Figure 19.3. They are, from top to bottom, a clock with a calendar, a program that displays the phase of the moon, a program that monitors CPU usage, and a program that monitors network traffic. Users of Mac OS X might find the operation of these applications familiar because their functionality resembles that of the Dock in OS X (which is a descendant of the NextSTEP Dock on which the dock in WindowMaker is based). Running applications have an icon in the dock, and applications can be kept there even when not running for quick access at any time.

Like KDE, WindowMaker supports virtual desktops, which can be accessed by clicking the arrows next to the paperclip in the upper-left corner.

Blackbox

Blackbox is a no-frills window manager that is quite popular on servers and also on many people's workstations. Figure 19.2, shown earlier, illustrates the Blackbox window manager.

Blackbox's main selling point is that it requires very few resources, and, as such, it will run well even on slow systems. Blackbox can also run applications created for the Windowmaker dock.

XFCE

XFCE is a desktop environment that is loosely based on the CDE window manager (the standard UNIX desktop for Sun, AIX, and HP). Figure 19.4 shows XFCE.

FIGURE 19.4

The XFCE desktop environment.

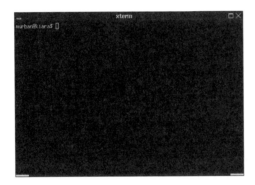

XFCE is based on the GTK toolkit, which is the same toolkit that GNOME is based on. This means that it integrates well with applications that use GTK. (GTK is a popular programming toolkit for designing graphical applications for X Windows.) GTK applications will inherit such things as color preferences from XFCE.

IceWM

IceWM is another window manager with a relatively small footprint. It resembles Windows 95 and OS/2, but is not as easy to configure. It also doesn't support all the features of these two desktops.

One nice thing about IceWM is that it works well with GNOME. We didn't cover GNOME in this book, but as far as full-featured desktop environments go, GNOME is the most significant competitor to KDE. However, unlike KDE, GNOME does not have its own window manager. Instead, it relies on an external window manager that is "GNOME aware". Such window managers include Enlightenment, Sawfish, and

19

Metacity; each of these is available in the ports. However, IceWM is one of the most GNOME-compliant window managers available.

FVWM 95

FVWM 95 is another attempt at cloning the Windows 95 interface. Once again, although the interface looks similar to Windows 95, much of the underlying functionality is missing. For example, no built-in support exists for icons, and the Start menu must be edited by hand from a text file. In addition, the appearances of the windows and such are also controlled from a text configuration file. Figure 19.5 shows the FVWM 95 window manager.

FIGURE 19.5

The FVWM 95 window manager in action.

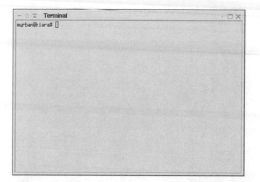

Installing and Configuring Alternative Window Managers

If you've found a window manager in this hour that caught your eye, you can install it from the FreeBSD ports collection. All the window managers and desktop environments covered in this hour are available in the x11-wm directory of the FreeBSD ports tree. See Hour 7 for instructions on installing new software in FreeBSD.

After you have installed the new window manager, you will need to configure it (although most of them can be started in a default state with no configuration first). Each of these window managers has a different method of configuration, so we are not going to go into them here. However, check the Web site for the window manager for more documentation on how to configure the window manager. All of the window managers listed in this hour have Web sites: go to the FreeBSD Web site at www.freebsd.org, click the Ported Applications link, scroll down to x11-wm, and then look for the entry of the window manager you want to try. There will be a link from here to the window manager's home page.

Changing Your Default Window Manager

If you would like to change your default window manager to one of these, you need to edit your .xinitrc file and tell it which window manager you want to use. Here are the window managers talked about in this hour, along with their corresponding entries that you should add to .xinitrc:

Window Manager	.xinitrc Entry
Windowmaker	wmaker
Blackbox	blackbox
XFCE	xfwm
IceWM	icewm
FVWM 95	fvwm95

After you have modified and save the .xinitrc file, the next time you start up X, the new window manager should be active.

Summary

In this hour, we took a brief look at some of the alternative window managers available besides KDE. We looked at the difference between window managers and desktop environments, and saw examples of each. We then looked at how to change the default window manager by editing the .xinitrc file.

Q&A

Q Why are there so many different window managers and desktop environments for me to worry about? Why can't FreeBSD just have one simple, predictable user interface like Windows or the Mac?

A That's a good question. Part of the problem is that by its open-source nature, FreeBSD (and by the same token, Linux) attract many users who each have their own individual, strongly-held beliefs about how computers should work. Many of these users are programmers, and if something doesn't work quite the way someone thinks it should, he will often harness the easy programmability of the X Window System to develop a solution that works for him. Hundreds of these competing ideas, with no single corporate vision guiding them or providing financial incentives to consolidate their efforts, lead to the kind of proliferation of different windowing systems we have before us today.

19

Q Seriously, what's the *best* windowing system available for FreeBSD?

A Unfortunately, that question is hard to answer. KDE is certainly the best developed and most advanced complete desktop environment for Linux, but its implementation on FreeBSD remains spotty. GNOME is more complex to set up and work with than KDE, but its implementation under FreeBSD is more complete and better supported. Unless you're a serious power user, you probably won't want to deal with any of the more bare-bones window managers if you seriously want to make a go of it with FreeBSD on the desktop.

Q Where can I obtain more information on the various window managers and desktop environments available for FreeBSD?

A An excellent Web site is available at `www.xwinman.org` that contains reviews and information of various window managers, along with screenshots of many of them.

Workshop

This section is designed to test your knowledge of the material covered in this hour with quiz questions, and to provide some exercises for further exploration of the subject of the available window managers for FreeBSD.

Quiz

1. The name of the file in which you can change your default window manager is

    A. `.xinitrc`

    B. `.xstart`

    C. `XF86Config`

    D. None of the above

2. The WindowMaker window manager is based on and attempts to embrace the design principles of what computing platform?

    A. Windows 95

    B. Mac OS X

    C. NextSTEP

    D. Windows XP

3. How does FVWM 95 differ from the Windows 95 that it attempts to emulate?

    A. The contents of the Start menu must be edited by hand in order to add new entries

    B. There are no desktop icons built-in

    C. There is no built-in graphical file manager

    D. Changing the appearance of windows requires you to edit a text file

    E. All of the above

4. Where can I find these various window managers if I want to install them and try them out?

    A. `http://www.xwinman.org`

    B. `/usr/ports/x11-wm`

    C. All over the Web

    D. The Packages menu in `sysinstall`

    E. All of the above

Quiz Answers

1. The correct answer is A.

2. The correct answer is C; although if you said B, you'd get partial credit because Mac OS X descends in large part from NextSTEP.

3. The correct answer, which should come as no surprise, is E.

4. The correct answer is E.

Exercises

1. It won't hurt your system to install as many window managers as you would like and to experiment with switching between them to see how you like each one. It's generally a simple matter of changing .xinitrc to reflect which window manager you want before you start up X. You can even switch window managers from within X; a window manager is just a process that runs in the background, handling the window-management tasks that X itself leaves unhandled. From within an X session, try killing the process that represents your current window manager (for instance, `wmaker`); then, from the command line in a terminal window (which cannot be moved around without a window manager running), start up another window manager (for instance, by typing **icewm**). The new window manager should take over your existing windows without a second thought.

2. If you find a window manager that you really like, consider contacting the developer (or the organization that develops it) and giving him some positive feedback. This is a tough world in which to be writing graphical user interfaces, particularly for free; with so many window managers out there, and with Windows and Mac OS X making such strides in comprehensive user experience, it can be a discouraging job. Make sure that they know their efforts are appreciated!

19

Hour **20**

Productivity in the X Window System

Not many people use a computer simply for the sake of using a computer. A computer is only useful if it can help you do your work more efficiently. Fortunately, many applications are available for FreeBSD and X in just about every area imaginable. Also, a great number of very good applications are available free because they are developed by the community.

In this hour, you will learn about:

- Word processors and spreadsheets available for FreeBSD and X
- Graphics applications available
- Internet applications available

Office Software

Of course, one of the staple applications for any workstation operating system is an office package. If you have KDE installed, you already have an

office package, called KOffice, installed on your FreeBSD system. KOffice is a fully featured office package that includes the following features:

- A word processor that also serves as a quite capable desktop publishing program
- A spreadsheet
- A presentation program similar to PowerPoint
- A charting program
- An illustration and drawing program

Starting KOffice

You can start KOffice applications in two ways. The first is by running the KOffice
Workspace program, which is located under the Office sub-menu of the K menu in KDE.
This will bring up a window that looks like Figure 20.1.

FIGURE 20.1

*The KDE Workspace
provides an integrated
environment for
working with the
KOffice applications.*

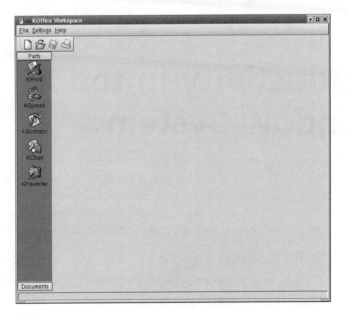

If you click on one of the applications on the left side of the window, it will open within
the window, as shown in Figure 20.2.

If you don't like the Workspace feature, you can also start each of the applications by
themselves so that they run outside of the Workspace. The individual applications can be
accessed from the K menu under the Office sub-menu.

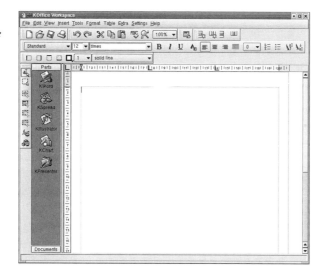

FIGURE 20.2

The KOffice Workspace with the KWord word processor loaded into it. Notice that you can still open the other applications from the menu on the left side.

KWord

KWord is a fully featured word processor that also has powerful desktop publishing functionality. Figure 20.03 shows a screenshot of KWord.

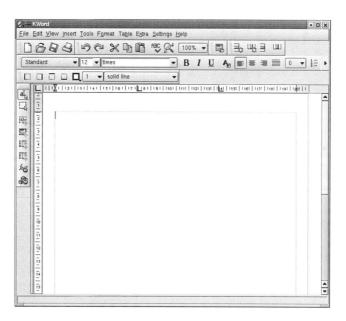

FIGURE 20.3

The KWord word processor.

20

KWord is a frames-based system in the same sense as Adobe Framemaker. For basic word processing, this doesn't really matter to you except that the terminology is a little different. For example, in the Insert menu, instead of saying Insert Page Break to force a new page, it says Hard Frame Break. However, this option performs the same function as inserting a page break in Microsoft Word, for example.

For the most part, KWord uses a standard user interface that is similar to the interface used by Windows and Macintosh word processors. Because of this, it shouldn't take most readers very long to become comfortable with KWord.

> By default, the rulers in all the KOffice applications are in millimeters. You can change this by right-clicking on one of the rulers and then selecting the unit of measure that you want in the pop-up menu.

KSpread

KSpread is a basic spreadsheet program that supports most common trigonometric functions and can also generate basic graphs and charts. Figure 20.4 shows a screenshot of KSpread.

FIGURE 20.4

The KSpread spreadsheet with a chart.

Although KSpread contains a fair number of basic financial functions for calculating such things as nominal interest, its support for statistical functions such as regression testing is very limited. Hopefully the KOffice people will address this problem in the future, but for now, KSpread is pretty much limited to basic number crunching. For a fuller suite of features, you might want to obtain StarOffice from Sun, which contains a spreadsheet application that can interoperate with Microsoft Office files. However, this program is commercial, and until the open-source edition of it (OpenOffice) is fully ported to FreeBSD, you will probably not be able to get it free. Personally, I think it's well worth the asking price.

KPresenter

KPresenter is a PowerPoint-like program that allows you to create slideshow presentations. Figure 20.5 shows KPresenter editing a slide.

FIGURE 20.5

The KPresenter slide program.

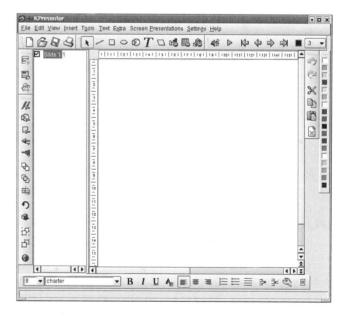

20

 At the time of this writing, KPresenter was extremely buggy and usually didn't display the slide shows correctly. Because of this, I recommend against using KPresenter for any actual presentations at this time. OpenOffice, when it is available, will have a full-featured presentation application that will provide an alternative to KPresenter.

KIllustrator

KIllustrator is a basic drawing program for creating illustrated figures. Figure 20.6 shows the KIllustrator program.

FIGURE 20.6

The KIllustrator program editing a figure.

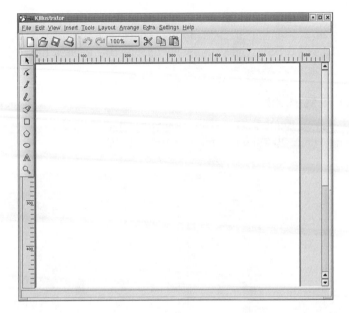

Once again, readers who are familiar with drawing programs should have a fairly easy time adjusting to KIllustrator.

StarOffice

StarOffice, available from Sun Microsystems, is a full-featured desktop productivity suite that offers better integration with Microsoft Office than any of the KOffice applications do. However, as discussed before, StarOffice is commercial software that you must order on CD, buy off the shelf, or download from Sun's Web site (www.sun.com/staroffice). The download file is very large, and you might decide that paying the full fee (about $40) for the CDs in the mail is a bargain for what you get.

StarOffice contains not only full-featured word-processing and spreadsheet applications with almost all the core functionality of Microsoft Office (as well as bi-directional file compatibility), but a desktop browser, an email client, a Web browser, and other tools as well. It has document templates, clip art, and most of the tools you are likely to need in a home or business context.

StarOffice is not technically available for FreeBSD; rather, it's a Linux-native software suite, and it runs under FreeBSD through its Linux compatibility layer. After you have downloaded the StarOffice installer file (`so-6_0-ga-bin-linux-en.bin`), move it into `/usr/ports/distfiles` and then use `cd` to go into `/usr/ports/editors/staroffice60`. After you have done this, you can type **make** and **make install** to install StarOffice into your system with the necessary FreeBSD patches. The installation procedure in the port will ask you a few questions, such as whether you want to do a "network install" or a "local install"; you will probably want to do a network install so you can put the StarOffice binaries into a location where all users can access them.

After this process has been completed, running StarOffice is a matter of typing **soffice** at the command prompt. You will be launched into the StarOffice Desktop, shown in Figure 20.7.

FIGURE 20.7

The StarOffice Desktop. The various icons represent tasks you can run, such as creating a new document of any of various types.

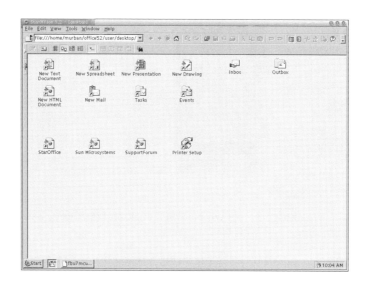

A full tutorial on how to use StarOffice to its full potential can be found in Sams *Teach Yourself StarOffice 5 for Linux in 24 Hours*, or any of the many books on StarOffice that have been written recently. These texts will cover how to use StarOffice for every task you're accustomed to using Microsoft Office for, plus a good deal more.

Image Editing

FreeBSD has a very powerful image editing program available for it, called *The GIMP*— which stands for Gnu Image Manipulation Program. The GIMP is powerful enough for all but the most complex image editing tasks, and it rivals Adobe Photoshop in features. Also, like all the other applications discussed in this hour, GIMP is available free.

Installing and Starting GIMP

GIMP is available in the Graphics directory of the FreeBSD ports tree. See Hour 6, "Adding and Removing Third Party Software," for detailed information on installing software from the FreeBSD ports collection.

After GIMP has been installed, you can start it from within KDE by clicking on K button, Run Command, and in the box that opens, type `gimp`. The first time you run GIMP, it will ask you some setup questions. In general, you can accept the default answers that it provides. Once setup has been completed, the GIMP control panel will be displayed (see Figure 20.8), as well as other dialogs and windows which you can close for now.

FIGURE 20.8

The main control panel in GIMP.

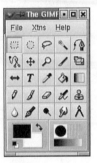

To open an image for editing in GIMP, click on File, Open. This will bring up the dialog box shown in Figure 20.9.

On the left side of the open file dialog box is a list of directories. On the right side is a list of files in the selected directory. Also note that there is a built-in primitive file manager. You can delete and rename files, as well as create a new directory.

After you have loaded an image into GIMP, it will appear in a new window such as the one in Figure 20.10.

As mentioned previously, GIMP's user interface does not follow the norms of most software that you have most likely used. The most important thing to keep in mind when working with GIMP is that the majority of image manipulation functions are not to be found in visible window menus, but instead are accessed by right-clicking on the image window, and then selecting one of the options from the pop-up menu. If you keep this one point in mind, you should be able to adjust to GIMP relatively quickly.

FIGURE 20.9

Opening an image for editing in GIMP.

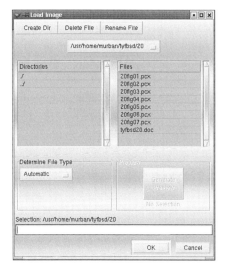

FIGURE 20.10

GIMP with an image loaded into a window for editing.

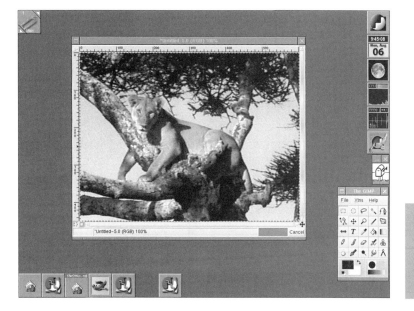

For example, to save a file in GIMP, you right-click on the image you want to save (in its display window), and then select File, Save from the pop-up menu.

Image editing functionality works in a similar fashion. Right-click on an image, and then select Edit to obtain a list of the available editing commands. Selecting Image from the right-click menu gives you options such as changing the image mode, brightness, contrast, and other such functions that apply to the entire image. Use the Dialogs sub-menu to access any of the various floating windows that make up the GIMP user interface, including the toolbox (with its twenty-five selectable image-editing tools) and the GIMP Control Center window, which you can use to open new images and control GIMP's settings.

Internet Applications

The KDE desktop comes with a few Internet applications that are reasonably full featured. The main ones that most people will be interested in are Konqueror, the built-in Web browser, and KMail, the built-in email program.

Konqueror Web Browser

Konqueror is KDE's built-in Web browser. It behaves very much like Microsoft Internet Explorer or Netscape Navigator. Figure 20.11 shows the Konqueror Web browser.

FIGURE 20.11
The Konqueror Web browser.

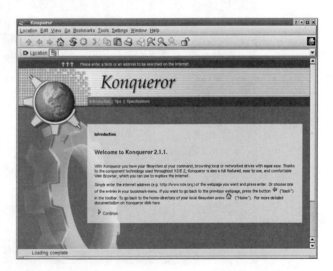

The one non-standard menu item in the Menu bar is Location. However, it really serves the same function as the File menu you are used to in Internet Explorer and Netscape. From the Location menu, you can open a new Web site, save the Web page to a file, and so on.

Note that Konqueror does not have any built-in Java support. If you want to be able to run Java applets in Konqueror, you will need to have the Java Runtime Environment installed. This is also available in the ports tree under the Java directory, /usr/ports/java/jdk13. Refer back to Hour 7 for details on how to install software from the ports or packages.

Much of the Web assumes that you will be using either Internet Explorer or Netscape for your browsing; indeed, these days you're lucky to find sites that explicitly take Netscape into account. Konqueror does a good job of emulating both browsers, and it can masquerade as either one for the purpose of getting into sites that require one of the "accepted" browsers. However, Konqueror doesn't have all the features of the mainstream browsers, and it won't be up to all tasks.

Fortunately, Mozilla—the open-source descendant of Netscape Navigator—is available for FreeBSD and can take you places where Konqueror can't. You can install Mozilla from the ports (/usr/ports/www/mozilla) or packages; type **mozilla** at the command line to launch it within KDE after it's installed.

KMail

KMail is KDE's built-in email client. Figure 20.12 shows its main screen.

FIGURE 20.12

The main screen of the KDE mail client KMail.

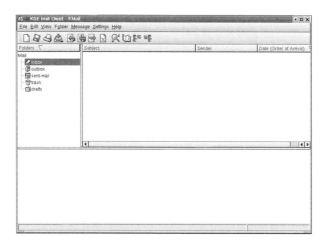

20

Before you can use it, of course, you need to tell KMail about your email account. To do this, click on Settings, Configuration. This will bring up the dialog box shown in Figure 20.13.

FIGURE 20.13

Configuring your email account information in KMail.

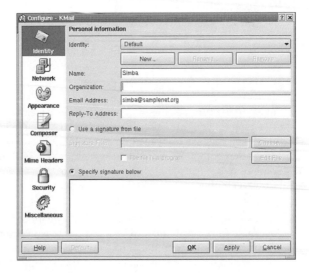

In this screen, simply enter your email address, your name, and any signature information that you want to append on the end of your email.

Next, you need to tell KMail about your mail servers. To do this, click on the Network icon on the left side of the configuration dialog box. This will bring up the dialog box in Figure 20.14.

FIGURE 20.14

Configuring out going email server information.

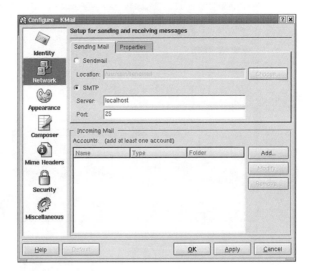

Unless you access your mail spool file directly (if you don't know, you probably don't), you will want to select the SMTP option, and then enter the address of your outgoing mail server. If you don't know what your outgoing mail server is, ask your ISP or system administrator. Unless you are specifically told otherwise, you should leave the port set to 25.

Now that you have configured the server that you send mail through, you must configure at least one incoming server—that is, a server you receive mail from. To do this, click the Add button in the Incoming Mail section of the dialog box. This will bring up the dialog box in Figure 20.15.

FIGURE 20.15

Adding an incoming mail server.

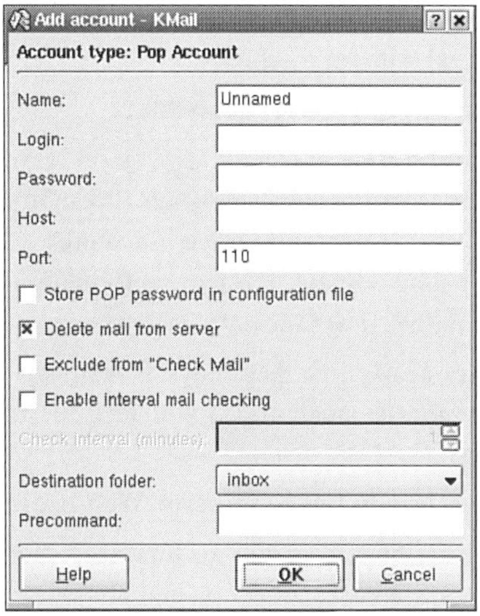

Here, you need to specify the name of the incoming mail server, as well as your login name and password for getting mail from the server. If you check the box that says Store POP Password in Configuration File, you will not be asked for the password each time you start KMail.

When you are done making configuration changes, click OK on the dialog boxes until you are back at the main KDE window.

20

Summary

In this hour, you looked at some of the basic productivity applications available for FreeBSD and the KDE desktop environment. You learned about the various office applications bundled with KDE's KOffice and about the GIMP image editing program. Finally, we closed the hour with a look at two popular Internet applications for browsing the Web and reading and sending email.

Q&A

Q Are the files created by KOffice applications compatible with Microsoft Office files?

A No. KWord can read documents created by most versions of Microsoft Word, but KWord's saved files cannot be read directly by Microsoft Word. One way to get around this is to save your KWord documents in HTML format, which Microsoft Word can generally read without trouble.

Q Are any free alternatives to KOffice available?

A At the time of this writing, a team is hard at work on porting OpenOffice to FreeBSD, so hopefully it will be available soon. OpenOffice is a fully featured office suite that truly rivals Microsoft Office in features; it's based on StarOffice, but developed in the public domain. For more information on OpenOffice, visit the project's Web site at www.openoffice.org.

StarOffice itself is very nearly free these days as well. All it really costs is time and effort. It's certainly worth the small cost if you need file-format compatibility with Windows applications.

Q Are there any alternatives to the Konqueror Web browser?

A Netscape and Mozilla are both available for FreeBSD. Both of these can be installed from the FreeBSD ports collection and are located in the www directory.

Q Can I run KMail if I'm not using KDE?

A Probably not. KMail is a closely integrated part of the KDE environment, and it shares many libraries with KDE's built-in window manager and applet framework. For instance, the address book utility that KMail uses depends on KDE's structure in order to run properly. If you're using GNOME or a different window manager, you might be best served by the email client found in Netscape Communicator or Mozilla.

Q Where can I learn more about KMail or KOffice?

A Both packages have their own Web sites. KMail is documented at http://kmail.kde.org, and KOffice's site is at http://koffice.kde.org.

Workshop

In this interactive section, we will test your knowledge of the material covered in this hour with quiz questions, as well as present a few exercises for further exploration of productivity under X.

Quiz

1. Where do I get KWord, KSpread, and the rest of KOffice?

   A. They're available in the ports, under `/usr/ports/kde`.

   B. They're installed automatically as part of KDE.

   C. They're available as off-the-shelf software in any computer store.

   D. They're still under development and not available yet.

2. How do I activate menu functions within the GIMP?

   A. Right-click on the object you want to manipulate, and then select from the options that are relevant to that object.

   B. Right-click anywhere on the screen, and the menus will appear.

   C. Double-click on a picture, and contextual menus will drop down from the mouse pointer.

   D. Type `menu` while the program is in the foreground to activate the floating menu toolbar.

3. How do you run KWord?

   A. Type `kword` at the command line.

   B. Double-click on a KWord document in the file browser or on the desktop.

   C. Open the KOffice Workspace from the K menu, and then select KWord from the set of icons on the left.

   D. Either B or C.

4. How do you run the GIMP?

   A. Type `gimp` at the command line.

   B. Double-click on an image file in the file browser on the desktop.

   C. Add the GIMP application to your K menu or the taskbar, and then double-click on it there.

   D. Any of the above.

20

5. Which of the applications discussed in this hour are available for Windows as well as for FreeBSD and Linux?

   A. The GIMP

   B. Konqueror

   C. KMail

   D. KOffice

   E. Mozilla

Quiz Answers

1. The correct answer is B.

2. The correct answer is A.

3. The correct answer is D.

4. The correct answer is D, though "very carefully" would also have been an acceptable answer.

5. The correct answers are A and E.

Exercises

1. KMail is very configurable. Try setting it up for secure IMAP operation using SSL/TLS—if your mail server supports it.

2. It's a sad fact that aside from StarOffice, not many applications exist for FreeBSD or the open-source community in general that can interoperate bidirectionally with Microsoft Office. However, many clever workarounds exist as possibilities. We have already discussed using HTML as a middle-man format for exporting word-processing files from KOffice to Word. See if you can come up with others. Remember, you can peruse the tools available in /usr/ports/textproc to see if anything useful is there; there might well be.

HOUR 21

Multimedia in FreeBSD

Although it is still not nearly up to par with Windows and Macintosh, multi-media support in FreeBSD is getting better. For example, today FreeBSD supports most popular sound cards, and thus can play back MP3s, audio CDs, and so on. In this hour, you will learn:

- How to configure sound support in FreeBSD
- Various applications available for playing media files in FreeBSD
- How to burn (record) CDs in FreeBSD
- How to play video files in FreeBSD

Configuring Sound Support in FreeBSD

To add sound support for FreeBSD, there are two things you have to do. The first is recompile the kernel with the sound device in it since it is not included by default. The second is to make the device nodes for the sound system. See Hour 10 for details on how to configure the kernel and build a new one. The line you need to add to the kernel configuration file in order to support sound is

```
device pcm
```

The pcm device supports most common sound cards and can also detect where most of them are located.

After you have added the pcm device to the kernel configuration and rebuilt the kernel, you need to create the device nodes for sound support. This is very simple to do. As the root user, change to the /dev directory (use the command cd /dev), and then type the following command exactly as shown:

`./MAKEDEV snd0`

Remember that FreeBSD is case sensitive, so make sure that you type it exactly as shown. This will create the necessary device nodes for accessing the sound card. In general, you don't need to worry about this because you don't interact with these device nodes directly. They are simply used by the sound applications to send data to the sound card. However, you do need to make sure that the sound device nodes exist.

Sound Applications

After you have finished configuring sound support in FreeBSD, you are ready to look at some applications for playing sounds in FreeBSD. Of course, one of the most common things that people want to do is play MP3 files. Yes, there are several options for playing MP3s in FreeBSD, including both command line and graphical MP3 players.

mpg123

mpg123 is a popular, no frills command-line MP3 player. It is available in the FreeBSD ports collection under the Audio directory.

After mpg123 has been installed, you can play MP3s with it by simply typing **mpg123** followed by the name of the MP3 file that you want to play. You can also provide a list of MP3 files, and mpg123 will play them in the order listed. The program also accepts wildcards. For example, mpg123 *.mp3 will play all the MP3 files located in the current directory. For more information on the features of mpg123, see its man page.

XMMS

XMMS is a popular MP3 player for X. It is basically a clone of Winamp, and, in fact, it even supports the use of Winamp skins. Figure 21.1 shows the Winamp MP3 player.

XMMS is available in the ports collection under the Audio directory.

FIGURE 21.1

*The XMMS MP3
player. Windows users
who have used
Winamp in the past
will not have any
problem getting used
to XMMS.*

CD Player

KDE also comes with a CD player. The CD player supports the CDDB system, which
means that it can automatically download album and track information from the Internet.
Figure 21.2 shows the KDE CD player.

FIGURE 21.2

The KDE CD player.

Mixers

FreeBSD comes with a mixer that can be accessed from the command line. To simply
display the current mixer settings, just type **mixer** at the command prompt, and press
Enter. Here is some sample output from the mixer command:

```
Mixer vol      is currently set to  90:90
Mixer bass     is currently set to  75:75
Mixer treble   is currently set to  75:75
Mixer synth    is currently set to  75:75
Mixer pcm      is currently set to  75:75
Mixer speaker  is currently set to  75:75
Mixer line     is currently set to  75:75
Mixer mic      is currently set to  32:32
Mixer cd       is currently set to  75:75
Mixer mix      is currently set to   0:0
Mixer igain    is currently set to  75:75
Mixer ogain    is currently set to  75:75
```

To change one of the settings, type **mixer**, followed by the name of the setting that you
want to change, followed by a number from 1 to 100. For example, the command

```
mixer vol 50
```

21

will set the main mixer volume to 50%. If you want to set the left and right levels differently, use two numbers separated by a colon. For example,

```
mixer vol 50:40
```

sets the left volume to 50 and the right volume to 40.

If you don't like the command-line mixer, KDE also has a mixer built in to it that can be accessed from the Multimedia sub-menu of the K menu. Figure 21.3 shows the KDE sound mixer.

FIGURE 21.3

The KDE sound mixer.

CD Burning

If you have a CD-R (CD Recordable) or CD-RW (CD Rewritable) drive, you can take part in what's becoming the favorite multimedia pastime in today's computer age: creating your own music CDs that are mixed however you like.

CD burning in FreeBSD is still a command-line affair, however. The recordable optical drive you have installed is most likely an IDE/ATA drive; if so, the tool you will be using is burncd. (If, however, you have a SCSI drive, you will need to use cdrecord; because SCSI burners are far less common these days than IDE burners, we will focus on burncd in this hour's lesson.)

Unlike the process of creating data CDs, which we covered in Hour 8, "Storage Systems and Backup Utilities," the creation of standard audio disc CDs doesn't involve a two-step process. You don't need to create an ISO disk image first using mkisofs. Instead, you can use the burncd command directly to write audio files in WAV format onto the disc.

First, convert the songs you want to burn into WAV format. You can use dagrab (available in the ports at /usr/ports/audio/dagrab) to rip audio tracks directly from audio CDs into WAV format. If your songs are in MP3 format, you can use the "Disk Writer" plugin—part of XMMS—to convert them to WAV format.

Many audio CDs that are being published today have copy-protection features that prevent even legitimate owners of the discs from "space-shifting" the discs' contents onto other media, such as software MP3 players or recordable CDs. If you can't rip audio from these discs using the dagrab utility, this is probably the reason.

After you have converted all the songs you want to burn onto a CD into WAV files, you can use burncd to write them all with a single command:

```
# burncd -f /dev/acd0c audio track1.wav track2.wav track3.wav fixate
```

You can list as many files as you want on this command line, provided they don't total more playback time than there is space on the disc. Bear in mind that CDs hold either 650MB or 700MB of data; if the WAV files you want to burn add up to more than that, you must remove some.

The -f switch specifies the drive device; the fixate keyword tells burncd to "close the session," meaning that after the process completes, the CD is completely burned and able to be mounted as a disk under FreeBSD or played in a standard CD player.

You can also create "MP3 CDs," which can be played back in an increasing number of mainstream audio players (including some in-dash players in cars). An MP3 CD is simply a standard ISO 9660 CD-ROM that contains a number of compressed MP3 files. You can fit some 12 times as many songs onto an MP3 CD as you can onto a regular CD, or more, depending on the compression level of your files.

To burn an MP3 CD, you will need to follow the two-step procedure that you would normally use to create a data CD, as we discussed in Hour 8. First, use mkisofs to create an ISO disk image from the MP3 files stored in a particular directory (/path/to/directory):

```
# mkisofs -o diskimage.iso -J -R /path/to/directory
```

This command will create an ISO 9660 disk image from all the MP3 audio files in the directory you specified; the -J and -R switches tell mkisofs to make the disc compatible with Windows (with the Joliet long-filename extensions) and with UNIX (with the Rock Ridge extensions). After the disk image is created, you can burn the CD using burncd:

```
# burncd -f /dev/acd0c -s 4 data diskimage.iso fixate
```

The -s 4 switch tells burncd to burn at 4x speed; you can set this number higher if your drive supports higher speeds.

21

Viewing MPEG Video Files

FreeBSD has a number of tools available in the ports that can read MPEG video files; MPEG represents a fairly large proportion of the video content that's available on the Internet today and because it's an open standard with freely available codecs (unlike Windows Media Player and older versions of QuickTime), shareware tools that can read MPEG files are plentiful.

Probably the best bet for viewing most modern MPEG files is mpeg2play, which is available in the ports at /usr/ports/graphics/mpeg2play. This utility, which runs (naturally) under X, will play back both the MPEG-1 files that one usually finds online and MPEG-2 files which can be extracted (though usually illegally) from DVD discs.

Running mpeg2play is fairly self-explanatory; simply feed it the name of a file to play:

```
# mpeg2play myfile.mpg
```

This will open the movie in a new window in your desktop environment, with controls available in another window.

The mpeg2play port is rather old, however, and has not been updated in some time. Look in /usr/ports/graphics for other tools with mpeg in their names; new MPEG playback utilities might become available with time.

DivX Video Files

Possibly the most common format on the Internet today for the openly traded video content that makes up most file-sharing traffic is DivX. This codec, usually embedded in Windows AVI files, is based on the emerging MPEG-4 standard and offers very good compression rates while preserving good quality. The codec is developed by volunteers whose Web site is at http://www.divx.com.

To play back DivX content, you will need to install linux-divxplayer. This program is available in the ports in /usr/ports/graphics/linux-divxplayer. It operates using FreeBSD's built-in Linux compatibility mode; although programs written for Linux usually pose no problems to FreeBSD, some applications that are heavy on graphics, sound, or other intensive device manipulation—which indeed describes DivX video—might cause some instability. Be aware that this might be the case, particularly considering that at the time of this writing, the version of linux-divxplayer is only 0.2.0!

After installing the linux-divxplayer port, which will install a few related dependency ports, you will be able to open DivX AVI files as follows:

```
# divxPlayer myvile.avi
```

Enjoy!

Playing DVDs

It used to be only a pipe dream that users could watch DVD video discs under Linux or FreeBSD; however, this is no longer the case, thanks to the developers of a program called Ogle.

The first thing you need in order to run Ogle, naturally, is a DVD drive. FreeBSD will recognize most common IDE/ATA DVD drives as `/dev/acd0`, just as with regular CD-ROM drives.

Armed with this equipment, all you should need to do is install the Ogle port, which includes its GUI, available at `/usr/ports/graphics/ogle-gui`. (This port implicitly installs the command-line `/usr/ports/graphics/ogle` port.) Once this is done, type **ogle** to start up the Ogle GUI.

With the DVD you want to watch in the drive, use the menu command Open to open the device `/dev/acd0`. (You can also use the Open dialog to open the contents of a `VIDEO_TS` folder, if you have copied the contents of a DVD to your hard drive, by specifying `/path/to/VIDEO_TS` as the target.) You might also be able to use the Open Disc menu command, which will automatically open the DVD in the drive without your having to specify the device name.

Ogle has many features that you are probably accustomed to using in standard DVD players, including menus, full-screen mode, title/chapter search, and a number of high-quality audio formats. However, a few features are missing at this time, such as the ability to seek back and forth through the video with a slider, and reverse playback. Ogle will undoubtedly continue to evolve however; and in the meantime, the basics ought to work quite well.

Summary

In this hour, you learned how to configure sound support in FreeBSD by adding the `pcm` device driver to the kernel, and also creating device nodes for sound support. We then looked at a small sample of the sound applications available for FreeBSD.

Multimedia hardly stops with sound playback, however; and so we looked at the basics of CD burning, MPEG and DivX video playback, and DVD playback—all features that are central to *multimedia* as we are accustomed to it today.

21

Q&A

Q FreeBSD doesn't support my sound card. What can I do?

A All may not be lost. There is a third-party vendor that makes sound drivers for FreeBSD. You can check them out at `www.opensound.com`. These sound drivers support more cards than the native FreeBSD drivers. The drivers are not free, but the cost might be worth it if they are the only way you can get sound support working in FreeBSD.

Q I have a SCSI CD burner. The `burncd` utility doesn't seem to work.

A That's because SCSI drives need to use the `cdrecord` utility, not `burncd`. Install it from `/usr/ports/sysutils/cdrtools`; then, refer to the `man cdrecord` page for details on using it, or refer back to Hour 8 when we discussed it in the context of storage systems.

Q MPEG video files don't seem to have any sound, or the sound behaves very oddly.

A MPEG is rather odd, as a format, in that its video and audio tracks are "multi-plexed"—they don't exist as separate tracks, but instead are woven together in a way that often confounds playback software. You might try the `splitmpg` port (`/usr/ports/graphics/splitmpg`) to separate out the audio and video tracks, and then play them back through separate utilities at the same time. This can have very odd results, though, such as the audio and video playing back at slightly different speeds.

Q Ogle crashed my machine!

A DVD playback is a very device-intensive process; support for DVD drives is still quite new in FreeBSD, and there is bound to be some instability as complete func-tionality for playing back DVD content is integrated into the system. Keep an eye on the FreeBSD mailing list (such as `freebsd-stable` or `freebsd-current`, either of which you can subscribe to by sending a message to `majordomo@freebsd.org`), and watch for others posting questions or reporting similar problems. The more people who use FreeBSD to watch DVDs, the more pressure there will be on the developers to make it stable.

Q My DVD of *The Matrix* won't play properly.

A This is to be expected; certain DVDs won't even play properly in many hardware DVD players! As Ogle continues to develop, it will likely support more and more advanced playback features. As it is, however, your best bet is to trust it only with the more bare-bones DVDs in your collection.

Workshop

In this interactive section, we will test your understanding of multimedia in FreeBSD with quiz questions and exercises designed to pique your curiosity about what else can be discovered within this hour's topic.

Quiz

1. The line that needs to be added to the kernel configuration file for sound support is

    A. `device sound`

    B. `device snd`

    C. `device pcm`

    D. None of the above

2. The command to create the sound device nodes is

    A. `./MAKEDEV snd`

    B. `./MAKEDEV snd0`

    C. `./MAKEDEV pcm`

    D. `./MAKEDEV sound`

3. The utility you need in order to create an ISO disk image to burn onto a data or MP3 CD is what?

    A. `burncd`

    B. `cdrecord`

    C. `mkisofs`

    D. Ogle

4. If you have an IDE/ATA CD-R or CD-RW drive, what tool will you use to burn CDs?

    A. `cdrecord`

    B. `mkisofs`

    C. XMMS

    D. `burncd`

5. How much data can you typically fit onto a CD-R?

    A. 650MB

    B. 4.7GB

    C. 700MB

    D. 250MB

21

6. What's the device name for a typical DVD-ROM drive in FreeBSD?

    A. /dev/acd0

    B. /dev/dvd0

    C. /dev/dvd

    D. /cdrom/cdrom0

Quiz Answers

1. The correct answer is C.

2. The correct answer is B.

3. The correct answer is C.

4. The correct answer is D.

5. Either A or C is correct.

6. The correct answer is A. C is typically the answer for Linux.

Exercises

1. MPEG-4 is likely to be the wave of the future when it comes to open video formats widely traded on the Internet. Research which utilities you might use in FreeBSD to play back MPEG-4 content, and also see if you can discover which tools available for other platforms can create MPEG-4 files. Knowing what most of the world will likely be using ought to help you keep prepared with your own system.

2. Experiment with Ogle, using the command-line version of the program; for instance, you can start Ogle with the `ogle -u cli /dev/acd0` command rather than going through the graphical menu. See the Ogle Web site for further details and documentation, at `http://www.dtek.chalmers.se/groups/dvd/`.

3. Determine what steps are necessary for creating either standard audio CDs or MP3 data CDs; try writing a script, in shell or Perl, that lets you select audio files from a list until their combined size would be too large to fit on a CD. Then, have the script burn the CD using the appropriate commands, as we have discussed in this hour's lesson.

PART V
FreeBSD as a Server

Hour

Hour **22**

Configuring a Basic Web Server

FreeBSD makes an excellent Web server platform. In fact, this is one of its most popular uses. Many large Web sites, including Yahoo! and Sony Japan, rely on FreeBSD to serve up millions of pages a day. You might not have any ambitions of serving quite so many visitors, but this just shows what FreeBSD is capable of handling. And when that capability is available free, why not take advantage of it? In this hour, you will learn:

- How to install Apache on your FreeBSD system
- Basic configuration of Apache
- Basic access control and security

What Is Apache?

Apache is freely available and open source Web server software. It is available for many platforms including most flavors of UNIX, including FreeBSD, MacOS X, OS/2, and more recently, Windows. Apache is the most popular Web server software in the world. According to a Netcraft survey, approximately 64% of the world's Web sites are running Apache.

Requirements for Running Your Own Web Server

Before you start installing Apache, you might first want to make sure that it makes sense for you to run your own Web server. For example, if you have a dial-up Internet connection, it probably is not practical for you to run a Web site off that. You are going to want at least a cable or DSL connection for running a Web site. Also remember that with most cable and DSL providers, your upstream bandwidth will usually be less than your downstream bandwidth, which basically means that you can receive files faster than you can send them. That's not usually an issue for normal Internet use, but a Web server spends most of its time sending files. So for this, it is a very big issue. If you expect your Web site to be busy, or you plan to have high bandwidth content such as streaming video on the site, cable or DSL will probably not be fast enough. The next step up is a dedicated T1 line, which can cost around a thousand dollars a month.

 If you intend to serve Web content from your FreeBSD machine on a cable or DSL connection, be aware that some providers block incoming HTTP requests (on TCP port 80) to all customers except those who have specifically paid for a "business account" that allows Web serving. Make sure that you know what capabilities your provider allows you.

In addition, there is the maintenance involved with running your own Web server. This involves such things as keeping on top of security issues, hardware maintenance, and so on.

If all you want to do is host a small Web site for your business or organization, it might make more sense for you to rent space on someone else's server. For around $10 to $20 a month, you can get a lot of bandwidth, you can get someone else to worry about the maintenance and server administration for you, you can get redundant backup systems and backup power supplies, and so on. This allows you to concentrate on the design of the site rather than on the maintenance and administration of the server itself.

Of course, there are also some drawbacks to renting space on someone else's server. The first is that you will have a lot less flexibility. You will generally be stuck with whatever software the hosting service has installed on their servers. If you are currently using one database for example, and later you decide to switch to a different one, you might find yourself having to find a different hosting service if your existing one doesn't support the new database.

The other major drawback is that you will be sharing space and bandwidth with other sites. This is usually not a problem, but it can cause slow response times during heavy traffic periods if several sites are getting hit hard.

If your site will be large and complex or you want to sell your hosting services to others, it might make more sense to set up your own Web server.

In addition to a broadband Internet connection, you will need the following:

- **A static IP address.** Most Internet service providers give you a dynamic IP address, which means that your IP address can change. If your IP address changes on a regular basis, people will not be able to find your site.

- **A registered domain name.** This is not strictly necessary, but if you don't have a domain name, site visitors will have to access your site by entering the IP address. For example, instead of http://www.mycompany.com, they will have to enter something like http://145.162.134.11. People are generally much better at remembering names than numbers, so you will probably want to register a domain name with a registration authority. A list of domain name authorities that you can register with can be obtained at http://www.internic.net/alpha.html.

- If you want to use a domain name, you will also need to provide a primary and secondary DNS server to host your domain name. The DNS server is what translates your domain name into an IP address. Running your own DNS server is a complex topic that is beyond the scope of this book. You might want to consider using a domain registration authority that can provide DNS services for you for a small monthly fee.

Before you actually set up a Web server on your broadband Internet connection, make sure that you read your user agreement with the Internet provider. Many providers will have "consumer access only" clauses in their basic Internet service plans. This basically means that you can only use the service to receive content and not to provide it. If your agreement has such a clause and you get caught running a Web server (there are ways they can tell if you are running one), you might get your account canceled.

Once you've taken care of all the preliminaries discussed previously, you are ready to install the Apache Web server.

Installing Apache

Apache is included in the FreeBSD ports collection in the /usr/ports/www directory. As of this writing, the most recent version of Apache is 2.0.40. Make sure that you install the production version and not the beta version; both might be available in the ports collection. To install the port, simply change to the correct directory in /usr/ports/www and type **make**, followed by **make install** after the build process has completed. A startup script will be installed for you in /usr/local/etc/rc.d that will cause Apache to load automatically on each system startup.

> Be aware, as with all services that you install or enable, that Apache is a software package that undergoes rapid development in order to add features and to fix bugs and security flaws. Every so often, a security hole will be found in Apache, and a new version will be released. Be sure to keep on top of the reports of these developments; subscribe to the freebsd-security mailing list (send a message to majordomo@freebsd.org with the line subscribe freebsd-security in the body), and pay frequent visits to Apache's Web site: http://www.apache.org.
>
> When a new version of Apache is released, synchronize your ports tree and rebuild the Apache port, as described in Hour 6, "Adding and Removing Third-Party Software."

Basic Apache Configuration: What You Need to Edit

Like almost everything else in UNIX, Apache's configuration is controlled by—you guessed it—text-based configuration files. Apache stores its configuration files in the directory /usr/local/etc/apache. There are several files in this directory, but the only one we are interested in here is httpd.conf. This is the main Apache configuration file; thus it is where you will control the majority of Apache's configuration options.

At first glance, the httpd.conf file might look quite complicated and intimidating. Fortunately, however, most of the options can be left at their default values. The file is also well commented so that you can tell what each configuration line is for.

For a basic server configuration, you will want to change the following lines:

`ServerAdmin: you@your.address`

The address that is listed for `ServerAdmin` will appear on error messages that are automatically generated by Apache and sent to visitors' browsers when something goes wrong. This gives visitors a way to contact you regarding problems they had with the site. This address should be replaced with whatever address you want to use to receive email regarding server problems.

`ServerName: new.host.name`

You should generally set the name of your host here, with the first part aliased to www. For example, if your full hostname is `simba.mycompany.com`, the name you should place here in the configuration file is *www.mycompany.com*. This is sometimes used when the server needs to look up its own hostname.

`DocumentRoot: /usr/local/apache/htdocs`

This directory is the root directory in which Web pages are stored. In other words, if someone enters *www.mycompany.com*, the file `/usr/local/apache/docs/index.html` is what will be sent to them. If you don't want to store your Web pages in this directory, you should change this path to whatever directory you do want to keep your Web pages in.

> Any files or directories located in the directory indicated by the `DocumentRoot` directive will be available for the Web server to read and send out over the Internet. Because of this, only documents intended to be displayed on the Web site should be stored in `/usr/local/apache/htdocs` or any of its subdirectories.

To get a basic Web server up and running, these are generally the only options you have to worry about initially. More information on the rest of the file can be found on the Apache Web site at `www.apache.org`.

Starting and Stopping the Apache Server

As mentioned previously, the Apache server will automatically start each time you boot your system because the installation process installed a startup script in

/usr/local/etc/rc.d. However, if you want to start the server manually at any time, you can use the apachectl program. For example,

```
#apachectl start
/usr/local/sbin/apachectl start: httpd started
```

The apachectl program can also be used to stop the server, and it is the easiest and best way to do this. For example,

```
#apachectl stop
/usr/local/sbin/apachectl stop: httpd stopped
```

If you want to restart the server, apachectl also has a command to do this rather than having to issue two commands:

```
#apachectl restart
/usr/local/sbin/apachectl restart: httpd restarted
```

Note that Apache only reads its configuration files once when it first starts. So any changes you make to them while Apache is running will not take effect until it has been restarted by issuing the previous command.

If you look at the process list while Apache is running, you will see multiple httpd processes because the main Apache process spawns several child processes to handle the incoming httpd requests. Apache always keeps several processes running to handle the requests—even if there currently is no Web site traffic. If, for whatever reason, you want to kill the Apache server by issuing a kill command directly to the process, you must make sure that you issue the command to the parent process. If you kill one of the child processes, the parent process will simply spawn a new one to replace it.

> The apachectl restart command will immediately kill the parent process as well as all the child processes, even if the child processes are currently handling a request. This means that any visitors to your site who are currently receiving or sending data to your Web server will basically "have the rug pulled out from under them." Because of this, the apachectl program also provides the graceful option that you can use instead of the restart option (for example, apachectl graceful). This command will restart the server but will not interrupt any transactions that are currently in process. Processes that are currently handling transactions will not be restarted until the current transaction has been completed.

By default, Apache runs on network port 80, and for a public Web server, you probably won't want to change this. Web browsers assume port 80 unless otherwise specified in the URL.

As a general security measure in the operating system, port numbers lower than 1024 can only be opened by the root user. Because of this, the parent Apache process needs to be run as root. However, the child processes are usually run as nobody, which is an account that has no special privileges and cannot log in to the system.

Note that Apache is subject to UNIX file permissions. Thus, in order for files and directories to be available to visitors to your site, they need to be readable by the user nobody. Usually, this will not be an issue because the files can just be world readable.

After the Apache server has been installed and started, you should be able to access it loading the following address into your Web browser (if you are attempting to access it from the same machine the Web server is running on.)

```
http://127.0.0.1
```

If the server is running, you should get the default Apache welcome page. Of course, you will want to replace this page with whatever the home page of your Web site will be.

Note that if the server is currently on a network, you should also be able to access the Web server from a different computer by entering the IP address of the Web server machine into the Web browser.

CGI

CGI stands for *Common Gateway Interface*. It is a method through which Web servers can run external programs and even pass data entered on a Web page form to an external program. The external program can also send output back to the Web server, which can then be displayed on a Web page, for example.

Although these external programs are commonly referred to as CGI scripts, they do not necessarily have to be scripts. CGI programs can be written in any language. The most common language for writing CGI scripts in UNIX is Perl. However, CGI can also be written in Python, TCL, shell script, AWK, SED, Java, or even a fully compiled language such as C. A discussion of how to write and use CGI scripts in your Web pages is beyond the scope of this book. However, we will cover how to enable CGI in the Apache server, as well as how to ensure that they don't end up compromising the security of your system.

Configuring Apache for CGI

CGI scripts generally have addresses that look something like the following:

```
http://www.mycompany.com/cgi-bin/myscript.pl
```

In general, Apache will only allow scripts located in the cgi-bin directory to be executed. The cgi-bin directory should not be located in the same directory that normal Web pages are served from because you do not want visitors to be able to load the CGI scripts like normal Web pages.

In the httpd.conf file, a line begins with ScriptAlias that determines where CGI scripts are stored. For example,

```
ScriptAlias /cgi-bin/ "/usr/local/www/cgi-bin/"
```

This line means that the CGI programs are actually stored in /usr/local/www/cgi-bin. The alias to that directory is the Web server root directory followed by the directory cgi-bin (for example, www.mycompany.com/cgi-bin). All of your CGI scripts need to be stored in /usr/local/www/cgi-bin. CGI scripts stored in normal Web page directories will be treated as normal HTML files and simply displayed rather than executed.

Note that CGI scripts are programs that are actually executed on the Web server. Normally, they will be run as the same user who the Web server process is running as, which means that the CGI scripts will normally be run as the user nobody.

As mentioned previously, we are not going in to an in-depth discussion here about how to use CGI; however, the following is a very simple CGI program that you can use just to test whether you have Apache's CGI support configured properly:

```
#!/bin/sh
echo "Hello. The current date and time is: "
date
```

Save this file in the /usr/local/www/cgi-bin directory as something with a .sh extension. For example mycgi.sh. Make sure that the file is set to be executable (recall Hour 5's lesson, "Users and Groups").

To prove that this is a normal file that can be executed directly from the FreeBSD command prompt, simply run it like normal. Note that because this directory will not be in your path, you will need to specifically tell FreeBSD that the file is located in the current directory. This can be done by preceding the command with a leading ./—for example, ./mycgi.sh. Here is a sample of what the program will display:

```
$ ./mycgi.sh
Hello, the current date and time is:
Tue Jul 23 23:14:12 CDT 2002
```

Now load the page into a Web browser. If the Web browser is located on the same system that that Web server is on, you should be able to use the following address to access the page:

```
http://127.0.0.1/cgi-bin/mycgi.sh
```

However, if you are accessing the page from a different system connected to the Web server over a network, use the IP address of the Web server system followed by `/cgi-bin/mycgi.sh`.

If CGI support is configured correctly, you should get a simple Web page that displays the `"Hello, the current date and time is:"` message followed by whatever the current date and time is.

Troubleshooting CGI

If you don't get the expected results, there are two common problems you might have run into. The first is that instead of displaying the `"Hello"` message followed by the current date and time, the Web page displays the source code for the CGI script. In other words, you get a Web page that displays the following:

```
#!/bin/sh
echo "Hello. The current date and time is: "
date
```

This probably means that the directory is configured as a normal Web site directory and not as a CGI directory. Apache will only allow scripts to be executed if they are located in a directory that is configured as a CGI directory in `httpd.conf` (which is done by following the procedures mentioned previously). If the directory in which the script is stored is not configured as a CGI directory, Apache will treat it as a normal file and simply send its contents over the Internet to the visitor's browser.

The second problem you might run into is that you get a Web page that says something like the following:

```
Forbidden
You don't have permission to access the requested resource
```

This message generally indicates one of two things:

- The script you are trying to load does not have the executable bit set. Therefore, Apache cannot run it.
- The user who the Web server runs as (`nobody` unless you changed it) does not have permission to execute the script. Therefore, Apache cannot run it.

Check the permissions on the file, as you learned in Hour 5, and try again.

Poorly written CGI scripts are one of the biggest sources of security holes on Web servers—especially if the script receives data from a form on a Web site. It's possible, for example, for a hacker to pass bogus information to the script through the form and cause the script to do something you never intended it to do. Because of this, you need to be extremely careful when writing your CGI scripts. Also, it is safer to write CGI scripts in a language such as Perl or Python rather than as shell scripts; these languages provide better runtime environment protection than shell programs and ensure a consistent security model.

Apache Modules

Apache modules can be used to extend the functionality of the Web server. For example, the mod_php module allows you to embed a scripting language into your Web page. The PHP language is a fully featured programming language with one of its strongest points being database access. This can allow you to build Web based front ends to such services as search engines, library card catalogs, and online stores.

The Apache modules can be compiled into the Apache server, or they can be dynamically loaded at runtime. Most of the modules are available these days in dynamically loadable versions so that one does not have to recompile the Apache software. These modules are called Dynamic Shared Modules, or more commonly, DSOs.

Quite a few Apache modules are available in the ports collection. These modules can be found in the /usr/ports/www directory. For example, one of the modules available here is the PHP module that we discussed earlier.

After you have installed the PHP port, you need to tell Apache about the new module. This is done by adding configuration options to the httpd.conf file that we introduced earlier. Edit the httpd.conf file and look for the following lines, which will probably be commented out. Simply uncomment them.

```
AddType application/x-httpd-php .php
LoadModule php4_module        libexec/libphp4.so
```

The preceding lines might not be exact, but look for something similar. If you can't find anything in httpd.conf that matches (you might try using your text editor's search function or the command-line grep utility to look through the file for the string php), look for a section that has a long series of lines starting with AddType and LoadModule. Add the AddType and LoadModule lines shown here to the ends of these blocks of directives, respectively.

The first line mentioned previously tells Apache which files should be handled by this module. Normal Web page files end with the extension `.html` or `.htm`. However, by convention, PHP-enabled pages end with the extension `.php`. So, for example, if the home page of a site contained PHP code, it would be named `index.php` instead of `index.html` or `index.htm`.

The second line gives the name of the module and the path to where the module is located. Once again, this could be slightly different depending on the most current version of PHP when you install this.

After the previous two statements have been added or uncommented, restart the Apache server using the `apachectl restart` command discussed earlier. (If the server is not currently running, the `restart` option will start it anyway.) The PHP interpreter should now be running.

Basic Security and Access Control

Apache includes some basic built-in security features that allow primitive access control to Web sites on the server. There are two ways that you can control access to various parts of the Web server. The first is by hostname or IP address. In this case, only hosts that have a certain name or IP address will be allowed to access the protected areas of the site.

The second is by username and password. In this case, a valid username and password is required to access the protected areas of the site.

The file that is used to control access to a directory is `.htaccess`. First, we will look at how to control access based on hostname or IP address.

Controlling Access by Hostnames or IP Address

Two complementary commands can be used to control access to a directory—`Allow` and `Deny`. The order in which these directives are read by Apache is important; it determines whether you want to create a policy of "*exclude* all visitors except those I specify" or "*include* all visitors except those I specify." This ordering is done with the `Order` directive in the `.htaccess` file. The `Order` directive tells Apache which set of lines—either `Allow` or `Deny`—to read first, regardless of how they are listed in the file. For example, to have the `Deny` statements read before the `Allow` statements, the line in `.htaccess` would look like this:

```
Order Deny.Allow
```

You can then simply specify what hosts and addresses you want to allow and deny access to. Here are some sample statements that could exist in the .htaccess file following the Order statement:

```
Deny from all
Allow from mycompany.com
Allow from lion.simba.org
```

In this case, almost all addresses are denied access to the directory where the .htaccess file is located. The only exceptions to the Deny from all rule are hosts located inside the mycompany.com domain, and hosts in lion.simba.org.

There might be other times when you want to allow access to everyone except those from a few specific domains. In this case, you will want to change the Order statement to tell Apache to read the Allow statements first and then the Deny statements (Order Allow,Deny). The rest of the file might look something like the following:

```
Allow from all
Deny from lamespammer.com
Deny from 122.101.122.211
Deny from spammer.mail.com
```

In this case, everyone is allowed except for people from the domains lamespammer.com, spammer.mail.com, and the host with the IP address 122.101.122.211.

Restricting Access by Username and Password

Controlling access by hostnames or IP address doesn't work for all situations. For example, most users have dynamic IP addresses from their ISP. That is, their IP address is assigned randomly from a pool of IP addresses available to their ISP. In this case, you can't rely on access by hostname or IP address to provide these users with access to protected areas of the site. In this case, you can use usernames and passwords.

To create a password protected directory, once again you will want to place an .htaccess file in the directory that you want to have protected. The file must contain, at a minimum, the following four entries:

AuthType

This will almost always be set to "Basic".

AuthName

This is simply the name of the protected area in quotation marks. It can be anything you want and is the name that will display in the browser's authentication box.

AuthUserFile

22

This lists the name of the file that contains the username and password combinations allowed to access this directory. Of course, for security reasons, this file should not be placed anywhere within the directory structure that the Web server can access.

> Require

This tells Apache how it should authenticate users. It can contain the keyword valid-user, which means that any user present in the AuthUserFile will be authenticated (assuming that they enter the correct password). It can also contain a list of usernames.

The following is a sample .htaccess file for controlling access to a directory by username and password:

```
AuthType Basic
AuthName "Top Secret Stuff"
AuthUserFile /usr/local/www/.htpasswd
Require valid-user
```

Once you have saved the .htaccess file, you need to create the password database.

Creating the Password Database

The htpasswd command is used to create and update the Apache password database (which, by the way, should *not* be confused with the FreeBSD user database, /etc/master.passwd). The first time you run htpasswd, you need to use the -c option to tell it to create the new password database file that doesn't yet exist. I also suggest you use the -m option, which will use MD5 encryption. MD5 is stronger than the default crypt()-based form of encryption. Here is an example for a first run of the command:

```
htpasswd -cm /usr/local/www/.htpasswd foobar
```

You will then be asked to supply the password that the user foobar will use to access the restricted directory.

There are two security issues you need to be aware of. The first is that the .htpasswd file should not be placed inside the same directory you are trying to protect, nor anywhere else within the directory tree that is accessible to the Web server. Doing so could potentially allow a Web site visitor to have the file sent to him by asking for it as a URL. Of course, sending your password file to a Web site visitor is probably not something you want to do.

The second thing you need be aware of is that this form of protection is rather primitive. For one thing, passwords sent over the Internet using this system are only garbled with a hash sequence, which is relatively easy to crack for someone snooping your Web site traffic to get a password. Also, the documents transferred after the user has been authenticated are not encrypted when sent, thus potentially allowing someone to intercept them. This means that this form of authentication only provides a basic level of security that cannot be trusted to keep sensitive documents secure. For a greater level of protection that is suitable for e-commerce and such, you will want to look into SSL, which is beyond the scope of this book. It, and other more advanced configurations for Apache under FreeBSD, can be found in *FreeBSD Unleashed* from Sams Publishing, as well as in many other books specifically dedicated to Apache, such as O'Reilly's *Apache: The Definitive Guide*.

Summary

In this hour, we looked at how to configure a basic Web server suitable for simple Web hosting. The Apache Web server, however, is highly complex and capable of far more than we were able to cover here. Advanced topics such as virtual hosting and secure sites were not covered. For more information on the advanced capabilities of Apache, please see the online documentation at the project's Web site (www.apache.org), or consult one of the books that is dedicated to Apache.

Q&A

Q I've used Apache on Linux and other UNIX platforms; the files all seem to be in different places under FreeBSD. What gives?

A It's a common problem with the variation in different UNIX systems: Each one seems to have its own idea about which files go where. Some Linux distributions, for instance, put the Apache installation into a single directory structure under /var/lib/httpd. FreeBSD attempts to adhere to a strict conceptual layout; Web content and executables don't go into /var, which is supposed to contain *variable* files (such as PID files, databases, and logs). Instead, Apache's binaries go into /usr/local/sbin and /usr/local/bin (depending on whether they alter system behavior or not), logs are kept in /var/log, documentation is at /usr/local/share/doc/apache, Web content goes into /usr/local/www, and configuration files go into /usr/local/etc/apache. This means that the installation sprawls across the whole system, but the files are all organized according to function. The ports keep a packing list so that they can all be cleanly uninstalled.

Q You've only talked about Apache 2.0. What about Apache 1.3? I thought that was the standard version.

A Apache 1.3 has only just now reached the end of its lifetime; Apache has been in the 1.x series now for almost seven years, and the transition to 2.0 as a stable platform is now complete enough that there is no reason to learn 1.3 if you're new to Apache. The only reason to know how 1.3 works is if you are managing a legacy installation. In any event, the configurations of the two versions are really quite similar and fully documented at the Apache Web site.

Q How do I enable CGI in regular users' directories (for example, not in the `cgi-bin`)?

A Use the `Options +ExecCGI` directive to enable the `ExecCGI` option for a location or directory specified in a `<Location>` or `<Directory>` block. You will also need to use `AddHandler cgi-script .cgi` to map all executable files whose names end in `.cgi` to the CGI script handler.

Q What about server-side includes?

A You can enable "parsed HTML" —HTML files that are processed by the server before being sent out, executing embedded program calls—using the `AddType` and `AddHandler` directives. Consult the Apache Web site for full documentation on how this is done. With SSI enabled, you can do things like embedding program output into HTML files or altering the page's appearance with basic flow control. It's like a built-in precursor to PHP.

Q Which is correct—`.html` or `.htm`?

A The original extension was `.html`, which completely reflects the acronym HTML (Hypertext Markup Language). The only reason `.htm` exists as a valid extension is because of Windows, which at the time the Web was becoming popular didn't support filename extensions longer than three characters. (Many Windows applications still don't.) This is why UNIX supports `.html` variations such as `.shtml` and `.phtml`, whereas Windows is stuck with such meaningless abbreviated versions as `.stm` and `.ptm`. You're using UNIX; use the longer extensions, just because you can.

Workshop

This interactive section has quiz questions and exercises which are designed to test your understanding of Web services with Apache and to point the way toward more advanced exploration of the subject.

Quiz

1. The program you use to start and stop the Apache server is

    A. `apache`

    B. `httpd`

    C. `apachectl`

    D. `htserv`

2. The name of the file that contains options restricting access to a directory is

    A. `htaccess`

    B. `.htpasswd`

    C. `htsecure`

    D. None of the above

3. The main file that controls Apache configuration options is

    A. `/usr/local/etc/apache.conf`

    B. `/usr/local/etc/httpd.conf`

    C. `/usr/local/etc/apache/apache.conf`

    D. `/usr/local/etc/apache/httpd.conf`

4. What is the purpose of Apache modules?

Quiz Answers

1. The correct answer is C.

2. The correct answer is D. Answer A is incorrect because it does not begin with a leading period. Answer B is incorrect because it is the name of the file that stores usernames and passwords, not the name of the file that contains the options that restrict directory access.

3. The correct answer is D.

4. The purpose of modules is to extend Apache capabilities beyond the normal base server. For example, `mod_php` provides an embedded scripting language that can be used to create dynamic Web pages and access databases.

Exercises

1. Apache is infinitely extensible. Look through the various modules that are available (all the ports whose names start with mod_ in /usr/ports/www) and see which ones might be useful to you. mod_perl lets you embed a Perl interpreter into Apache, speeding up execution of frequently-used Perl scripts; mod_frontpage lets you support users who want to use Microsoft FrontPage to author their sites; and mod_dav lets you create a WebDAV server (as is used by Apple's iCal software). You can install as many of these modules as you want. Experiment until you have a module loadout that matches your needs.

2. Enable server-side includes using the documentation found on Apache's Web site. Learn how to create a simple if/then statement, printing out different HTML content depending on the outcome of some condition (such as, for instance, the browser that a visitor is using).

3. Learn how to use .htaccess files to control configuration options at different places all throughout the system. What benefits does this have over making your changes globally in httpd.conf?

4. The same goes for /usr/local/etc/apache/mime.types. What benefits are there in specifying new file types in this file rather than in httpd.conf?

22

Hour 23

Basic Email Services

Any multiuser operating system on the Internet must give its users the ability to send email messages to users of other systems. This is one of the oldest uses of the Internet, and certainly it has lately become an integral part of any computer user's life. However, in its current form, email is a bit different from how it used to be.

FreeBSD is configured "out of the box" to provide email services for local users of the system; if you make certain changes to the default configuration, it can also act as a relay so that people on dial-up machines can use your server to convey their messages to their destination servers. However, this also means that mass mailers ("spammers") can also use your server as a broadcasting station without your permission.

In this hour's lesson, we will cover Sendmail, the venerable *Mail Transfer Agent (MTA)* that still transmits the majority of the world's email and that is bundled as part of FreeBSD. You will learn

- Using the various files that comprise the configuration of Sendmail
- Customizing the Master Config file and regenerating Sendmail's runtime configuration file

- Adding aliases to the system
- Starting and stopping Sendmail
- Viewing the message queue and seeing what messages are waiting to be delivered
- Fighting spammers by controlling mail relaying

SMTP and Sendmail

The *Simple Mail Transfer Protocol (SMTP)* is responsible for transferring email messages from one server to the next. It's a simple protocol, as its name suggests, designed only for establishing the identity of the sender and the recipient, and transmitting a message's contents. The sender and recipient are each specified by an email address, which consists of a username and a hostname, separated by the at symbol, @; if the SMTP server that receives the message has the same hostname as the one in the email address, it knows the message is intended to reach a recipient there. If not, it knows it must *relay* the message to another host.

In the simplest case, this is the way an email message travels from one user to another; in the olden days, when everybody had a shell account on a server, a user on one server could email a user on another server simply by opening up a mail program on the local machine (a Mail User Agent, such as Pine, Elm, or Mutt), writing a message, and telling the program to deliver it. The MUA would then open up an SMTP connection to the remote user's mail server (which was usually the same machine on which that user had a shell account) on port 25. The remote server would read the email address, realize that the message was intended for a local user, and dump the message into the user's mailbox. The user could then open up his own MUA and read the message.

These days, it's usually a little more complicated, as shown in Figure 23.1. A complete email delivery path usually takes two or more network hops before it reaches its destination.

Today, the most common situation is for the sender of an email message not to be a local shell user right on the mail server machine, but a dial-up user communicating through an *Internet service provider (ISP)*. This user's MUA might be Microsoft Outlook, Apple Mail, Eudora, or any of their popular cousins. When the MUA sends the message, it opens up an SMTP connection to the SMTP server furnished by the user's ISP—*not* to the remote user's mail server directly.

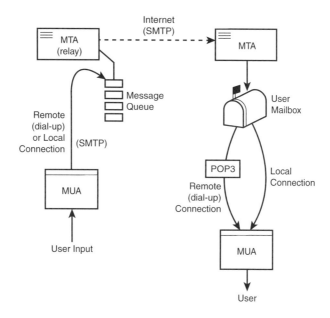

FIGURE 23.1

Diagram of an email message's path from one user to another, showing the roles of MUAs and MTAs.

MUAs don't send messages directly to the recipient's SMTP server because MUAs have very limited mail sending capacity. They don't have such features as message queues or the capability to keep retrying a connection. Most MUAs operate through a real SMTP server, which handles all the mail sending tasks much more efficiently.

The sending MTA, the ISP's SMTP server, receives the message and places it in the *message queue*. Realizing that the recipient is not a user on the network for which it's a mail server, it will immediately try to transmit the message on to the recipient's SMTP server. If the MTA can't send it immediately, the message remains in the message queue for up to five days, constantly retrying, before the MTA deletes it. Upon successful transmission, though, the receiving MTA takes the message and appends it to the recipient user's mailbox—/var/mail/<user> if it's a FreeBSD machine.

Email recipients today are also usually not local shell users on the receiving MTA. They're dial-up users as well, and must get their mail either through POP3 (Post Office Protocol version 3) or IMAP (Internet Message Access Protocol), both methods for downloading messages to a local MUA such as the ones we discussed before.

You can execute a completely valid SMTP transaction purely from the command line; SMTP is a plain-text interactive protocol that uses simple four-letter, English-like commands, and you can send someone a simple message without even having access to an MTA or an email program:

```
# telnet destination.com 25
Trying 64.41.134.166...
Connected to destination.com.
Escape character is '^]'.
220 destination.com ESMTP Sendmail 8.11.1/8.11.1; Wed, 16 May 2001
22:55:37
➥ -0700 (PDT)
HELO stripes.sender.com
250 destination.com Hello w012.z064002043.sjc-ca.dsl.cnc.net
[64.2.43.12],
➥pleased to meet you
MAIL From: frank@sender.com
250 2.1.0 frank@sender.com... Sender ok
RCPT To: bob@destination.com
250 2.1.5 bob@destination.com... Recipient ok
DATA
354 Enter mail, end with "." on a line by itself
From: frank@sender.com
To: bob@destination.com
Subject: Testing, 123...

This is a test message.
.
250 2.0.0 f4H5uCu53501 Message accepted for delivery
QUIT
221 2.0.0 destination.com closing connection
Connection closed by foreign host.
```

This is hardly user-friendly, though. If it weren't for MTAs and MUAs, this is how we would be doing all of our email—and it wouldn't be nearly as useful or fun.

Basic Sendmail Configuration

FreeBSD comes with Sendmail installed and already configured to serve basic email needs right out of the box. All you have to do to enable Sendmail (so that it starts at boot time) is add the following line to /etc/rc.conf:

```
sendmail_enable="YES"
```

Once the system is up and running, you can send a message to anyone on the Internet, and they can send one to you—provided that you have a few things set up properly. For the most part, these aren't configuration items for Sendmail itself, but for the system in general—Sendmail relies on the system to have a few guarantees in place before it will operate without a hitch.

Sendmail File Layout

There are three places in the system that concern Sendmail:

- /etc/mail—Configuration files for Sendmail
- /var/mail—User mailboxes
- /var/spool/mqueue—Message queue files

Sendmail itself is located at /usr/sbin/sendmail, and its log files are written to /var/log/maillog (which is automatically rotated and archived on a daily basis so that old logfiles are available as maillog.0.gz, maillog.1.gz, and so on).

The mailbox files (mail spools) in /var/mail are plain-text files—each named for the user who owns it and with permissions set to 600 (readable and writable only by the owner). New messages are appended to the end of the recipient's mail spool file. There are also temporary POP lock files, which have zero length and a name of the form .username.pop. They receive the contents of the corresponding mail spool file while a POP3 connection is open, and any untransferred remnants are then copied back into the mailbox.

Using the Sendmail Configuration Files

Sendmail is controlled through a number of different configuration files—all found in /etc/mail. Each file has its own purpose, allowing you to control a particular set of Sendmail functions.

Making General Configuration Changes

The main Sendmail config file—the one that it reads upon startup containing all the operating options and filter rules—is /etc/mail/sendmail.cf. However, unlike just about every other config file for every other program, you're not intended to edit this file to alter Sendmail's behavior. Rather, you should make changes at a higher "macro" level in the Master Config (.mc) file, and then compile a sendmail.cf file from that. It's best to leave sendmail.cf alone unless absolutely necessary.

Your actual configuration changes should be made in /etc/mail/freebsd.mc, the Master Config file. Think of it as the config file *for the config file*. It contains a list of features and options that override the defaults in the standard config file—much in the same fashion that /etc/rc.conf overrides /etc/defaults/rc.conf. To make your changes to the Sendmail configuration, you will want to make them in this file, using the otherwise mostly unknown m4 macro language, and then compile a new sendmail.cf file from it.

The contents of freebsd.mc look like this (the dnl that marks the commented-out lines stands for *delete through newline*):

```
dnl Uncomment the first line to change the location of the default
dnl /etc/mail/local-host-names and comment out the second line.
dnl define(`confCW_FILE', `-o /etc/mail/sendmail.cw')
define(`confCW_FILE', `-o /etc/mail/local-host-names')
```

As you can see, the contents of these lines are designed to be read by a program, but not so much by a human. Believe it or not, the sendmail.cf file that is generated from this is even less readable.

There's a Makefile in /etc/mail, which allows you to create a new .cf file from the freebsd.mc file simply by typing **make cf** from inside that directory. Then, install this output file (freebsd.cf) into sendmail.cf using make install.

```
# make cf
/usr/bin/m4 -D_CF_DIR_=/usr/share/sendmail/cf/
➥/usr/share/sendmail/cf/m4/cf.m4  freebsd.mc > freebsd.cf
# make install
install -c -m 444 freebsd.cf /etc/mail/sendmail.cf
```

The /etc/mail/Makefile has a number of other uses, as you'll see in a moment.

Creating Mail Aliases

A mailbox exists in /var/mail for every user on the system; however, someone isn't required to have an account in order to have an email address on your machine. You can always set up *aliases* to map incoming email addresses to any other address, whether it's another account on your machine, an address somewhere else on the Internet, or even a pipe to a file or program. The default /etc/mail/aliases contains examples of all these. An alias line contains the alias name, a colon, a space or tab, and the target address or pipe:

tiger: bob@stripes.com	Redirects to bob@stripes.com
fsmith: frank	Goes into frank's mailbox instead of fsmith's
pager: "|/usr/local/bin/pageme"	Sends the message as input into /usr/local/bin/pageme

`dump: ">>/home/frank/dump2me"`	Appends the message to the `dump2me` file
`mylist:include:/home/frank/list.txt`	Expands to include all the addresses in `list.txt`

After you make any change to `/etc/mail/aliases`, you have to rebuild the `aliases.db` file, which is a faster *hash table* version of the `aliases` file. You can use the traditional `newaliases` command to do this; or for consistency's sake with the rest of the maintenance tasks, use `make aliases`:

```
# make aliases
/usr/sbin/sendmail -bi
/etc/mail/aliases: 22 aliases, longest 10 bytes, 213 bytes total
```

> Global aliases aren't the only way to redirect mail from one local address to another or to an external address. For instance, if a user wants all his incoming mail to be forwarded automatically to some external address, you could use `/etc/mail/aliases` to do the trick, but this involves root access; there's a better way if the user has a full account on the system.
>
> All a user has to do to forward mail to another address is to create a `.forward` file in his home directory, containing the forwarding email address. This can be done with any text editor, or even simply with `echo`:
>
> `# echo "frank@somewhereelse.com" > .forward`
>
> Removing this file will cause mail forwarding to stop.

Blocking and Allowing Specific Senders

The *access database*, `/etc/mail/access`, provides a way to apply certain rules to single hosts, subnets, or whole groups of addresses—an excellent anti-spam provision. Applicable rules include `OK`, `REJECT`, `RELAY`, `DISCARD`, or `550 <message>`. The contents of the default `/etc/mail/access` file show examples of how the address/hostname field can be formatted:

```
cyberspammer.com              550 We don't accept mail from spammers
FREE.STEALTH.MAILER@          550 We don't accept mail from spammers
another.source.of.spam        REJECT
okay.cyberspammer.com         OK
128.32                        RELAY
```

23

- OK accepts messages from the specified host, regardless of whether that host might fail other checks in the system (such as the anti-relaying provisions that we will discuss shortly).
- REJECT refuses connections initiated by the specified host.
- DISCARD silently drops messages after accepting them, making the sender think that the message has been successfully delivered.
- RELAY enables relaying for the specified host, overriding other checks (as with OK).
- 550 <message> specifies a "rejection" message that is displayed to a sender, matching the host specification. This message will appear during the SMTP session, and will be included in an error email message that is sent back to the sender.

After you've made changes to /etc/mail/access, the access.db file must be regenerated. This is done with the make maps target, which regenerates any of the feature map files that have been changed since the last time make maps has been run. Follow this command with make restart to restart the Sendmail master process with the new access.db file:

```
# make maps
/usr/sbin/makemap hash access.db < access
# make restart
/bin/kill -HUP `head -1 /var/run/sendmail.pid`
```

Other Configuration Files

There are more files in /etc/mail that control Sendmail's operation: /etc/mail/virtusertable and /etc/mail/local-host-names are both important for advanced Sendmail configuration, such as an installation in which your server hosts email services for multiple domains. The virtusertable file allows you to set up mappings of usernames at other hosted domains to go to other local users' mailboxes at your normal domain; think of it as an aliases file on steroids. The local-host-names file allows you to specify which domains you're hosting mail for.

The complete documentation for how to use the virtual-hosting database and other configuration files can be found at http://www.sendmail.org, the Sendmail Consortium's Web site.

Controlling Sendmail

Sendmail operates by keeping a single *master* process running and listening on port 25 for incoming connections—as well as additional processes for handling queue runs, sending messages to remote recipients, and other tasks. The master process is started at boot time from /etc/rc. Starting and stopping the Sendmail master process is made easy by `Makefile` and the integrated nature of the resource configuration files in `/etc`. To start the Sendmail server, simply go into `/etc/mail` and enter **make start**:

```
# make start
(. /etc/defaults/rc.conf; source_rc_confs;  if [
➥"${sendmail_enable}" = "YES" -a -r /etc/mail/sendmail.cf ];
➥then  /usr/sbin/sendmail ${sendmail_flags}; fi  )
```

Because this command echoes its actions, you can see that it pulls in relevant configuration details from the systemwide resource configuration files—in which flags such as -q30m (do a queue run every thirty minutes) and -bd (run as a background daemon) are centrally specified. It will even refuse to start the process if the `sendmail_enable` variable in the `rc.conf` files is set to `NO`.

Restarting or stopping the master process is equally simple:

```
# make restart
/bin/kill -HUP `head -1 /var/run/sendmail.pid`
# make stop
/bin/kill -TERM `head -1 /var/run/sendmail.pid`
```

You can see what state each Sendmail process is in by using `ps` in wide mode in conjunction with `grep`; each process reports its position in the queue as an argument against its name in the process table. The following example shows the master process (51248) and a process in the middle of a queue run (54150):

```
51248  ??  Ss    0:00.17 sendmail: accepting connections (sendmail)
54150  ??  I     0:00.02 sendmail: ./f4GKwVW16827
➥mail.backstreetboys.com.: user open (sendmail)
```

The Message Queue

Messages waiting to be sent by Sendmail sit in `/var/spool/mqueue`. In Sendmail's default configuration, a new `sendmail -q` process is started every 30 minutes, stepping through each queued message and attempting to deliver it to its destination. This continues for five days: At the end of which, an undeliverable message is returned to the sender with the relevant error headers attached.

If you have some messages in your queue, which you almost certainly will if you've been using the system for any length of time, you can browse through them at will. Unlike opaque systems such as Microsoft Exchange in which queue files are kept in a database without an easy way to tweak or even see the files waiting to be sent, Sendmail provides both. Queued messages are just plain-text files, capable of being read and edited by regular text editors. This gives the administrator great control over how the mail system operates; however, it also provides an opportunity for the administrator to abuse his power by looking through pending messages' contents. If you run a system in which you trust your users, be sure that they can trust you too!

The first such tool that comes with Sendmail is called `mailq`, and it's a way to list the current state of all messages waiting in the queue.

```
# mailq
                /var/spool/mqueue (2 requests)
——Q-ID—— —Size— ——-Q-Time——· —————Sender/Recipient——————
f4H1Ahu36976    6246 Wed May 16 18:10 MAILER-DAEMON
                (Deferred: Operation timed out with mlists.acmecity.com.)
                                    <fred@acmecity.com>
f4GKwVW16827     706 Wed May 16 13:58 www
                (host map: lookup (hotamil.com): deferred)
                                    bob@hotamil.com
```

Using `mailq`, you can keep an eye on what kind of mail transfer errors frequently occur on your system. If people often forget to specify complete email addresses or misspell common mail server hostnames, you can address that problem through education and tutorials that you send to your users or make publicly available; if you're getting a lot of hostname lookup errors, it might point to a configuration problem on your end. It's an excellent diagnostic tool.

The queue also gives you the ability to fix mistakes in messages on the way out. Let's say, for instance, that you had an entry like the second one in the `mailq` output shown earlier. The erroneous recipient domain is the result of a simple typo; you can either wait five days for Sendmail to give up trying to find `hotamil.com` and send it back to you as an error, or you can fix this problem right in the queue.

To do this, go into `/var/spool/mqueue` and look for the files matching the ID of the entry in the `mailq` output. These would be the files `dff4GKwVW16827` and `qff4GKwVW16827`; the first contains the message body, and the second contains the message headers in an interim format. Simply open up the file with the headers (`qff4GKwVW16827`) in a text editor, replace all occurrences of `hotamil.com` with `hotmail.com`, save the file, and wait for the next queue run. The message will go through cleanly this time.

If you can't wait that long, force a queue run by running `sendmail -q -v`. This gives you the added bonus of a look into exactly how Sendmail does its SMTP transactions with all the remote systems; with each message it processes, it will echo to the session all the output from the transaction, just as in our example at the beginning of the chapter. You'll get to see all the interesting greeting messages that various administrators program into their MTAs, visible only to other MTAs, and therefore often quite creative and silly. You can use Ctrl+C to exit at any time—messages are removed from the queue only after they've been successfully transferred.

Mail Relaying and Spam Control

You can't have a mail server online on the Internet without it being probed by spammers to see if they can use it for broadcasting their junk mail all over the world—and if they can, they will. *Relaying* mail means passing on messages that neither originate from nor end up on the local system. That's what most spammers do: They connect from a remote, anonymous location to any "open" mail server that they can find that imposes no restrictions on who can connect to them and relay mail through to other servers.

For a legitimate dial-up or remote user to use your SMTP server to send a message to another remote recipient, your server has to act as a relay, forwarding the message to the recipient even if the message didn't originate from and wasn't addressed to anyone on its machine. Functionally, as illustrated in Figure 23.2, this is exactly how a spammer would send an unsolicited message to the same recipient through the same SMTP server: It must relay.

FIGURE 23.2

Relaying. Spammers and legitimate users, if they're not local to S1, must use S1 as a relay to forward their messages to S2.

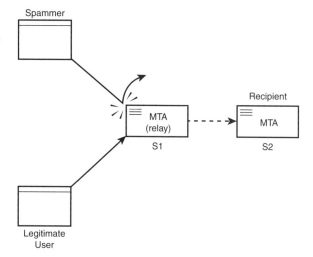

Relaying is usually allowed by what's known as the *MX record*, a line in the SMTP server's network DNS database (either served from the same machine as the SMTP server or another server in the same network) that tells all the machines within that network that your SMTP server (S1) is a legitimate Mail eXchanger for them. Sendmail, in its default configuration on FreeBSD, will accept mail from senders whose MX record points to S1, defining it as the MTA for the network. This prevents people outside the network from using S1 as a relay; if they try, their messages will be bounced back with a `Relaying denied` error.

> You can find out what the registered MX host is for a domain by using the `host` command:
>
> ```
> # host somecompany.com
> somecompany.com has address 164.199.3.78
> somecompany.com mail is handled (pri=30) by mail-1.somecompany.com
> ```
>
> You can then connect directly to this host, `mail-1.somecompany.com`, to perform raw SMTP transactions (for testing purposes, for example).

The problem commonly faced, though, is that this setup is great for ISPs or enterprise networks that have a fully defined network, DNS entries for all its hosts, and a proper MX record pointing to the relaying SMTP server. But what about standalone Internet hosts, which might have users all over the world trying to use it to transmit mail? Each of these users, when trying to send a message through S1 from wherever they happen to be, will get a `Relaying denied` error back unless S1 has been specifically configured to allow them to relay. There are a number of ways to do this; each method has its benefits and drawbacks, but because they all decrease the security of your system to some degree, you should consider them only if absolutely necessary and appropriate to your system's role as a mail server.

- Add "trusted" sender domains to the file `/etc/mail/relay-domains`, which doesn't exist in the default installation. Any host within a listed domain will be permitted to relay through your server. You have to restart Sendmail after modifying this file. This is easy and effective, but as soon as you add a large, popular domain to this file that might contain spammers as well as legitimate senders, its benefit is lost.

- Use the access database (`/etc/mail/access`). This feature allows you to set up an `OK` or `RELAY` rule for each known host or domain from which your users will be connecting. This works well for small impromptu networks or for a few remote hosts at easily identifiable addresses, but it doesn't scale well for a lot of users on dynamic addresses.

- Enable any of the five or six relaying exception features available in Sendmail by adding them to `/etc/mail/freebsd.mc` and regenerating the `sendmail.cf` file (as shown earlier). There's a feature that enables you to allow relaying based on whether the `From:` header is set to an address at your domain (`relay_local_from`)—though this is easily forged by spammers and therefore the feature isn't usually advisable. There's also an optional feature to perform a check against one of the *Realtime Blackhole Lists*, which are centrally maintained databases of known spammers (and which often require you to subscribe for a fee).

This feature is in the default `freebsd.mc`, but commented out; to enable it, remove the `dnl` comment and rebuild the config file.

- As an absolute last resort, turn off relay checking altogether by enabling the `promiscuous_relay` feature. This will allow any valid user to send mail through your Sendmail server; however, it will also allow any spammer to do the same. There are independently run databases on the Internet that keep records of all "open" mail servers, and some service providers use these databases as "black hole" lists of their own. You don't want your server to end up in these databases! If it does, some legitimate mail from your users or their correspondents might be blocked because of their ISPs blocking mail to or from your server. It's an incredibly bad idea to run an open mail server. However, if your server is in a secure network environment (for example, inside an enterprise network protected by a NAT firewall), it can eliminate a great deal of unnecessary hassle associated with securing the server.

As a general rule, the best solution to the relaying problem is simply to instruct all your users to use the SMTP servers provided by their own dial-up ISPs. These services will always have their own SMTP servers that are open to their own customers. Because the headers in a mail message (such as the `From:` address) are all derived from the message body and therefore completely under the control of the email client program, there's no reason for a remote user to want to use your SMTP server if he already has one of his own.

The Sendmail Consortium has an excellent page on relaying rules and your various available configuration options at `http://www.sendmail.org/tips/relaying.html`.

Summary

In this hour, you learned the basics of running an SMTP server using Sendmail. You saw how SMTP is structured, how messages travel from one user to another via SMTP and POP/IMAP, and you saw how to tweak Sendmail to behave according to your personal tastes.

Sendmail is one of the largest and most complex beasts in UNIX. A full treatment of Sendmail-based email services would cover the numerous methods for customizing Sendmail in a large ISP or enterprise configuration. It would also discuss how to set up POP3 and IMAP servers for that "last mile" of the connection, as well as discussing MTAs that are designed as better, faster, more scalable, and easier-to-use alternatives to Sendmail. But what you have seen here is the core of what makes Sendmail itself the workhorse of the Internet: an unglamorous job, but one that it does very well nonetheless.

Q&A

Q Mail is bouncing back to me with an error of `"Cannot resolve hostname"`. What do I do?

A Make sure that your FreeBSD machine has a valid reverse DNS lookup record. Type `nslookup 111.112.113.114`, using your machine's IP address instead of 111.112.113.114. If you don't get your machine's correct hostname back, talk to your network administrator and get the reverse DNS record fixed (generally by making sure that there is a valid record for your machine's IP address that points to resolvable hostname).

Q I added some aliases to `/etc/mail/aliases`, but sending mail to those addresses doesn't obey the aliases I set up.

A You need to regenerate the alias database. Go into `/etc/mail` and type `make aliases`, or use the `newaliases` command.

Q I'm trying to send mail through my server, and I keep getting `Relaying denied` errors!

A Sendmail is behaving the way it should in the Internet age: It's not letting your mail through if you're not a local user and aren't sending *to* a local user. You will need to exempt yourself from the anti-relaying rules by adding your desktop machine's IP address or subnet address to `/etc/mail/access`, with a `RELAY` rule, just as one example of a solution.

Q Sendmail is too big and ugly. I feel confident in my ability to install and use something else. What do you recommend?

A The most popular Sendmail replacement is Postfix, written by Wietse Venema. See `http://www.postfix.org` for more; you can install it from the ports (`/usr/ports/mail/postfix`). FreeBSD is designed to allow Postfix to be installed as a drop-in replacement for Sendmail, via `/etc/mail/mailer.conf`. See `man mailer.conf` for details. You might also want to look into Qmail, which is faster and more secure than Sendmail.

Workshop

This section is designed to answer common questions that come up about Sendmail and SMTP concepts, as well as to solidify your understanding of email services with quiz questions and exercises for further exploration.

Quiz

1. What is the location of the Sendmail binary on FreeBSD?

   A. `/usr/bin/sendmail`

   B. `/usr/local/sbin/sendmail`

   C. `/usr/sbin/sendmail`

   D. `/usr/libexec/sendmail/sendmail`

2. What file do I edit to add aliases to the system?

   A. `/etc/aliases`

   B. `/etc/mail-aliases`

   C. `/usr/local/etc/mail/aliases`

   D. `/etc/mail/aliases`

3. What file do I edit to make general Sendmail configuration changes?

   A. `/etc/mail/freebsd.mc`

   B. `/etc/mail/sendmail.cf`

   C. `/usr/sbin/sendmail`

   D. `/etc/mail/mailer.conf`

4. What port does Sendmail communicate on?

   A. 10

   B. 23

   C. 25

   D. 110

5. What's the best (but least convenient) way to protect against spam relaying?

   A. MX record restriction

   B. `/etc/mail/access`

   C. The `promiscuous_relay` feature

   D. Realtime Blackhole Lists

6. What's the worst (but most convenient) way?

   A. MX record restriction

   B. `/etc/mail/access`

   C. The `promiscuous_relay` feature

   D. Realtime Blackhole Lists

23

Quiz Answers

1. Either C or D are correct—trick question! `/usr/sbin/sendmail` is what you would call from a program or the command line; but it's really a "wrapper" that calls `/usr/libexec/sendmail/sendmail`. If you were to "drop in" Postfix as a replacement, `/usr/sbin/sendmail` would simply change where it pointed.

2. The correct answer is D.

3. The correct answer is A. Remember to compile a new `sendmail.cf` and restart Sendmail after editing the Master Config file.

4. The correct answer is C.

5. The correct answer is A; use per-host exceptions to prevent `Relaying denied` errors on your own messages.

6. The correct answer is C. Don't use this unless you absolutely have to, or if you're positive that your server is in a situation in which it's at no risk of being made into a spam relay.

Exercises

1. Explore the myriad uses for the `aliases` database. Try creating a mailing list that's really just an alias which reads in the contents of a text file full of email addresses.

2. Try creating a *real* mailing list; install Majordomo or Mailman from the ports (`/usr/ports/mail/majordomo` or `/usr/ports/mail/mailman`) and explore how they use extremely complex aliases to accomplish such feats as archiving, resending, parsing, bouncing, and approval by the administrator.

3. This hour doesn't cover POP3 and IMAP, the common protocols for providing mail delivery services at the recipient end. Look into Qpopper (`/usr/ports/mail/qpopper`) and IMAP-UW (`/usr/ports/mail/imap-uw`) and explore their potential usefulness to your system. Both packages have Web sites with URLs listed in their ports' `pkg-descr` files.

HOUR 24

File Sharing

You have now learned almost all that you need to know in order to run a FreeBSD machine as a fully functional workstation or server on the Internet. However, there is one final puzzle piece before the picture is complete: file sharing. This is the subject of the final hour.

Any computer on the Internet can handle email and Web surfing. Those are the two biggest and most commercialized segments of the Internet, and they are all that many Internet users ever experience. However, a truly networked computer must have a third aspect of its networking in place before it can be considered truly *complete*, and that is the capability to share files with other computers across the network. This kind of connectivity dates back to the earliest days of the Internet—yet it occurs not over a single simple protocol as with email or the Web, but over a number of different platform-specific protocols that keep changing over time. From the rudimentary FTP through the proprietary AppleTalk and NetBIOS/SMB, to the most modern peer-to-peer applications, file sharing has evolved into a myriad of different forms over the years (not least because the materials that some people choose to share involve illegal copyright violations). The benefits of file sharing are mitigated somewhat by the "underground" mystique it still retains.

Yet file sharing is essential for downloading legitimate software and working in clustered environments in which documents must be available to everyone quickly and conveniently. In this hour, you will learn

- How to set up an FTP server and share files over FTP
- How to set up an NFS server and allow users of other UNIX machines to share your files over NFS
- How to use NFS to access files on another UNIX machine
- How to use Samba to share files with Windows machines

File Sharing Through FTP

The *File Transfer Protocol (FTP)* is probably the oldest form of file sharing available to computer users, and it is also one of the most rudimentary—though it is still used widely for tasks such as downloading large binary files (usually software archives).

A user connects to an FTP server using a specialized program, usually simply called `ftp` on most systems, although many more full-featured graphical FTP clients are available (including Web browsers, which incorporate some FTP functionality). FTP is also built in to the standard windowing filesystem of Windows and Mac OS X.

When the FTP program connects to the server, it prompts for a username and a password; if what the user enters is correct for a user that exists on the server, he can then browse his home directory using the `ls` command, download files with `get`, and upload them with `put`. Many other commands are available, allowing the user to rename files, create and remove directories, and navigate through the remote and local filesystem. Finally, when the user is done, the `quit` command exits the FTP program. FTP is interactive and session based, and the user must know the server name and the location of the file he wants to retrieve in order to use it effectively. This is part of what makes it such a primitive protocol, although its ubiquity means that it is still very important to life on the Internet.

FreeBSD comes with an FTP server built in (the standard BSD `ftpd` daemon), configured out of the box to enable FTP access to authenticated users. The built-in server is quite complete and secure, and it allows you to transfer files to and from your FreeBSD machine without any additional setup. Nonetheless, you will need to know how to run an FTP server properly to prevent unauthorized access and use of your machine, especially if you choose to enable "anonymous FTP" access—the ability of any random user to come to your server and download files from a specified "public" location.

You can replace FreeBSD's default FTP server with any of a number of other choices—some of the more popular being WU-FTPD and ProFTPd. These are available in the ports (`/usr/ports/ftp`) or the packages (under `ftp`).

The file layout of the FTP server, in the default configuration, is integrated with the system in the same way that most other core services are. Several configuration files are in `/etc`—some of which do double duty as systemwide resource files used by other services. Individual users' home directories are considered part of the FTP server layout because each authenticated user connects directly into his home directory.

Because anonymous FTP requires a bit more configuration and maintenance than regular authenticated FTP, though, we must examine the difference between them a little more in depth.

Authenticated and Anonymous FTP

When a user who has an account on the server logs in via FTP with his username and password, the server provides access to the user's home directory and all its files. The user can enter an `ls` command to verify this. Each regular user thus connects to a different point on the FTP server when logging in as a user: his home directory. However, anonymous FTP provides a way for a user without an account to connect. An anonymous user opens the connection, enters `anonymous` or `ftp` as his username, and any text string (conventionally the user's email address, though this usually isn't enforced or authenticated in any way) for the password. The user is then given access to a *public* FTP area: `/var/ftp`, the home directory of the `ftp` user (which is also created when anonymous FTP is enabled), as shown in Figure 24.1.

FIGURE 24.1

Authenticated and anonymous FTP users.

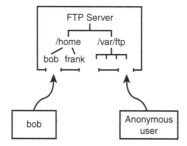

A fundamental difference exists between regular account users and anonymous FTP users, though. Anonymous FTP is in a `chroot` *jail* by default (`chroot` means "change effective filesystem root"), meaning that to the user, /var/ftp appears to be the server root /. Nothing outside /var/ftp is accessible or even visible. A regular account user can enter a command such as cd /usr/local to move to any part of the system and access files with the same readability permissions as in a terminal session, but an anonymous FTP user can't get out of /var/ftp at all. An anonymous user who enters cd /pub will be taken to /var/ftp/pub.

Enabling Anonymous FTP Access

By default, anonymous FTP is not enabled; the easiest way to enable it, if you choose to do so, is through sysinstall. Run /stand/sysinstall; then enter the Configure and Networking sections. Scroll to the Anon FTP option, and press the spacebar to enter the Anonymous FTP Configuration screen, as shown in Figure 24.2.

FIGURE 24.2
Anonymous FTP configuration options.

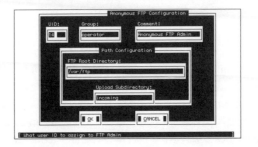

The default options are generally appropriate for a typical FreeBSD system. The UID, Group, and Comment fields control how the new ftp user will be created. This user's home directory is set to /var/ftp, which is how anonymous FTP works—the ftp login is treated as a regular user that behaves as if it's listed in /etc/ftpchroot, so anybody logging in as ftp (or its alias, anonymous) will be put into a chroot jail at /var/ftp.

You can change any of the fields to suit your system (for instance, if you already have a user with a UID of 14, or if you want a name for the upload directory that's different from incoming). When you select OK at the bottom of the screen, the ftp user will be created, as will the /var/ftp tree with its necessary subdirectories.

Disabling Anonymous FTP Access

The /stand/sysinstall program doesn't provide the capability to disable anonymous FTP after it's been enabled, but you can do this a number of ways (any of the following will do the job):

- Remove the /var/ftp tree.

- Remove the `ftp` user.
- Add the `ftp` user to `/etc/ftpusers` (probably the easiest and cleanest method). We will discuss the use of this file shortly.

Similarly, you can disable the upload (`incoming`) directory by simply removing it, or else by changing its permissions to 755 (the default directory permissions in which only the owner—root—can write into it). Re-enable it (or any other directory to which you want anonymous users to be able to upload files) by changing its permissions to 1777—for instance, `chmod 1777 /var/ftp/incoming`.

Controlling FTP Access

It's essential to have some control over who is allowed to access your FTP server. FTP operates in cleartext, meaning that the usernames and passwords sent across the network when an FTP session is started up can be "sniffed" by an eavesdropper watching packets on the network. Also, perhaps you want only certain authenticated users to be able to connect to the server and others to be locked out.

This can be done in a number of ways. The two most convenient ways involve the `/etc/ftpusers` and `/etc/shells` files. A third way, `/var/run/nologin`, controls whether the server accepts connections at all.

The `/etc/ftpusers` File

The simplest way to forbid a certain individual user or a group of users from connecting to the FTP server is to add that user's login name to the `/etc/ftpusers` file, which exists in the default FreeBSD installation and contains the names of the various system pseudo-users (such as `operator`, `bin`, `tty`, and so on). These users have null passwords, and `ftpd` will not allow anyone with a null password to connect; keeping the usernames in `/etc/ftpusers` provides an extra layer of security.

You can add any username to the file, and because `ftpd` reads all relevant configuration files with each new connection, there's no need to restart any processes. Try connecting to the FTP server as a disallowed user, and you should get a response like the following:

```
# ftp localhost
Connected to localhost.somewhere.com.
220 stripes.somewhere.com FTP server (Version 6.00LS) ready.
Name (localhost:frank): frank
530 User frank access denied.
ftp: Login failed.
ftp>
```

24

Note that the `access denied` message appears immediately after the server receives the username—it doesn't prompt for a password. This prevents passwords from being sent over the wire, providing an extra security precaution in case you've disabled a user out of concern regarding an eavesdropper sniffing for passwords.

You can also add any group name to `/etc/ftpusers`; simply precede the name with an at symbol (@): for example, `@users`. Any user who is part of any group listed in the file will be disallowed access.

The `/etc/shells` File

After seeing whether the user is listed in `/etc/ftpusers`, `ftpd` checks the shell associated with the user and sees whether it's listed in `/etc/shells`. If it isn't, the user will get the same kind of `access denied` message as with `/etc/ftpusers`. You can leverage this functionality to prevent a user from logging in with a terminal program *or* with FTP by changing the user's shell to `/sbin/nologin` (which simply prints out an `account not available` message and exits, and is not listed in `/etc/shells`) or something similarly constructed.

The /var/run/nologin File

To turn off FTP logins completely, without modifying `/etc/inetd.conf` or any other such config files, you can simply place a file called `nologin` in `/var/run`; if `ftpd` sees this file, it will respond to all connections as follows:

```
# ftp localhost
Connected to localhost.somewhere.com.
530 System not available.
ftp>
```

You can use `touch /var/run/nologin` to create the file (with zero length) and disable FTP logins. Remove the file (`rm /var/run/nologin`) to re-enable the FTP server.

Basic NFS Configuration

A somewhat more advanced form of file sharing, built in to all UNIX operating systems, is the *Network Filesystem (NFS)*. Unlike AppleTalk and Windows networking, NFS is not a peer-to-peer protocol. It's a client-server model—where one machine has *shares* (or specific folders in the filesystem that are *exported*, or made available over the network), and another machine connects to that machine requesting access to its shares. The client then mounts the desired share into its own filesystem, as though the NFS share were simply another UNIX disk or partition, and the user can list the files in it and work with them at the shell command line.

Like FTP, NFS has no built-in means for *browsing*, or the ability to get a listing of what servers or shares are available on a local network. An NFS client must know which servers it can connect to and what the available shares' names are before it can do anything useful.

An NFS server can control exactly which clients are able to connect to it—for example, by hostname or IP address; or by centralized login, as with NIS or Kerberos. Another feature of NFS is that because it does not depend on LAN broadcasts for server discovery, it can be used across the Internet just as easily as across the LAN. A client in Boston can mount a share from a server in San Francisco, if necessary. By contrast, NetBIOS/SMB and AppleTalk only can operate within *domains* or *zones* on the local network (though AppleTalk/IP can cross the Internet freely).

The client-server structure of NFS is designed so that you can centralize the resources in your network. For example, an enterprise might give all its employees home directories on a central UNIX machine: Every other system in the network that supports NFS will be able to mount those home directories and access them remotely, rather than requiring each machine to have its own copy of every home directory. Figure 24.3 shows this kind of network topology in action. The same can be done for build directories (in a software development environment) or shared applications that are centrally installed (as in a university workstation cluster). NFS mounts can be used in conjunction with NIS (centralized login management) to provide the entire network with user authentication; then, file ownership and permissions on every file in a mounted share will work just as on the NFS server machine itself. You can even install FreeBSD over NFS if you mount the installation CD-ROM on the NFS server and point `sysinstall` toward it.

NFS doesn't have any built-in security or encryption, so it should be used over the Internet only if you're working with files that can safely be exposed to the public. Mission-critical or sensitive data should never be sent over wide-area NFS except inside a LAN protected by a firewall or through an encrypted VPN tunnel.

A FreeBSD machine can be configured to be an NFS server, an NFS client, or both. We'll talk first about setting it up as an NFS server and then about configuring it as a client.

24

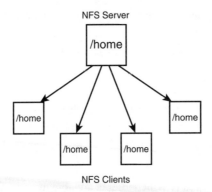

FIGURE 24.3

An enterprise network with central NFS-mounted home directories.

Configuring an NFS Server

Setting up your FreeBSD machine to be an NFS server involves adding the following two lines to /etc/rc.conf:

```
nfs_server_enable="YES"
rpcbind_enable="YES"
```

When you set the nfs_server_enable option and reboot, FreeBSD starts three different kinds of daemon processes after reading the contents of the /etc/exports file to determine what to share via NFS. These processes—nfsd, mountd, and rpcbind—each has its own role to play in NFS and can be tweaked for maximum performance by experts. The default configuration, however, should be adequate for most users' needs.

Setting Up Shares: The /etc/exports File

The /etc/exports file lists what directory trees should be shared via NFS and who should be allowed to access them. If /etc/exports does not exist or is not readable when the network is started, the nfsd and mountd processes are not started.

The full format of /etc/exports is defined in man exports. A basic export line specifies one or more directories that should be exported (shared), any of several options, and then an optional list of hosts (by IP address, network, netgroup, or hostname) that are allowed to share the specified directories. For example, the following line shares the /home directory and all its subdirectories to anybody who connects:

```
/home -alldirs
```

Note that the -alldirs option can only be specified if the share is the mount point of a filesystem (for example, /usr or /home). If it isn't, for example if /home is not the point at which a filesystem is mounted (if your /home is just a directory inside /usr), the share will not be made available.

A share that can be accessed only by three specified hosts and is read-only would look like this:

```
/usr2 -ro -alldirs stripes.somewhere.com spots.somewhere.com 64.41.131.165
```

> You can create groups of hosts (*netgroups*) by specifying them in the file `/etc/netgroup`. A group can be specified in the following form:
>
> `groupname (host, user, domain) (host, user, domain) ...`
>
> For instance, to create a group called `desktops` that contained three particular hosts (named `sol`, `luna`, and `terra`), the line would look like this:
>
> `desktops (sol,,) (luna,,) (terra,,)`
>
> A netgroup defined on usernames would look like this:
>
> `developers (,frank,) (,bob,) (,alice,)`
>
> You can then use any of these netgroup names instead of hostnames in `/etc/exports` to confine an NFS share to members of that group.

File ownership in an NFS share is mapped based on the UIDs of each file and directory. If the usernames and UIDs on the server and client machines are the same (for instance, if the machines' logins are synchronized via NIS or Kerberos), the permissions will match. However, if the UID 1045 maps on the server to the username `bill`, but UID 1045 on the client is `john`, John will own the files in the share that the server thinks Bill owns. When exporting a share containing files owned by many different users, make sure that the infrastructure is in place to provide consistent mappings between UIDs and usernames on all the machines on your network.

You can use the `-maproot=<username>` or `-maproot=<UID>` options to map ownership so that the username matching `<username>` or having the user ID `<UID>` on the client machine will have full root permissions in the share. For example, to share the entire filesystem of the NFS server with anybody in the `64.41.131` network, with the client user `frank` having full read/write access to all the files, use the following:

```
/ -maproot=frank -network 64.41.131 -mask 255.255.255.0
```

After making any changes to `/etc/exports`, you need to restart the `mountd` process. Do this by accessing the runtime PID file:

```
# kill -HUP `cat /var/run/mountd.pid`
```

> You can't have multiple export lines for mount points within the same partition or filesystem. This is to prevent problems in cases where the export permissions for different shares in the same filesystem would conflict. If you want to create multiple shares that are within the same filesystem, you must put them all on the same line. The following setup is illegal:
>
> ```
> /home/frank 64.41.131.102
> /home/joe 64.41.131.102
> ```
>
> But the following setup is correct:
>
> ```
> /home/frank /home/joe 64.41.131.102
> ```

You can use the showmount program to display the valid shares and their permissions. This is how you can tell whether your /etc/exports setup is valid:

```
# showmount -e
Exports list on localhost:
/usr                              Everyone
/home/frank                       64.41.131.102
/home/joe                         64.41.131.102
/                                 64.41.131.0
```

Starting NFS Services Without Rebooting

The cleanest way to start NFS services is to reboot the system. However, if you need to start the services and you don't want to reboot, simply issue the following commands as root (omitting the rpcbind command if it's already running):

```
# rpcbind
# nfsd -u -t -n 4
# mountd -r
```

Then, use showmount -e to make sure that the NFS shares are being exported properly.

Configuring an NFS Client

If your FreeBSD machine will be mounting NFS shares from other servers, you will need to configure it as a client. Technically this isn't really necessary—you can mount an NFS share in a rudimentary fashion right out of the box. However, configuring the system as an NFS client gives you a few features that ensure speedy and reliable performance.

To set up an NFS client machine, simply enable the following line in /etc/rc.conf:

```
nfs_client_enable="YES"
```

This setting enables the NFS Input/Output Daemon, `nfsiod`, which helps to streamline NFS client requests and tunes a few kernel settings to improve access time. This is all handled automatically in the `/etc/rc.network` script at boot time, along with the NFS server settings (that you saw earlier).

Mounting Remote Filesystems

Mounting an NFS share is done with the `mount_nfs` command, which is a shorthand command for `mount -t nfs` (as you saw in Chapter 8, "Storage Systems and Backup Utilities"). In its most common form, you would pass to it two arguments: the host and share names in a combined string, as well as the local mount point:

```
# mount_nfs spots:/home /home2
```

A successful mount will result in no output. Check that the mount was successful with the `df` command:

```
# df
Filesystem           1K-blocks     Used     Avail Capacity  Mounted on
/dev/ad0s1a             992239    54353    858507      6%    /
/dev/ad0s1f           26704179  4872963  19694882     20%    /home
/dev/ad0s1e            9924475  1642343   7488174     18%    /usr
procfs                       4        4         0    100%    /proc
spots:/home           9924475  1642343   7488174     18%    /home2
```

If you go into the `/home2` directory, you'll see all the directories within `/home` on the NFS server, with each file's ownership mapped based on UID, as we discussed earlier. The filesystem will remain mounted until you explicitly unmount it with the `umount` command:

```
# umount /home2
```

 Remember to leave any NFS-mounted directory before you try to unmount it with `umount`. You will get a `device busy` error if you try to unmount a filesystem while you're still inside it.

NFS shares can be mounted in a great variety of different ways, and the options are laid out in the `man mount_nfs` page. Some of the more useful are the `-T` option, which forces TCP transport rather than UDP (useful for mounts done over long-distance WAN links); and the `-s` and `-x <seconds>` flags, which allow the mount to timeout and disappear after a specified period and fail (a *soft* mount).

```
# mount_nfs -s -x 60 spots:/home /home2
```

Another useful option is -i, which enables interruptibility. Normally, if you have mounted an NFS share and the server becomes unresponsive or unreachable, any filesystem calls you make (commands that deal with the shared files, such as ls) can hang in such a way that even pressing Ctrl+C won't stop them. The -i option makes it so that Ctrl+C (the termination signal) will force the command to fail, returning control to you.

As with other filesystem types, you can add NFS mounts to /etc/fstab to set up predefined mount points, simplifying the mount process. Place any options you would otherwise pass to mount_nfs in the Options column, separated by commas:

```
# Device              Mountpoint     FStype  Options           Dump    Pass#
spots:/home           /home2         nfs     rw,-T,-i,noauto 0        0
```

With a table entry like this, you can mount an NFS filesystem with the mount command:

```
# mount /home2
```

Mounting Remote Filesystems Automatically at System Boot

All filesystems in /etc/fstab are automatically mounted at boot time unless the noauto option is present. You can specify that remote NFS shares should be mounted at startup by simply adding them to /etc/fstab, as you just saw. However, there are a few things to watch out for.

Most notably, NFS has an extremely long default timeout period, and the phase during startup when filesystems are mounted is a synchronous, blocking process. If your NFS server or servers cannot be found—for instance, if the server machine isn't running, or if your own machine's network connection is not configured properly—the boot process can hang for an intolerably long period before giving up and finishing the boot procedure.

You can solve this problem by placing the noauto option in /etc/fstab, as you saw in our earlier example. However, this means that you have to mount each NFS share manually after the system is fully booted. There's a better way to handle this: the -b option.

```
# Device              Mountpoint     FStype  Options    Dump    Pass#
spots:/home           /home2         nfs     rw,-b      0        0
```

The -b option tells mount to make a quick attempt to contact the server and, if it can't, to fork off a child process to continue trying to connect while the boot process continues on. Similarly, if you mount a share from the command line using -b, the process forks into the background and returns you to the command prompt. The following is the output you would get when trying to mount the share specified in the preceding example /etc/fstab line after trying for 60 seconds:

```
# mount /home2
spots:/home: nfsd: RPCPROG_NFS: RPC: Port mapper failure - RPC: Timed out

nfs: Cannot immediately mount spots:/home, backgrounding
```

The background mount_nfs process will keep trying to mount the share until it's successful. This method is particularly useful in computing clusters or labs in which NFS-mounted resources are nice to have but not required for correct operation—for example, a cluster in which an NFS mount contains popular user programs or games, but all critical system functions are available on disks on the local system.

Samba and Windows File Sharing

FTP and NFS are good for communicating and sharing files between two UNIX machines. But the fact is that this is a Windows world, and no matter what kind of network environment your machine will be in, it will probably be surrounded by Windows machines. If you want to share files with your Windows using friends, you're going to have to play by their rules.

Fortunately, FreeBSD has the capability to do Windows-style file sharing with all the functionality that a Windows machine would have. Specifically, it has Samba, a software package that allows a UNIX machine to appear to be just another Windows machine on the local network; Windows machines can connect to it just as they would to another Windows machine. Samba even handles printer sharing and domain logins, and can act as a Windows domain controller in its own right.

An advantage that Windows NetBIOS/SMB protocol has over systems such as NFS is that it supports automatic server discovery, or browsing. In Windows, if you open the Network Neighborhood or My Network Places window, it will display the names of all available SMB servers on the local network. This way, you know which servers you can connect to without having to know their names in advance.

The name of each machine, as it appears in the network browser window (as shown in Figure 24.4), is its *NetBIOS name*, a designation that Windows allows to be up to 15 characters long. Although Windows requires you to input a NetBIOS name in uppercase, it shows up in the network browser window in initially capitalized, lowercase form. Under other operating systems (such as FreeBSD), the NetBIOS name is the same as the machine's hostname, truncated to 15 characters if necessary.

24

FIGURE 24.4

The Windows network browser window, showing a FreeBSD machine running Samba.

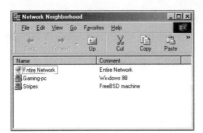

NetBIOS names are handled by a form of name service, somewhat like DNS names, but mapping the displayed NetBIOS machine names to particular machines is based on other criteria as well as the IP address (because NetBIOS isn't restricted to IP). Samba's name server component is separate from the actual SMB data server, as you will see.

One drawback to NetBIOS is that it operates only on a LAN; NetBIOS packets are broadcast based, and therefore aren't forwarded by routers. The *WINS (Windows Internet Name Service)* protocol exists to link Windows sharing zones on different networks, mitigating this issue somewhat.

Installing and Configuring Samba

Samba is available in the ports at `/usr/ports/net/samba` or in the packages. Refer to Hour 6, "Adding and Removing Third-Party Software," for details on how to install a package or port.

After you have installed the Samba package, a variety of new items will be installed: daemon executables (in `/usr/local/sbin`), administrative tools (in `/usr/local/bin`), documentation and examples (in `/usr/local/share`), and configuration files that go into `/usr/local/etc`. Some of the possible config files don't exist in the default installation; you have to create them from scratch if you want to take advantage of their functionality. There are also code pages (in `/usr/local/etc/codepages`) that map Windows character sets to UNIX ones.

The only configuration file that exists in the package is `/usr/local/etc/smb.conf.default`, which you must rename to `smb.conf` for it to work. Similarly, the `/usr/local/etc/rc.d/samba.sh.sample` startup script must be renamed to `samba.sh`. In the very easiest way to get Samba running, you only need to edit `smb.conf` and modify the `workgroup` line to reflect the workgroup or domain of which your machine is a part. For instance, if your workgroup is called MYGROUP, change the `workgroup` line as follows:

```
# workgroup = NT-Domain-Name or Workgroup-Name, eg: REDHAT4
  workgroup = MYGROUP
```

Samba will now be started automatically when the system boots. To start it manually, run the `samba.sh` script with the `start` parameter:

```
# /usr/local/etc/rc.d/samba.sh start
 Samba#
```

> Note that there is no line break in the script output after the service name Samba. This cosmetic flaw exists because during startup, each service in /usr/local/etc/rc.d is started sequentially, and the echoed output of each startup script all goes onto the same line. Being able to start services from the rc.d startup scripts is a convenience feature, not the primary intended functionality.

24

The `smbd` and `nmbd` Daemons

If the `samba.sh` script runs successfully, you will notice two new processes running: `smbd` and `nmbd`:

```
# ps -waux | grep mbd
root    3855  0.0  1.5  2368 1816  ??  Is    2:43PM  0:00.00
➥/usr/local/sbin/smbd -D
root    3857  0.0  1.2  1940 1496  ??  Ss    2:43PM  0:00.02
➥/usr/local/sbin/nmbd -D
```

The `smbd` daemon is the actual data server, the process that handles SMB/CIFS requests from connected Windows clients—file transfers, print jobs, listings, and so on. Unlike NFS, SMB doesn't require a separate process to be running for each simultaneous connection; the master `smbd` process forks off a new copy of itself for each new client session and handles all that client's requests for the duration of the session. The `-D` option specifies that `smbd` should operate as a standalone daemon, listening for requests on TCP port 139.

Operating in parallel with `smbd` is `nmbd`, the NetBIOS name server. It's the process that allows Windows clients to see the FreeBSD machine in the network browser view, as you saw in Figure 24.4. It also has the job of responding to client requests for a particular NetBIOS host if it's specified by name; if a Windows client uses the \\<name> syntax to connect to a particular server by name, the client sends out a broadcast name request asking for the IP address of the server with that NetBIOS name. It's the job of `nmbd` to send back a response with the requested host's IP address so that the client can open an SMB request directly to the server. It's somewhat like DNS (in that it maps a common name to a direct address), and also has a lot in common with ARP (in that it operates on a LAN through broadcast name requests, rather than to a designated central name server).

Creating Samba Shares

Many examples for how to configure a shared directory can be found in
`smb.conf.default`. To enable any of them, remove the comment mark (#) from the beginning of the appropriate lines in `smb.conf`.

Example shares are displayed below the `===== Share Definitions =====` line in
`smb.conf`. Each share's name is listed in brackets, and the configuration lines following it apply until the next bracketed block. The `smb.conf` file begins with a `[global]` block, allowing you to set global parameters that affect all shares on the system; the rest of the blocks each define a share whose settings override the previously defined global settings.

After making any configuration change in `smb.conf`, you will need to restart Samba by stopping and restarting it:

```
# /usr/local/etc/rc.d/samba.sh stop
# /usr/local/etc/rc.d/samba.sh start
```

> The man `smb.conf` page lists all available configuration parameters and describes in detail what each does. However, you might find it easier to view the page in HTML format—in which headings and examples are set apart with text formatting and made easier to read, as well as being contextually hyperlinked. Refer to the online documentation at
> `http://samba.org/samba/docs/man/smb.conf.5.html` for the formatted version.

Sharing Directories

To share a regular public directory, define a share block like this:

```
[my-public]
   comment = Public Stuff
   path = /usr/local/share/samba-stuff
   public = yes
   writeable = yes
   printable = no
   write list = @staff
```

With this share enabled, a client will see a share called my-public at the top level of the server's share listing. However, unless the user is authenticated and is a member of the UNIX group staff, the files in the share will be read-only. Remove the write list line to make the share writeable by all users. Note that writeable = yes is equivalent to saying read only = no.

By default, a [homes] share is defined and enabled; this special share is built-in, allowing access to each user's home directory on the Samba server if the Windows client connects to it with the proper credentials.

```
[homes]
    comment = Home Directories
    browseable = no
    writeable = yes
```

Because this share is set as not browsable, home directories not owned by the client user are not displayed; if a client connects as a valid user with a home directory on the Samba server, his home directory (labeled with his username because that's the name of the directory in UNIX) appears as one of the available shares. No other users' home directories appear.

Sharing Printers

Like [homes], [printers] is a special share that behaves a little differently from regular shares. Under FreeBSD, all attached printers defined in /etc/printcap are available to Samba users. Chapter 9, "The FreeBSD Printing System," explains how to set up your FreeBSD machine to support local printers in /etc/printcap.

By default, the [printers] share is set up like this:

```
[printers]
    comment = All Printers
    path = /var/spool/samba
    browseable = no
# Set public = yes to allow user 'guest account' to print
    guest ok = no
    writeable = no
    printable = yes
```

Set browseable = yes to allow connected users to see and use your printers.

As stated in the embedded comment, you can make your printers public so that anyone on the network can use them. This involves the use of a *guest user*, which you can set up using *share-level* security. Note that public is a synonym for guest ok, so you would change the guest ok line to yes instead of adding a public = yes line to allow the guest user to print. Guest users and share-level security are a somewhat advanced topic; refer to the Samba Web site, or to the how-to guide at `http://samba.linuxbe.org/en/samba/config/share-1.html`, for further documentation on how to use it.

Access Control

The default method for controlling access to Samba shares is called *user-level* security. In this scheme, the client presents a username/password pair to the server upon the initial setup of the connection. The server determines whether to accept the client based on the username/password pair and the identity of the client machine itself. If it accepts the client, all shares are accessible.

It can be tricky to set up user-level security properly. The Windows username, which is defined either when the Windows user logs in to a local profile or to a domain controller, must exist on the Samba server as a regular UNIX user (or mapped to a UNIX user). For instance, if the Windows user Harris logs on to his Windows machine, opens up the Network Neighborhood window, and tries to connect to our Samba server, he will be denied access (and given a password prompt for a share called `\\STRIPES\IPC$`) unless the user `harris` exists on the UNIX machine.

> In Windows NT/2000, the password prompt allows you to enter a username as well as a password. However, in Windows 95/98/ME, all you get is a password prompt, and the username is derived from the login name.

Samba users must exist in a password database at `/usr/local/private/smbpasswd`, which is similar to `/etc/master.passwd` in that encrypted passwords are stored in it for each local UNIX user. When Samba is installed, users from `/etc/master.passwd` are converted into Samba format and placed into `/usr/local/private/smbpasswd` with both the LANMAN password and the Windows NT password (both are present for compatibility) set to strings of 16 X characters—an invalid password, indicating that the user cannot log in.

To enable a user, you must set the password to something valid. This is done with the `smbpasswd` program. It works similarly to `passwd`, prompting you for your old Samba password and then requiring you to enter a new one twice unless you're root—in which case, you need not supply the old password, and you can change any user's password as well as your own.

```
# smbpasswd harris
New SMB password:
Retype new SMB password:
Password changed for user harris.
```

Accessing Shared Files on a Windows System (The smbfs Filesystem)

SMB file sharing can work both ways. Samba allows you to set up your FreeBSD machine as an SMB server only, but there is a way to set it up as a client and mount a remote SMB share like any other filesystem. This is smbfs, available as a standard kernel module as of FreeBSD 4.4, and in the ports (/usr/ports/net/smbfs) in earlier versions.

The smbfs implementation in FreeBSD includes an smbfs.ko kernel module in /modules and a mount_smbfs tool in /sbin that works like all the other mount_* tools available for mounting various filesystems. The best documentation for smbfs is found in the man mount_smbfs page.

To mount an SMB filesystem using smbfs, use mount_smbfs with a few basic options. The -I flag specifies the hostname or IP address, and the two remaining arguments are the remote share name (of the form //<user>@<NetBIOS name>/<share name>) and the local mount point. To mount the share called public from a Windows machine called gaming-pc onto the local /smb/public directory, use the following syntax:

```
# mount_smbfs -I 64.41.131.139 //guest@gaming-pc/public /smb/public
```

You will be prompted for a password. Use a blank password if the share is set to allow full access; use the appropriate password if the share is set to read-only or password-protected mode.

> The smbfs.ko kernel module is loaded automatically when needed by mount_smbfs. If you want to, you can load it at boot time by adding the following line to /boot/loader.conf:
>
> smbfs_load="YES"
>
> However, this is probably not necessary.

To add an SMB share to /etc/fstab, use the following syntax:

```
//guest@gaming-pc/public   /smb/public      smbfs  rw,noauto 0   0
```

The mount -a process that occurs during startup will mount this share automatically when the FreeBSD system boots.

Summary

In this, the final hour of our course on FreeBSD, you learned how to turn your machine into a file-sharing server and client using a variety of protocols. You learned how to set up an FTP server, both for authenticated and anonymous users. You learned how to use NFS, sharing files back and forth over a networked filesystem. Finally, you learned how to set up a basic Samba configuration in order to communicate with Windows machines on a local network.

Each of these protocols, particularly NFS and Samba, is a great deal more flexible than our coverage here indicates; if you find that you have the need and the desire, you will be able to extend your knowledge of these protocols to the point at which you can increase the performance and convenience (as well as the security) of your file-sharing mechanisms to whatever level you prefer.

Q&A

Q What's the point of using FTP to serve files? Why not just use HTTP?

A HTTP has indeed supplanted much of the purpose for FTP's existence, particularly in the case of large binary downloads (such as software archives). However, FTP has advantages in its dual-channel connection model (which allows it to operate through firewalls), its built-in user authentication, the ability to upload files and perform filesystem operations on the server, and the fact that its transport mechanism is tuned to support large binary files rather than small text/HTML files (as with HTTP).

Q My /var partition is too small to hold a large public anonymous FTP archive.

A You can create a location in another, larger partition to hold the content that would normally go into /var/ftp. For example, move the contents of /var/ftp to /usr/ftp, and then make a symbolic link there with the following command: ln -s /usr/ftp /var/ftp.

Q Isn't there a way to browse NFS shares on a local network?

A There is, actually. A system called Service Location Protocol (SLP) is available to help machines on a LAN track each other's NFS services. You can install OpenSLP (a free implementation of SLP) from the ports, at /usr/ports/net/openslp.

Q My NFS mounts sometimes freeze up; sometimes they take forever to come unstuck, and until then my terminal session is locked.

A Make sure that you're using the `-i` option when you mount NFS shares. This is usually not necessary on local networks; but if you're mounting shares over the WAN, and the connection occasionally causes the mount to stall, the `-i` option might be your best bet.

Q How do I share files with Macintosh machines over AppleTalk?

A You will want to install the netatalk port, located at `/usr/ports/netatalk`. Note that Mac OS X can use NFS and SMB to share files as well as AppleTalk.

Q Isn't there a more user-friendly way to configure Samba?

A There is a Web-based administration tool called SWAT, which is installed along with the Samba port. See Samba's Web site (`http://www.samba.org`) for more information on how to use it. Be aware that because it has to be able to modify system configuration files and thus has to run as a privileged user, running SWAT opens up a number of potential security holes. These are documented in the package if you install SWAT; be sure to heed the cautions.

24

Workshop

This interactive section is designed to solidify your understanding of FTP, NFS, and Samba with quiz questions, and to extend your horizons for the use of these tools through exercises.

Quiz

1. What's the default FTP server that comes with FreeBSD?

    A. WU-FTPD

    B. ProFTPd

    C. BSD `ftpd`

2. What file do I add usernames to in order to prevent them from logging in via FTP?

    A. `/etc/ftpusers`

    B. `/etc/ftp/users`

    C. `/etc/ftpbanned`

    D. `/var/ftp/etc/ftpusers`

3. Which NFS mount option is used for "backgrounding" mount processes so that they don't block the system?

   A. -i

   B. -b

   C. -T

   D. noauto

4. What is the nmbd daemon used for?

   A. It does name services for Samba.

   B. It services incoming NFS connection requests.

   C. It services incoming Samba connection requests.

   D. It maps incoming RPC calls to an unused server port.

5. What command is used to mount an SMB filesystem onto a FreeBSD machine?

   A. mount

   B. mount_nfs

   C. mount_smbfs

   D. mount -t smbfs

Quiz Answers

1. The correct answer is C.

2. The correct answer is A.

3. The correct answer is B, though A is useful as well.

4. The correct answer is A.

The correct answer is either C or D.

Exercises

1. You might find that the built-in FTP server in FreeBSD doesn't suit your needs. You might want to do sophisticated per-directory access control, for example, or you might want to give users the capability to fetch Zip archives of whole directory trees on-the-fly. You can do this by installing alternate FTP servers such as ProFTPD and WU-FTPD; both are available in the ports, in /usr/ports/ftp. Try installing ProFTPD and seeing what benefits its configuration model provides you.

2. You can set up Samba to do a lot more than simply share files with peer Windows machines. You can use it to join your FreeBSD machine to a Windows domain or even to serve as a domain controller for a whole Windows network. Try creating a domain for your home network and subscribing various Windows machines to it if you have them handy. It's not easy, but it's a great skill to have if you can manage it!

3. This chapter discusses the standard, built-in methods for sharing files inherent to UNIX and Windows. However, the form of file sharing that is getting all the press these days is the content-centric, peer-to-peer kind, which was pioneered by Napster and continues in dozens of different popular applications such as KaZaA, Morpheus, and Gnutella. Many of these applications are available for FreeBSD, either as a direct port or running through the Linux binary compatibility layer. In /usr/ports/net, you will find such ports as eDonkey, gtk-gnutella, LimeWire, and Mutella. Experiment with these if you're interested in file sharing of the kind that keeps the RIAA up at night. Note that most of these clients require KDE or GNOME.

24

PART VI
Appendixes

Hour

APPENDIX **A**

Resources for FreeBSD Users

This appendix contains a list of resources that FreeBSD users will find helpful.

Web Sites

The following Web sites may be of interest to FreeBSD users. The list includes both FreeBSD specific sites as well as sites not specifically related to FreeBSD, but that might still be useful.

FreeBSD Specific Sites

The following Web sites are specific to FreeBSD and the FreeBSD project.

www.freebsd.org

This is the official Web site of the FreeBSD project. Among other things, you will find announcements of the latest releases here, as well as other important announcements. It is also the place to start when looking for FreeBSD software, additional documentation, and more.

www.freshports.org

This site contains the latest news and updates to FreeBSD software ports. It's a good way to keep track of when software you are using has been updated and such. The newest software that has been ported to FreeBSD as well as the latest updates to existing software will be highlighted here.

www.freebsddiary.org

This site contains tons of how to articles and FAQs for many areas of FreeBSD use. It also includes forums for FreeBSD users, including the "FreeBSD Pets" forum where you can post pictures of your pet for all FreeBSD users to see.

www.freebsdmall.com

This is the primary place for ordering FreeBSD stuff. You can order official CD releases here that help support the project. You can also order clothing, caps, pins, coffee cups, and more with your favorite little daemon on them.

www.daemonnews.org

This is primarily a news site containing items of interest to BSD users. It contains items relating to all versions of FreeBSD. In addition, there are often tutorial articles on this site for performing tasks under different versions of BSD, including FreeBSD.

Other Web Sites

The following Web sites are not specifically related to the FreeBSD project. However, you might find them useful anyway because they contain information on common FreeBSD software and UNIX in general.

www.apache.org

This is the home page of the Apache Web server project, which is the software that we use in this book to configure a Web server with FreeBSD. Here you will find complete documentation for the server, as well as information on the latest Apache releases.

www.xfree86.org

This is the home page of the XFree86 project. It is a freely available implementation of the X Window System that is included with FreeBSD to provide graphical user interface capabilities. This site contains information on the latest XFree86 releases, as well as documentation for XFree86.

www.postfix.org

Postfix is a popular alternative mail server that can be used as a drop-in replacement for sendmail. Postfix is the mail server that we use in this book. You will find complete documentation for the Postfix server at this site, as well as information on latest releases and such.

www.kde.org

KDE is the graphical user environment that we have been using in this book. This is the home page for the KDE project. You will find more information about the project such as the latest release information here.

www.gnome.org

Gnome is the biggest competitor to KDE for the standard UNIX desktop environment. If you don't like KDE, or if you are just curious, you can check it out here. Gnome is available for FreeBSD in the ports collection.

Mailing Lists

To subscribe to any one of the following mailing lists, send an email to majordomo@freebsd.org that contains the following in the body of the message:

    subscribe list-name

where *list-name* is any one of the lists given later. If you want to unsubscribe from any of the lists, send the following command to the same address given above:

    unsubscribe list-name

Some of the lists given later are quite busy and will generate a great deal of email. If you don't want this but still want to get messages from the lists, you can subscribe to them in digest form. In this case, you will be sent a single message containing all the messages that have been posted each time the number of messages posted has exceeded 100K in size.

General Lists

General lists can be subscribed to and posted to by anyone. However, before posting to a list, you should read the guidelines that are sent to you when you subscribe. This will help you determine what kinds of messages should be posted to this list, and which messages would be better posted on some other list.

- **freebsd-advocacy:**

  This list is basically a forum for discussing ways of advocating and promoting FreeBSD.

- **freebsd-arch:**

  This list discusses hardware architectures and design.

A

- **freebsd-bugs:**

  This list contains all the bug reports that are filed for FreeBSD. You should not actually send bug reports to this list, but rather you should submit a bug report using the form located at `http://www.freebsd.org/send-pr.html`. The submitted problem reports are then automatically posted to the freebsd-bugs list where anyone who subscribes can view them.

- **freebsd-chat:**

  This is a general discussion list. It's not intended for technical discussion or the posting of problems and questions about how to do things in FreeBSD. It's mostly just intended as a social list.

- **freebsd-commit:**

  Any change made to the FreeBSD source tree is posted to this list. It is a read-only list, so you can't post anything to it. It probably isn't of much interest to you unless you are really interested in the nuts and bolts of FreeBSD.

- **freebsd-config:**

  This is a list for discussing FreeBSD installation and configuration tools. Some of the discussion on this list involves potential replacements for the current tools, including a graphical installer that is in the works.

- **freebsd-current:**

  You **need** to be subscribed to this list if you are attempting to work with FreeBSD CURRENT. Note that this is not the place to post general how-to questions about FreeBSD, even if you are asking the question in relation to CURRENT. Such questions will be ignored, and you won't get answers. Only technical questions specifically related to CURRENT should be posted here. General technical questions should be posted to the freebsd-questions list.

- **freebsd-isp:**

  This is a discussion list for FreeBSD users who are providing Internet services. This is not the place for you to post questions about connecting to an Internet service provider with FreeBSD. Rather, it is a discussion list for the providers themselves. Questions about connecting to an ISP should be posted to the freebsd-questions list.

- **freebsd-jobs:**

  This is pretty much a list of job postings for FreeBSD related jobs. If you are looking for a job, you can search this list. If you have a position that you need to fill, you can post a message here.

- **freebsd-newbies:**

  This is a list for users new to FreeBSD to discuss their experiences. It is not a forum for getting answers to how-to or technical questions. These types of questions should be sent to the freebsd-questions list.

- **freebsd-policy:**

  This list contains announcements regarding policy decisions that have been made by the FreeBSD core team. For example, decisions about procedures for submitting new code to the FreeBSD source tree. It is read-only and has very little traffic.

- **freebsd-questions:**

  This is the place to post technical questions regarding problems you are having with FreeBSD. When posting questions, make sure that you are specific. For example, "I can't get the Internet to work" will not be enough information for anyone to help you with the problem. Also, try to be courteous when asking questions on this list. The people on this list answering questions are doing so on their own free time and without pay, so don't get upset if you don't get an answer right away. You do not need to be susbscribed to this list in order to post questions to it, but if you are not subscribed to the list, make sure that you provide a valid email address so that people will be able to contact you with answers.

- **freebsd-stable:**

  If you are following the STABLE tree of FreeBSD, you should be subscribed to this list because important information is sometimes posted here (such as messages that the STABLE tree is currently broken; this doesn't happen as often as with CURRENT, but people can and do make mistakes). Also, an "all clear" will be posted to this list when the tree is working again. Like CURRENT, this is not the place to post general technical or how-to questions about FreeBSD unless they are specifically related STABLE. General technical or how-to questions should be posted to freebsd-questions.

- **freebsd-security-notifications:**

  Every FreeBSD user should be subscribed to this list. This is where notifications of security holes will be posted. There will also be instructions for fixing the holes posted here.

USENET Newsgroups

The USENET news system is a worldwide system of forums on just about every subject imaginable. There are two ways you can access the system. The first is with a newsreader program. Ask your ISP what the name of the news server you should use is. The second is through Google Groups, which can be reached from the Google home page (www.google.com) by clicking on the Groups link. Like directories, USENET groups are organized by categories and subcategories that are separated by periods. Here is a list of groups that might be of interest to FreeBSD users:

- comp.unix.freebsd.announce
- comp.unix.bsd.freebsd.misc

In addition to these FreeBSD specific newsgroups, some general UNIX related newsgroups also might be of interest to FreeBSD users. These are listed here:

- comp.unix
- comp.unix.questions
- comp.unix.admin
- comp.unix.programmer
- comp.unix.shell
- comp.unix.user-friendly
- comp.security.unix
- comp.source.unix
- comp.unix.advocacy
- comp.unix.misc

There are also some newsgroups specifically related to the X Window System. These are listed here:

- comp.windows.x.i386unix
- comp.windows.x
- comp.windows.x.apps
- comp.windows.x.announce
- comp.windows.x.intrinsics
- comp.windows.x.motif
- comp.windows.x.pex
- comp.emulators.ms-windows.wine

That last entry might cause some confusion. What is MS Windows doing in a list of UNIX related newsgroups? Basically, WINE is a Windows emulator for UNIX that allows you to run SOME Microsoft Windows applications under the X Window System.

WINE is available in the FreeBSD ports collection if you want to play with it, but its use is beyond the scope of this book. (Note that WINE actually stands for WINE Is Not an Emulator. The GNU people seem to love recursive acronyms.)

IRC Channels

IRC is a near real time chat network where you can interact with other users in forums. I say near real time because lag times on IRC can often be somewhat high (as in there is a delay between the time you send your message and the time that others actually get it).

Here are some IRC channels of interest to FreeBSD users. Note that there are different networks of IRC channels. In order to log in to one of these channels, you must be logged in to a server for the correct network.

- EFNet: `#freebsdhelp`
- Undernet: `#freebsd`

For Windows, a good IRC client is Mirc. For X Windows in FreeBSD, you might like X-Chat, which is available in the `irc` category of the FreeBSD ports tree.

Like the USENET newsgroups and mailing lists, it's important to remember that no one on IRC is paid to help you, so once again, be courteous. These people are helping you in their free time. It is also important to remember that IRC lag times can sometimes be high and that some people might be logged in to the channel but doing other things and not currently actually watching the IRC channel. Because of this, if you don't get an answer right away, don't assume that people are ignoring you. They probably aren't. They probably just haven't seen your message yet.

A

APPENDIX B

FreeBSD Quick Reference

This appendix contains a list of common FreeBSD commands for quick reference. These commands are grouped by functional area: shell commands, file and directory manipulation commands, system utilities, and so on. Refer to this appendix to remind yourself of which commands to use whenever you are confronted with a task to perform in the shell and you're not sure which command you need.

This guide also contains a list of useful configuration files for various services and system behaviors. Note that in the configuration files whose names begin with a dot (which are per-user configuration files), the prefixed tilde character (~) represents the path to an individual user's home directory. For example, FreeBSD expands ~/.login to /usr/home/*myname*/.login, and ~frank/.login becomes /usr/home/frank/.login.

Command	Action
	File and Directory Manipulation
cd *dirname*	Changes to the directory *dirname*. If the directory does not begin with a /, it is assumed to be relative to the current directory. (For instance, cd public_html changes to the public_html directory within the current directory.) If it does begin with a /, it is assumed to be an absolute path. (cd /usr takes you directly to /usr.)
ls	Lists the contents of the current directory except for hidden files. Add the option -a if you want to list the hidden files as well.
cp *file1 file2*	Copies *file1* to *file2*. Use the option -r to recursively copy a directory and all its files, and the -i option to prevent the command from clobbering existing files.
mv *file1 file2*	Moves *file1* to *file2*. These can either be names of files or directories. Like the cp command, -i can be used to prevent the command from clobbering existing files.
rmdir *dir1*	Removes a directory from the FreeBSD file system. However, for this command to work, the directory must be empty.
touch *file1*	Updates the last accessed time on the file. If the file does not already exist, it will be created.
mkdir *dir1*	Creates a new directory named *dirname*.
ln *file1 file2*	Creates a link from *file1* to *file2*. By default, it creates a hard link. Use the -s option to create a soft link.
chmod [permissions] *file1*	Changes the access permissions on the file.
chown *username file1*	Changes the ownership of the file to the user *username*. Usually only root can change file ownership.
chgrp *groupname file1*	Changes the group that the file belongs to. Normal users can only change the group to another group they belong to.
passwd	Changes your login password. Normal users can only change their own password. The root user can specify a name after the password to change anyone's password (for example, passwd frank).
	Common Utilities
grep [pattern] *file1*	Searches the file for the specified pattern. This command should only be used on text files, or on text output from other commands (for example, cat /var/log/messages | grep "httpd").
more *file1*	Displays the contents of a file one screen at a time or the output of a command that has been piped to it one screen at a time.

Command	Action
	Common Utilities
cat *file1*	Displays the contents of the file. Can also be used to combine two files into one using redirections (for example, cat file1 file2 > file3).
wc *file1*	Displays the number of words, characters, and lines in the file.
diff *file1 file2*	Compares the contents of the two files and displays the differences between them.
fmt *file1*	Formats the file into a format that is suitable for emailing. By default, it writes to STDOUT, which is normally the screen.
cut [option] *file1*	Allows you to display only a particular column or field of a file.
head *file1*	Displays the first 10 lines of a file.
tail *file1*	Displays the last 10 lines of a file.
sort *file1*	Sorts the contents of the file into alphabetical order and displays it to STDOUT, which is normally the screen.
cal	Displays a calendar for the current month.
date	Displays the current date and time. The root user can also use this command to set the date and time.
man *command*	Displays the manual page for the command.
ee	Invokes the FreeBSD Easy Editor text editor.
vi	Invokes the vi text editor.
	System Utilities and Maintenance
ps	Displays a list of processes running on the system.
top	Displays a list of processes and resource usage that is updated every couple of seconds.
kill *n*	Kills the process number specified by n.
killall *process*	Kills a process by name instead of process number.
at	Schedules a command or shell script to run at a specified time.
crontab	Schedules a command or shell script to run periodically at a specified time.
shutdown	Shuts down the system in an orderly way and notifies users of the shutdown.
	Printer Related Commands
lpr	Sends a print job to the printer.
lprm	Removes a print job(s) from the queue.

B

Command	Action
Common Utilities	
`lpq`	Displays a list of jobs currently in the printer queue.
`lpc`	Controls print daemons and print queues.
Software Installation and Removal	
`pkg_add name`	Installs a new software package on the system.
`pkg_delete name`	Deletes a software package from the system.
`pkg_info`	Gives information on software packages.
`make`	If given from a directory in a ports tree, it downloads and builds the necessary files for installing the software port.
`make install`	Installs a software port that has already been built. If the port has not yet been built, this command will usually obtain and build it first.
`make deinstall`	Removes installed software from the system.
`make clean`	Removes the work directory containing all the files created during the port building process.
`make distclean`	Removes the work files as well as the original archive of source code that was downloaded.
Configuration Files	
`~/.profile`	Configuration file for bourne style shells (sh, ksh, bash).
`~/.login`	Configuration file for C style shells (c, tcsh).
`~/.cshrc`	Configuration file for C style shells that also applies to subshells.
`~/.forward`	Email forwarding control file.
`~/.xinitrc`	Controls X Window System configuration options on a per-user basis.
`/etc/rc.conf`	Main FreeBSD configuration file.
`/etc/X11/XF86Config`	Main (global) configuration file for the X Window System.

INDEX

How can we make this index more useful? Email us at indexes@samspublishing.com

FreeBSD Installation Instructions

FreeBSD can be installed by booting directly from the CD-ROM or by booting from floppies. Other types of installations are covered in the INSTALL.TXT file on the top-level directory of the CD-ROM.

Start Installation with a Bootable CD-ROM

Insert the CD-ROM in your CD drive and restart your computer. Hit the DEL or the F2 key to access the BIOS setup utility while the computer is starting up. Once in the BIOS setup utility, look for a boot priority option. If your computer is capable of booting from a CD-ROM, your CD-ROM drive will be listed. Make sure the CD-ROM drive has a higher boot priority than your hard drive(s) to enable booting from a CD-ROM.

Start or reboot your machine with the disc in your CD-ROM drive. After a few moments, you should see the FreeBSD installation routine. For more details on the installation routine, please see the section Installation Quick Start Guide.

Create a Boot Diskette

To start the FreeBSD install process from a diskette, you will need two formatted 1.44 MB 3.5" diskettes or one formatted 2.88 MB 3.5" diskette. Label the two disks appropriately, such as BOOT and MFS ROOT, or label the one disk as BOOT.

1. Insert the FreeBSD 4.7 CD-ROM into your computer's CD-ROM drive. If you are using UNIX without a volume manager, you will need to mount the disc.

2. Go to the command line.

3. Navigate to the TOOLS directory on the CD-ROM.

4. Insert one of the two formatted diskettes (BOOT) and type `fdimage ../FLOPPIES/KERN.FLP a:` [ENTER], if using DOS or Windows or type `dd if=../floppies/kern.flp of=/dev/floppy` [ENTER], if using UNIX.

5. When the first image has been written, remove the first diskette and insert the second diskette (MFS ROOT). Use the same command as in Step 4, but this time use MFSROOT.FLP.

If you formatted one 2.88 MB 3.5" diskette, use the same command as in Step 4, but use the BOOT.FLP image instead. When you are through creating the boot diskette(s), leave the FreeBSD CD-ROM in your CD-ROM drive and see the section Start Installation with a Boot Diskette.

Start Installation with a Boot Diskette

Insert the CD-ROM in your CD drive and the BOOT diskette in the floppy drive and restart your computer. Hit the DEL or the F2 key to access the BIOS setup utility while the computer is starting up. Once in the BIOS setup utility, look for a boot priority option. Make sure the floppy drive has a higher boot priority than your hard drive(s) to enable booting from the diskette.

Start or reboot your computer. If you are using the two diskette option, you will be prompted to insert the MFS Root diskette after a few moments to a few minutes. After a few moments, you should see the FreeBSD installation routine. For more details on the installation routine, please see the section Installation Quick Start Guide.

Installation Quick Start Guide

Once the root file system has been loaded, you will be presented with the Kernel Configuration Menu. While a detailed walkthrough is not presented here, we can offer a few installation tips. If your system is pretty standard, you can probably just press Q and continue with the installation. If your system hung and you are at this step again or you have a non-standard system, you should choose the full-screen visual mode kernel configuration. Go through the menus and determine if the hardware listed matches your system. Pay special attention to anything flagged with CONF in reverse video as this signifies that one or more drivers in the default configuration conflict with the resources you have in your system. Once you are done, press Q to continue installing.

If everything went well, you will be presented with the FreeBSD Installation Main Menu (called /stand/sysinstall Main Menu). The Usage menu option will describe the installation options in detail, so you should read this guide before you do anything else.

Once you choose an installation option, follow the on-screen prompts to finish the installation.